MODERN HUMANITIES RESEARCH ASSOCIATION

TUDOR & STUART TRANSLATIONS

VOLUME 12

General Editors
ANDREW HADFIELD
NEIL RHODES

ARTHUR GOLDING'S *A MORAL FABLETALK* AND OTHER RENAISSANCE FABLE TRANSLATIONS

ARTHUR GOLDING'S *A MORAL FABLETALK* AND OTHER RENAISSANCE FABLE TRANSLATIONS

Edited by

Liza Blake and Kathryn Vomero Santos

MODERN HUMANITIES RESEARCH ASSOCIATION
2017

Published by
The Modern Humanities Research Association
Salisbury House
Station Road
Cambridge CB1 2LA
United Kingdom

© The Modern Humanities Research Association, 2017

Liza Blake and Kathryn Vomero Santos have asserted their right under the Copyright, Designs and Patents Act 1988 to be identified as the authors of this work.

Parts of this work may be reproduced as permitted under legal provisions for fair dealing (or fair use) for the purposes of research, private study, criticism, or review, or when a relevant collective licensing agreement is in place. All other production requires the written permission of the copyright holder who may be contacted at rights@mhra.org.uk

First published 2017

ISBN 978-1-78188-606-9 (hbk)
ISBN 978-1-907322-25-9 (pbk)

Copies may be ordered from www.tudor.mhra.org.uk

MHRA TUDOR AND STUART TRANSLATIONS

GENERAL EDITORS

Andrew Hadfield (University of Sussex)
Neil Rhodes (University of St Andrews)

ASSOCIATE EDITORS

Guyda Armstrong (University of Manchester)
Fred Schurink (University of Manchester)
Louise Wilson (Liverpool Hope University)

ADVISORY BOARD

Warren Boutcher (Queen Mary, University of London); Colin Burrow (All Souls College, Oxford); A. E. B. Coldiron (Florida State University); Patricia Demers (University of Alberta); José Maria Pérez Fernández (University of Granada); Robert S. Miola (Loyola College, Maryland); Alessandra Petrina (University of Padua); Anne Lake Prescott (Barnard College, Columbia University); Quentin Skinner (Queen Mary, London); Alan Stewart (Columbia University)

For details of published and forthcoming volumes please visit our website:

www.tudor.mhra.org.uk

TABLE OF CONTENTS

General Editors' Foreword viii

Acknowledgements ix

Abbreviations xii

List of Illustrations xvi

Introduction 1

Further Reading 48

Table of Fables 54

Arthur Golding, *A Moral Fabletalk* 61

William Caxton, from *The Subtle Histories and* 313
Fables of Aesop

Richard Smith, from *The Fabulous Tales of* 349
Aesop the Phrygian

John Brinsley, from *Aesop's Fables Translated* 391
Grammatically

John Ogilby, from *The Fables of Aesop* and *Aesopics* 411

Textual Notes 501

Glossary 515

Bibliography 545

Index 561

GENERAL EDITORS' FOREWORD

The aim of the *MHRA Tudor & Stuart Translations* is to create a representative library of works translated into English during the early modern period for the use of scholars, students and the wider public. The series will include both substantial single works and selections of texts from major authors, with the emphasis being on the works that were most familiar to early modern readers. The texts themselves will be newly edited with substantial introductions, notes, and glossaries, and will be published both in print and online.

The series aims to restore to view a major part of English Renaissance literature which has become relatively inaccessible and to present these texts as literary works in their own right. For that reason it will follow the same principle of modernisation adopted by other scholarly editions of canonical literature from the period. The series will have a similar scope to that of the original *Tudor Translations* published early in the last century, and while the great majority of the works presented will be from the sixteenth century, like the original series it will not be rigidly bound by the end-date of 1603. There will, however, be a very different range of texts with new and substantial scholarly apparatus.

The *MHRA Tudor & Stuart Translations* will extend our understanding of the English Renaissance through its representation of the process of cultural transmission from the classical to the early modern world and the process of cultural exchange within the early modern world.

Andrew Hadfield
Neil Rhodes

ACKNOWLEDGEMENTS

The moral of the fable of this volume is that it pays to surround yourself with a menagerie of smart and generous colleagues. We are grateful especially to Alan Stewart, who alerted us to the existence of Arthur Golding's manuscript in the Columbia University Rare Book & Manuscript Library, and who also suggested that the *MHRA Tudor & Stuart Translations* series might be the ideal home for an edition of Golding's fable translations. Alan, this book literally would not exist without you. We would also like to thank the editors of the *MHRA Tudor & Stuart Translations* series for their support and assistance throughout the development of this project. Neil Rhodes, Andrew Hadfield, Gerard Lowe, and Simon Davies always offered prompt and thoughtful responses to our many conceptual and practical queries.

Completing the textual work on our authors required a great deal of travel to archives in North America and the UK, and we are therefore also happy to acknowledge the generous financial support of the following libraries, who offered travel fellowships that enabled us to complete the necessary research: the Huntington Library, the University of California Los Angeles Special Collections (Thayer Fellowship Program), the University of Illinois Urbana-Champaign (UIUC) Rare Book and Manuscript Library, the University of Minnesota Libraries (Elmer L. Anderson Research Scholarship Program), and the University of Texas at Austin Harry Ransom Center. We have also received support from a Renaissance Society of America Research Grant, as well as institutional support from the New York University Animal Studies Initiative (who gave funding for travel and for the costs of including images of animals in the volume), the University of Toronto Mississauga Office of the Vice-Principal, Research, Research and Scholarly Activities Fund (which funded travel and research assistants), a University of Toronto Mississauga SSHRC Institutional Grant (which funded travel), the University of Toronto Mississauga Research Opportunity Program (which funded travel and research materials), and the Texas A&M University-Corpus Christi Research Enhancement Grant (which funded travel, research materials, and research assistants).

This heavily illustrated volume would not have been possible without the help of librarians and imaging assistants across the globe. We would like to thank the National Library of Scotland, the Royal

Library at Windsor Castle, and the Columbia University Rare Book & Manuscript Library for providing images for this volume, and allowing them to be reproduced. We would like to single out three libraries in particular for their generous policies regarding photographic reproduction. Because the Huntington Library, the Rare Book and Manuscript Library at UIUC, and Bristol Public Library allowed us to take our own photos and use them in this edition, we have been able to create an enriched reading experience that includes the visual as well as the textual elements of Renaissance fables. These photos were taken by Liza Blake; all images in the volume were formatted and prepared for publication by Philly Vasquez, Kathryn Vomero Santos, and Diane Blake. Diane Blake in particular put countless hours into photo editing work; we are grateful that she gave birth to one of the editors, which allowed us to exploit her Photoshop expertise.

For those libraries we were not able to travel to, colleagues and librarians across the world photographed pages on our behalf so we could complete a more full collation of Ogilby's text. We are therefore grateful to Elizabeth Bradtke, Stuart Butler, Alexander Paulsson Lash, Q Sarah Ostendorf, and Steven Rozenski, as well as librarians at the University of Michigan Library, the William Andrews Clark Memorial Library, the Clark Art Institute Library, and the Yale Center for British Art.

Other colleagues offered their time and expertise. We would like to thank Kathryn Will for helping us decipher heraldic terms; Kevin J. McGinley, Simon Stern, and Andrew Zurcher for their knowledge of early modern laws; Jeannie Miller for help unpicking an Arabic citation; and Kara Gaston and Audrey Walton for offering Latin consultations. Puck Fletcher and Ambereen Dadabhoy helped us enormously by checking minute textual details on our behalf in books at the British Library and Huntington Library, respectively, and Kirk Melnikoff generously shared his unpublished work on Richard Smith with us. We also gratefully acknowledge the following research assistants, who gave their time, intelligence, and diligence to this volume: Michael Baichoo, Edna Bovas, Paul Harrison, Mehak Kawatra, Melanie Simoes Santos, and Kelsey Willems.

We had the great fortune to participate in a number of Folger Institute, Mellon, and NEH programs related to both translation and textual editing. We hope that our colleagues and mentors from these experiences will see the impact of our conversations in this volume. We are especially grateful to Jacques Lezra for his support during the

ACKNOWLEDGEMENTS

early stages of the project and to Anne Coldiron for championing our edition as it neared completion.

Finally, we are grateful to our cats, to whom this volume is dedicated: Marston (who lives with Liza Blake), and Lexington and Hudson (who live with Kathryn Vomero Santos). In addition to their companionship, our cats were a constant 'help' with Skyping and editing, and any errors that remain in the text can be attributed to paws walking across keyboards. Our cats also helped us remember, as we worked on these fables, that most animal actions are, in reality, impossible to moralize.

ABBREVIATIONS

1484   William Caxton, *Here begynneth the book of the subtyl historyes and Fables of Esope whiche were translated out of Frensshe in to Englysshe by Wylham Caxton at Westmynstre in the yere of oure Lorde. M.CCC.lxxxiij* (Westminster: William Caxton, 1484) [Caxton's translation of Aesopian fables, and the basis of our edition.]

1518   *Fabularum quae hoc libro continentur interpretes, atque authores sunt hi. Guilielmus Goudanus. Hadrianus Barlandus. Erasmus Roterodamus. Aulus Gellius. Angelus Politianus. Petrus Crinitus. Ioannes Antonius Campanus. Plinius Secundus Nouocomensis. Nicolaus Gerbellius Phorcensis. Aesopi Vita ex Max Planude excerpta. & aucta* (Strasbourg, apud Matthias Schürer, 1518) [A book of fables in Latin; the section of fables by Goudanus contains the same Latin text that served as the basis of Brinsley's translation. All abbreviations from this book are silently expanded.]

1570   Robert Henryson, *The Morall Fabillis of Esope the Phrygian, compylit in eloquent, and ornate Scottis meter, be Maister Robert Henrisone, scholemaister of Dunfermeling* (Edinburgh: Robert Lekpreuik, 1570) [An early printed version of Henryson's fables, and a possible source for Smith's translation.]

1571   Robert Henryson, *The Morall Fabillis of Esope the Phrygian, compylit in eloquent, & ornate Scottis meter, be M. Robert Henrisone, scolmaister of Dunfermling. Newlie corectit, and vendicat, fra mony errouris, quhilkis war ouersene in the last prenting, quhair baith lynes, and haill versis war left owt* (Edinburgh: Thomas Bassendyne, 1571) [An early printed version of Henryson's fables, and a possible source for Smith's translation.]

ABBREVIATIONS

1577   Robert Henryson, *The Fabulous Tales of Esope the Phrygian, compiled moste eloquently in Scottishe metre by Master Robert Henrison, and now lately Englished. Euery tale moralized most aptly to this present time, worthy to be read*, trans. by Richard Smith (London: Richard Smith, 1577) [Smith's translation of Henryson's Aesopian fables, and the basis of our edition.]

1617   John Brinsley, *Esops Eables [sic] translated grammatically, and also in propriety of our English phrase; and, euery way, in such sort as may bee most profitable for the Grammar-schoole. The vse of it is according to the directions in the prefaces, and more fully set downe in Ludus Lit. or the Grammar-schoole* (London: H. L. for Thomas Man, 1617) [One of the surviving editions of Brinsley's fable translations.]

1624   John Brinsley, *Esops Fables translated both grammatically, and also in propriety of our English phrase; and, euery way, in such sort as may be most profitable for the Grammar-schoole. The vse of it is according to the directionrs [sic] in the prefaces, and more fully set downe in Ludus Lit. or the Grammar-schoole* (London: by I. D. for Thomas Man, 1624) [One of the surviving editions of Brinsley's fable translations.]

1651   John Ogilby, *The Fables of Aesop paraphrased in Verse, and adorn'd with sculpture* (London: Thomas Warren for Andrew Cook, 1651) [The printings of the first set of Ogilby's fable translations from 1651.]

1665   John Ogilby, *The Fables of Aesop paraphras'd in verse: adorn'd with sculpture, and illustrated with annotations. The second edition. By John Ogilby, Esq; Master of His Majesties Revells in the Kingdom of Ireland* (London: Thomas Roycroft for the author, 1665) [The printings of the first set of Ogilby's fable translations from 1665.]

1668	John Ogilby, *The Fables of Aesop paraphras'd in verse: adorn'd with sculpture, and illustrated with annotations. The second edition. By John Ogilby, Esq; Master of His Majesties Revells in the Kingdom of Ireland* (London: Thomas Roycroft for the author, 1668); and John Ogilby, *Aesopic's: or a second collection of fables, paraphras'd in verse: adorn'd with sculpture, and illustrated with annotations. By John Ogilby, Esq; Master of His Majesties Revells in the Kingdom of Ireland* (London: Thomas Roycroft for the author, 1668) [The printings of Ogilby's first and second sets of fables from 1668.]
1673/5	John Ogilby, *The Fables of Aesop. Volume 1. Paraphras'd in verse, adorn'd with sculpture, and illustrated with annotations. By John Ogilby Esq;, His Majesty's Cosmographer, Geographick Printer, and Master of the Revels in the Kingdom of Ireland. The Third Edition* (London: John Ogilby, 1673); and John Ogilby, *Aesopicks: or, a second collection of fables, paraphras'd in verse, adorn'd with sculpture, and illustrated with annotations. By John Ogilby Esq; His Majesty's Cosmographer, Geographick Printer, and Master of the Revels in the Kingdom of Ireland. The Second Edition* (London: John Ogilby, 1673) [The printings of Ogilby's first and second sets of fables from 1673. A few copies of these texts exist with a title page from 1675, but the text behind the 1675 title pages is identical to that of 1673, so we consider the date of the 1675 title pages to be spurious; see part IV of our introduction for more details.]
Aesopics	All early printings of the second set of Ogilby's fables (for those textual features that do not vary across editions). If it is not qualified (e.g., '1668 *Aesopics*'), this word simultaneously cites 1668 and 1673/5 in this list.
Barnes	Arthur Golding, *A Moral Fable-talk*, ed. by Richard G. Barnes (San Francisco: The Arion Press, 1987) [A previous edition of Golding's translation.]

ABBREVIATIONS

EEBO	*Early English Books Online*
The Fables of Aesop	All early printings of the first set of Ogilby's fables (for those textual features that do not vary across editions). If it is not qualified (e.g., '1651 *Fables of Aesop*'), this phrase simultaneously cites 1651, 1665, 1668, and 1673/5 in this list.
Field	Arthur Golding, 'Arthur Golding's *A Morall Fabletalke*: An Annotated Edition', ed. by Nora Rooche Field (unpublished doctoral dissertation, Columbia University, 1979; abstract in *Dissertation Abstracts International*, 40 (1979), 3314A) [A previous, unpublished edition of Golding's translation.]
Freitag	Arnold Freitag, *Mythologia Ethica, hoc est, moralis philosophiae per fabulas brutis attributas, traditae, amoenissimum viridarium: in quo humanae vitae labyrintho demonstrato, virtutis semita pulcherrimis praeceptis, veluti Thesei filo docetur. Artificiosissimis nobilissimorum sculptorum iconibus ab Arnoldo Freitagio Embricensi, latin explicatis, aeri incissum* (Antwerp, excudebat Christopher Plantin: Philip Galle, 1579) [Golding's Latin source. All abbreviations from this book have been silently expanded.]
Kindrick	Robert Henryson, *The Poems of Robert Henryson*, ed. by Robert L. Kindrick (Kalamazoo, MI: Medieval Institute Publications, 1997) [An edition of Henryson's *Morall Fabillis*. References are to Kindrick's notes in this edition.]
NRSV	*The New Oxford Annotated Bible: New Revised Standard Version, with the Apocrypha*, ed. by Michael D. Coogan et al. (Oxford: Oxford University Press, 2010)
OED	*The Oxford English Dictionary*, online edition

LIST OF ILLUSTRATIONS

1. Illustration of 'The Fox and Ape', in John Ogilby, ... Cover
   The Fables of Aesop. By permission of the Bristol
   Public Library

2. Title page of Arnold Freitag, *Mythologia Ethica*. 3
   By permission of the University of Illinois
   Urbana-Champaign Rare Book and Manuscript
   Library

3. Title page of Peeter Heyns (?), *Esbatement moral des* 17
   animaux. By permission of the Columbia University
   Rare Book & Manuscript Library

4. First page of fables in John Brinsley, *Aesop's Fables* 20
   Translated Grammatically. By permission of the
   Huntington Library, San Marino, California

5. First page of 'The Argument Between Aesop and the 25
   Translator' from Richard Smith, *The Fabulous Tales
   of Aesop the Phrygian*. By permission of the National
   Library of Scotland

6. First page of fables in Arthur Golding, *A Moral* 34
   Fabletalk. By permission of the Columbia
   University Rare Book & Manuscript Library

7. Title page of Arthur Golding, *A Moral Fabletalk*. 61
   By permission of the Columbia University Rare
   Book & Manuscript Library

8. Illustrations from Arnold Freitag, *Mythologia* 62–311
   Ethica. By permission of the University of Illinois
   Urbana-Champaign Rare Book and Manuscript
   Library

9. Illustrations from William Caxton, *The Subtle* 313–347
   Histories and Fables of Aesop. By permission of the
   Royal Collection Trust / © Her Majesty Queen
   Elizabeth II 2016, and the Huntington Library, San
   Marino, California

LIST OF ILLUSTRATIONS

10. Illustrations from John Ogilby, *The Fables of* 411–499
    Aesop and *Aesopics*. By permission of the University
    of Illinois Urbana-Champaign Rare Book and
    Manuscript Library

INTRODUCTION

In the late sixteenth century, Arthur Golding, a prolific Tudor translator perhaps best known today for his English version of Ovid's *Metamorphoses*, translated a collection of fables that he entitled *A Morall Fabletalke*. The manuscript of Golding's translation, now located in the Columbia University Rare Book & Manuscript Library, was never printed and is little known. In order to make the text available to a wide range of readers, we present an edition of the translation in full in this volume. We also include selections from four other English Renaissance translations of moral fables: William Caxton's 1484 translation, Robert Henryson's translation in Middle Scots, 'Englished' in 1577 by Richard Smith ('English' was an early modern verb meaning 'to translate into English'), a 1617 school-text translated by John Brinsley, and John Ogilby's politically motivated fable translations from 1651 and 1668.

Our choices cover a broad historical range (from Caxton in 1484 to Ogilby in 1668) that reaches from the beginning to the end of the English Renaissance. The various translators present fables in several forms and formats: in prose and in poetry; linked to biblical verses; provided with more or less explicit morals; illustrated with images of animals in nature, or animals walking upright in seventeenth-century dress; with footnotes guiding a student to translate the fable back into Latin; and with paratextual poems reflecting on translation. We include translators who aim to carry across the literary qualities of Aesop, as well as translators who have political, biblical, national, and pedagogical purposes. Within this book you will find a full picture of the variety and aesthetic power of the widespread practice of fable translation in the period.

This introduction falls into four main sections. We begin with an overview of the fable in the early modern period and give a history of the early modern idea that a fable or *fabula* could be a carrier of deep philosophical meaning as well as a pleasant narrative with a moral attached to it. The second section discusses fables in translation, making special reference to where our five translators fit into the wider cultures of translation in Renaissance Europe. The third section builds on the first two, moving from how early modern readers might have thought about and encountered fables to offering some suggestions to our modern readers on how to read the fables within. We end with editorial notes, describing the material conditions in which each of these early texts survive, and describing our editorial practices. Throughout the introduction we make frequent reference to the fables found within this volume, using the first letter of the translator's last name (Golding = G; Caxton = C; etc.), followed by the fable number within that translator (so, 'O7' indicates the seventh fable in the fables by Ogilby).

I. FABLE, *FABULA*, *MYTHOS*: A HISTORY

The fables in this volume share many common features. Each has a short narrative, and most have some kind of moral or lesson attached to that narrative. Many are about beasts (hence this kind of fable is frequently called a beast fable), though fables may also star gods, humans, plants, and objects. Most, though not all, are or have at one time been attributed to Aesop or his followers and imitators. Giving a timeless, formal definition of what makes a fable a fable is not always easy; even Ben Edwin Perry, the founding figure of modern fable studies, struggles to define what makes a fable a fable, or even to determine whether fable is a genre, a mode, or something else entirely.[1] The broadest definition he is able to give comes from 'the rhetoricians of the first century and later [... who] define it in four words as λόγος ψευδὴς εἰκονίζων ἀήειαν, "a fictitious story picturing a truth."'[2]

The best approach, therefore, might be to define fables not formally, but historically. This is the approach taken by Edward Wheatley, whose book on medieval fables argues that we need to move beyond 'formalist definitions of fable as a genre [because they ...] are superfluous to a historicized understanding of the medieval phenomenon of the elegiac Romulus collection' (that is, the poetic collection of fables translated into Latin by Romulus, the group of fables most commonly read and cited in the Middle Ages).[3] Here we plan to follow the lead of Wheatley, attempting not to write a transcendent, timeless definition of 'fable', but to give a basic sketch of the contours of a historical definition. Golding's manuscript,

---

[1] Ben Edwin Perry, 'Fable', *Studium generale* 12 (1959), 17–37.
[2] Perry, 'Fable', p. 22.
[3] Edward Wheatley, *Mastering Aesop: Medieval Education, Chaucer, and His Followers* (Gainesville: University Press of Florida, 2000), p. 5. Wheatley continues, 'For [medieval] readers, the form of the fable was more accidental than essential [...]. All-encompassing formal definitions tell us more about our own desires to master fable than medieval reception of the literary form.'

INTRODUCTION

A Morall Fabletalke, is a translation of Arnold Freitag's Latin book of fables entitled (in part) *Mythologia Ethica, hoc est, Moralis philosophiae per fabulas brutis attributas* [*Ethical* Mythologia, *that is, moral philosophy by means of fables, attributed to beasts*] (see Figure 1 below). How and why Golding might translate Freitag's *Mythologia* as *Fabletalke*, and what it means for how we read Renaissance fables, is the subject of this section.

FIGURE 1. Title page of Arnold Freitag, *Mythologia Ethica*. By permission of the University of Illinois Urbana-Champaign Rare Book and Manuscript Library.

The word 'fable' in Renaissance England was a translation of the Latin word *fabula*, which was in turn a translation of the Greek word μῦθος (*mythos*), meaning 'word', 'story', or 'myth'. When modern readers see the word 'fable' we think almost exclusively of the short, moral story that has come to be associated primarily with the Ancient Greek figure Aesop, who may or may not have actually lived. But thanks to the plasticity of translation, Renaissance thinkers thought of the word *fabula* as referring not only to Aesopian fables, but also to what we would call myths. Natale Conti's 1567 *Mythologiae* [literally, myth-talk or myth-speeches] is a huge, ten-book study of what he refers to within as *fabulae*.[4] In this volume he reveals the deeper meanings — including philosophical, natural, and moral truths — that lie hidden in the myths and fables of ancient cultures.[5] Though Conti sometimes distinguishes *fabula* (meaning myth) from what Aesop wrote,[6] other early modern writers did not make this distinction; 'fable' and 'myth' (and their Latin cognates) are frequently used interchangeably. Georg Sabinus, for example, refers to the mini-myths in Ovid's *Metamorphoses* as 'fables' in his mythographic *Fabularum Ovidii interpretatio* [*The Interpretation of the Fables of Ovid*] (1555).[7] Arthur Golding, whose manuscript is at the heart of this edition, writes that the mythological writer Ovid sometimes communicates 'by way of fabling',[8] and Ogilby, the last author included in this volume, refers to the fable writer Aesop as 'Old Aesop, that renowned mythologist' (O17, l. 56).[9]

The fact that 'fable' and 'myth' could be used interchangeably in early modern England is significant because the mythographic tradition, which had flourished for centuries before the Renaissance,

---

[4] Natale Conti, *Mythologiae*, trans. by John Mulryan and Steven Brown, 2 vols (Tempe: Arizona Center for Medieval and Renaissance Studies, 2006). Mulryan and Brown call attention to the difficulty of translating Conti's word *fabula* for modern readers; see p. 1, n. 3. References to Conti's text in English translation will include the book and chapter number, followed by the page number in this edition.

[5] For a thorough history of the mythographic tradition before Conti, see John Mulryan and Steven Brown, 'Introduction', in Conti, pp. xi–xlvi (pp. xxv–xxvi).

[6] Conti, I.4, p. 6.

[7] Georgio Sabino, *Fabularum Ovidii interpretatio* (Witeberge, 1572).

[8] Arthur Golding, 'Epistle to Leicester', in Ovid, *Metamorphoses*, trans. by Arthur Golding, ed. by Madeleine Forey (New York: Penguin Books, 2002), l. 450.

[9] See also Ogilby's dedicatory letter, and James Shirley's commendatory poem to Ogilby, 'To my Worthy Friend', l. 19, both in this volume. In O11, l. 28n, Ogilby refers to Ovid's myth of Pygmalion as a 'fable'.

INTRODUCTION

was founded on a core belief: that ancient writers encoded deep philosophical truths in poetic *fabulae*. Conti puts it as follows: 'not so many years before the times of Plato, Aristotle, and other philosophers, the ancients did not openly teach the principles of philosophy: instead they found a secret mythological disguise for disseminating these truths.'[10] The Greek sages, he claims, used 'stories [*fabulas*] to conceal their philosophical directives.'[11] Francis Bacon's mythographic text *The Wisdome of the Ancients* (1609 in Latin; English translation 1619) is explicitly built on the belief that early writers communicated through fables: 'Therefore in the first ages all things were full of Fables[,] aenigmaes, parables, and similes of all sortes: by which they sought to teach and lay open, not to hide and conceale knowledge.'[12] In the middle of the seventeenth century Thomas Sprat, member of and historiographer for the scientific Royal Society, describes the ancient 'fabulous Age', in which thinkers 'set [ideas] off with the mixture of Fables, and the ornaments of Fancy [...] the first Masters of knowledge among them, were as well Poets as Philosophers.'[13] Roger L'Estrange in his 1692 fable collection likewise argues that ancient fiction was 'Philosophical Mythology', which therefore authorizes him in his own 'Symbolical Way of Morallizing upon Tales and Fables'.[14]

The idea that ancient writers used fables, in the sense of *fabula*, to convey deep philosophical truths was frequently brought out as a way of justifying sometimes tortuous interpretations of classical writers.[15] But it was sometimes turned into a kind of justification of poetry, or of fictional activity itself.[16] Sabinus pushes this reasoning to its

---

[10] Conti, I.1, p. 1.

[11] Ibid., I.1, p. 2. The Latin in brackets is supplied from Natale Conti, *Mythologiae sive explicationum fabularum libri X* (Venice, 1581), sig. A1r.

[12] Francis Bacon, *The Wisedom of the Ancients, written in Latine by the right honourable Sir Francis Bacon Knight, Baron of Verulam, and Lord Chancelor of England*, trans. by Arthur Gorges (London, 1619), sigs a10v–11r. For a detailed study of Bacon's understanding of mythology, see chapter 3, 'George Sandys, A Translator between Two Worlds', in Lee T. Pearcy, *The Mediated Muse: English Translations of Ovid 1560–1700* (Hamden, CT: Archon Books, 1984), pp. 37–70.

[13] Thomas Sprat, *History of the Royal Society*, ed. by Jackson I. Cope and Harold Whitmore Jones (Saint Louis: Washington University Studies, 1958), p. 6.

[14] Roger L'Estrange, *Fables of Aesop and other Eminent Mythologists: with Morals and Reflections* (London, 1692), sig. A2v.

[15] Bacon lambasts previous attempts to 'wrest' meaning from 'many poeticall Fables' even before he embarks on his own interpretation; see *Wisedome*, sigs a6r–v.

[16] The second chapter of Wheatley's *Mastering Aesop*, 'Theories of the Fable: Telling

absolute and logical limit when he states authoritatively, *Poetica nihil aliud est nisi Philosophia numeris & fabulis concinna* [poetry is nothing other except philosophy arranged in metrical feet and fables].[17] He does not claim that some poetry contained philosophy in it, but that poetry is *nothing other than* philosophy decorated either with verse (*numeris*), or with story (*fabula*). The theory of the *fabula* in general, and of the Aesopian fable in particular, was closely bound up with thinking about literary works in the middle ages and Renaissance. Even Philip Sidney in his famous and influential *Defense of Poesy* (c. 1580) argues that poetry cannot be said to 'lie', because at no point does it claim to be telling the truth, and then follows this claim up with Aesopian fables as a prime example: 'so think I none so simple would say that Aesop lied in the tales of his beasts; for who thinks that Aesop writ it for actually true were well worthy to have his name chronicled among the beasts he writeth of.'[18]

The link between Aesopian fable, *fabula*, *mythos*, and poetry may have been forged as early as Plato's *Phaedo*, when he describes Socrates' decision to translate Aesopian fables into poetry while he was in prison. Socrates describes himself as having a dream in which he was instructed to make music; he decides to do so, and 'considering that a poet, if he is really to be a poet, must compose myths and not speeches (ποιητὴς εἶναι, ποιεῖν μύθους), since I was not a maker of myths (μυθολογικός), I took the myths (μύθους) of Aesop, which I had at hand and knew, and turned into verse the first I came upon.'[19] In this moment, hugely influential in the Renaissance, Socrates claims that to make poetry is to make myths: ποιητὴς εἶναι, ποιεῖν μύθους (*poietes einai, poiein mythous*) — a maker (poet) to be, to make myth.[20] Even the claim itself is poetic: some form of the

---

Truth, Fearing Falsehood' (pp. 33–51), is a study of the Latin word *fabula* insofar as it signifies fiction more generally; he covers medieval theories about the usefulness of fiction.

[17] Sabino, sig. A6r; the translation is our own.

[18] Philip Sidney, *The Defense of Poesy*, in *Sir Philip Sidney: Selected Writings*, ed. by Richard Dutton (New York: Routledge, 2002), pp. 102–48 (p. 130).

[19] Plato, *Plato: Euthyphro, Apology, Crito, Phaedo, Phaedrus*, vol. 1, trans. by Harold North Fowler (London: William Heinemann, 1926), 61B, pp. 212–13.

[20] In S. K. Heninger Jr.'s *The Subtext of Form in the English Renaissance: Proportion Poetical* (University Park: The Pennsylvania State Press, 1994), he devotes an entire chapter ('Socrates and his Versified Aesop', pp. 33–68) to tracing the topos of Socrates translating Aesop as a way of thinking about early modern poetic theory,

verb ποιεῖν [to make] appears as the first and third word, while the infinitives cluster around the comma, forming a chiasmus. And the *myths* that Socrates chooses to (re)make, in this moment, are the fables of Aesop.

The word 'fable', then, could refer not only to a short Aesopian narrative about beasts but also, more broadly, to fictional activity in general, or to a work of narrative pointing to a deeper philosophical truth. The Aesopian fable was not separate from this more broad definition of 'fable', but was a subset of it; it is for this reason that early modern authors and translators frequently take Aesopian fables so seriously. However, it is also the early modern period that begins the systematic devaluation of 'fable' that would eventually split *fabula* from its deeper, more mythological associations. The English word 'fable', like *fabula*, could mean myth or fiction, but it could also, in the middle ages and Renaissance, mean 'a fiction invented to deceive; a fabrication, falsehood.'[21] The line between fable as literature and fable as lie had always been carefully negotiated — Plato's *Republic* allows fables into the ideal city because 'the fable is, taken as a whole, false, but there is truth in it also,'[22] thereby distinguishing the lie of fiction from the more fundamental truth within. But the new and burgeoning epistemological paradigms of the seventeenth century tried to eliminate fictional or imaginative forms of truth.

The scientific revolution of the seventeenth century was spurred by Francis Bacon, who argued that science must eliminate the fable and focus on facts. In his *New Organon*, his text outlining the plan for his *Great Instauration* or re-founding of the sciences, the former mythographer purges *fabula* from his future scientific program: 'There is a great number of [...] false associations. As for fables, they should be completely exterminated.'[23] In the same text in which he argues for the importance of natural history as a way of gathering the data for inductive reasoning, he also warns that real, historical

---

particularly about the relationship between poetry as *mythos* and poetry as verse. Ogilby mentions Socrates' translation as a way of shoring up the importance of Aesop in the dedicatory letter that precedes his fables in this volume. See also the next section of this introduction for a fuller discussion of how early modern authors used Socrates to think about translation.

[21] *OED*, s.v. 'fable, n.', 1.d.

[22] Plato, *The Republic*, vol. 1, trans. by Paul Shorey (London: William Heinemann, 1930), 377A, pp. 175–77.

[23] Francis Bacon, *The New Organon*, ed. by Lisa Jardine and Michael Silverthorne (Cambridge: Cambridge University Press, 2000), II.50, p. 218.

memory is 'diminished because it has sometimes been damaged and violated by fables.'[24] Bacon's great posthumous propagandist Thomas Sprat, as mentioned earlier, describes in his long history of knowledge how early learning was wrapped up in fables. But Sprat's history is teleological, and the future of knowledge, for him, can succeed only if people can be persuaded 'to separate the knowledge of Nature, from the colours of Rhetorick, the devices of Fancy, or the delightful deceit of Fables.'[25] Fables used to instruct obliquely; now, in an inversion of the Horatian maxim to delight and instruct,[26] they make deceit delightful. Although Aesopian fables flourished in the latter part of the seventeenth century, thanks largely to their reinvention and vigorous reanimation in the middle of the century by John Ogilby, 'fable' would eventually part ways from *fabula* and *mythos* in common understanding.

But the *fabula* took a long time to kill; as late as 1692, Roger L'Estrange's *Fables of Aesop and other Eminent Mythologists* continues to insist on the link between fables and mythology, and claims that fables are suitable for the education of young children and the instruction of adults alike. L'Estrange accepts the premise of people like Bacon and Sprat, admitting in what may be a direct reference to Bacon's early mythography that 'the Wisdom of the Ancients has been still Wrapt up in Veils and Figures'.[27] However, having accepted that premise, he then makes a passionate argument for those 'Veils and Figures', claiming that fables and mythologies gain their power *because* they are oblique: 'This Contrivance of Application, by Hints, and Glances, is the Only way under the Heavens to Hit it […] and what cannot be done by the Dint of Authority, or Persuasion, in the Chappel, or in the Closet, must be brought about by the Side-Wind of a Lecture from the Fields, and the Forests.'[28] According to L'Estrange, fables gain their power precisely from going about everything indirectly; their artistic indirectness is not what makes them outmoded, but what makes them the most useful, the most effective. Though by the end of the seventeenth century the English word 'fable' had largely split from its mythological roots, for much of the English Renaissance

---

[24] Bacon, *New Organon*, I.87, p. 72.
[25] Sprat, p. 62.
[26] Horace, *Ars Poetica*, in *Satires, Epistles, and Ars Poetica*, trans. by H. Rushton Fairclough (Cambridge, MA: Harvard University Press, 1966), l. 343: *utile dulci*.
[27] L'Estrange, sig. A2v.
[28] L'Estrange, sig. B1r.

'fable' carried with it the meanings and connotations of *fabula* (meaning myth, fable, or fiction).

The idea that fables in general carried deeply embedded knowledge, that a fable was a narrative with a deeper message or purpose, was presumably what made Aesop's fables so perfect for various forms of use, application, and appropriation in the early modern period. In addition to carrying deep meaning, fables were also thought to serve as a kind of spoonful of sugar to help the medicine of moral and other truths go down. Again, Philip Sidney turns to Aesopian fables as a prime example of the usefulness of all literary production:

> For conclusion, I say that the philosopher teacheth, but that he teacheth obscurely, so as the learned only can understand him; that is to say, he teacheth them that are already taught. But the poet is the food for the tenderest stomachs; *the poet is indeed the right popular philosopher, whereof Aesop's tales give good proof*: whose pretty allegories, stealing under the formal tales of beasts, make many (more beastly than beasts) begin to hear the sound of virtue from these dumb speakers.[29]

The fables of Aesop not only contain philosophical lessons, but also make those lessons easy to understand and digest; in this they serve as the prime example of all poetic or literary production. The idea that fables are the most basic blend of pleasure and instruction, that old Horatian statement of the purpose of poetry, is what made them crucial to the curriculum of medieval and early modern schoolboys learning Latin. Early modern authors knew there was classical precedent for fables being used in instruction, whether that instruction be in mastering Latin translation, in practicing rhetorical skills, or in the imparting of basic moral lessons.[30] Plato in his *Republic* advocates, as Conti puts it, 'that boys should begin their studies with an examination of honest fables';[31] they had indeed been doing so since the middle ages. The fact that most children encountered fables

---

[29] Sidney, *Defense*, pp. 115–16; italics added for emphasis.

[30] For more on the use of Aesop in schools, especially for the instruction of Latin translation, see part II of this introduction below. On fables as a useful tool for teaching rhetoric, see Joel B. Altman, *The Tudor Play of Mind: Rhetorical Inquiry and the Development of Elizabethan Drama* (Berkeley: University of California Press, 1978), p. 45. On moral lessons, see the next note.

[31] Conti, I.2, p. 3. See Plato, *Republic*, 377A.

so early in their literate life is perhaps the reason that references to Aesopian fables are more or less ubiquitous in Renaissance literature, and in Renaissance writings more generally.

More importantly, what those children learned in the schoolroom were not only the moral lessons that Aesop taught, but also a mode of reading literary works for hidden meanings. This mode of reading taught children to read not only for content and form, but for *application*. What matters is not just what a fable says, and what it can teach you about using language, but also how you can apply the lesson that the fable imparts. It was also possible to modify that lesson, and in this respect especially, fables were not only for children. In the mid-seventeenth century fables received a new life thanks to John Ogilby (the latest translator in this volume), who fitted them out as an ideal literary form to work through the new political and social environment of the English Civil War and its aftermath. Jane Elizabeth Lewis' study of the Augustan fable argues that in this new environment, 'A fable that earned its keep, apparently, had somehow to be at once plain and devious'.[32] Mark Loveridge claims that Ogilby is a political fabulist *par excellence*, not in that he uses his fables to advocate a particular position, but in that he uses his fables in a way that almost redefines what it means for a literary text to be political.[33] Many of the most important studies of the Renaissance fable are interested not just in how early modern authors understand fables, but what they do with them. In her early and paradigmatic study *Fables of Power*, Annabel Patterson places Ogilby not at the beginning, but in the middle of a long line of fabulists that includes writers such as John Lydgate, Philip Sidney, Edmund Spenser, and John Lyly, all of whom use the fable as a means for political analysis.[34]

Renaissance fables left themselves open to so many uses partly because of the flexibility of what counted as an 'Aesopian' fable in the period. Aesop is unique among classical authors as they were received by Renaissance humanists, because his corpus — if you believe 'him' to have existed at all — was distributed and uncertain.

---

[32] Jayne Elizabeth Lewis, *The English Fable: Aesop and Literary Culture, 1651–1740* (Cambridge: Cambridge University Press, 1996), p. 5.
[33] Mark Loveridge, *A History of Augustan Fable* (Cambridge: Cambridge University Press, 1998).
[34] Annabel Patterson, *Fables of Power: Aesopian Writing and Political History* (Durham, NC: Duke University Press, 1991). Patterson discusses Ogilby most extensively in the chapter '"The Fable is Inverted": 1628–1700', pp. 81–110.

INTRODUCTION

Early modern authors were aware that Aesop's fables were closer to a swarm than a defined body of work; hence even Caxton's early set of fables carefully demarcates and distinguishes among fables by Aesop, Avianus, Alfonso, and Poggio. Conti noted that 'Aesop' was more of a useful idea or tradition than a genuine author: 'Although fables were made by many different men, custom prevailed and all fables were called "Aesopic"'.[35] In the middle ages, three Latin versions of fables dominated the Latin curriculum: Latin prose translations of the Greek fabulist Phaedrus by Romulus; Latin verse translations of the Greek fabulist Babrius by Avianus; and later the elegiac Romulus, sometimes referred to as the fables of Walter the Englishman, a Latin verse translation based on the Romulus collection.[36] But by the sixteenth century there were many different groups or families all competing, or sometimes joining forces, with one another.

In the late fifteenth and early sixteenth centuries, with the rise of printing presses in Europe, a number of competing versions of fables sprang up. In 1476/7 Heinrich Steinhöwel's collection of fables by Romulus, Avianus, and Alfonso would create an entire branch, on which perches Caxton's fables from 1484.[37] In 1505 the Aldine press produced an edition of 192 Greek and Latin fables in poetry and prose ascribed to 'Gabriae' or Babrius; these Greek fables sometimes appear in bilingual editions, or sometimes with only Greek or Latin translation, well into the seventeenth century. In the 1510s another different set of Latin fables began to travel together, usually under the title *Fabularum quae hoc libri continentur interpretes atque authores sunt hi* [*The translators and authors of the fables that are contained in this book are these*]; this set initially included 45 fables translated by Guilielmus Goudanus (or Guilelmus de Gouda), as well as fables by Hadrianus Barlandus (or Adriaan van Baarland), Guilielmus Hermanus (or Hermannus), Desiderius Erasmus, and other early

---

[35] Conti, I.3, p. 5.
[36] This concise potted history of medieval fables is taken nearly verbatim from Seth Lerer's pithy overview in his *Children's Literature: A Reader's History from Aesop to Harry Potter* (Chicago: University of Chicago Press, 2008), p. 43. For more on the elegiac Romulus see Wheatley, pp. 7–31; for more on Avianus see William F. Hodapp, 'The Fables of Avianus', in *Medieval Literature for Children*, ed. by Daniel T. Kline (New York: Routledge, 2003), pp. 12–28.
[37] For more details on this branch, see Lenaghan's introduction in William Caxton, *Caxton's Aesop*, ed. by R. T. Lenaghan (Cambridge, MA: Harvard University Press, 1967), pp. 3–21 (pp. 13–18).

humanists.[38] It is this grouping, including 139 fables in all, that would serve as the basis for countless other editions in the Renaissance, including editions from the 1520s, at which point they had picked up an additional one hundred fables by Laurentius Abstemius (or Lorenzo Astemio), thirty-three fables by Laurentius Vallensis (or Lorenzo Valla), and one hundred fables by a translator named as 'Rimicius' in the early texts (perhaps Rinuccio d'Arezzo). In addition, they moved into editions published in the mid-sixteenth century in France, and also seem to have served as the basis for the edition of Latin fables that began to be printed in England in 1618, where more fables were added still.[39] The 1618 book of fables, *Aesopi phrygis fabulae*, would go through approximately twenty more printings before 1689, when L'Estrange would cite it as a standard Aesopian Latin textbook in his work.[40]

As this very preliminary sketch of what 'Aesop' meant in early modern Europe should make clear, to speak about translating 'Aesop' is different than to speak about, for example, translating Ovid, the text of whose fifteen-book *Metamorphoses* had been carefully edited and established by Raphael Regius by the end of the fifteenth century. There is not one core corpus of Aesopian fables; rather, there is a kind of nebulous crowd, with some groups and some translations more heavily used and relied on than others. Whether our authors are doing strict linguistic translations of a clear and established source, or whether they are basing fundamentally new poems on older plots and ideas, 'translation' seems to mean something different when it comes to Aesopian fables — or perhaps we might say that the tradition of fable translation helps us understand the complexity and variety of Renaissance translation practices more widely.

---

[38] Enrique González González credits Martinius Dorpius for this collection; see his 'Martinus Dorpius and Hadrianus Barlandus Editors of Aesop (1509–1513)', *Humanistica Lovaniensia: Journal of Neo-Latin Studies* 47 (1998), 28–41 (p. 28). See also Paul Thoen's 'Aesopus Dorpii. Essai sur l'Esope latin des temps modernes', *Humanistica Lovaniensia* 19 (1970), 241–89, which González González cites as the definitive article on this collection.

[39] *Aesopi phrygis fabulae: iam recenter ex collatione optimorum exemplarium emendatius excusæ, cum nonnullis eiusdem & Poggij fabulis adiectis: et indice correctiori adiuncto* (London: Excusae pro Societatis Stationariorum, 1618).

[40] L'Estrange, sig. B1v. The count of editions is taken from a search of the database *EEBO*.

INTRODUCTION

II. FABLES IN TRANSLATION; FABLES AND TRANSLATION

In his influential book on children's literature, which takes Aesop's fables as its starting point, Seth Lerer contends that '[t]he history of the fable is [...] the history of its translation'.[41] This volume not only charts some key moments in that history, but also illustrates how wide-ranging and influential translation practices were during a period that was shaped by the invention of the printing press, the Reformation, the rise of humanist education, and the political upheaval of civil war. In other words, we build on Lerer's claim by showing how the history of the fable is not just the history of *its* translation, but that of translation itself. By the time they were translated into English during the Renaissance, fables had already been transformed by the readers and writers who had encountered them in the centuries since they were first recorded. A closer look at the audiences and translation practices that fuelled early modern English engagement with fables reveals just how capacious the term 'translation' was during this period. The goal of this section is to provide an overview of the diversity of fable translation practices, which ranged from literal grammatical construing, to literary expansion, to cultural and political projects that reflected contemporary events and developments in Renaissance England. Although our five translators take very different approaches to rendering fables into their vernacular language, this section will also highlight several commonalities among their efforts to revive and reshape this ancient tradition.

The earliest of our translators, William Caxton (1422–1492), was also, as Anne Coldiron has described him, 'the first of England's printers without borders.'[42] In most accounts of English literary and print history, Caxton is celebrated as the earliest printer of Chaucer's works, but the vast majority of his output was translated from other languages. In many cases he translated the texts himself, while in others he printed the work of other translators. Translation, Coldiron explains, became the essential means by which Caxton generated content for his new press.[43] Having spent time in Bruges and Cologne

---

[41] Lerer, *Children's Literature*, p. 42.
[42] A. E. B. Coldiron, *Printers Without Borders: Translation and Textuality in the Renaissance* (Cambridge: Cambridge University Press, 2015), p. 36.
[43] Coldiron has written extensively on the role of translation in Caxton's printing activity. In addition to *Printers Without Borders*, see 'The mediated "medieval" and Shakespeare', in *Medieval Shakespeare: Pasts and Presents*, ed. by Ruth Morse,

as a merchant and diplomat, Caxton learned both French and Dutch, but most of his translations were of French and Latin texts. Caxton's one known translation from Dutch, the well-known medieval beast epic *Reynard the Fox* (1481), demonstrates an early interest in tales about animals that comment on human behaviour.

Caxton's *The Subtle Histories and Fables of Aesop* (1484) is based on a text with its own rich translation history. As was typical for Caxton, he translated from a French source, Julien Macho's *Les subtilles fables d'Esope* (Lyon, 1482), and we can see the clear influence of the French language in French loan-words such as 'sapience' and 'aiguise' (C1; Caxton, Book 1 Prologue). Moreover, Caxton sometimes links these French words with English counterparts in doublets, pairs of words that establish synonyms between the language of his source and the English language (e.g., 'aiguise and sharpen', Book 1 Prologue). Macho's text was itself a translation of Heinrich Steinhöwel's Latin-German translation of several fable collections, including those of Romulus, Avianus, Babrius, and Poggio. First printed as a bilingual text in Ulm in 1476/7 and again in German only in 1477/8 in Augsburg, Steinhöwel's translation would go on to be translated into several other languages during the next 150 years, including French, Spanish, Czech, and, of course, English.[44] The longevity and multilingual success of this collection is a testament not just to the popularity of fables themselves but also to the rise and spread of print technology throughout Europe.

The fables that Arthur Golding (*c.* 1532–1606) translated followed a similarly multilingual and multinational trajectory. As mentioned above, Golding's immediate source text was Arnold Freitag's *Mythologia ethica* (1579), a Latin translation of a French translation of a Dutch text derived from earlier French sources that drew not just on European fable traditions but also on the popular genre of the emblem (on emblems, see part III of this introduction). While Golding's manuscript lacks the printed illustrations that accompanied his source text and its predecessors, the images played an important role in shaping the translational and formal journey that this text took

---

Helen Cooper, and Peter Holland (Cambridge: Cambridge University Press, 2013), pp. 55–77; and 'William Caxton', in *The Oxford History of Literary Translation in English*, Vol. 1: *To 1550*, ed. by Roger Ellis (Oxford: Oxford University Press, 2008), pp. 160–68.

[44] On Steinhöwel's edition and its long international life, see Pack Carnes, 'Henrich Steinhöwel and the Sixteenth-Century Fable Tradition', *Humanistica Lovaniensia* 35 (1986), 1–29.

INTRODUCTION

before it came to his attention.[45] In 1567, Flemish engraver Marcus Gheeraerts the Elder initiated and financed a book entitled *De warachtighe fabulen der dieren* [*The Truthful Fables of the Animals*], for which he also created the copper engravings; Eduard de Dene supplied the Flemish poetic translations of Gilles Corrozet's *Des fables d'Esope Phrygien* [*The Fables of Aesop the Phrygian*] (Paris, 1542) to accompany Gheeraerts' illustrations.[46] Corrozet's text, like several other European vernacular translations of the period, was illustrated with woodcuts, but what distinguished the Gheeraerts-de Dene Flemish version from its source was the fact that the images were also accompanied by an emblematic tag — a short pithy phrase summing up the lesson of the fable (e.g., 'Wickedness punished.') — and a corresponding biblical citation, thereby giving rise to what scholars have described as the hybrid genre of the emblematic fablebook.[47] As fables moved between languages and across borders, they were also transforming genres and inspiring experiments with both textual and visual media.

The emblematic fablebook featuring Gheeraerts' engravings would

---

[45] It is uncertain whether or not Golding had access to the images as he translated the text. Paul J. Smith assumes that Golding was working from a manuscript copy that Freitag gave to him when he visited England in 1579; see Smith, '*Dispositio* in the Emblematic Fable Books of the Gheeraerts Filiation (1567–1617)', in *Emblems of the Low Countries: A Book Historical Perspective*, ed. by Alison Adams and Marleen van der Weij (Glasgow: Glasgow Emblem Studies, 2003), pp. 149–70 (p. 151). Richard G. Barnes, on the other hand, posits that Golding was working from a printed edition and was therefore familiar with the images (Arthur Golding, *A Moral Fable-Talk*, ed. by Richard G. Barnes [San Francisco: Arion Press, 1987], p. 27). However, as Barnes notes elsewhere in his edition, there are some fables that seem to have been translated without access to images, such as the fable where Golding mistakenly translates *ceruus* as 'servant' rather than 'stag' (the image depicts a stag); see Barnes, pp. 338–39.

[46] Dirk Geirnaert and Paul Smith, 'The Sources of the Emblematic Fable Book *De warachtighe fabulen der dieren* (1567),' in *The Emblem Tradition and the Low Countries: Selected Papers of the Leuven International Emblem Conference, 18–23 August, 1996*, ed. by Karel Porteman, Marc Van Vaeck, and John Manning (Turnhout: Brepols, 1999), pp. 25–38. On the importance of Gheeraerts as an illustrator, see Edward Hodnett, *Aesop in England: The Transmission of Motifs in Seventeenth-Century Illustrations of Aesop's Fables* (Charlottesville: The University Press of Virginia, 1979): 'A remarkable aspect of the seventeenth-century illustration in England is that the chief figures — Francis Cleyn, Wenceslaus Hollar, and Francis Barlow [—] were all etchers, all illustrators of *Aesop's Fables*, and all indebted to Marcus Gheeraerts' (p. 8).

[47] See Geirnaert and Smith, p. 25, and Barbara Tiemann, *Fable und Emblem: Gilles Corrozet und die französische Renaissance-Fabel* (Munich: Fink, 1974), p. 108.

return to the French language in 1578 with the publication of *Esbatement moral des animaux* [*Moral Entertainment of the Animals*], but this anonymous translation did not originate from France. A prefatory poem composed by the Flemish schoolmaster and French language instructor Peeter Heyns offers some explanation, as it claims that the translation was started in London and finished in Antwerp (*A Londres entonnez & finiz en Anvers*).[48] Although the text does not explicitly name Heyns as the translator or offer any further information about why the fable collection was translated into French at this particular moment, Paul J. Smith speculates that it was the persecution of Protestants in the Low Countries that led to this French version.[49] In 1568, Gheeraerts fled Bruges for London and would return to Flanders one year before the publication of the *Esbatement moral*. Given the fact that Heyns' name is the only one present in the text, it is possible that Gheeraerts commissioned this fellow Dutch Protestant and French language instructor, who would himself go into exile in 1585, to translate his collection of fables. What this possible scenario reminds us is that the motives for translating a text from one language into another were numerous, and could be connected to the political and religious turmoil of early modern Europe.

In addition to amplifying its source with eighteen more fables and rendering the Flemish poems into sonnets, the *Esbatement moral*, as its title suggests, added the metaphor of entertainment and theatricality to the collection. The title page, which features an illustration of animals on a stage with a human audience below (see Figure 2), brings this metaphor to life, suggesting that this form of moral entertainment performed by animals is like a play that amuses audiences as it delivers truths or lessons.

It is indeed telling that Heyns' prefatory poem is addressed *au spectateur & lecteur* [to the spectator and reader], targeting first the spectator who will watch the animals perform various scenarios in the process of reading about them. Neither Freitag nor Golding has a title page that describes or depicts theatrical entertainment, but both retain traces of theatricality within the fables themselves, which refer to the collection as a 'theatre of fablespeeches' (G80), a theatre whose doors shut with the conclusion of the final tale (G125). The strain of texts that led to Golding's *A Moral Fabletalk* recognized and

---

[48] Peeter Heyns (?), *Esbatement moral* (Antwerp, 1578), sig. A2v.
[49] Paul J. Smith, *Dispositio: Problematic Ordering in French Renaissance Literature* (Leiden: Brill, 2007), pp. 154–58.

INTRODUCTION

FIGURE 2. Title page of Peeter Heyns (?), *Esbatement moral des animaux*. By permission of the Columbia University Rare Book & Manuscript Library.

exploited the very reason for their popularity: fables were effective precisely because they used entertainment to instruct.

Because it survives only in a single unsigned manuscript, *A Moral Fabletalk* has been left out of many accounts of Golding's career as a prolific translator, but his interest in such a text is hardly surprising. In fact, situating this translation within his larger body of work helps to tease out the connections between what seem to be distinct threads in his translation practices. He is most famous today for his translation of Ovid's *Metamorphoses* (published in part in 1565, and in whole in 1567). He is also well known for having translated large amounts of John Calvin's theological writings from French, but he also translated numerous Latin and French texts, from the historical *Commentaries* of Julius Caesar, to the dramatic poetry of Theodore Beza's *Tragedie of Abrahams Sacrifice*, to numerous theological treatises. Although Elizabeth Oakley-Brown has been careful to point out that Golding's oeuvre includes 'an arguably secular strand of translated texts',[50] most scholars of Golding, usually working from the prefatory poems he attaches to his translation of Ovid's *Metamorphoses*, emphasize his morality and extensive religious translations. As a text that blends a moralizing literary tradition with biblical citations, *A Moral Fabletalk* brings together both strands of Golding's interests and belies the common narrative about Golding that he repudiated his Ovid translation upon its completion in the 1560s and turned only to more serious, non-literary texts thereafter.

The moral and didactic nature of fables made them undoubtedly appealing to teachers of the period, who could use these tales to teach their pupils essential lessons about human behaviour. But equally as important as their educational content was the fact that they could also be used to teach young schoolboys how to read and write in Latin. Following the humanist grammar school practice of 'double translation' that Roger Ascham famously describes in his 1570 treatise *The Scholemaster*, students would translate Latin texts into English and back again. Schoolmaster John Brinsley (fl. 1581–1624) explains the value of this pedagogical method in more detail in his *Ludus Literarius, Or the Grammar Schoole* (1612):

> [T]his may be a most profitable course as they proceed to cause them to translate of themselves Aesop's *Fables* or Tully's *Sentences* or the like into plain, natural English so as was showed, and to cause them the next day for their exercise to bring the same thus in English, and to be able without book first to make a report of it (striving in the *Fables* who shall tell his tale in best words and

---

[50] Elizabeth Oakley-Brown, 'Arthur Golding', in *The Encyclopedia of English Renaissance Literature*, vol. 2, ed. by Garrett A. Sullivan, Jr. and Alan Stewart (Chichester: Wiley-Blackwell, 2012), pp. 386–88.

manner) and then to read it into the Latin of the author out of the English and be able to prove it, and where they have read the hard words. And after all these to try (if your leisure will serve) how they can report the same in Latin, either in the words of the author, or otherwise, as they can of themselves, which all who are pregnant and will take pains will be able to do very readily. By this you shall find great increase.[51]

In other words, the students would translate the Latin text into plain English and then bring a summarized version with them to school the next day, when they would practice putting it back into Latin. In order to guide schoolmasters and their students through this process, Brinsley published a series of textbooks that featured the works of Cato, Virgil, Cicero, Ovid, Corderius, and Aesop, all 'translated grammatically'. Throughout these texts, Brinsley experimented with the mise-en-page by using columns and elaborate marginal annotations as he attempted to replicate and teach the process of translating. *Aesop's Fables Translated Grammatically* (1617 and 1624) is a translation of a standard set of forty-five Latin fables ascribed to the fifteenth-century humanist Guilielmus Goudanus in the sixteenth century; based on the number of educational texts that orient themselves to these fables, we assume these were the standard Latin fables taught to schoolchildren in the sixteenth and seventeenth centuries. Brinsley rendered this popular series of Latin fables into English and then provided a series of grammar and vocabulary notes in the margins that would help the young pupil retranslate the fables back into Latin. As you can see in Figure 3, the marginal annotations take up as much, if not more, of the page as the fable itself. We have not been able to reproduce this format exactly in our edition, but, as you will see in our Brinsley selections, the notes are key to the reader's engagement with these fables.

Brinsley's method was not strictly focused on grammar and vocabulary, however. As he explains in the instructions written for 'the painful schoolmaster' (see his 'Epistle to the Reader' in this volume), before students could focus on issues of 'construing, parsing, making, and proving the Latin,' they should first identify the 'matter' or content of the fables, explain what wisdom is learned

---

[51] John Brinsley, *Ludus Literarius*, in *English Renaissance Translation Theory*, ed. by Neil Rhodes (London: Modern Humanities Research Association, 2013), pp. 435–47 (pp. 445–46).

> **1**
>
> ✻ The fables of
> Esop. *r* tales or
> ✻ *r* Esops Fables. fained deuises.
> *Foolish contempt*
> *of learning.*
>   **I**   ✻ Of a cocke fee-
> ✻ *Of a Cocke.* [*This fable set-* ding hens: or of a
> *teth out the foolish contempt of* dunghill cocke.
> *learning and wisedome.*]   *Gallinaceus*] signi-
>   fyeth, belonging
>   to a cock or a hen,
> ✻WHen on a time a cock or hennish, see-
> * ✻ scratched in a dung- ming to be added
> hill, hee found a precious only to distinguish
> stone: *r* saying, what, doe I *Gallus* signifying a
> finde ✻ so gay a thing? If a French man.
> ✻ Ieweller had found [*it*] ✻Whilst a cock &c.
> ✻ none ✻ could haue beene ✻ turned ouer a
> more ✻iocund than hee, *r* as dunghill viz. scrat-
> who knew the price [of it.] it vp by little and
> [But] ✻ intruth *r* it is ✻*of no* little. *r* what quoth
> vse to mee, neither doe I he. ✻ a thing so
>   bright or shining.
>   ✻ a lapidary or one
> that trimmeth and selleth pretious stones. ✻ no thing.
> ✻ could be. ✻ merry or, ioyfull. *r* because hee knew the
> worth of it. ✻ truly. *r* it will serue me for no purpose. ✻ to
> me or for me to ⁿo vse.
>   ✻*r* greatly

FIGURE 3. First page of fables in John Brinsley, *Aesop's Fables Translated Grammatically*. By permission of the Huntington Library, San Marino, California.

from such matter, and make a 'report', or summary, of the fable in both English and Latin. In addition to giving us insight into early modern pedagogical practices, Brinsley's Aesop, along with his other classical school texts, illustrates how translation practices prompted experimentation with format and mise-en-page that allowed for the kinds of annotations frequently found in manuscripts while also capitalizing on the speed of print technology to reshape and standardize the way translation could be taught.

Brinsley was not alone in recognizing the pedagogical potential of translating Aesop's fables. Using the same set of fables as Brinsley, Simon Sturtevant aimed to guide the translator by publishing a version of them in Latin with a 'construing' or translation of each individual word or phrase.[52] For schoolmaster and phonetician William Bullokar, fables proved to be an important testing ground for his new ideas about spelling during a time when orthography was not yet standardized. In 1585, he published *Aesops fabl'z in tru ort'ography with grammar-nóts*, which he hoped, however wishfully, would both model and teach proper spelling.[53] Pierre Lainé's *The Princely Way to Teach the French Tongue* (1677) shows that fables retained their value to teachers of language well into the seventeenth century. Following several pages of notes on pronunciation, spelling, grammar, vocabulary, common phrases, and dialogues, Lainé's text includes 'Some choice Fables of Aesop put into Burlesque French', presumably so that the language learner could test his or her knowledge by reading these familiar tales.[54] What is striking about these fables is that, unlike the rest of the manual, which often pairs French and English translations, the fables are in French only and seem to invite the student to read them fluently in their newly acquired foreign language, or to translate them back into English.

The translation of fables was not limited to precise grammatical and linguistic replication, however, as many writers and teachers

---

[52] Simon Sturtevant, *The Etymologist of Aesop's Fables, containing the construing of his Latine fables into English: also the etymologist of Phaedrus fables, containing the construing of Phaedrus (a new found yet auncient author) into English, verbatim* (London, 1602).

[53] *Aesops fabl'z in tru ort'ography with grammar-nóts He'r-vntoo ar al'so iooined the short sentenc'es of the wýz Cato im-printed with lýk form and order: bóth of which autorz ar transláted out-of Latin intoo E'nglish by William Bullokar* (London, 1585).

[54] At the beginning of this section, Lainé explains that the fables were first prepared 'for the use of her Highness the Lady Mary, when a Child,' referring to the daughter of King James II (Pierre Lainé, *The princely way to the French tongue as it was first compiled for the use of Her Highness, the Lady Mary, and since taught her royal sister, the Lady Anne: to which is added a chronological abridgment of the Sacred Scripture by way of dialogue: together with a larger explication of the French grammar, choice fables of Aesop in burlesque French, and lastly some models of letters French and English. By P. D. L., Tutor for the French to both Their Highnesses* [London, 1677], sig. X1r).

engaged in the practice of retelling or paraphrasing these tales. William F. Hodapp explains that Latin fable collections, especially those of Avianus, were used to teach medieval children not only Latin grammar and vocabulary but also how to retell stories.[55] Twelfth-century teacher and scholar Alexander Neckham demonstrates these various methods in his *Novus Aesopus* as well as in his *Novus Avianus*, as he retells fables 'apparently to illustrate for pupils how to work with a source text to master syntax, vocabulary, and metrics.'[56] For the second fable in the *Novus Avianus*, Hodapp observes, Neckham 'offers three versions — *copiose, compendiose*, and *subcincte*', a practice that seems to follow 'a pedagogy outlined by Quintilian, who suggested that retelling fables in various ways is useful for developing facility with the language.'[57] The fables of antiquity, then, taught young students both to translate between Latin and their vernacular languages and to engage in acts of literary creation.

It was perhaps these or similar practices that inspired the fourteenth-century Scottish poet Robert Henryson (fl. *c.* 1460–1500), whose *The Morall Fabillis of Esope the Phrygian* first circulated in manuscript, and then in printed texts in 1570 and 1571. Judging from his 'Prologue to the Reader' alone, we might assume that his version is a straightforward 'grammatical' translation that promises '[i]n mother tongue, out of Latin, to prove | To make some manner of translation'.[58] But while it is certainly the case that Henryson translated from the elegiac Latin collection of fables popular in the late middle ages,[59] the fables themselves show that he was also clearly

---

[55] Hodapp, pp. 12–28.

[56] Hodapp, p. 17.

[57] Hodapp, pp. 17, 19. Quintilian says that 'pupils should learn to paraphrase Aesop's fables [...] in simple and restrained language [...] and finally proceed to a freer paraphrase in which they will be permitted now to abridge and now to embellish the original [...] the pupil who handles it successfully will be capable of learning everything' (*Institutio Oratoria*, vol. 1, trans. by H. E. Butler [London: William Heinemann, 1921], I.ix.2–3, p. 157).

[58] Robert Henryson, 'The Argument or Prologue', in this volume (Smith fables), ll. 32–33.

[59] See Wheatley, p. 149, and Jill Mann, *From Aesop to Reynard: Beast Literature in Medieval Britain* (Oxford: Oxford University Press, 2009), p. 262. Mann notes that not all of Henryson's fables are Romulan; some seem to come from the collection of tales about a mischievous fox known in the middle ages as the *Roman de Renart* (pp. 265–67). Of the four fables from Henryson that we include in this volume, three come from the Romulus tradition (S1, S2, S4); S3 may derive from Steinhöwel's fables, the ultimate source for Caxton's fable translation (see Mann, p. 264 n. 5; see

engaging in a translation practice that resulted in long poetic expansions of the short tales attributed to Aesop.

In 1577, not long after Henryson's *Morall Fabillis* appeared in printed editions in Scotland, a London printer and bookseller named Richard Smith (fl. 1552–1598) published an 'Englished' version of Henryson's text under the title *The Fabulous Tales of Aesop the Phrygian, Compiled Most Eloquently in Scottish Metre by Master Robert Henryson, and Now Lately Englished*. Smith seems to have started his career in the cloth trade as a draper's apprentice before turning to books, and the limited information we know about him is largely pieced together from the details that survive in this particular translation.[60] We do not have birth or death dates for Smith, but the fact that he concludes this translation with the phrase 'Finished in the vale of Aylesburie the thirteenth of August. Anno Domini. 1574' suggests that he had some connection to Buckinghamshire, a county just to the northwest of London. His bookselling and printing practices do not demonstrate a particular pattern, but he seems to have established an interest in translation with his first publication, which was another translator's 'Englished' version of Boccaccio's *Il Filocolo* (1567). When he takes on his own translation project, Smith invokes the modesty topos popular among early modern translators, writing apologetically in his epistle to Richard Stonley that he 'very rudely [...] obscured the author,' and did not publish his translation for two years after he 'turned it into English [... because he was] hoping some else of greater skill would not have let it lie dead' (see Smith's 'Epistle' in this volume).

Indeed, reviving and spreading the fame of the dead was one of the primary motivating forces for Smith's translation. In a prefatory poem entitled 'The Argument between Aesop and the Translator', he even goes so far as to imagine an encounter with the ghost of Aesop, who appears to him '[a]pparellèd both brave and fine, | After the Scottish guise' while he was walking through St Paul's Churchyard, one of the primary sites of the London book trade (ll. 5–6). Drawing on two popular metaphors used to think about translation in the period — of ghosts, and of texts that change languages like people change

---

also R. J. Lyall, 'Henryson's *Morall Fabillis* and the Steinhöwel Tradition', *Modern Language Studies* 38 [2002], 362–81).

[60] For more on Smith, see Kirk Melnikoff, *Elizabethan Publishing and the Makings of Literary Culture* (Toronto: University of Toronto Press, forthcoming 2017); we are grateful to him for sharing his work with us prior to publication.

clothes — Smith conjures the spectre of the original author in order to authorize his text. The poem alternates between two different typographies (see Figure 4 below): Aesop's ghost's language is rendered in roman type, and Smith's voice is rendered in black letter, or, as it was known in the English Renaissance, 'English' type. Steven K. Galbraith has shown the association between the English language and English typography in the sixteenth century; as he argues, 'type and language were inextricable for English readers', so much so that books appearing in multiple translations would change their typography as well: 'It wasn't enough to translate the *language*; they also had to *translate* the *type*.'[61] The text of Smith's translation is likewise in black letter, translating the typography of the 1571 Scots *Morall Fabillis*, Smith's most likely source: 1571 uses an unusual type called *civilité*, a font made to look like cursive that was associated with simple, homely instruction.[62] Unlike some early modern translators, Smith does not present himself as the new Aesop, but uses visual elements such as typography to distinguish himself from the classical author and highlight the distance between the two of them.

The way typography works in this poem fits with what makes Smith's project, as a whole, unusual for thinking about translation in the period: in this case, the act of translation is almost unnecessary. Though Smith modifies Henryson's spellings to spellings more recognizable in Elizabethan English (for example, Henryson's 'Scraipand' becomes Smith's 'Scraping'; his 'quhyle' becomes 'while', etc.), Middle Scots was not so unintelligible in Renaissance England that it necessarily needed a translation. Smith's Englishing, then, is a somewhat strange instance of translation in this period: instead of bringing two cultures together, using translation as a linguistic bridge, Smith's translation creates a gulf: suddenly Henryson's fables, and his language, are considered to be inaccessible without an intermediary. This use of translation to create distance between two close cultures is apparent even in Smith's prefatory poem, where Aesop explains to the translator that he hopes to 'meet

---

[61] Steven K. Galbraith, '"English" Black-Letter Type and Spenser's *Shepheardes Calender*', *Spenser Studies* 23 (2008), 13–40 (p. 21; italics original).

[62] See David J. Parkinson, 'Introduction', in *Robert Henryson: The Complete Works*, by Robert Henryson, ed. by David J. Parkinson (Kalamazoo: Medieval Institute Publications, 2010), p. 8, citing Denton Fox, ed., *The Poems of Robert Henryson*, by Robert Henryson (Oxford: Clarendon Press, 1981), p. li, and Harry Carter and H. D. L. Vervliet, *Civilité Types* (London: Oxford University Press, 1966), p. 34.

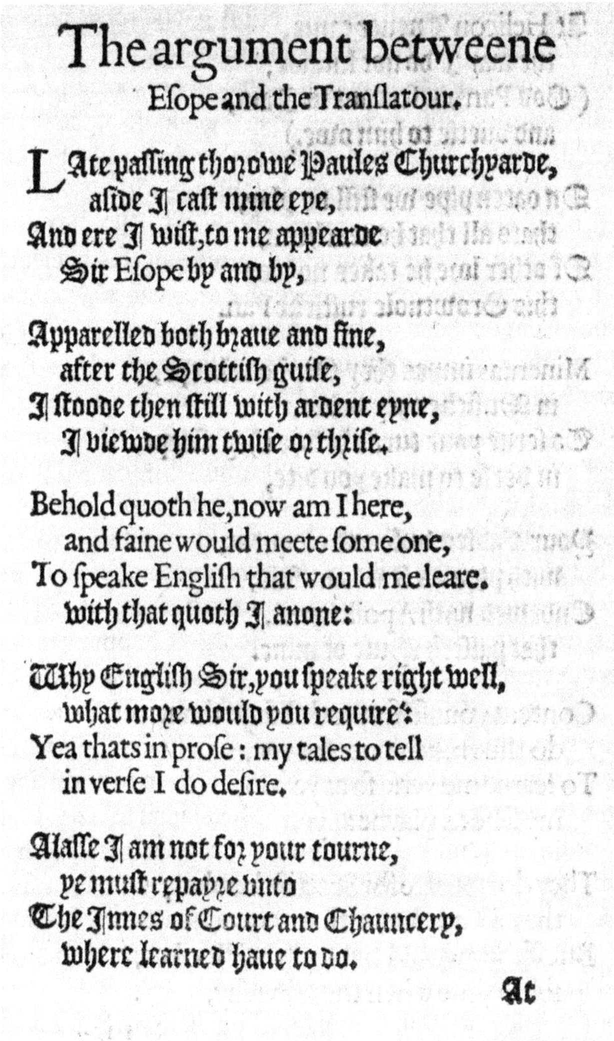

The argument betweene Esope and the Translatour.

Late passing thorowe Paules Churchyarde,
 aside I cast mine eye,
And ere I wist, to me appearde
 Sir Esope by and by,

Apparelled both braue and fine,
 after the Scottish guise,
I stoode then still with ardent eyne,
 I viewde him twise or thrise.

Behold quoth he, now am I here,
 and faine would meete some one,
To speake English that would me leare.
 with that quoth I anone:

Why English Sir, you speake right well,
 what more would you require?
Yea thats in prose: my tales to tell
 in verse I do desire.

Alasse I am not for your tourne,
 ye must repayre vnto
The Innes of Court and Chauncery,
 where learned haue to do.

       At

FIGURE 4. First page of 'The Argument Between Aesop and the Translator', from Richard Smith, *The Fabulous Tales of Aesop*. By permission of the National Library of Scotland.

someone | To speak English that would [him] lere' or teach (ll. 10–11). When the translator responds that Aesop already speaks English 'right well', referring not just to the present conversation but to earlier English translations such as Caxton's, the ghost protests that he has only been taught to speak in English prose and that he desires another layer of translation into English verse. Henryson is therefore simultaneously deserving of praise for his poetic renderings of these ancient tales, and in need of English redemption.

The expansive translation practices that Henryson employed in the fourteenth century would appear again in the middle of the seventeenth century with fellow Scotsman John Ogilby's two lushly illustrated collections of 'paraphrased' English fables, entitled *The Fables of Aesop* (1651) and *Aesopics* (1668).[63] For Ogilby (1600–1676), translating Aesop was an opportunity to redeem this ancient author, who had been 'dishonoured by unworthy translators',[64] and to apply the lessons from the texts to the fraught political situation of his time by building the context right into the fables themselves. A staunch Royalist, Ogilby recognized the political potential of Aesop's fables and produced lengthy 'paraphrased' versions of them in order to comment on the events and aftermath of the English Civil War. One of the clearest examples is 'The Battle of the Frog and the Mouse' (O2): Ogilby not only expands the well-known fable attributed to Aesop, but also merges it with the *Batrachomyomachia*, or *The Battle of Frogs and Mice*, a mock epic poem sometimes attributed to Homer that was translated into English by George Chapman in the early seventeenth century.[65] In the most basic version of the Aesopian fable, a frog offers to help a mouse across some water then tries to drown it; as they struggle, a kite devours them both. In Ogilby's version, the struggle is transformed into an epic battle between two warring armies led by the characters Frogmorton and Moustapha. No doubt inspired by the political tumult that divided his own nation, the moral of Ogilby's militarized version of the fable is that 'factions with a civil war imbrued' are doomed to be 'subdu'd' 'by some unseen aspirer' (O2, ll. 225–26). Civil wars, Ogilby warns in the middle of England's Civil War, make countries vulnerable.

Before turning to translation, Ogilby had built a career as a dancing-master and courtier and was responsible for opening the first

---

[63] The Ogilby portrait frontispiece was engraved by William Faithorne and modeled after the work of the Dutch painter Sir Peter Lely (Pieter van der Faes). The fable illustrations were largely designed by Francis Barlow and Franz Clyen. Most of the images were engraved by Wenceslaus Hollar while others were engraved by Dirck Stoop and Richard Gaywood. See Edward Hodnett, *Francis Barlow: First Master of English Book Illustration* (Berkeley: University of California Press, 1978).

[64] John Ogilby, 'To the Right Honorable Heneage Finch Earl of Winchilsea and Viscount Maidstone, and the Right Honourable Henry Seymour Lord Beauchamp', in this volume.

[65] George Chapman, *The crowne of all Homers workes Batrachomyomachia or the battaile of frogs and mise* (London, 1624).

theatre in Ireland in 1637.[66] In 1649 he published his translation of Virgil, for which James Shirley later praised him in a commendatory poem to his *Fables of Aesop* using language that bears a striking resemblance to the imagined encounter with Aesop's ghost that Smith described above:

> Methinks I see
> The learned shade of Virgil rise to thee,
> Taught our own language, with that soul, and sense,
> As hath not shamed his Roman eloquence[.][67]

Anticipating critiques for 'descend[ing] to Aesop' after having 'the honour of conversation with Virgil,' Ogilby uses his dedicatory letter to situate himself in a rich genealogy of the 'wisest' who have 'highly esteemed' the 'ancient mythologist', a list that includes both Macrobius and Socrates, 'who was judged by the oracle the wisest man then living, [and who] followed [Aesop] in all his ways of persuasive oratory, not disdaining to translate him into verse.'[68] As described in section I above, Socrates was said to have translated Aesop into verse while in prison, an activity that Ascham folds into his description of metaphrasis, or metaphrase: 'This kind of exercise is all one with *paraphrasis*, save it is out of verse either into prose or into some other kind of metre, or else out of prose into verse, which was Socrates' exercise and pastime (as Plato reporteth) when he was in prison, to translate Aesop's *Fables* into verse.'[69] Raising the ghost of Aesop and presenting 'the old philosopher in a modern and poetical dress' once more during England's crisis of governance proved to be an apt decision on Ogilby's part: the morals these fables offered seemed to be more alive than ever before.

This volume forms part of the *MHRA Tudor & Stuart Translations* series, not merely because it contains early translations, but also because, as this section has shown, the history of fable translation can also teach us a great deal about histories of translation more broadly. Taken together, the translators discussed in this section demonstrate

---

[66] Charles W. J. Withers, 'Ogilby, John (1600–1676)', in *Oxford Dictionary of National Biography* (Oxford: Oxford University Press, 2007) <http://dx.doi.org/10.1093/ref:odnb/20583>.
[67] James Shirley, 'To my Worthy Friend Mr. John Ogilby', in this volume, ll. 9–12.
[68] John Ogilby, 'To the Right Honorable Heneage Finch', in this volume.
[69] Roger Ascham, *The Schoolmaster*, in *English Renaissance Translation Theory*, ed. by Neil Rhodes (London: Modern Humanities Research Association, 2013), pp. 411–25 (p. 425).

how capacious the category of translation was in the early modern period. It is no small coincidence that the same stories that schoolboys learned to translate at a young age would also inspire writers to think about the aesthetic, pedagogical, and political potential of translating literary texts into English. Further, the variety of approaches that our translators brought to these tales suggests that there was no single way to read a fable, and that translating and re-translating them were means by which to generate new ways of reading and to find new readers for these age-old tales.

III. READING RENAISSANCE FABLES

A fable typically has two main parts: a narrative, and a 'moral', or a concise summation of the lesson to be learned from that narrative. While this model defines nearly all fables, the variety of literary work that can fall under that broad umbrella definition is truly remarkable. Some authors or translators may wish to put more emphasis on the *narrative* part of the fable: the true literary interest is in the story, and attention is paid to plot, characterization, and descriptions whose details often exceed what is needed to convey the moral. In our volume, Ogilby is the best example of this. His long narrative poems contain a wealth of detail, learned references, and jokes, and can stretch into many pages (the narrative part of the fable of the frog and the mouse, O2, is 222 lines); however, each ends with a compact four-line moral. It is clear when reading Ogilby that narrative triumphs over the simple moral.

Henryson (as Englished by Smith) is closest to Ogilby in terms of the wealth of detail included in his narratives, though he also gives equal weight and care to his morals. In the long moral that follows his own version of the fable of the frog and the mouse (S4), each detail that may have seemed gratuitous becomes significant: the frog's ugly features are explained allegorically, as is the mouse's naïveté, as is the kite's rapaciousness, as is the water's constant motion — and so on. Narrative detail becomes important for Henryson because it feeds the allegorical reading that the 'moral' section of the fable entails. Fables are more than mere didactic texts for Henryson, who probably comes closest to an understanding of *fabula* as a means to express the deeper truths that were described in the first part of this introduction.

Ogilby and Henryson also share an interest in narrative that stretches not only within fables but across fables: each includes

INTRODUCTION

characters who appear more than once and explicitly move from one moralizable adventure to another. Henryson's larger fable collection includes a series of three fables (none included in this volume) that all feature the same fox, and in Ogilby's sequences, the fables frequently follow causally on one another: the fight of words that takes place between 'The Lion and the Forester' (O8) leads to a compromise and dinner invitation in the next fable, 'The Lion, the Forester, and His Daughter' (O9); the death of the lion over dinner in this second fable leads to the forester's commission to kill another large beast in 'The Forester, the Skinner, and the Bear' (O10). We have included three set sequences in this volume (O8–10, 11–13, and 15–17) to illustrate this tendency of Ogilby, though there are more in the larger collections from which these fables are taken.

However, Ogilby goes still further by embedding cross-fable references that stretch across the volume, not just short sequences. When the forester agrees to kill the bear in 'The Forester, the Skinner, and the Bear' (O10), one of the bold justifications for his plan comes from a desire to revenge himself on the bear; this is a reference to the earlier fable 'The Bear and the Bees' (O6), where a bear — as it turns out, the same bear who will be hunted later — attacks a hive of bees. In the fable that immediately precedes 'The Lion and the Forester' (O8, which begins with an announcement that there will be a universal peace, especially between humans and animals), a fox spreads the news of the peace to a cock, who wisely refuses to believe the news until it is corroborated further. This kind of cross-referencing strains against the basic makeup of the fable, which is usually a self-contained and portable unit exemplifying a lesson. Ogilby's fables are more like smaller pieces of a larger story about the animal kingdom — and, simultaneously, the human political landscape — than they are like individual lessons.

On the other side of the spectrum of fables are those that place more weight on the *exemplarity* of the fable, or the lesson to be learned. The fables of Caxton and Brinsley, when contrasted with those of Henryson and Ogilby, are incredibly short and shorn of detail: the translators give the minimum amount of plot required to relay a message, and seldom do details or points of interest appear that are gratuitous to the message the fable is intended to convey, or the segment of learning that the narrative is meant to demonstrate. The interpretation and analysis of these two translators, therefore, requires different skills and focuses than does an analysis of the two narratively inclined translators. While Ogilby and Smith's translation of Henryson can be read with a somewhat standard set of tools for literary analysis (paying great attention to the texture of language, metre, characterization, speed of narration, level of detail, and figures of speech), Caxton and Brinsley reward those who ask different kinds of questions: What kinds of patterns appear in terms of what morals are offered, what animals appear, and so on? What is the relationship between narrative, however brief, and moral?

The project of these shorter kinds of fables is to worry the question of exemplarity itself: an example must be at once exceptional, an unusual or especially paradigmatic instance of something, and representative, able to represent or stand in for other similar instances. The ingenuity and creativity, in these shorter fables especially, is in the jump from narrative to moral. The authors seek to seal, or conceal, the gap between the example (the specific narrative) and the exemplary lesson it conveys. When the dog refuses to take bread from, and so successfully turns away, a thief in G33, C6, B5, and O4, the lesson must go beyond the merely reiterative or literal ('Do not take bread from thieves if you are guarding a house'), and must be abstracted into a larger message: Don't trust people who flatter or try to bribe you, as they are probably trying to get something more from you (Brinsley); Pay attention to where gifts are coming from and why they are given (Caxton). Tracking and questioning the jump from a story to a moral is the interpretive puzzle in these shorter fables, a task that also raises larger questions of how examples function, and how we abstract from particular instances to general kinds of knowledge — questions that would become important in the scientific revolution of the seventeenth century as scientific reformers like Francis Bacon insisted that true knowledge could only be built on data and concrete observations gradually abstracted, via inductive reasoning, into larger theoretical claims about nature.

At the absolute end of this side of the spectrum — the side that places most weight on the moral rather than the narrative — lies Arthur Golding's *A Moral Fabletalk*. The *Fabletalk* as it comes down to us is a hand-written manuscript, divorced of its context, but the text from which he was translating, Freitag's *Mythologia Ethica*, is a cross between a fable book and an emblem book. Emblems were an art form that combined visual and verbal media, and typically consisted of at least three parts: a short motto or phrase, an image, and a slightly longer poem or inscription. As scholar of emblems Peter M. Daly describes, these three elements often fit together in a mosaic of meaning: 'a general moral is enunciated in the motto, embodied in

INTRODUCTION

the picture [...], which in turn is elucidated in the epigram [...]. [T]he three parts — motto, picture, and epigram — cooperate in communicating a complex notion, which is not fully contained in any one of the parts.'[70] Emblems frequently rely on an allegorical understanding of the world: hence the phoenix described in the Golding's emblematic fable G124 is both an exotic bird and a figure or allegorical representation of Christ.[71] Daly, in a survey of contemporary understandings of the emblem, argues that in the earliest versions of emblem books the images were seen as optional, but for later writers images are definitive of what makes an emblem.[72]

Fables and emblems overlap and interact in interesting ways in the early modern period. Andraeas Alciatus, whose *Emblamata* of 1531 invented the emblem book, explicitly notes that some of his emblems are drawn from fables. He notes that his emblem about a sick kite is *ex apologo Gabriae* [out of the apologue or fable of Gabrius or Babrius, an ancient Greek fable translator]; likewise his emblem about the beaver who castrates himself to escape the hunter is the *Apologus Aesopicus de Castore* [Aesopian apologue or fable of the beaver].[73] Fables are also the basis of many of the emblems of Geffrey Whitney, author of the first English emblem book, though Whitney, like other emblem authors, frequently collapses fables, removing or only gesturing to their implicit narrative elements. Take, for instance, the fable of the dog and his reflection (G56, B4). In this fable, a dog

---

[70] Peter M. Daly, 'Emblems: An Introduction,' in *Companion to Emblem Studies*, ed. by Peter Daly (New York: AMS Press, 2008), pp. 1–24 (p. 3). See also Huston Diehl, *An Index of Icons in English Emblem Books 1500–1700* (Norman and London: University of Oklahoma Press, 1986).

[71] Mary V. Silcox notes in her 'The Emblem in the United Kingdom and America,' in *Companion to Emblem Studies*, ed. by Daly, pp. 369–91, that English emblems 'developed from a joining together of native allegorical religious representations with imported epigrammatic models of witty creation, largely secular, and imprese [devices or emblems]. The result is an emblem tradition with two streams, religious and secular' (pp. 369–70). Golding's fables clearly participate in the religious emblem tradition more than in the secular.

[72] Peter M. Daly, 'Emblem Theory: Modern and Early Modern', in *Companion to Emblem Studies*, ed. by Daly, pp. 43–78. His overview of Renaissance emblem theory is pp. 66–78.

[73] Andreas Alciatus, *Emblemata V.C. Andreae Alciati Mediolanensis iurisconsulti; cum facili & compendiosa explicatione, qua obscura illustrantur, dubiáque omnia soluuntur* (Antwerp, 1584), pp. 281, 331. For more on the relationship between emblem books and fable collections, see Mason Tung, 'A Serial list of Aesopic Fables in Alciati's *Emblemata*, Whitney's *A Choice of Emblemes* and Peacham's *Minerva Britanna*', *Emblematica* 4.2 (1989), 315–29.

with a piece of meat in his mouth sees his reflection in water, opens his mouth to try to take the 'other' dog's meat, and loses the meat he had because of his greediness. Whitney's emblem book includes an emblem about this dog, but it seems to assume that the reader already knows this canine fable: the only gesture to story in Whitney is in a single couplet: 'Let suche beholde, the greedie dogge to moane, | By brooke deceau'd, with shaddow of his boane.'[74] In emblems that draw on fables, it is typically the animal, rather than an animal's actions or interactions, that stands for something or relates a lesson.

Things went the other way as well in the sixteenth century: some of the 'fables' that Golding translates seem to come from the emblem tradition rather than from the fable tradition. In particular, his fable 'Of the Chameleon' (G78) has almost no narrative at all, but is a description of the physical attributes of the chameleon. The description of the animal comes from Pliny, a Roman natural historian who described a number of different animal species; the idea that a chameleon's ability to change his skin colour likens him to a flatterer can be found in Alciatus' fifty-third emblem, whose image of a chameleon is given the motto *In adulatores* [Of flattering sycophants].[75] It is possible that Alciatus' emblem book, or an imitation thereof, is the source of this 'fable'.[76] Other Golding fables,

---

[74] Geffrey Whitney, *A choice of emblemes, and other deuises, for the moste parte gathered out of sundrie writers, Englished and moralized. And diuers newly deuised, by Geffrey Whitney. A worke adorned with varietie of matter, both pleasant and profitable: wherein those that please, maye finde to fit their fancies: bicause herein, by the office of the eie, and the eare, the minde maye reape dooble delighte throughe holsome preceptes, shadowed with pleasant deuises: both fit for the vertuous, to their incoraging: and for the wicked, for their admonishing and amendment* (Leyden, 1586), p. 5.

[75] Alciatus, *Emblamata*, p. 127. Though the description of the chameleon in G78 seems to come directly from Pliny, many of the fables in Golding's collection also draw on medieval Christian bestiaries, books that describe the divine significance of animals and natural objects. For example, the late medieval text *Physiologus* argues that the 'Phoenix represents the person of the Savior' or Jesus (*Physiologus: A Medieval Book of Nature Lore*, trans. by Michael J. Curley [Chicago: University of Chicago Press, 1979], p. 14); compare G124: 'The phoenix beareth the figure of our saviour Christ.' Bestiaries, natural history, emblem books, and fables frequently traded tropes, including both natural facts and natural interpretations.

[76] To further complicate the issue, later editions of Alciatus' emblem book would change their images to match Gheeraerts' engravings. As Edward Hodnett explains, Christopher Plantin, who printed a late-sixteenth-century edition of Alciatus, seems to have purchased Gheeraerts' fable plates at some point in the 1570s; see Hodnett, *Marcus Gheeraerts the Elder of Bruges, London, and Antwerp* (Utrecht: Haentjens, Dekker & Humbert, 1971), pp. 13–14.

such as G122, likewise seem to come ultimately from emblem books,[77] and near the end of the collection, narrative seems to fall away entirely: the last two fables in the collection merely describe attributes of two birds, and explain the moral significance of those descriptions.

Because Golding's fable text is closer to emblem than to narrative — in that each fable requires the reader to evaluate the relationship between emblematic image and text — his fables are more self-enclosed than those of Henryson and Ogilby. Golding, therefore, as a fabulist closer to the moral end of the spectrum than the narrative end, requires the same set of questions that Brinsley and Caxton do, but his fables are more complicated still: the discerning reader must determine not only the relationship between narrative and moral, but the relationship between narrative, moral, motto, and biblical citation. Golding's translation is only of Freitag's Latin prose, so his manuscript looks very different in its handwritten form than it does in this volume — see Figure 5 below. However, because images are so central to this emblematic family of fables, we have included the engravings from Freitag's *Mythologia Ethica* in this volume. In so doing, we have given readers a chance to grapple with all five elements (the four verbal elements and the one visual element) that go into each fable in this rich tradition.

Of course, to put too much weight on the word *moral*, as an adjective implying ethical imperatives, is also to misunderstand the fascinating uses to which fables are put in the early modern period. The moral of a fable, as is mentioned above, is best understood as a concise summation of the lesson or point of the narrative. Often these lessons were moral in the sense that we would use the word today, but, as has been described in the previous sections, fables were thought to contain other kinds of lessons too: political, philosophical, social, linguistic, territorial, or natural philosophical. What may be unexpected to readers who pick up a volume of moral fables, then, is the range of instruction on offer across these fables. Lessons are ethical, but they also describe effective ways for ruling over others, interacting with friends and with enemies, thinking about learning and the nature of knowledge, seeing biblical lessons and the work of God in everyday events, exploring the features of human nature, and

---

[77] See Alciatus, *Emblemata*, p. 191, whose image of the ass loaded with food and eating thistles is remarkably similar to Gheeraerts' both before and after Gheeraerts' images start to be used as models in the 1570s.

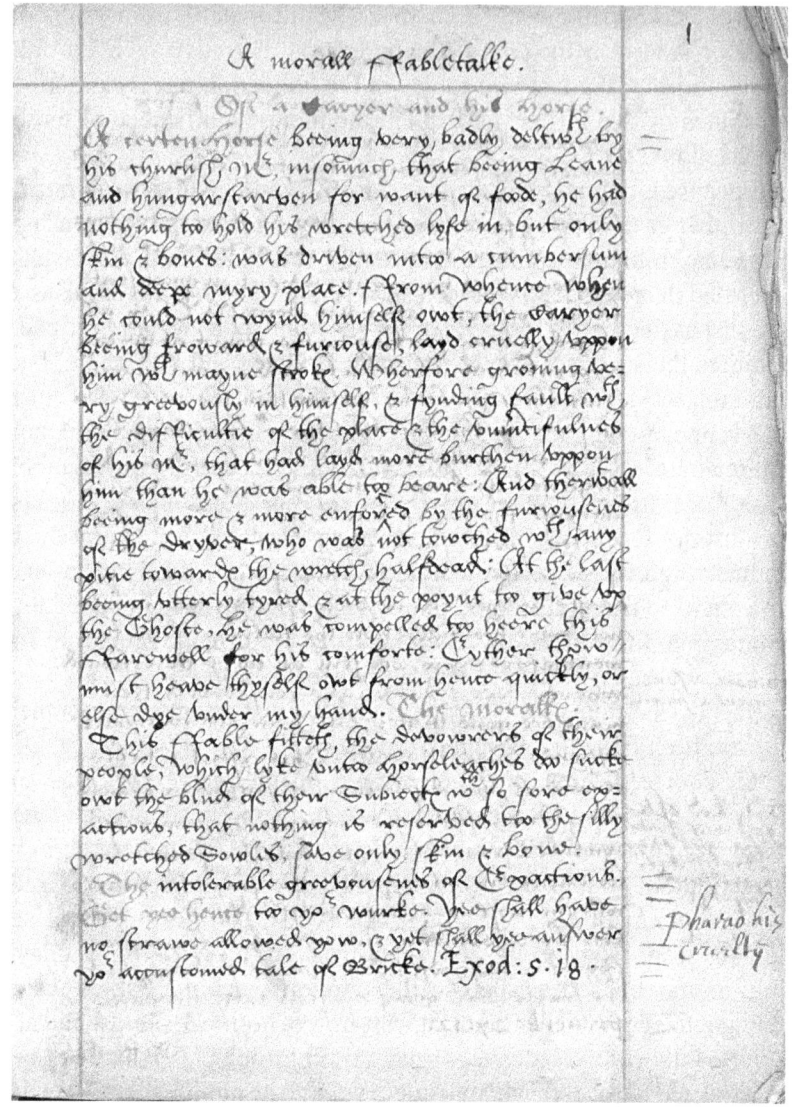

FIGURE 5. First page of fables in Arthur Golding's *A Moral Fabletalk*. By permission of the Columbia University Rare Book & Manuscript Library.

stretching the boundaries of poetic forms and genres — to name only a few.

Reading these fables, therefore, means not only taking in a wide variety of lessons, but also exploring the puzzle that is the Renaissance fable. What are its parts; how do they fit together; what

INTRODUCTION

in the narrative escapes the moral; or how does the moral exemplify the narrative, elevating it to something more than itself? In the following volume you will find the text of Golding's manuscript *A Moral Fabletalk*, in full, transcribed, edited, and annotated; because it survives only in one handwritten copy, we have made it available in its entirety in an affordable volume for the first time. From our four other fabulists we have included selections made according to a number of different criteria. As the reader, you may select different authors and read within one author's selection of fables; we have attempted to include from each author a representative selection of animals, kinds of morals, and writing styles, as well as selecting some of the 'best' or most interesting fables (in our subjective opinion) from each — the 'Exemplative Tale of the Lion and the Mouse' (S2) has a fable within a dream vision; C11, 'Of the Wolf which Made a Fart' is remarkable for its length and strangeness; O11, 'Of the Young Man and the Cat', translates the Pygmalion myth (the artist who prays that his statue might come to life so he might marry her) to a man who prays (successfully) to have his cat transformed into a woman that he might marry.

We have also attempted to include fables that were popular in the middle ages and Renaissance, and that appear in other authors and kinds of texts as well, to allow our readers to enrich their readings of early literary texts: William Shakespeare's use of the fable of the limbs and the belly (see C9, B9, O7) in his play *Coriolanus*, for example, or Geoffrey Chaucer's incorporation of the fable of the man and the lion (see C10, O3) into the *Canterbury Tales*' Wife of Bath's famous haunting question about fair representation in art: 'who peyntede the leon, tel me who?'[78] We also included, from Caxton, fables that contain no morals and show the plasticity of the fable in the period. Though we have tried to include fables that are unique to each translator (Caxton's list of monsters, C17, or Ogilby's transforming cat, O11) we have also provided overlapping fables so that readers can read across authors for comparative readings as well: the fable of the cock and the precious stone appears in each of our authors (G51, C1, S1, B1, O1), as do the fables about the mouse and the frog (G37, C2, S4, B3, O2), and about the lion and the mouse (G12, C1, S2, B6, O3). Cross references to fables that appear in multiple versions can be found in the 'Table of Fables' immediately

---

[78] Geoffrey Chaucer, *Wife of Bath's Prologue*, in *The Riverside Chaucer*, ed. by Larry Benson (Boston, MA: Houghton Mifflin, 1987), l. 692.

following the 'Further Reading' section. Whatever your path through the fables in this book, we hope you find them challenging, intriguing, pleasing, and, of course, instructive.

IV. EDITORIAL POLICIES AND NOTES

Arthur Golding, *A Moral Fabletalk*

The manuscript of Arthur Golding's *A Morall Fabletalke*, located in the Columbia University Rare Book & Manuscript Library (Western Manuscript 16), is a quarto bound in dark leather with gold tooling on the front, back, and spine. The cover once had two ties made of green ribbon, which have now mostly worn away. The main text runs to 132 numbered pages — written in Golding's neat and spiky secretary hand with occasional embossing italic script — and contains 125 fables in English prose, each of which has a 'morall' or 'moralles' attached to it. After Golding's text, another hand has added fourteen more pages of fables (until the 146th numbered page); pages 147–84 have page numbers and ruled margins but are left blank. Later pages and the flyleaves contain a number of miscellaneous readers' marks. The manuscript's provenance can be traced back only to 1930, when it appeared in an auction along with two other sixteenth-century manuscripts; it was eventually purchased by Hollywood screenwriter and rare book collector Jules Furthman in 1936. Furthman is the one who attributed the (unsigned) manuscript to Golding. Furthman then approached Hugh G. Dick, a professor at the University of California, Los Angeles (UCLA) with the manuscript; Dick identified Freitag as the source and worked on the manuscript for several years, apparently intending to produce an edition, though he never did so. We have compared the handwriting in the manuscript to several documents written by Golding, including three receipts, a memorandum, a petition, and a letter.[79] We have no doubt that the manuscript is in

---

[79] One receipt is held at the Folger Shakespeare Library in Washington, DC: 'Receipt from Arthur Golding of Little Birch, Essex, Esq., to Lady Golding, his sister-in-law' [manuscript], May 20, 1590, X.d.318. The rest of the papers were accessed through *State Papers Online, 1509–1714* (Gale, Cengage Learning, 2016) <http://gale.cengage.co.uk/state-papers-online-15091714/part-i.aspx>; all are held in the National Archives of the UK: 'Receipt by Arthur Goldyng', May 22, 1563, SP 12/28, f. 175; 'Receipt by Arthur Goldyng', May 26, 1563, SP 12/28, f. 184; 'Memorandum of money received by Arthur Goldyng for the use of the Earl of Oxford', May 22, 1563, SP 12/28, f. 176; 'Petition of Arthur Golding', June 28, 1563, SP 12/29, f. 11; and 'Arthur Golding to Myldemay', 1585, SP 46/33, f. 349.

INTRODUCTION

Golding's hand; in this we are supported by most scholars.[80] Columbia University acquired the manuscript in 1959 when it was presented as a gift by the Class of 1923.

As mentioned above, Golding's source for this text is Arnold Freitag's Latin *Mythologia Ethica*. The date of the manuscript is uncertain, but the translation must have been produced between 1579, when Freitag's translation was published, and 1605, when Golding died.[81] According to David G. Hale, Hugh G. Dick estimated that the translation might have happened *c.* 1580.[82] Richard G. Barnes conjectures that the translation may have been initiated after 1586, when the engraver Gheeraerts was in England (based on the fact that Gheeraerts seemingly commissioned other translations).[83]

Two other editions of Golding's text exist. One is an unpublished PhD dissertation by Nora Rooche Field, and the other, by Barnes, is a specialty edition produced in a very limited print run (325 copies) by a small San Francisco press. Field gives a critical old-spelling text and has a number of useful footnotes tracing the sources of natural and biblical ideas, with a long introduction; we frequently refer to her findings in our notes.[84] Barnes' modernized edition, like ours, publishes Golding's manuscript as it might have been printed, adding engravings from Freitag's *Mythologia Ethica* and laying the text out to match the layout of Freitag. Barnes' edition is also annotated, with reference to the notes of Dick and to Field's edition. His edition includes a genealogy of Golding's fables (showing their place in the

---

[80] Hugh G. Dick's papers include a letter from the famous bibliographer W. W. Greg dated January 7, 1939, which affirms, 'The text of the "Fables" manuscript is in the same hand as the memorandum of debt signed by Arthur Golding' (Hugh Gilchrist Dick papers, 1937–1974, UCLA Special Collections, Charles E. Young Research Library, University of California, Los Angeles, Box 21, Folder 7, Item 18). Dick also thought the MS was in Golding's hand (Letter dated July 1, 1946, in Dick papers, Box 21, Folder C, Item 2), and he wrote in a letter dated June 13, 1966 that he and early modern paleographer Giles Dawson 'were of one mind on it' (Dick papers, Box 21, Folder 7, Item 22).

[81] For the first major discussion of this question, see David G. Hale, 'The Source and Date of Golding's "Fabletalke"', *Modern Philology: A Journal Devoted to Research in Medieval and Modern Literature* 69.4 (1972), pp. 326–27 (p. 326).

[82] Hale, p. 326. Dick's correspondence includes a letter saying that he believes 'the MS was written sometime between 1579 and 1586' (Letter to Richard C. Horne, dated June 13, 1966, in Dick papers, Box 21, Folder 7, Item 22).

[83] Barnes, p. 27.

[84] Arthur Golding, 'Arthur Golding's *A Morall Fabletalke*: An Annotated Edition', ed. by Nora Rooche Field (unpublished doctoral dissertation, Columbia University, 1979; abstract in *Dissertation Abstracts International*, 40 [1979], 3314A).

larger circulation of this particular set of fables), as well as a genealogy of Gheeraerts's engravings and images influenced by them. It also contains a detailed description of the annotations in the manuscript, with a few transcriptions. We note whenever our text differs from that of Field or Barnes.

Because Golding's manuscript only exists in one copy, our editorial practice is fairly conservative. We transcribed the main text of the manuscript in full, and have modernized its spelling (to match *OED* headwords), capitalization, and punctuation in accordance with the practice in the rest of the *MHRA Tudor & Stuart Translations* series. We have also updated its formatting, regularized moments in the manuscript where Golding switches scripts for emphasis, and expanded his abbreviated biblical citations. However, we deviate in one way from the series standards. Golding regularly compounds words that would be either separate (naughty pack), or hyphenated (fable-talk) according to modern standards. Because Golding was invested in the study of (the quasi-Germanic) Anglo-Saxon, and because he so consistently compounds words throughout the entire manuscript, we have maintained these compound words when they are made up of two nouns (fabletalk), or of an adjective and a noun (naughtypack). We have used a hyphen when Golding has a compound word that is made up of two adjectives (gross-witted), an adverb and an adjective (over-heady), or a noun and an adjective (orator-like); in a few cases this meant going against *OED* practice (so, e.g., we give 'over-swollen' despite the *OED* listing the headword 'overswollen'). In three exceptional cases we have also used a hyphen when the compound word produced would have been, in our opinion, particularly awkward: wheatharvest, wolfwhelp, firstfruit.

In some cases, Golding's biblical citations no longer correspond to modern bibles; for our readers' ease of reference, we have left these citations as they are when they correspond to Freitag or to a contemporary bible, and have added a note giving the reference in the modern NRSV. In some cases, Golding has not supplied a reference while Freitag has, or has made an obvious error. Golding often incorrectly transcribes Freitag's '9' and '6' as '0', and in Fable 42 he gives 'Pro: 3.23' when both Freitag and contemporary bibles have Proverbs 3:32. In these exceptional cases we have emended Golding's citation. We list all changes to Golding's biblical citations among our emendations; a full list of all emendations to the text can be found in the Textual Notes at the end of this volume.

We have included images to correspond to each of Golding's fables

INTRODUCTION

in order to give our readers a sense of what Golding's translation might have looked like if it had been printed, and to allow our readers to encounter Golding's text as a part of the larger tradition of emblem books. Because Golding's manuscript does not contain these engravings, we have supplied images from the copy of his source, Freitag's *Mythologia Ethica*, held in the Rare Book and Manuscript Library at the University of Illinois Urbana-Champaign. All images were taken from the UIUC's copy of Freitag by Liza Blake, and prepared for publication by Philly Vasquez, Kathryn Vomero Santos, and Diane Blake; we gratefully acknowledge the UIUC's Rare Book and Manuscript Library for allowing their use in our publication.

William Caxton, *The Subtle Histories and Fables of Aesop*

William Caxton printed his translation of fables in 1484; its title reads, in part, [*T*]*he subtyl historyes and Fables of Esope whiche were translated out of Frensshe in to Englysshe by Wylham Caxton*. This edition, which also includes the life or biography of Aesop, served as the basis of two later editions printed by Richard Pynson in 1497 and again in 1500, as well as for other printings in the sixteenth and seventeenth centuries. Caxton's 1484 edition is a folio with signature gatherings consisting of 8 leaves (except for the 'S' signature, of which only six leaves are extant). The main text is printed in a black letter typeface.

Caxton's text exists in two scholarly editions, one by Joseph Jacobs published in 1889, and a more modern scholarly edition by R. T. Lenaghan, published in 1967. Joseph Jacobs' edition is in two volumes; the first volume is a study of the history of fables, and the second is an old-spelling edition of Caxton's text.[85] We checked Jacobs' edition and found it to contain several textual errors. R. T. Lenaghan's illustrated old-spelling edition, which retains Caxton's original punctuation and marks page breaks, is a scrupulous critical edition, and we highly recommend it for anyone seeking to read more deeply in Caxton.[86] His introduction includes a detailed account of the textual history of Caxton's fables, and his notes make regular reference to Julien Macho, Caxton's immediate source, and to Steinhöwel, the original collector of this set of fables.

---

[85] William Caxton, *The Fables of Aesop, as first printed by William Caxton in 1484 with those of Avian, Alfonso, and Poggio*, ed. by Joseph Jacobs (London: David Nutt in the Strand, 1889).

[86] Caxton, *Caxton's Aesop*, ed. by Lenaghan, cited above.

Our editorial practice for Caxton's fables grants textual priority to Caxton's original 1484 edition, though we have consulted later editions in preparing our text, including those of Pynson from thirteen and sixteen years later. Caxton's 1484 edition survives in three copies: a complete copy at the Royal Library at Windsor Castle (W), and two partial copies at the British Library (B) and Bodleian Library (O), respectively. We have examined each of the three surviving copies of Caxton's 1484 edition, and have completed a partial collation of the text, which revealed very few differences among the three copies. Most differences were variations in accidentals that would be erased in the modernization process (for example, fallen spaces, places where letters and virgules were only partially inked or not inked at all, spacing differences). In our partial collation (which included every fable to be included in our edition) we found only three significant differences: W and O label the sixty-third folio as 'Folio lx' while B corrects to 'Folio lxiii' (f. 63r); W and O give the word 'hane' while B corrects to 'haue' (i.e., 'have'; f. 72r); and B and O give the word 'loyn' while W corrects to 'lyon' (f. 75r). As with Golding, our edition of Caxton's fables is a fairly conservative one. However, we have modernized Caxton's spelling (to match *OED* headwords), capitalization, and punctuation in accordance with the practice in the rest of the *MHRA Tudor & Stuart Translations* series. Caxton's punctuation is particularly far from modern practice — most of his clauses are divided by virgules — and we have had to take a few liberties in deciding where to break clauses to make complete sentences. A full list of all emendations to the text can be found in the Textual Notes at the end of this volume.

We have also included images to correspond to each of Caxton's fables that were illustrated in his 1484 edition. Three of the images (the initial woodcut of Aesop, the image of the cock and the precious stone, and the image of the frog and the rat) are supplied from the Royal Library at Windsor Castle's copy of 1484, by that library's imaging department. The rest of the images are supplied from the copy of Richard Pynson's 1497 reprint of Caxton's text held at the Huntington Library; photographs from the Huntington Library's copy of Pynson were taken by Liza Blake, and were prepared for publication by Kathryn Vomero Santos and Diane Blake. We gratefully acknowledge the Royal Collection Trust (© Her Majesty Queen Elizabeth II 2016) and the Huntington Library for allowing us to use these images in our publication.

INTRODUCTION

Richard Smith, *The Fabulous Tales of Aesop the Phrygian*

Henryson's *Morall Fabillis* exists in manuscript copies in London and in the National Library of Scotland in Edinburgh; these manuscripts have been collated with later print editions and edited in original spelling in modern editions. The fables also exist in four early print editions: a 1570 Edinburgh printing by Robert Lekpreuik; a 1571 Edinburgh printing by Thomas Bassendyne; a 1577 London printing by Richard Smith (published as *The Fabulous Tales of Esope the Phrygian*); and a 1621 Edinburgh printing by Andro Hart. Each of these early printed editions exists in only one surviving copy; the 1570 edition is held at the British Library, and the rest are held at the National Library of Scotland. Smith's edition claims to be an 'Englishing' (or a translation into English) of Henryson's text; the fables are printed in black letter typeface.

Our edition of the *Moral Fables* is of Richard Smith's 1577 edition specifically, and we have therefore adopted the sole surviving print copy of Smith's edition as our copy text. We have compared the edition with the other printed editions from which Smith might have been working, but have granted the Smith edition textual priority over the others. Three noteworthy variants appear when comparing Smith's 1577 edition to the two printed Edinburgh editions. In the 'Argument or Prologue', l. 60, Smith has the phrase 'Lack the disdain'; 1571 reads 'Lak the disdane' (p. 5), and 1570 reads 'Lak the wisedom' (sig. A3r). In S2, l. 288, Smith has the phrase 'These rural men'; 1571 reads 'rurall' here (p. 66), and 1570 reads 'cruell' (sig. H1r). In S4, ll. 170ff., Smith includes a stanza that exists in 1571 (p. 117) but not in 1570 (sig. N3v). We therefore have tentatively concluded that if Smith was working from a printed version of Henryson's text, he was most likely working from the 1571 edition rather than from the 1570 edition. We note any interesting changes and variants between Smith's edition and others in our notes to the fables themselves.

Henryson's *Moral Fabillis* has been edited in multiple modern scholarly editions from the medieval manuscripts (and taking account of the later print editions). For an excellent edition of Henryson's *Moral Fabillis* in Middle Scots, we recommend that of Robert Kindrick from 1997, or the updated TEAMS edition from 2010.[87]

---

[87] Robert Henryson, *The Poems of Robert Henryson*, ed. by Robert L. Kindrick (Kalamazoo, MI: Medieval Institute Publications, 1997); Henryson, *Robert Henryson: The Complete Works*, ed. by David J. Parkinson, cited above.

However, ours is the first edition specifically of Smith's 1577 'Englishing' with its fascinating changes and paratexts.

We have modernized Smith's spelling (to match *OED* headwords), capitalization, and punctuation in accordance with the practice in the rest of the *MHRA Tudor & Stuart Translations* series. In many cases, making these modernizations did damage to the relatively regular metre of Smith's translation, or to his rhymes. We have noted in our text each instance in which we have altered Smith's metre; readers should generally assume that imperfect rhymes in Smith are a result of our modernizations. A full list of all emendations to the text can be found in the Textual Notes at the end of this volume.

John Brinsley, *Aesop's Fables Translated Grammatically*

There are two surviving editions of John Brinsley's *Esops Fables*, one from 1617 and one from 1624. Only one copy survives of each of the two editions: the 1617 edition is held at the Huntington Library, and the 1624 edition is held at the British Library. The 1624 edition is currently bound with five other educational texts. Brinsley's translation is of Guilielmus Goudanus' Latin translation of 45 Aesopian fables; we were able to identify them as coming from Goudanus' set because Brinsley occasionally cites specific Latin words from his source to explain them to his reader (B1, *Gallinaceo*; B8, *puerpera*); these words appear in Goudanus's translations but not others. The Goudanus translations were reprinted more than almost any other set in sixteenth- and seventeenth-century Europe, often as parts of larger collections including other groups of fables as well; some versions of the fable of the cock and the precious stone say that the cock *verrit* [sweeps] the dirt, and others say that the cock *vertit* [turns over] the dirt. We know from Brinsley's notes that he must have been translating from one of the editions that reads *vertit*. No modern edition of Brinsley's fables exists.

We have completed a full collation of all differences in spelling and punctuation between the two volumes. The two texts are very close to one another, though with a few minor differences in capitalization, punctuation, and typography. We believe both editions (1617 and 1624) have textual authority, as the changes made to the 1624 edition suggest a revising author (or very informed editor) and not just a re-setting compositor. Brinsley himself announces his intention to revise in his 'Epistle to the Reader', included in our volume: 'Vouchsafe me your better derection, in love; and what is defective, I shall (God willing) labour to supply in the next edition.' The biggest change between the two editions is that Brinsley modifies his citation system; in 1617, Brinsley uses the letter 'r' as a symbol marking notes that teach his readers about the 'variety of English phrase' (what we give in the volume as **B/V**),[88] while in 1624 he marks these notes using lowercase letters of the alphabet in alphabetical order (1624, sig. A5v). Changes between the two editions also include reinsertion of a missing line (sig. B6v), a change of an incorrect animal (sig. D6v), and comparable changes on sigs A6v and B6r. There are enough small changes in format, lineation, font, etc., to indicate that the text was reset, but the fact that the pages have almost identical catchwords throughout suggests that the compositor was closely following the earlier printed text as his model. It is most likely that Brinsley (or someone else) made corrections to a copy of the 1617 edition for the new printing. As with any new edition, resetting the type also introduces obvious errors not present in an earlier edition.

In general, we have considered each difference between the two texts individually, and chosen what we think to be the best option in each case. In producing our composite text, we tended to lean towards accepting readings from the 1624 edition, as coming closer to representing Brinsley's final intentions. Other principles in making editorial decisions included: a desire for fullness or an additive principle (if a word is present in one text but not another, we tried to include it; partly this follows Brinsley's own practice in supplying his readers with as many synonyms as possible); and clarity or 'correctness' (Brinsley designed his text to help schoolchildren translate from English back to Latin, so any obvious errors or confusions would have been corrected; many of the changes between the editions are corrections for clarity). A list of all significant variants between the two editions can be found in the Textual Notes at the back of our volume, below the list of emendations we have made to the text. We have also modernized Brinsley's spelling (to match *OED* headwords), capitalization, and punctuation in accordance with the practice in the rest of the *MHRA Tudor & Stuart Translations* series. Brinsley's text contains many square brackets, which he has used to provide information to his translators; we have retained his square brackets throughout.

---

[88] See Figure 3 above for an illustration of Brinsley's mise-en-page, including his use of asterisks and lowercase 'r's to mark different kinds of footnotes.

John Ogilby, *The Fables of Aesop* and *Aesopics*

John Ogilby's fables have a complicated publishing history. In 1651 Ogilby published a first set of eighty-one fables entitled *The Fables of Aesop*, with a dedicatory letter and two commendatory poems, in quarto. The fables were reprinted in folio in 1665 with an additional fable and with long and learned marginal annotations added to many fables. In 1668 he reprinted the first eighty-two fables again, and also released a second set of fifty fables, entitled *Aesopics*, which also included two longer poems in parts: *Androcleus, or the Roman Slave*, and *The Ephesian Matron*. Both of the 1668 printings were also in folio. Both collections of fables (plus the longer poems in *Aesopics*) were printed again, this time in octavo, in 1673, and apparently again in 1675, also in octavo.[89] In total, 123 copies of either *The Fables of Aesop* (hereafter *Fables*) or *Aesopics* are known to survive, held in libraries across North America, the UK, Europe, and Australia. Of the 123 surviving copies, we have examined 106 copies, and completed partial collations (including all fables included in this volume plus eleven additional fables) of seventy-two copies. The *Fables* and *Aesopics* are sometimes bound together, sometimes bound separately but as clear companions, and sometimes isolated and circulating as individual texts. In some libraries, they are catalogued as two separate books, while in others, they are catalogued as two volumes or parts of one larger text. In certain copies some of the images are missing (the image accompanying 'The Young Man and the Cat', O11 in this volume, is the image that is most often absent), and in some copies there are no images.

The only modern version of Ogilby's text is a photographic reprint of his 1668 *Fables of Aesop*, published by the William Andrews Clark

---

[89] As Earl Miner notes, a scholar named Max Plessow asserted that there was another version of *The Fables of Aesop* from 1653, but there is no evidence to support this assertion and we believe it to be erroneous. See Miner, 'Introduction,' in John Ogilby, *The Fables of Aesop Paraphras'd in Verse* (London: Thomas Roycroft for the author, 1668; repr. Los Angeles: William Andrews Clark Memorial Library, 1965), pp. i–xiv (p. xiii, n. 6), citing Max Plessow, *Geschichte der Fabeldichtung in England bis zu John Gay (1726)* (Berlin: Mayer & Müller, 1906), p. LXXII. Two octavo title pages also survive in an album of solitary title pages at the British Library, indicating that the fables were perhaps reprinted in the 1680s: one is a title page for *The Fables of Aesop*, 'Printed for Tho. Basset in Fleet-Street, Robert Clavel and Rich Chiswell in St Paul's Church-Yard', dated London, 1683; the other is a title page for *Aesopics*, 'Printed for T. Basset, R. Clavel, and R. Chiswell', dated London, 1684 (British Library, London, Harley MS 5923, fols 78, 76). For our theory that the 1675 reprint is only apparently a reprint, see below.

Memorial Library in 1965 with an introduction by Earl Miner.[90] This reprint, being a facsimile, makes no collation between the 1668 edition and other historical forms. In his introduction, Miner hypothesizes that the 1668 editions of each of the two texts was the last authorial edition: 'The fact that the last two editions were printed the year before Ogilby's death, in octavo, and by other publishers suggests that Ogilby had little supervision of them. What I have designated as the third edition [of *Fables*] may be thought therefore as the last which he certainly supervised.'[91] Katherine S. Van Eerde likewise finds that the edition from 1675 'falls far short of the 1665 and 1668 editions, with reworked and poor cuts,' and posits, 'It may have been a pirated edition.'[92] However, we have no reason to believe that Ogilby would not have had a hand in the copies from the 70s, both of which were published before his death; the title pages from 1673 both state that the books were 'Printed by the Author, at his House in *White-Friers*'. In any case, many of the changes made in these copies are improvements, especially to the metre of the fables, and we have therefore frequently accepted a change made only in the 70s.

Our collation revealed a few interesting things about the original printings of Ogilby's text. For the 1668 *Aesopics*, the first eight pages of fables were reset at some point; there are no substantive differences, but there are enough tiny changes in spelling and punctuation to indicate that the pages were completely reset. The 1670s *The Fables of Aesop* and *Aesopics* are bound together in a copy at the Huntington Library (call number 430929) that contains a total of 4 title pages bound within its covers: at the front is a title page for *The Fables of Aesop* dated 1673, immediately followed by a title page for *Aesopics* dated 1675. There is another 1673 *Fables of Aesop* title page inserted at the end of the main text of *The Fables of Aesop*, and at the start of the second volume of fables there is a second title page for *Aesopics* dated 1673. The editions of *Fables* and *Aesopics* from 1673 and 1675 are virtually identical, including occasional irregular or broken typography; in addition, stop-press corrections are distributed evenly across the supposedly different editions of 1673 and 1675. This suggests that these two editions are in fact one edition,

---

[90] See full citation for this edition above.
[91] Miner, p. iii.
[92] Katherine S. Van Eerde, *John Ogilby and the Taste of His Times* (Folkestone, UK: Dawson, 1976), pp. 46–47.

and one print run, perhaps with a new title page printed in 1675, with recycled or leftover pages behind it. We therefore refer to these 'two' editions as one single edition (1673/5) in our textual notes.

Because each edition introduces both changes and errors, we have considered variants among editions and chosen what we think to be the 'best' option in each case. This is often subjective, but in general we allowed regular metre to triumph over irregular, and have adopted corrections of obvious errors. We have also modernized Ogilby's spelling (to match *OED* headwords), capitalization, and punctuation in accordance with the practice in the rest of the *MHRA Tudor & Stuart Translations* series. Ogilby frequently spelled his words to indicate pronunciation (e.g., he will write 'skill'd' if he wishes the word to be pronounced with one syllable, and 'skilled' if it is to be pronounced with two syllables). Though we have modernized his spelling, we have tried to indicate intended pronunciation where possible (so for the examples above we would modernize to 'skilled' assuming a one-syllable pronunciation, and would modernize to 'skillèd' where the word seems to require two syllables). Where spelling varies in a way that would affect metre among editions, we have noted it in our list of variants in our Textual Notes.

We have also regularized Ogilby's typography, removing hundreds of single italicized words, with a few exceptions. Throughout each of his editions, Ogilby will sometimes italicize entire lines or couplets; usually these lines or couplets are particularly proverbial, or removable from their immediate context. For example, in O3 the mouse steps back from describing an encounter with an elephant to state a wider truth: '*True valour best is without witness shown.*' When entire lines or couplets were italicized in every edition, we have maintained the italics, assuming them to mark particularly portable lessons or morals (and it is worth noting that in each of Ogilby's early printings, the four-line morals that end each fable were set in italic type). Where lines are italicized only in some editions, we have noted them in our list of variants. The 1651 *Fables* sets certain lines in black letter; we have not attempted to reproduce this practice. A list of all significant variants between (or among) the editions can be found in the Textual Notes at the back of our volume, below the list of emendations we have made to the text.

We have included images to correspond to each of Ogilby's fables, as his fables were published with illustrations in each of his editions, despite changing format twice (from quarto to folio and then from folio to octavo). We have also included the two large engravings that appear in the 1668 editions (in different places in different copies): an engraving of Aesop surrounded by animals, accompanied by a short poem, and an engraving of Ogilby. We have photographed the engravings from copies of the 1668 *Fables* and the 1668 *Aesopics* held in the Rare Book and Manuscript Library at the University of Illinois Urbana-Champaign. All photographs were taken from the UIUC's copies by Liza Blake, and were prepared for publication by Philly Vasquez, Kathryn Vomero Santos, and Diane Blake; we gratefully acknowledge the UIUC's Rare Book and Manuscript Library for allowing their use in our publication. The cover image for this volume is from a copy of Ogilby's *Fables* held at the Bristol Public Library; almost all of the images in this copy were coloured in with watercolours at some point in the book's history. The photograph was taken by Liza Blake, and prepared for publication by Diane Blake. We are grateful to the Bristol Public Library for allowing us to use the image on our cover.

At the end of this volume is a glossary of obscure words, and common words being used in usual ways; throughout, we mark any word that is defined in the glossary with a degree symbol (°) the first time it appears in each translator's text.

FURTHER READING

The full list of books discussed and cited in the introduction, and in the footnotes to the fables themselves, can be found in the Bibliography at the end of this book. Below you can find suggested further reading on Renaissance fables in general (especially English fables), and for each of our authors in particular.

I. (MEDIEVAL AND) RENAISSANCE FABLES

Acheson, Katherine O., 'The Picture of Nature: Seventeenth-Century English Aesop's Fables', *Journal for Early Modern Cultural Studies* 9 (2009), 25–50

Cottegnies, Line, 'The Art of Schooling Mankind: The Uses of Fable in Roger L'Estrange's Aesop's Fables (1692)', in *Roger L'Estrange and the Making of Restoration Culture*, ed. by Anne Dunan-Page and Beth Wynn (Aldershot: Ashgate, 2008), pp. 131–48

DuBruck, Edelgard, 'Aesop's Weeping Puppy: Late-Medieval Migrations of a Narrative Motif', *Early Drama, Art, and Music Review* 22 (1999), 1–10

Finch, Chauncey E., 'The Renaissance adaptation of Aesop's "Fables" by Gregorious Corrius', *Classical Bulletin* 49 (1973), 44–48

Fudge, Erica, *Perceiving Animals: Humans and Beasts in Early Modern English Culture* (Champaign: University of Illinois Press, 2002)

——, ed., *Renaissance Beasts: Of Animals, Humans, and Other Wonderful Creatures* (Champaign: University of Illinois Press, 2004)

Hale, David G., 'Aesop in Renaissance England', *Library* s5-XXVII (2) (1972), 116–25

Hodapp, William F., 'The Fables of Avianus', in *Medieval Literature for Children*, ed. by Daniel T. Kline (New York: Routledge, 2003), pp. 12–28

Hodnett, Edward, *Aesop in England: The Transmission of Motifs in Seventeenth-Century Illustrations of Aesop's Fables* (Charlottesville: University Press of Virginia, 1979)

Lerer, Seth, 'Aesop, Authorship, and the Aesthetic Imagination', *Journal of Medieval and Early Modern Studies* 37.3 (2007), 580–94

——, 'Ingenuity and Authority: Aesop's Fables and Their Afterlives', in *Children's Literature: A Reader's History, from Aesop to Harry Potter* (Chicago: University of Chicago Press, 2008), pp. 35–56

Lewis, Jayne Elizabeth, *The English Fable: Aesop and Literary Culture, 1651–1740* (Cambridge: Cambridge University Press, 1996)

Loveridge, Mark, *A History of Augustan Fable* (Cambridge: Cambridge University Press, 1998)

Mann, Jill, *From Aesop to Reynard: Beast Literature in Medieval Britain* (Oxford: Oxford University Press, 2009)

Patterson, Annabel, *Fables of Power: Aesopian Writing and Political History* (Durham: Duke University Press, 1991)

Perry, Ben Edwin, *Aesopica: A Series of Texts Relating to Aesop or Ascribed to Him* (Urbana: University of Illinois Press, 1952)

——, 'Fable', *Studium generale* 12 (1959), 17–37

——, 'Introduction', in *Babrius and Phaedrus*, trans. by Ben Edwin Perry (Cambridge, MA: Harvard University Press, 1964), pp. xi–cii

——, *Studies in the Text History of the Life and Fables of Aesop* (Haverford: The American Philological Association, 1936)

Tung, Mason, 'A Serial list of Aesopic Fables in Alciati's *Emblemata*, Whitney's *A Choice of Emblemes* and Peacham's *Minerva Britanna*', *Emblematica* 4.2 (1989), 315–29

Wheatley, Edward, *Mastering Aesop: Medieval Education, Chaucer, and His Followers* (Gainesville: University Press of Florida, 2000)

II. ARTHUR GOLDING'S *A MORAL FABLETALK*

Golding, Arthur, 'Arthur Golding's *A Morall Fabletalke*: An Annotated Edition', ed. by Nora Rooche Field (unpublished doctoral dissertation, Columbia University, 1979; abstract in *Dissertation Abstracts International* 40 (1979), 3314A)

——, *A Moral Fable-talk*, ed. by Richard G. Barnes (San Francisco: The Arion Press, 1987)

Golding, Louis Thorn, *An Elizabethan Puritan: Arthur Golding the Translator of Ovid's* Metamorphoses *and also of John Calvin's* Sermons (New York: Richard R. Smith, 1937)

Hale, David G., 'The Source and Date of Golding's "Fabletalke"', *Modern Philology: A Journal Devoted to Research in Medieval and Modern Literature* 69.4 (1972), 326–27

Hodnett, Edward, *Marcus Gheeraerts the Elder of Bruges, London, and Antwerp* (Utrecht: Haentjens Dekker & Gumbert, 1971)

Nelson, William, 'A Morall Fabletalke', *Columbia Library Columns* 9.1 (1959), 26–32

Smith, Paul J., 'Arnold Freitag's *Mythologia ethica* (1579) and the Tradition of the Emblematic Fable', in *Mundus Emblematicus: Studies in Neo-Latin Emblem Books*, ed. by Karl A. E. Enenkel and Arnoud S. Q. Visser (Turnhout: Brepols, 2003), pp. 173–200

——, '*Dispositio* in the Emblematic Fable Books of the Gheeraerts Filiation (1567–1617)', in *Emblems of the Low Countries: A Book Historical Perspective*, ed. by Alison Adams and Marleen van der Weij (Glasgow: Glasgow Emblem Studies, 2003), pp. 149–70

——, *Dispositio: Problematic Ordering in French Renaissance Literature* (Leiden: Brill, 2007)

Wortham, James, 'Arthur Golding and the Translation of Prose', *HLQ* 12 (1949), 339–67

III. WILLIAM CAXTON'S *THE SUBTLE HISTORIES AND FABLES OF AESOP*

Caxton, William, *Caxton's Aesop*, ed. by R. T. Lenaghan (Cambridge, MA: Harvard University Press, 1967)

——, *The Fables of Aesop, as first printed by William Caxton in 1484 with those of Avian, Alfonso, and Poggio*, ed. by Joseph Jacobs (London: David Nutt, 1889)

Coldiron, A. E. B., 'The mediated "medieval" and Shakespeare', in *Medieval Shakespeare: Pasts and Presents*, ed. by Ruth Morse, Helen Cooper, and Peter Holland (Cambridge: Cambridge University Press, 2013), pp. 55–77

——, *Printers Without Borders: Translation and Textuality in the Renaissance* (Cambridge: Cambridge University Press, 2015)

——, 'William Caxton', in *The Oxford History of Literary Translation in English*, Vol. 1: *To 1550*, ed. by Roger Ellis (Oxford: Oxford University Press, 2008), pp. 160–68

Hosington, Brenda M., 'The Role of Translations and Translators in the Production of English Incunabula,' in *Renaissance Cultural Crossroads: Translation, Print and Culture in Britain, 1473–1640*, ed. by S. K. Barber and Brenda M. Hosington (Leiden: Brill, 2013), pp. 3–20

Wilson, Robert H., 'The Poggiana in Caxton's *Esope*', *The Philological Quarterly* 30 (1951), 348–52

IV. RICHARD SMITH'S *THE FABULOUS TALES OF AESOP THE PHRYGIAN*

Clark, George, 'Henryson and Aesop: The Fable Transformed', *ELH* 43.1 (1976), 1–18

Fox, Denton, 'Henryson and Caxton', *Journal of English and Germanic Philology* 67 (1968), 586–93

Gray, Douglas, *Robert Henryson* (Leiden: Brill, 1979)

Henderson, Arnold Clayton, 'Having Fun with the Moralities: Henryson's *Fables* and Late Medieval Fable Innovation', *Studies in Scottish Literature* 32 (2001), 67–87

Henryson, Robert, *Morall Fabillis. The Poems of Robert Henryson*, ed. by Denton Fox (Oxford: Clarendon, 1981)

——, *The Poems of Robert Henryson*, ed. by Robert L. Kindrick (Kalamazoo: Medieval Institute Publications, 1997)

——, *Robert Henryson: The Complete Works*, ed. by David J. Parkinson (Kalamazoo: Medieval Institute Publications, 2010)

Higgins, Iain Macleod, 'Master Henryson and Father Aesop', in *Author, Reader, Book: Medieval Authorship in Theory and Practice*, ed. by Stephen Partridge and Erik Kwakkel (Toronto: University of Toronto Press, 2012), pp. 198–231

Khinoy, Stephan, 'Tale-Moral Relationships in Henryson's *Moral Fables*', *Studies in Scottish Literature* 17 (1982), 99–115

Lyall, R. J., 'Henryson's *Morall Fabillis* and the Steinhöwel Tradition', *Modern Language Studies* 38 (2002), 362–81

Mann, Jill, 'Henryson: the Epicized Fable', in *From Aesop to Reynard* (see section I above), pp. 262–305

Melnikoff, Kirk, *Elizabethan Publishing and the Makings of Literary Culture* (Toronto: University of Toronto Press, forthcoming 2017)

Powell, Marianne, *Fabula docet: Studies in the Background and Interpretation of Henryson's Morall Fabillis*, Odense University Studies in English 6 (Odense: Odense University Press, 1983)

Wheatley, Edward, 'Robert Henryson's *Morall Fabillis*: Reading, Enacting, and Appropriating', in *Mastering Aesop* (see section I above), pp. 149–89

V. JOHN BRINSLEY'S *AESOP'S FABLES TRANSLATED GRAMMATICALLY*

Enterline, Lynn, *Shakespeare's Schoolroom: Rhetoric, Discipline, Emotion* (Philadelphia: University of Pennsylvania Press, 2012)

Green, Ian, *Humanism and Protestantism in Early Modern English Education* (Farnham: Ashgate, 2009)

Salmon, Vivian, 'John Brinsley: 17th-Century Pioneer in Applied Linguistics', *Historiographia Linguistica* 2.2 (1975), 175–89

——, *The Study of Language in 17th-Century England* (Amsterdam: John Benjamins, 1988)

VI. JOHN OGILBY'S *THE FABLES OF AESOP* AND *AESOPICS*

Eames, Marian, 'John Ogilby and his Aesop: The Fortunes and Fables of a Seventeenth-Century Virtuoso', *New York Public Library Bulletin* 65 (1961), 73–88

Hodnett, Edward, *Francis Barlow: First Master of English Book Illustration* (Berkeley: University of California Press, 1978)

Kishlansky, Mark, 'Turning frogs into princes: Aesop's Fables and the political culture of early modern England', in *Political Culture and Cultural Politics in Early Modern England: Essays Presented to David Underdown*, ed. by Susan D. Amussen and Mark A. Kishlansky (Manchester: Manchester University Press, 1995), pp. 338–60

Lewis, Jane Elizabeth, 'Aesopian examples: the English fable collection and its authors, 1651–1740', in *The English Fable* (see section I above), pp. 14–47

FURTHER READING

Loveridge, Mark, 'The fable in the wars: Ogilby and after', in *A History of Augustan Fable* (see section I above), pp. 102–42

Ogilby, John, *The Fables of Aesop Paraphras'd in Verse*, intro. by Earl Miner (Los Angeles: William Andrews Clark Memorial Library, 1965)

Patterson, Annabel, '"The Fable is Inverted": 1628–1700', in *Fables of Power* (see section I above), pp. 81–110

Pennington, Richard, *A Descriptive Catalogue of the Etched Work of Wenceslaus Hollar, 1607–1677* (Cambridge: Cambridge University Press, 2002)

Van Eerde, Katherine S., *John Ogilby and the Taste of his Times* (Swindon: Dawson, 1976)

TABLE OF FABLES

ARTHUR GOLDING, *A MORAL FABLETALK*

1. Of a Carrier and his Horse 62
2. Of the Lion and the Fox 64
3. Of the Oak and the Elm 66
4. Of a Lion and an Ass 68
5. Of a Man that Called for Death 70
6. Of a Cockatrice and a Weasel 72
7. Of an Ape and his Imps 74
8. Of a Lion and a Horse 76
   Compare to C7
9. Of the Fox and the Crane 78
10. Of the Peacock and the Nightingale 80
11. Of the Sheep, the Wolves, and the Dogs 82
12. Of a Lion and a Dormouse 84
    Compare to C3, S2, B6, O3
13. Of the Northwind, the Sun, and a Wayfarer 86
14. Of the Grasshopper and the Ant 88
15. Of the Wolf and the Crane 90
16. Of the Ash and the Reed 92
17. Of a Shepherd that without Cause Had Oft Cried out 94
    for Help against Wolves
18. Of a Wolf and a Great-Bellied Sow 96
    Compare to B8
19. Of a Woman and her Hen 98
20. Of a Mule 100
21. Of a Wether and a Wolf 102
22. Of a Neatherd Breaking his Idol 104
23. Of a Fox and of Cats 106
24. Of a Snake and a Stith 108
25. Of Two Seacrabs 110
26. Of the Hare and the Snail 112
27. Of a Raven and a Sheep 114
28. Of a Fox and of Bees 116
29. Of the Eagle and the Fox 118
30. Of a Couple of Friends and a Bear 120
31. Of an Ass and a Little Dog 122

TABLE OF FABLES

32. Of a Wolf and a Lamb 124
    Compare to B2
33. Of a Thief and a Dog 126
    Compare to C6, B7, O4
34. Of a Spiteful Cur and an Ox 128
    Compare to C12
35. Of a Horse and an Ass 130
36. Of the Raven and the Fox 132
37. Of the Frog and the Mouse 134
    Compare to C2, S4, B3, O2
38. Of a Frog and an Ox 136
39. Of a Hart that Beheld Himself in a Water 138
40. Of the Doves and the Goshawk 140
    Compare to C5
41. Of a Hart and a Horse 142
42. Of a Fox and a Goat 144
43. Of the Lion and the Bear 146
44. Of the Housemouse and the Fieldmouse 148
    Compare to B5
45. Of a Fowler and a Turtledove 150
46. Of a Mountain that Travailed with Child 152
47. Of the Peacock and the Rest of the Birds Choosing 154
    Him King
48. Of an Ox and a Calf 156
49. Of a Bittern and a Crow 158
50. Of the Eagle and the Raven 160
51. Of a Cock that Found a Precious Stone 162
    Compare to C1, S1, B1, O1
52. Of a Boar and an Ass 164
53. The Battle between the Birds and the Beasts 166
54. Of the Frogs Craving a King 168
    Compare to C4
55. Of a Wolf and a Goat 170
56. Of a Dog Deceived by a Shadow in the Water 172
    Compare to B4
57. Of a Woodward and a Wood 174
    Compare to B10
58. Of a Jay that Decked Himself with Peacocks' Feathers 176
59. Of a Stag and of Oxen 178
60. Of a Lion Dividing a Prey among his Attendants 180
61. Of a Wolf and a Sheep 182

62. Of Hares Stricken with Great Fear 184
63. Of a Fox that Would Eat No Grapes 186
64. Of an Ape and a Cat 188
65. Of a Horse and an Ass 190
66. Of a Smith and his Dog 192
67. Of a Fox that Had Lost his Tail 194
68. Of the Falcon and of Other Birds 196
69. Of a Lion that Was Spent with Age 198
70. Of the Goat, the Lamb, and the Wolf 200
71. Of a Fly and an Emmet 202
72. Of the Dragon and the Elephant 204
73. Of a Bear and of Bees 206
    Compare to O6
74. Of a Raven and a Scorpion 208
75. Of a Wolf Clad in a Sheep's Skin 210
76. Of a Wolf and a Hedgehog 212
77. Of a Serpent and an Urchin 214
78. Of the Chameleon 216
79. Of a Ram and a Bull 218
80. Of a Hen and her Chickens 220
81. Of a Ploughman and a Mouse 222
82. Of a Fowler and a Ruddock 224
83. Of a Clown and a Satyr 226
84. Of the Greater Mouse and an Oyster 228
85. Of an Eagle and a Snail 230
86. Of a Kite and a Cuckoo 232
87. Of the Puttock and the Nightingale 234
88. Of a Countryman and an Adder 236
89. Of a Lion and a Man 238
    Compare to C10, O8
90. Of the Lion, the Fox, and the Ass 240
91. Of the Lion and the Fox 242
92. Of the Lion, the Boar, and the Vulture 244
93. Of the Wolf and the Fox 246
94. Of a Fox Commending Hare's Flesh 248
95. Of a Bull and a Dormouse 250
96. Of the Ape and the Fox 252
    Compare to B12, O5
97. Of a Wolf and a Man's Head Carved 254
98. Of a Stag and a Sheep 256
99. Of a Shegoat and a Wolf's Whelp 258

TABLE OF FABLES

100. Of a Cat and a Cockerel 260
     Compare to O12
101. Of an Old Lame Cat and of the Mice 262
102. Of a Lame Dog and his Master 264
103. Of a Husbandman and his Dogs 266
104. Of an Ass and his Three Masters 268
105. Of an Ox, an Ass, a Mule, and a Camel 270
106. Of a Handicraftsman, an Ape, and a Monkey 272
107. Of a Young Unthrift and a Swallow 274
108. Of a Drunken Servant 276
109. Of a Fowler and a Partridge 278
110. Of Cocks and of a Partridge 280
111. Of a Husbandman and a Stork 282
112. Of a Sheep and a Wolf 284
113. Of Jupiter and the Watersnake 286
114. Of Jupiter and the Bee 288
115. Of a Horse of War and Swine 290
116. Of an Ass and a Horse 292
     Compare to B9
117. Of a Horse and an Ass 294
     Compare to B9
118. Of a Turkeycock and a Dunghillcock 296
119. Of a Kite that Was Sick 298
120. Of an Ostrich and a Nightingale 300
121. Of an Old Impotent Stork 302
122. Of an Ass Loaden with Provision of Meat and Drink 304
123. Of a Swan and a Stork 306
124. Of the Phoenix 308
125. Of the Stork 310

WILLIAM CAXTON, FROM *THE SUBTLE HISTORIES AND FABLES OF AESOP*

Book 1 Prologue 315
  1. Of the Cock and of the Precious Stone 316
     Compare to G51, S1, B1, O1
  2. Of the Rat and of the Frog 317
     Compare to G37, S4, B3, O2
  3. Of the Lion and of the Rat 318
     Compare to G12, S2, B6, O3
Book II Proem 320

4. Of the Frogs and of Jupiter 321
      Compare to G54
  5. Of the Colombes or Doves, of the Kite, and of 322
      the Sparhawk
      Compare to G40
  6. Of the Thief and of the Dog 323
      Compare G33, B7, O4
  7. Of the Lion and of the Horse 324
      Compare to G8
  8. Of the Knight and of the Widow 325
  9. Of the Hands, of the Feet, and of the Man's Belly 327
      Compare to B11, O7
  10. Of the Man and of the Lion 329
      Compare to G89, O8
  11. Of the Wolf which Made a Fart 330
  12. Of the Envious Dog 336
      Compare to G34
  13. Of Phoebus, of the Avaricious, and of the Envious 337
  14. Of the Disciple and of the Sheep 338
  15. Of an Old Harlot or Bawd 340
  16. Of a Blind Man and of his Wife 343
  17. Of the Recitation of Some Monsters 345

RICHARD SMITH, FROM *THE FABULOUS TALES OF AESOP THE PHRYGIAN*

The Book's Passport 351
Epistle 352
The Argument between Aesop and the Translator 354
His Verdict on his Labour 357
The Argument or Prologue 358
1. The Tale of the Grosshead Chanticleer the Cock and 361
    the Precious Stone
        Compare to G51, C1, B1, O1
2. The Exemplative Tale of the Lion and the Mouse, with 365
    the Author's Prologue before
        Compare to G12, C3, B6, O3
3. The Merry Tale of the Wolf and the Wether 376
4. The Tale of the Woeful End of the Paddock and the 382
    Mouse, Showing the Mischief of Dissemblers
        Compare to G37, C2, B3, O2
The Epilogue 390

TABLE OF FABLES

JOHN BRINSLEY, FROM *AESOP'S FABLES TRANSLATED GRAMMATICALLY*

Epistle Dedicatory 393
Epistle to the Reader (To the painful schoolmaster) 396
   1. Of a Cock 397
        Compare to G51, C1, S1, O1
   2. Of a Wolf and a Lamb 398
        Compare to G32
   3. Of a Mouse and a Frog 400
        Compare to G37, C2, S4, O2
   4. Of a Dog and a Shadow 401
        Compare to G56
   5. Of a City Mouse and a Country Mouse 402
        Compare to G44
   6. Of a Lion and a Mouse 404
        Compare to G12, C3, S2, O3
   7. Of a Thief and a Dog 405
        Compare to G33, C6, O4
   8. Of a Wolf and a Young Sow 406
        Compare to G18
   9. Of a Horse and an Ass 407
        Compare to G116, G117
  10. Of a Wood and a Countryman 408
        Compare to G57
  11. Of the Limbs and the Belly 409
        Compare to C9, O7
  12. Of an Ape and a Fox-Cub 410
        Compare to G96, O5

JOHN OGILBY, FROM *THE FABLES OF AESOP* AND *AESOPICS*

To the Right Honourable Heneage Finch Earl of Winchilsea 413
and Viscount Maidstone, and the Right Honourable Henry
Seymour Lord Beauchamp
To my Friend Mr. Ogilby (by William Davenant) 415
To my Worthy Friend Mr. John Ogilby (by James Shirley) 418
   1. Of the Cock and Precious Stone 421
        Compare to G51, C1, S1, B1
   2. The Battle of the Frog and Mouse 427
        Compare to G37, C2, S4, B3

3. Of the Lion and the Mouse 437
    Compare to G12, C3, S2, B6
4. Of the Dog and Thief 443
    Compare to G33, C6, B7
5. Of the Fox and Ape 447
    Compare to G96, B12
6. Of the Bear and the Bees 449
    Compare to G73
7. Of the Rebellion of the Hands and Feet 453
    Compare to C9, B11
8. Of the Lion and the Forester 459
    Compare to G89, C10
9. Of the Lion, the Forester, and his Daughter 463
10. Of the Forester, the Skinner, and a Bear 469
11. Of the Young Man and the Cat 473
12. Of the Cat and the Cock 479
    Compare to G100
13. Of the Cat and the Mice 483
14. Of the Sheep and the Butcher 487
15. Of the Wolf and the Fox 491
16. Of the Same Wolf and Fox 494
17. Of the Same Wolf and Fox 497

ARTHUR GOLDING

A Moral Fabletalk

That is to say, a most delectable garden of moral philosophy, conveyed in fables, by speeches attributed to brute beasts.

Wherein the labyrinth or maze of man's life is set forth, and the way of virtue by most beautiful precepts (as it were by Theseus' clew° of yarn)[1] is directed. (c. 1580)

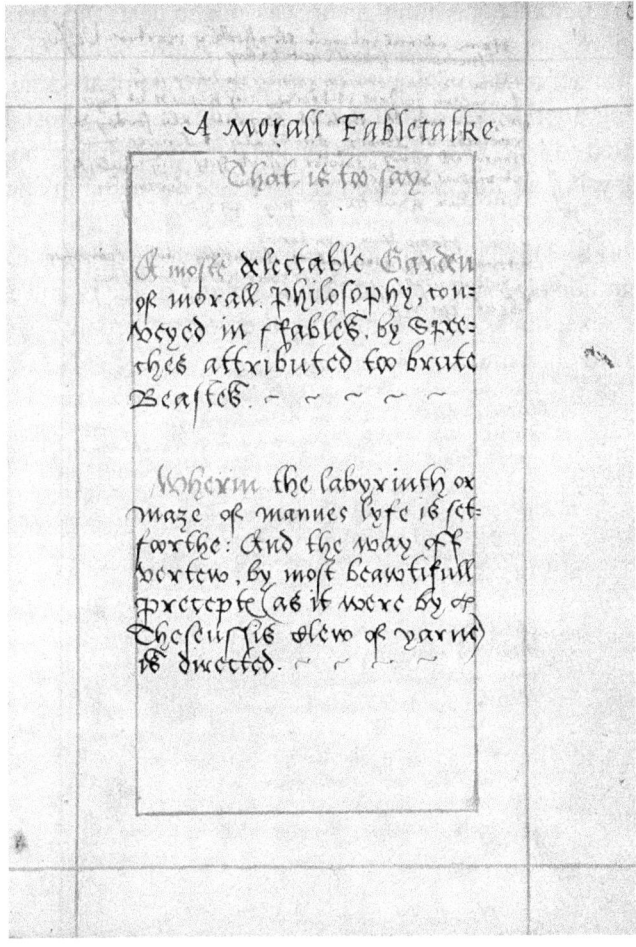

---

[1] At the recommendation of Ariadne, the mythical hero Theseus brought a clew, or a ball of thread, into the Minotaur's labyrinth and unwound it as he entered so he could find his way back out. There is also a possible pun on 'clue' here.

ARTHUR GOLDING

1. Of a Carrier° and his Horse

A certain horse, being very badly dealt with by his churlish master — insomuch that, being lean and hunger-starven° for want° of food, he had nothing to hold his wretched life in but only skin and bones — was driven into a cumbersome and deep miry place. From whence when he could not wind himself out, the carrier, being froward° and furious, laid cruelly upon him with main° strokes. Wherefore° groaning very grievously in himself, and finding fault with the difficulty of the place and the unmercifulness of his master that had laid more burden upon him than he was able to bear, and therewithal being more and more enforced by the furiousness of the driver, who was not touched with any pity towards the wretch half-dead, at the last being utterly tired and at the point to give up the ghost, he was compelled to hear this farewell for his comfort: 'Either thou must heave thyself out from hence quickly, or else die under my hand.'

The Morals: This fable fitteth° the devourers of their people, which like unto horseleeches° do suck out the blood of their subjects with so sore° exactions,° that nothing is reserved to the silly° wretched souls, save only skin and bone.

A MORAL FABLETALK

The intolerable grievousness of exactions.

Get ye hence to your work. Ye shall have no straw allowed you, and yet shall ye answer your accustomed tale° of brick. (Exodus 5:18)[1]

---

[1] This book of Exodus describes how the Pharaoh oppressed the Israelites, demanding that they produce a daily quota of bricks, but refusing to supply the straw from which bricks are made.

2. Of the Lion and the Fox

Upon a time, the lion (which among all beasts beareth the sovereignty), counterfeiting himself to be very sore° sick, summoned all beasts to be before him by a day² as it were to confer with them concerning the affairs of his kingdom, that he might leave it in quiet state to his posterity after his decease. They all obeyed and came flocking to the court at the day appointed, as it had been to hold a parliament. Only the fox, being wilier than the rest, when he saw in the dust that their footsteps were all thitherward and none homeward, neglected the king's commandment, and inveighing° against the fond° and unadvised rashness of the latter sort, said, 'Of a truth ye be out of your wits, and well worthy of the name of beasts as ye be indeed, for that ye mark not more heedfully how the footings of them that went afore you be still all to the courtward: whereby ye should have considered that many be gone thither, but none be come back again.'

The Morals: This present° fable commendeth the discretion of such as by timely advisedness eschew° the enticing tyranny of wicked princes (whereby the silly people, alas, too easily be entrapped) and so escape the snares wherein most men are caught.

---

² i.e., on a given day or within a day

Wisdom gotten by other men's harms.

A wily person spying a mischief hideth himself from it, but the simple ones going on still catch harm. (Proverbs 27:12)

3. Of the Oak and the Elm

After the example of a wicked prince followeth in very good order the fable of the oak and the elm. For on a time, the elm (like a bloody counsellor) not only earnestly advised but also, with reasons and arguments (to his own seeming) of great importance, laboured to persuade the oak that for the confirming and stablishing° of his state, he should pluck up all other trees by the roots. But the king (who, being of a mild disposition, had long borne with the cruel demands of the elm), being at length provoked to anger and put out of patience with his over-great importunity,° asked him by what means he might be able to withstand the force of tempests and whirlwinds when he had rooted up the rest of the trees. Whereunto when the elm (being at his wits' end) could make no reply, the king, charging him upon pain of the grievous indignation of His Royal Majesty, and of other punishments also, never thenceforth to trouble any of them, banished him from the company of the rest of the trees.

The Morals: The oak showeth a prince how to win the love of his commons,° and how he should be affected towards his subjects: namely° that he should as well be grieved at their adversity, as be partaker of their prosperity.

The welfare of the subjects is the stablishment° of the prince.

The dignity of a king consisteth in the multitude of his people, and the fewness of commons is the prince's dishonour. (Proverbs 14:28)

4. Of a Lion and an Ass

A lion, starkling° at the noise of a cock that crowed (for it is said to be the natural infirmity of that beast so to do),³ took him to flight. A certain gross-headed ass by chance beholding it, and not understanding the cause thereof, imputed° it to himself, and thereupon pursued the lion. When the lion was gone so far that he could no more hear the crowing of the cock, so as his heart was discharged of that fear, he turned back, and with a dry laughter fell upon the ass. Whom as he was tearing in pieces with his talons,°⁴ he reproved of his doltishness with these words: 'Ah thou witless fool, imaginest thou a lion to be so cowardly as to run away at the sight of an ass? Learn thou this day in my paws, by example unavailable to thyself, that it is a gross folly for an underling or a novice to thrust himself through rash headiness° into contention against his master, or through overweening° presumption to adventure upon anything that is above his power.'

The Morals: Besides that the conclusion of this fable carrieth the use thereof with it, I add this further: that it is a point of extreme madness for a man to be so bold (without considering what Nature hath given unto him) as to challenge another man, specially such a one as by many degrees doth surmount him.

---

³ Pliny describes lions as being afraid of the cock's crow in book 8, chapter 19 of his *Natural History*; see Pliny, *Natural History*, vol. 3, trans. by H. Rackham (Cambridge, MA: Harvard University Press, 1940), p. 41.
⁴ Golding originally mistranslated the Latin *inguibus* [talons] as 'teethe' and then crossed it out and wrote 'talentes', which we have modernized as 'talons'.

Undiscreet° is the provoking of a mightier than thyself.

Strive not with a man of might, lest thou fall into his hands.
(Ecclesiasticus 8:1)[5]
Withstand not a man of power to his face, nother° wade thou
against the sway of a stream. (Ecclesiasticus 4:32)[6]

---

[5] Ecclesiasticus, or Sirach, is considered apocryphal in some traditions, but was included in sixteenth-century versions of the Vulgate.
[6] In Golding's manuscript this verse was left without a citation; we have supplied the missing citation from Freitag for ease of reference.

5. Of a Man that Called for Death

An old man that was crooked for age, being weary of the weight of a great burden that he carried, and tired with the tediousness of his way, sank down and anon° called for Death, who, hearkening° to his call as being hard behind him, began by and by to level his dart at him. 'Nay, Death,' quoth° the old man, 'I called thee not to take away my life, but to ease me of my pain and of the weariness of my journey by helping me to bear some part of my burden.'

The Morals: Oftentimes it comes to pass that when some over-grievous inconvenience is like to ensue,° we forget the former encumbrance, and bear the present pinch° with the uprighter mind. And there is no man so forspent° with age, but that (as Cicero sayeth) he believeth that he may be able to live yet one year more.[7] Yea,° and I say thus much further, there is none also which could not find in his heart to endure continually even the greatest encumbrances that can be, so° he might live still. So careful° is Nature to maintain herself.

---

[7] Golding here refers to Cicero's *De Senectute* vii.24: 'for no one is so old as to think that he cannot live one more year.' See Cicero, *De Senectute*, in *De Senectute, De Amicitia, De Divinatione*, trans. by William Armistead Falconer (Cambridge, MA: Harvard University Press, 1946), p. 33.

Weariness of life pretended by such as are in adversity.

Better is death than a bitter life, and everlasting rest than continual languishing. (Ecclesiasticus 30:17)
A quick dog is better than a dead lion. (Ecclesiastes 9:4)

6. Of a Cockatrice[8] and a Weasel

A certain huge and cruel cockatrice, harbouring in a dreary and dusky den overgrown with bushes and keeping continual watch against all other living things, lay wilily in wait for a weasel that fed daily before his den, and went out many times to catch him up, hoping to obtain his purpose one time or another. But trimly° did the weasel still disappoint the practices of his enemy and wisely delude his eager desire of doing harm. For, being armed with his wonted° weapons, he entered without fear into the cockatrice's den, knowing well that by taking with him a small branch of rue° (which herb is reported to be a most present° remedy against poison), like as by rubbing his body all over with it he had often prevented his enemy aforetimes, so he should easily disappoint the force of his venom ever after.

The Morals: This fable warneth the weaker sort to arm themselves warely° and wisely against the stronger sort, and to advise themselves well aforehand, and to remember that the practices of such are to be dissolved and disappointed° not by force but by discreet° dealing.

---

[8] A cockatrice is a mythical creature that is either: a basilisk (a serpent capable of killing with its eyes); a monster with the head, wings, and feet of a cock and the tail of a serpent; or a crocodile. Although the Latin reads *Basilisci*, the engraving clearly depicts the hybrid creature, which also carried the 'venom' referred to in the fable.

A MORAL FABLETALK

Defence armed with policy against power.

Resist the devil and he shall flee from you. (James 4:7)
In any wise° take to you the shield of faith, whereby ye may quench
all the fiery darts of the wicked. (Ephesians 6:16)

7. Of an Ape and his Imps°

An ape, having two young ones, brought them up diversely. The one he cockered° most tenderly, and the other could do nothing that would please him. This therefore he removed from his company, but the other he held so dear and familiar° that he could not abide to have him out of his sight. To be short, in all his behaviour he found nothing amiss. He leaps where he listeth,° he fetcheth his gambols° and frisks,° and he tumbles about, forbearing° no kind of dissoluteness, unchecked or uncontrolled. Wherethrough° it came to pass that at last he thrust his hip out of joint. The sire, coming in at the mischance of his dear babe, filled all the house with shrieking, and catching him up in his arms, hugged him so hard that by and by he yielded up the ghost.[9] Thus, through undiscreet love, he procured to his bairn° death and to himself sorrow.

The Morals: This tale agreeth to such parents as, cockering their children with a blind and unlucky love, do by their over-much tenderness procure at the last to themselves sorrow, and to their children destruction.

---

[9] In book 8, chapter 80 of his *Natural History*, Pliny says, 'Tame monkeys kept in the house who bear young ones […] in a considerable number of cases they kill their babies by hugging them'; see Pliny, *Natural History*, vol. 3, p. 151.

The fond love of parents to their children.

He that spareth the rod hateth the child, but he that loveth him chastiseth him continually. (Proverbs 13:24)
An unnurtured son is a shame to his father, and a foolish daughter becometh a disparagement [of her stock].[10] (Ecclesiasticus 22:3)

---

[10] These square brackets are present in the manuscript.

8. Of a Lion and a Horse

A hungry lion, spying a horse in a large and open field, came craftily to him, and, feigning to be a horseleech, offered his service to the horse, if by any mischance or default° of body he were diseased, saying he had most present remedies against all maladies and diseases. The horse, smelling the lion's cozenage,° said, 'In good time, sir, are you come, of all leeches° most wished for, and in very good season hath father Apollo sent you his Asclepius[11] unto me. For one of my hinder° feet is festered with a privy° canker,° and hath need of surgery. It requireth your help, and I beseech you lay a plaster to it.' As the lion (making as though he would view the sore) stooped down to his hinderparts, the horse hit him such a blow with his heel that he set him beside his remembrance, and made him to sink in a swound° to the ground.

The Morals: It falleth out sometimes that such as go about to entrap other folks and to take them in a trip° are overtaken themselves with the like or with a greater guile, and, being served with the same sauce, do (as is said in the proverb) fall into the pit which they themselves made.[12]

---

[11] Asclepius was the Greek god of medicine and healing, son of Apollo (god of music, poetry, healing, and knowledge).
[12] The proverb is either a reference to Proverbs 26:27, 'Whoever digs a pit will fall into it', or to Erasmus' proverb, 'He fell into the pit which he had made'. The biblical quotation is from the NRSV; the proverb is from Desiderius Erasmus, *Adages, I.i.1 to I.v.100*, trans by Margaret Mann Phillips, vol. 31 of the *Collected Works of Erasmus* (Toronto: University of Toronto Press, 1982), I.i.52, p. 101.

Deceit disappointed by prudent policy.

Better be the woundings of a lover than the deceitful kisses of one that hateth. (Proverbs 27:6)

An enemy weepeth with his eyes, when with his heart he imagineth how to tumble thee into the pit. And if he find opportunity, he will not be satisfied with blood. (Ecclesiasticus 12:16)

9. Of the Fox and the Crane

A fox, bidding a crane to dinner, promised him good cheer. But when the crane was come, he set porridge before him in a platter. And when the crane could scarce get up wherewith to staunch his hunger, the fox gave him a dry mock for an amends.[13] The crane, putting up this scorn with silence, and purposing to serve the fox with the same sauce, bade° him again another time, and at his coming did set his meat° upon the table in a narrow-mouthed gourd,° desiring him to taste of his victuals° and spare not, for he had prepared them of purpose to cure the spleen.[14] And therewithal the crane, putting in his bill, fed lustily and filled his belly with the dainty meat. Which when he had done, then gibing° at the fox, he asked him how he liked his fare.° The fox confessed himself to be well dealt with, and, being touched with the conscience of his own misdealing afore, granted that guile was to be mocked out with guile, and that a crabbed° knot required a tough wedge,[15] and that (the world being so full of cozening mates as it was) there should not want° deceivers that would employ their whole endeavours in cozening° other men.

The Morals:[16]

---

[13] i.e., When the crane could not scoop enough to sate his hunger, the fox mocked him.
[14] i.e., to cure the fox's ill humour
[15] i.e., a difficult problem requires a forceful solution
[16] Freitag does not supply a moral for this fable, perhaps because the moral is built into the fable itself by the fox. We have included Golding's heading, which marks the absence of a moral.

Guile requited with guile.

He will deceive the deceivers, and give grace° to them that deal plainly. (Proverbs 3:34)

10. Of the Peacock and the Nightingale

When on a time the peacock, wondering at the sweet singing of the nightingale, hearkened attentively to her, and through envy blamed Nature that she had not bestowed that great benefit upon him, wherewith it had been meet° he should have been adorned for the beautifulness of his feathers, Nature, in defence of her providence, upbraided him with his unthankfulness, telling him that, instead of that sweet singing and melody, she had endued° him with another most noble gift (and therefore that he did her great wrong, seeing that the nightingale envied not his prerogative° and gifts),[17] adding that if she should daily give new shapes to things at everybody's pleasure and appointment, she should be ever new° to begin.

The Morals: The drift of this present fable is to counsel° every man to be contented with the gifts which he hath received of the sovereign God, the workmaster° of Nature, and not to be inquisitive in asking why other gifts are bestowed upon other men.

---

[17] We have added these parentheses to make the syntax clearer.

It is injury and unthankfulness to blame Nature for being
beneficial to other men.

Let your behaviour be clear from covetousness, and be contented
with that which you have. (Hebrews 13:5)

11. Of the Sheep, the Wolves, and the Dogs

Whenas the discord which hath been of old between the sheep and the wolves broke out on a time into cruel war, and that the sheep nevertheless lived safely under the defence of lusty stout mastiffs,° the wolves, distrusting their own strength, sued° for peace,[18] offering to give their young whelps° in hostage to the sheep, so they on the other side would yield them their dogs. The silly sheep, being void of deceit, accepted the condition, and so peace was concluded betwixt them with these articles: that neither part should annoy other by private or public force; and that if aught° happened to be done to the contrary by either of the parties, the same that offended should bear the blame according to the law of arms. As soon as the whelps of the wolves were grown big, they fell upon the sheep, and the wolves themselves fell upon the dogs, and, breaking their faith, worried° the sheep and devoured them ere° they were aware.

The Morals: This place forbiddeth us to believe our enemies overhastily, or to assure ourselves rashly of the faithfulness of those that are nuzzled° in deceit, willing us to crink with the crinker,[19] and (as the holy scriptures warn us) in no wise to trust a new-reconciled friend.

---

[18] i.e., appealed or asked for peace

[19] The *OED* gives the following definition for the word 'crinking': 'The use of intricate turns or twists of speech, thought, etc., esp. so as to deceive.' The only two attested uses of the word 'crinking' are in Golding's translation of John Calvin's *Sermons on Deuteronomy* (1583). Here this phrase means: to be deceptive with the deceiver (rather than be fooled by false friends, you ought to trick those who are trying to trick you). Freitag has the proverbial *Cretense Cretisandum*, which appears in a few other texts in the period and means: lie to those who lie to you (the Latin phrase alludes to the idea that people from Crete were proverbially liars).

Innocency is easily deceived.

Never believe thine enemy. For his malice fretteth° like the rust° of iron. And therefore if he come crouching and creeping to thee, bethink thee how to keep thyself from him.
(Ecclesiasticus 12:10–11)

12. Of a Lion and a Dormouse

Upon a time, a lion (I wot° not by what misfortune, whether chased by hunters or by some other casualty),° being fallen into a toil and having striven in vain to get out (for by his struggling he did but entangle himself the more), at length, greatly fearing the mischief that hung over him, did horribly roar out. With which noise the dormouse (whom he had afore made beholden° to him) woke out of his sleep, and, coming apace unto him, sheared asunder the cords and let him loose.

The Morals: It oftentimes befalleth that even the weakest and meanest° sort of men do hit upon occasion of gratifying and requiting, even towards those that are of greatest state. And therefore no man's degree is to be despised; nother is there so base an abject° or rascal which may not stand us in some stead° one time or other.

No man is barred from occasion of requiting.

When thou dost a good turn, consider to whom thou dost it, and then for thy well-doing thou shalt have thanks. Do good to a righteous man, and thou shalt find great recompense.
(Ecclesiasticus 12:1–2)[20]

---

[20] Golding originally wrote this citation as '12:12'. Another hand wrote a '0' over the second '1', and then included a superscript ':1:' above the new '0', changing the citation to 12:1:02 (i.e., 12:1–2). This second hand is correct: the citation is Ecclesiasticus 12:1–2.

13. Of the Northwind, the Sun, and a Wayfarer°

The northwind and the sun, falling at strife about their strength, stood stoutly° either of them upon his reputation. And the contention grew so great that for the deciding of it they would needs° choose an arbitrator who by experience should find which of them was the stronger. Whereupon they agreed that the next wayfaring° man should be he, and that which of them could bereave him of his cloak should obtain the honour of the victory. Blustering Boreas,[21] being the first that should assault him with his boistous° blast, was so far unable to bereave him of his cloak with all the force he had that he wound him up more and more in it. But the sun so scorched the traveller with his burning beams that anon, being unable to endure the heat, he cast his cloak from him.

The Morals: This fable commendeth the commodious°[22] dealing of such as procure men to yield to their opinion rather by reason and courtesy than by violence. For men can find in their hearts to be drawn, but not to be compelled.

---

[21] Boreas was the north wind, or the god of the north wind.
[22] A later annotator of the manuscript crossed out Golding's 'commodiouse' (advantageous or profitable) and wrote above it instead 'dextrous' (skilful or cunning).

Moderate power is better than heady° violence.

Not that we be lords over your faith. (2 Corinthians 1:24)
I became weak to the weaklings, that I might win the weaklings.
(1 Corinthians 9:22)

14. Of the Grasshopper and the Ant

When winter was come, the grasshopper, seeking succour° of the pismire,° besought her to relieve his penury° out of the heaps that she had hoarded up. The pismire, rubbing him with the remembrance of his neglecting of the pleasantest time of the year, upbraided him with his spending of the summer in sloth, idleness, and singing when he lived in the cornfields, saying: 'Then was the time that thou shouldest have been mindful of the time to come, when abundance of all things flowed unto thee. Therefore learn now by this thy want, that he which laboureth not in due time, ne° taketh occasion when it serveth, but runneth riotously at random in jollity and pleasure, shall one day die miserably in scarcity of all things, and pay too dear for those his untimely delights.'

The Morals: This fabulous° tale[23] showeth that the loss of time is most dear, and the gain thereof most honest, and therefore that occasion ought to be taken hold of, and pleasure not so much pampered that in prosperity men should be unmindful of adversity, but in the mids° of their joys bethink them of the sorrows that may ensue.

---

[23] i.e., this tale that is a fable, this fable-like tale

The rewards of slothfulness and painfulness are contrary.

The sluggard will not go to plough for cold, and therefore shall he beg in summer and not be relieved. (Proverbs 20:4)

15. Of the Wolf and the Crane

The wolf, being almost choked with a bone that stuck in his throat, and having sought help of many in vain, at length moved the crane with many fair promises to pull it out. The crane, being persuaded, put his head into the wolf's mouth and plucked the bone out of his throat. For his doing of which good turn, when he demanded his covenanted° reward, the wolf gave him this answer: 'Art thou so gross-witted° as not to consider that I could have taken away thy life when thy head was thrust into my throat, and yet that I of pity spared thee? Away, therefore, and think thyself beholden to me, that thou hast thy life, which I could have taken from thee.'

The Morals: Learn hereby that that benefit is worst bestowed which is bestowed on a churl,° and that thy labour and cost are never so lost indeed as when they be cast° away upon such kind of men.

Foul is the stain of ingratitude.

The promise of a thankless person will melt away like the winter's ice and wash away like overflowing water. (Sapience 16:29)[24]

---
[24] Elsewhere Golding uses 'Wisdom' to refer to this book of the Bible.

16. Of the Ash° and the Reed

As the ash on a time, despising the reed, did through a certain arrogant pride extol his own strength to the sky and flout° the reed for his overpliable weakness, bragging of his own force, how he of his own nature was able to withstand the brunts of tempests and the violence of whirlwinds, whereas the reed was shaken with every blast, suddenly there arose so great an alteration of the air and so hideous a wind that it rent° up the ash by the root and overthrew him to the ground. When the reed regarded[25] the ash fallen, 'How safe a victory,' quoth he, 'and how sure a strength is it, to yield to fury and force?'

The Morals: This setteth forth the fond boasting of the proud ash in his own power and strength, and by example thereof showeth that the vanity of such as rashly stand in contention doth for the most part come to a shameful end.

---

[25] Golding's manuscript is missing a verb here; Freitag has *contemplata* [observed, noticed, contemplated]. Field supplies 'observed', and Barnes supplies 'beheld'.

The stoutness° of the proud catcheth a crack.°²⁶

He hath scattered the proud in the imagination of their hearts. He hath put down the mighty from their seats and hath exalted the lowly and meek. (Luke 1:51–52)

---

²⁶ Barnes reads this word as 'crank'.

17. Of a Shepherd that without Cause Had Oft Cried out for Help against Wolves

A certain turncoat° shepherd, a notable craftsmaster° of cozenage and deceit, was wont° (of a certain delight in lying and not of any necessity) to cry out to the husbandmen° and to his fellow shepherds for help against the wolves as he was feeding his sheep. Now when his over-often doing thereof had made his crafty and cozening disposition known to the world, they made no more account of his outcries. Insomuch that it happened ere long after that when a wolf caught a sheep out of his flock indeed, and he, not now in jest as aforetimes° but in good earnest and of present necessity, fell to his accustomed manner of crying out, they, hearing him, made as though they had been deaf and suffered him to call for help in vain. And so for his lying, he was punished with the loss of his sheep.

The Morals: Sith° it is the reward of a liar not to be believed when he speaketh truth, it appeareth manifestly that the custom of lying is both shameful and hurtful.

It is the punishment of a liar to want credit
when he sayeth the truth.

The feeding of a man's self with lying seemeth sweet, but afterward
his mouth shall be filled with gravel. (Proverbs 20:17)

18. Of a Wolf and a Great-Bellied Sow

A wolf, perceiving a great-bellied sow to be near her faring time,° stepped unto her with a subtle device,° and, pretending to be a skilful midwife, offered her service to her. The sow, being not ignorant of the wolf's wiliness, told her roundly that she needed not her help, and therefore she should have leave to bestow it somewhere else. Notwithstanding this, the wolf, being sharp set upon the devouring of her fare,° would not be answered with that refusal, but, putting off shame, offered to serve her as a nurse. The sow, being chafed° with the importunateness of the wolf, bade her be packing, for she knew her to be a wolf even by her paws and by her coat, and that she meant nothing but treachery.

The Morals: The discretion of the sow in preserving her pigs teacheth us that it is a point of stark madness to commit our safety to lewd° folk nuzzled in craftiness, or to rest upon the defence of such as bend all the force of their wit to bring the state and welfare of their neighbours into extremity of danger.

No trust is to be given to feigned° friendship.

The man that speaketh to his friend with smooth and filed° words layeth a snare for his feet. (Proverbs 29:5)

19. Of a Woman and her Hen

A certain woman kept up a hen that laid her every day an egg of gold, which undoubtedly was a great maintenance to her house and household. Hereupon conceiving a covetous opinion (which blinded discretion) that her hen was full of such eggs, she, being allured by over-greedy desire of gain to her own undoing, in hope of more abundant increase ripped the hen's belly to find out the treasure of eggs that lay hidden there. But when she saw herself disappointed of the hope, both of the one egg and also of any mo,° she blamed her own blind and over-heady covetousness.

The Morals: It falleth out commonly, that when the unsatiable° gulf of covetousness beginneth once to overflow with too great a desire of riches, it both forgoeth the present benefits and also loseth the things which the daily trade did bring in. And this tale is not intended of a silly woman only, but also of all sorts of men, specially of merchants, who for desire of gain pass not to hazard° their money and substance unadvisedly, never giving over until they have shifted countries twice or thrice and have endangered their souls to all men.

All covet, all lose.[27]

A covetous person will not be satisfied with money, and he that is in love with riches shall take no fruit of them. (Ecclesiastes 5:9)

---

[27] The word 'all' here is the object, not the subject — 'Covet everything, lose everything.'

20. Of a Mule

A mule, in time past, being fed most finely° and daintily, and not pinched° with any toil or travail° as other beasts of burden were, waxed° weary of his over-quiet and idle life, and, boasting disdainfully of his kindred and ancestors with daily contention about it, bragged that he was descended of the most noble race of horses, wherethrough he was meet for justling,° running, and such other exercises of activity, and was not to be employed in so unhonourable kind of life. Whereupon it came to pass that after long and often repetition of such complaints, he obtained to be led out of the stable to the lists° and to the horseraces, there to make proof of his valour and swiftness. But when he saw the cunning of the goodly° horses in running, then acknowledging the slowness and dullness of his nature, 'Alas,' quoth he, 'now I find myself to be the foal° of a stale, forworn,° slow-paced ass.'

The Morals: Trial and experience bewray° what every man is able to do, and by most evident reasons doth show how great each man's ability is, and how far it may extend.

The work showeth what the workman is.

He that sayeth he knoweth Him and keepeth not His commandments is a liar, and the truth is not in him. (1 John 2:4)

21. Of a Wether° and a Wolf

A wolf, having disguised himself in a sheep's skin, came to a sheepfold and offered courtesy to a wether, persuading him to walk with him into the next laund,° which he said was very fine and pleasant. The wether told him he would willingly go with him, if he were a wolf and not a sheep, so as he might defend them both, being otherwise unarmed of himself, from the injuries and ravenousness of wild beasts. The wolf, being glad of that answer, did cast off his sheep's habit, saying, 'Lo, in good sooth° I am a wolf; therefore let us now to the wood together.' 'It was even you that I waited for,' quoth the wether, 'for I knew afore what thou wast. Therefore now get thee hence alone with a mischief. It is enough for me at this time to have learned this lesson, that the wolf changeth his hair but not his heart.'

The Morals: Even so, it is no novelty to have many ravening° wolves and bloodthirsty beasts clad° in sheep's skins dwelling among innocent persons.

Things are not to be deemed by the outward show.

Beware of false prophets, which come unto you in sheep's clothing, but inwardly be ravening wolves. (Matthew 7:15)

22. Of a Neatherd° Breaking his Idol

When a certain idolatrous cowherd that was poorer than Codrus[28] had daily resorted to his household god, whose image set up in his lobhole°[29] he used to worship, and after many instant° and importunate prayers had reaped no benefit or fruit of all his devotion, at the length being tired with the mercilessness of his idol and thereupon letting loose the bridle of his impatiency, he knocked him throughly°[30] with the head of a hatchet, and, suddenly unlooked for, a treasure of gold that lay hid in his belly issued out at a rift of him. Whereupon making himself sport at his own policy, 'Needs must thou be of a very bad disposition,' quoth he, 'which hadst rather to do good by compulsion than of thine own accord,° rather well beaten than being whole, and rather at reviling than at entreatance.'°

The Morals: Forasmuch as the good turn that is extorted deserveth no thanks, every man ought to strain himself to do good of his own free will and bounty.

---

[28] Codrus was a poor man described in Juvenal's *Satires* (in *Juvenal and Persius*, trans. by G. G. Ramsay [New York: G. P. Putnam's Sons, 1928], III.203–11). The phrase 'poor as Codrus' was proverbial, according to Erasmus (see Desiderius Erasmus, *Adages, I.vi.1 to I.x.100*, trans. by R. A. B. Mynors, vol. 32 of the *Collected Works of Erasmus* [Toronto: University of Toronto Press, 1989], I.vi.76, pp. 51–52).
[29] Freitag reads *larario* [dwelling place of the lar(s) or household god(s)]; Golding's 'lobhole' refers to the dwelling of a 'lob', or country bumpkin.
[30] i.e., knocked him all the way through

A good turn gotten by force.

For if we be dead with him, we shall also live with him. If we suffer with him, we shall also reign with him. If we deny him, he will also deny us. (2 Timothy 2:11)

23. Of a Fox and of Cats

A fox, going on the way with certain cats, did very proudly and arrogantly commend his own subtlety° and wiliness and therewithal so debase the wits of the cats, that he affirmed them to be good for nothing but only to delight some nice dames with their murlimewes,° or to stand watching° to catch mice. While this controversy was in debating to and fro,° and that the fox disgraced the mousing of the cats with very opprobrious° terms, suddenly at their backs they espied dogs, which are enemies to them both. The cats, skipping quickly up into trees, escaped the danger of tearing in pieces by the dogs. But the fox, finding no place of refuge, was caught. 'Alas,' quoth he, 'whereas all vain boasting is foolish, surely it is most folly of all to dispraise those which either have been or shall be beholders of our overthrow.'

The Morals: This fable taunteth the mockers and depravers of other men's lives, showing by example of the fox that such as delight in flouting others do commonly come to a shameful end, and are compelled to commend those highly whom they had scorned afore when they see them eschew the snares wherein they themselves are fast° hampered.

Virtue in words and not in deeds.

Suffer not pride to bear sway in thy mind or in thy words, for all destruction took his beginning thereat. (Tobit 4:14)

24. Of a Snake and a Stith°

A snake, being in malice with a stith, laboured to bite off a piece of it. But the more fiercely he bit, the more he hurt himself. For whilst that being blinded with the witchery of presumption, he considered not that the hardness and substantialness of the steel could not be overcome by the tenderness and brittleness of his teeth, and that his contending was against an enemy whose revenge he might not hope to scape,° and whose strength he was not able to impair. He unawares bereft himself of his teeth, and received of the stithy° such answer as this: 'O too, too mad and worse than mad! Although thy teeth were of brass, and as fast riveted in thy head as could be, yet could they nothing avail against the hardness and substantialness of my nature.'

The Morals: This fable reproveth the fondness of such as, being of no strength at all or having very little, contend with those that are of such force and power as is able to despise and subdue even the stoutest that be.

Arrogant is the presumption of a weakling.

I am Jesus whom thou persecutest. It is hard for thee to kick against the prick.[31] (Acts 9:5)

---

[31] i.e., It will go badly for you if you resist someone with more power.

25. Of Two Seacrabs

When a certain seacrab, of that kind which Pliny registreth among the cammars,[32] went about to teach a young one of his to swim after another manner than he was endowed withal by Nature and by his mother's bringing up, inveighing against their old manner of swimming backward as uncomely,[33] the young crab answered that he was not to be blamed, seeing that Nature had not taught him to swim otherwise. Nevertheless, he said he was willing to obey, if his mother would vouchsafe° to teach him any other manner by her own example. But now sith his parents dissented from themselves, swimming otherwise than they would have him to do, he must be fain° to fetch and learn the principles of that swimming from somewhere else.

The Morals: Hereby be noted such unjust censors and severe reprovers° as, being sharper-sighted than Lynceus[34] in carping° and rebuking other men's faults, are blinder than beetles in their own, and are most defiled with the same vices for which they reprehend others. For few there be that bear in mind this saying of the poet: 'That teacher justly merits double blame, | Which checking° others, faulteth° in the same.'[35]

---

[32] Pliny was a first-century Roman natural philosopher who compiled the encyclopedic *Natural History*. The word 'cammars' is perhaps Golding's attempt to coin a new English word that corresponds to Freitag's *cammaros* (*cammarus*, *cammari*), meaning lobsters or sea-crabs. Pliny writes about lobsters (*cammerus*) and crabs (*cancer*) in adjacent chapters (9.50 and 9.51) and sometimes in relation to one another (Pliny, *Natural History*, vol. 3, pp. 226–31), but does not actually categorize sea-crabs among the lobsters.

[33] Barnes reads this word as 'uncamly', and posits that it might be a coinage by Golding (p. 302), likely meaning 'not crab-like'. Field reads 'uncumly'; we also see the third graph as a 'u' rather than an 'a' (and have modernized accordingly).

[34] A figure from Greek mythology whose eyesight was especially keen. See Apollodorus' *Biblioteke*: 'Lynceus excelled in sharpness of sight, so that he could even see things under ground', in Apollodorus, *Library*, ed. and trans. by Sir James George Frazer, 2 vols (Cambridge, MA: Harvard University Press, 1921), III.x.3, p. 13. Erasmus gives as one of his *Adages*, 'Lynceo perspicacior | More clear-sighted than Lynceus', and notes that 'Lynceus' piercing sight was proverbial', in Erasmus, *Adages, II.i.1 to II.vi.100*, trans. by R. A. B. Mynors, vol. 33 of the *Collected Works of Erasmus* (Toronto: University of Toronto Press, 1991), II.i.54, pp. 48–49.

[35] Golding's translation of a Latin sentence from Cato's *Distichs* (I.30), a book of proverbial wisdom and popular medieval textbook; see *The Distichs of Cato: A Famous Medieval Textbook*, trans. by Wayland Johnson Chase (Madison, WI: University of Wisconsin Studies, 1922).

Example dissenting from doctrine.

Thou therefore which teachest other men, teachest not thyself.
Thou that preachest that men should not steal, stealest. Etc.
(Romans 2:21–23)[36]

---

[36] The 'Etc.' here refers to verses 22 and 23, which Golding adds to Freitag's citation. He does not, however, include the verses themselves.

26. Of the Hare and the Snail[37]

The hare, vaunting° himself against the snail for swiftness and nimbleness of foot, and upbraiding him with the slowness and lumpishness° of his body, challenged° sovereignty over him. The snail, scorning the hare's pride, lest he should in his own opinion prejudice himself by stooping° to his lure, demanded to bring the matter to trial and challenged his adversary to the encounter, avowing that he would not otherwise yield him that praise and preeminence than by being overcome. Hereupon the day and place were appointed for the encounter, and either of them came to the appointed mark. The snail, going on leisurely night and day, came to the race's end afore the hare, who, having no regard of the time, thought° to have prevented him at his ease alonely° by running. And so the snail won the wager.

The Morals:[38]

---

[37] In Freitag, *Leporis ac Testudinis* [The Hare and the Tortoise], a well-known Aesopian fable. The engraving clearly depicts a tortoise, not a snail. Golding's use of the word 'snail' may be an indication that he was completing his translation without the accompanying images, or he may be using 'snail' to mean tortoise (a rare and obsolete but attested definition of 'snail'; see *OED*, s.v. 'snail, n. 1,' 1b; see also Barnes, p. 321).

[38] Freitag supplies a moral for this fable, though Golding has not included it. The missing moral reads: *Vsvs fabulae est, In omni vitae actionisque genere assiduitatem quamplurimum posse, cunctaque ardua industria ac diligentia demum superari, ac lentè festinando, quod monet ille, plus effici quàm praematura properatione.* [The use of this fable is, that in all of life and actions, assiduousness is able to bring forth a great many things, and all arduous things are ultimately overcome by industry and diligence; and by making haste slowly, as this [fable] admonishes, more is brought about than by premature speed.]

Nature outgone by diligence.

Know ye not that they which run in a race, do all of them run, and yet but one of them winneth the prize? So run ye as ye may obtain the reward. (1 Corinthians 9:24)

27. Of a Raven and a Sheep

It cometh so to pass, that although the dispositions of naughtypacks° be diverse, and the manner of their naughtiness is not all one, no not even among those that are of one suit,° yet notwithstanding they jump° all in this point, that they always imagine mischief to them that are good. So is the silly and innocent sheep alway° assaulted. For when on a time a raven, lighting° upon a sheep's back, began to tire° upon him unmercifully with his hooked beak, the sheep, bewailing the wrong in himself, told the raven that as fierce as he was upon him, being feeble and unarmed, he durst° not try his strength upon the dog that suddenly at that time came in their sight. The raven, being no whit° moved therewith, answered that he knew well enough what he had to do.

The Morals: In vain do we make our complaints, or pretend right, before such as take pleasure in other men's harms and calamities.

It is a shame to assail an unweaponed man.

Ye shall not hurt the widow or the fatherless. If ye hurt them, they shall cry unto me and I will hear them, and my wrath shall wax hot, and I will smite you with the sword, and your wives shall be widows and your children fatherless. (Exodus 22:23)

28. Of a Fox and of Bees

A fox that was caught in a snare, being so stung with bees that he was outwardly all on a gore blood, was counselled by another fox to scare away the flies and cutfowls°[39] that sat upon him. Whereunto he answered that in his opinion that counsel was smally[40] to his behoof,° because that when he had driven away those that were already satisfied and full of his blood, other new hungry ones would come in their stead, and much more greedily suck the rest of the blood out of his body than those whose bellies were already full.

The Morals: It is an old proverb printed in all men's minds by the stamp of nature that of two evils the least is always to be chosen.

---

[39] The word 'cutfowl' means insect, though the word is now obsolete; the only other recorded use of it is in Golding's 1587 translation of Philippe Du Mornay's *Trewnesse of Christian Religion* (*OED*). Barnes notes that the manuscript is unclear here, and transcribes this word as 'Cutpolls' (p. 322).

[40] In his notes on the manuscript, Hugh G. Dick transcribed this as 'finally', but the initial letter is an 's', and 'smally' makes sense: the fox is saying that the advice is little (smally) to his benefit (Hugh Gilchrist Dick, 'Working Copy of Transcript', Box 21, Folder 5, in Hugh Gilchrist Dick Papers, 1937–1974, UCLA Library Special Collections, Charles E. Young Research Library, University of California, Los Angeles). The word 'smally' also appears in several other Golding translations (*EEBO*). Field and Barnes both read 'smally'.

Of two evils it is wisdom to choose the lesser.

It is better for me to fall into your hands without doing this deed than to sin in the sight of the Lord. (Daniel 13:23)[41]

---

[41] In most modern Bibles Daniel ends with 12 chapters; today, this citation would be written as Susanna 23. Where modern citations may differ from those of the sixteenth century, we have noted the modern reference as it appears in the NRSV.

29. Of the Eagle and the Fox

Upon a time the eagle, having lain in wait for the fox, had caught her cubs, and, soaring away with them, had carried them to his nest. The vixen,° coming in the meanwhile and beholding it, could at that time do nothing but fill the air with complaints and threats for the taking away of her whelps. The injury whereof sank so deep in her mind that, finding opportunity of revenge, she kindled a fire under the tree where the eagle bred, the smoke and flame whereof killed his birds. At whose cry their dam°[42] came flying in to them, and did what she could to have saved them, but it was to no purpose. Whereby the eagle to his own grief was taught that which he knew not afore, namely that the way of revenge is foreclosed to none.

The Morals: This place warneth us that oftentimes even the feeblest find occasion of revenge, and therefore that no man ought to provoke another to wrath without cause.

---

[42] The feminine 'dam' and following pronoun 'she' indicates either the presence of a second female eagle or that Golding has mixed up the gender of the bird (as he occasionally does in other fables).

Dangerous is the contempt of inferiors.

He that doeth wrong shall receive according to his wrong dealing, and there is no accepting of persons[43] with God. (Colossians 3:23)[44]

---

[43] i.e., no undue partiality
[44] Both Freitag and Golding give this citation; in the NRSV this verse is Colossians 3:25.

30. Of a Couple of Friends and a Bear

A couple of friends, going together on the way, as they were talking together to ease the weariness of their journey, by chance spied a great bear coming against them not far off. Whereat being stricken with fear, and having no long time to consult what to do, they separated themselves asunder, the one climbing up into a tree, and the other falling flat to the ground as if he had been dead. Therefore, when the bear came at him and saw him lie upon the ground without stirring, he kept on his way thinking he had been dead. For it is a thing commonly known that bears are wont to abstain from dead carrions.° Which thing the traveller's fellow beholding from the tree, when he saw all danger past, came down to his friend and asked him what it was that the bear had whispered in his ear. 'Marry,'° quoth he, 'that I should shun such friends as thou art, and have no trust in them that hold the law of friendship no longer than prosperity lasteth.'

The Morals: A sure friend is seen in necessity.[45]

---

[45] Freitag includes both a short moral and the tag above the image on the opposite page; Golding has omitted the tag. The missing text reads: *Fucatae amicitiae nota* [A sign of painted friendship]. In other words, perhaps, a sign that what was thought to be a true friend was in fact only a painted or artificial one.

Every friend will say, 'I also have joined friendship,' and there is a friend which is a friend but only in name. (Ecclesiasticus 37:1)

31. Of an Ass and a Little Dog

An ass, beholding a little spaniel fawning on his master, and therefore greatly in his favour, began to fall into an inward consideration of the luckless lot° of his own life, and to complain in himself that, whereas he himself was cudgeled° and beaten, the spaniel lived in delicacy and idleness, and was coyed° of his master for fawning upon him. Whereupon, finding fault with his own rudeness, he took upon him to purchase his master's favour the same way that he had lately seen the dog use. And so, braying and frisking° (full° finely you may be sure), he fell to fawning and pawing ill-favouredly at his master with his forefeet. At whose outcry, the servants, coming with all speed, did cudgel him well and surely, and afterward he was sold away to a crabbed° carle,° who held him slavishly to his labour.

The Morals: This fable is devised against counterfeiting and hypocrisy. And the ass's misfortune warneth us to walk aright,° and not to start aside unadvisedly from our proper calling and trade of life to another for which we be less meet.

The neglecting of a man's own vocation.

And the man in whom the wicked fiend was, running upon them and overmastering them, prevailed against them both, so as they fled out of the house naked and wounded. (Acts 8:19 and 19:16)[46]

---

[46] Although this citation appears in both Freitag and Golding, neither includes the text of Acts 8:19.

32. Of a Wolf and a Lamb

As a wolf and a lamb were drinking by chance both at one brook, the wolf on the upper part of the stream and the lamb on the nether part, as soon as the wolf spied the lamb, by and by like a crafty jack° and a cruel greedygut, he quarrelled that the lamb troubled the water and made it thick with mud, stepping to him with these or like words: 'I would never have thought, though thou haddest been an ox, that thou durstest° to have broken out into so great boldness.' The lamb, being too well acquainted with the cruelty of his enemy, and throughly° afraid of him in his heart, as he was about to excuse himself mildly, was repressed by the wolf with these words: 'Darest thou, Jack Sauce,[47] like an imp of thy father's brood, chop logic with me?[48] Darest thou so much as mutter one word? Thou shalt not scape it unpunished. For I promise thee that thy malapertness° shall by and by cost thee thy life.'

The Morals: It reprehendeth the malicious lust that quarrellers have to do harm, who, taking occasion upon every toy,° yea even where no cause at all is ministered, make a gain to their malice of the behaviours of innocents,[49] and never laugh more slyly in their sleeves than when they have brought the lives, good names, and goods of good men to destruction.

---

[47] We have followed the practice of the manuscript in making this phrase, 'Jack Sauce', appear like a name. However, Jack Sauce is not a character but a descriptive name: a 'Jack-sauce' is 'an impudent fellow' (*OED*).

[48] To chop logic means to argue in an annoying way, to bandy logical arguments.

[49] i.e., out of or from the behaviours of innocents. The 'of' here is Golding's awkward translation of the Latin *ex insontium moribus*.

The malice of the wicked hunteth after mischief.

Whereupon the princes and great personages sought occasion to find some fault in Daniel, on the behalf of the kingdom.
(Daniel 6:4)

33. Of a Thief and a Dog

A thief, having broken open a man's gate by night, cast bread to a dog that lay without,° lest he should bewray him while he was robbing the house. But the dog, being not forgetful of his charge, suffered not his mouth to be so stopped,° but with his barking and razing° bewrayed the presence of the thief, and, raising up the whole house, sharply rebuked the thief with these words: 'Thou rascal gallow-clapper,° thou utterly mistakest thy mark if thou think that any benefit or profit can allure me to hazard the loss of my credit by concealing thy crime, or if thou imagine that my good name and faithfulness are to be sold for the lickerousness° of a little gain.'

The Morals: It frayeth° servants from the wicked infamy of treachery and unfaithfulness, in that it painteth out the uncorruptible constancy of the dog, the faithfulest of all beasts, in defending his master's goods. By whose example all men should of right be moved to keep the halidom° of their faith unviolated and uncorrupted, seeing that the contrary sort of men never reap any good report, no, not even at the hands of those to whose benefit such treachery redoundeth.°

A MORAL FABLETALK

An example of uncorrupted trustiness in despising a man's own profit.

If thou have a faithful servant, let him be unto thee as thine own soul,[50] and use him as thy brother. (Ecclesiasticus 33:30)

---

[50] Golding originally (prematurely) wrote 'brother', then crossed it out and replaced it with 'Sowle'.

34. Of a Spiteful Cur° and an Ox

A certain mastiff that was wallowing,° frisking, and sporting himself with such other pleasures in a fair° meadow, espying an ox come thither to feed, laboured exceedingly to keep him from his accustomed grazing with his unmeasurable malapertness and vexation. The ox, bespeaking the troublesome dog, desired him gently° that he would not do him the wrong to bar him from the use of his right by keeping him from his feeding, both because those victuals were not for the dog's diet, and also for that he had not any interest in those pastures.° But it booted° not the ox to strive with the churl that regarded not the weight of reasons. For although he denied not that hay and grass served not his turn,° yet he said he took no small pleasure and delight in them.

The Morals: So froward are the dispositions of some men that they envy other men the use of the good things which themselves cannot enjoy, and had rather to make havoc and spoil of them than to permit those to enjoy them which have need of them.

A MORAL FABLETALK

The fervent desire of envy to work spite.

Again I beheld all the labours of men, and I perceived that their welldoings lay open to the envy of their neighbours.
(Ecclesiastes 4:4)

35. Of a Horse and an Ass

An ass, being laden with a great pack, and carrying moreover the horse's provender° that travelled with him, and being at the point to sink under his burden, besought the horse to help him. Who, being moved with no compassion towards the ass, but being over-pampered with idleness and the delights of easy life, gave no ear to his wayfellow's°[51] entreatance. By reason whereof, the ass, being over-pressed with the weight, died out of hand.[52] When the hackneyman° saw that, he fell into a great chafe° with the wanton° and prancing jade° for his refusing to undertake some part of the ass's pains, and, loading him with the same burden that the ass had borne,° tamed him with a store of stripes,° thereby teaching him to his great grief to lay aside his merciless cruelty, and with meek and mild affection to pity the miseries and sorrows of other folk.

The Morals: Justly be their adversities scorned, which are so puffed up with prosperity that they not only be not moved at the calamities of their neighbours, but also refuse to succour those that take most pains for the welfare and commodity° of their life.

---

[51] The word 'wayfellow', meaning fellow wayfarer, is Golding's coinage.
[52] i.e., immediately or suddenly

The just reward of unmercifulness.

The wicked man's heart is desirous of mischief, and will not have compassion upon his neighbour. (Proverbs 21:10)
Bear ye one another's burden, and so fulfil the law of Christ. (Galatians 6:2)

36. Of the Raven and the Fox

The fox, always like himself, making conscience to degenerate from the disposition of his ancestors — that is to say, making no conscience at all whom he overtake with his wiles — spareth not even those that are attainted° with the same interest of lewdness that he himself is.[53] And therefore, beholding a raven upon a tree with a lump of good fat cheese in his bill, he fell a-praising his feathers, exceedingly protesting like a flatterer that if the qualities of his untrained nature were answerable to the beauty of his feathers, he was worthy to be king of all birds and to have obedience at all their hands. The raven, taking pride at this praise, and being tickled with vainglory,° began to clap his wings at the commendation, and in going about to utter the sweetness of his voice in singing, did let the cantle°[54] of cheese slip out of his mouth. Which thing the fox perceiving, who stood at the receipt of the bait in reward of his flattery, caught it up and went his way.

The Morals: Such are the feats of flatterers, that by bewitching the minds of men that are desirous of praise and vainglory with the enticements of filed words, they swallow up their substance and wealth, and in the end give them a mock for their folly.

---

[53] i.e., The fox, being fox-like, and not wanting to deviate from the (devious) practices of his ancestors — that is to say, having no scruples about fooling anyone at all — does not even avoid fooling those who are also deceptive. To 'make conscience' is to have scruples about.

[54] Field's edition of the *Fabletalk* records this as 'cautle'. While the ambiguity of minims makes this a possible transcription, 'cautel' means a trick, while 'cantle' is a morsel or portion of food. Barnes also reads 'cantle'.

Flattery hurtful to the unadvised.

The man that speaketh fair and feigned speeches to his friend layeth a snare for his feet. (Proverbs 29:5)[55]

---

[55] The citation for this verse is missing in both Golding's manuscript and Freitag. We have supplied the citation from the NRSV for ease of reference.

37. Of the Frog and the Mouse

Look what strife was of old, in the time that is made renowned by the verses of Homer;[56] the same or not unlike (for discord seldom dieth among reconciled enemies) grew between a certain mouse and a frog, for all the former atonement. For when a certain frog, as he lope° here and there upon a pond's bank to seek his food and repast, espied a mouse, by and by he called to mind the old grudge, and thinking a fit time of revenge to be offered, desired the silly mouse to dinner, who mistrusted no evil, and, promising him to carry him on his back through the pond, did tumble him down in the mids of the water and drowned him. But whilst the mouse in his utter peril (bethinking himself of the ancient enmity) strove in vain to rid himself from the hold of his enemy, a kite° caught them both for his prey.

The Morals:[57]

---

[56] The Βατραχομυομαχία, *Batrachomyomachia*, or Frog-Mouse-Battle, was an early mock-epic version of this tale often attributed, probably incorrectly, to Homer.

[57] Freitag has a moral here, though Golding has not supplied it. The missing moral reads: *Habet ea in hominum moribus affabulatio energiam, vt improbos demonstret rarissimè vel nunquam supplicium euadere: nam quod ait Horatius, Raro antecedentem scelestum deseruit pede poena claudo: ita & mus exsoleti propemodum delicti, & rana praesentis muricidij luit poenas.* [This fable efficiently demonstrates that in the customs of human beings, wicked people very rarely or never escape punishment. For, as Horace says, 'Rarely does Vengeance, [though] with a lame foot, cease to be concerned with a wicked man, [though he has been] outstripping [her]'. Therefore both the mouse for a nearly faded away transgression, and the frog for the present muricide (mouse-killing), pay a penalty.] The embedded quotation comes from Horace's *Odes*, book III, ode 2, lines 31–32.

The enemy preyeth upon the discord of friends.

Every kingdom divided in itself shall be desolate, and house shall fall upon house. (Luke 11:17)

38. Of a Frog and an Ox

A frog, seeing a very fat ox in a very fine meadow, and taking spite at him for his great hugeness, with his horned brow and his stately dewlaps° dangling down to the show,[58] began to repine° at it, and, approaching to him as offended at his own littleness, strutted° himself so far beyond his power, of very pride and spite, to match the ox in bigness that he burst himself asunder, and by shedding° out his bowels and blood upon the ground, learned and taught that it was not for anybody to vaunt himself arrogantly by emulating another man's state, forgetting his own ability. Which doing of his was very fitly° taunted with this quip by the ox, laughing him to scorn: 'Tell me, wretch,' quoth he, 'what had it booted thee to have been equal with me in body? Truly thou dost not know how many labours and toils thou must have endured, from the which Nature hath privileged thee by the benefit of thy little body.'

The Morals:[59]

---

[58] i.e., dangling down to outward view or appearance. Barnes has difficulty reading this word (pp. 323–34); Field reads 'slope'. The word is a bit blotched, but clearly reads 'showe'. Golding originally wrote 'his' before 'showe', before crossing it out and replacing it with 'the'.

[59] Freitag has a moral here, though Golding has not supplied it. The missing moral is as follows: *Is oppidò omnium calculis felix censendus est, sua qui uiuit sorte contentus; tantoque est beatior in humili vitae genere, quàm in fastigio rerum collocatus, quanto paucioribus rebus indiget, quantoque eius venter minus, vt inquit ille, quàm alterius capit.* [By the calculations of all people, he should be exceedingly happy who lives content of his own lot; and so much as he is the more happy in his lowly kind of life, than settled at the peak of things, so he needs fewer things, and so much less his stomach takes hold of, as this [fable] says, than that [stomach] of another.] In other words, he who is happy with his place in life needs less to be satisfied.

Over-heady and unprofitable pride.

After pride cometh a fall, but the lowly-minded shall be taken up into glory. (Proverbs 29:23)
Thou hast meekened me as a new-weaned[60] child. (Psalms 88:11)

---

[60] Golding's coinage, meaning newly weaned (in other words, a very young child).

39. Of a Hart° that Beheld Himself in a Water

A hart, beholding his body and members very wistly° in a clear spring, dispraised and discommended° his feet more than was convenient, yielding all praise and commendation to his horns, glorying in them as the only ornament of beauty and majesty, not knowing as yet what his feet might avail him, or how greatly his horns might annoy him. For within a while after, when he had escaped the hands of hunters in the open field by the benefit of his feet, anon when he came among the thick and bushy groves, he was hampered by the horns and made a prey to the hounds. In whose rending of him in pieces, he blamed his former preposterous praisings, lamenting that he had found fault with his feet which had so often saved him afore, and so fondly praised those branches of his that had been the cause of his death and destruction.

The Morals: It is a vice bred for the most part in all men, by a certain peculiar corruption of nature, to despise the things that may stand us in most stead, and wilfully to work our own harm, and to open the gap of all calamities to ourselves, by our own overweening and swelling pride.

A foolish interchange of praise and dispraise.

Thine own overweening and the pride of thy heart[61] have deceived thee. (Jeremiah 49:16)
Woe be to you that call evil good, and good evil. (Isaiah 5:20)

---

[61] That the supporting biblical quote about a proud heart (Latin *cordis*) should follow a fable about a proud hart (Latin *cervus*) is a happy coincidence in English. The pun is more obvious in the manuscript, where Golding spells both the animal and the bodily organ as 'harte'.

40. Of the Doves and the Goshawk°

At such time as the kites and puttocks° were at deadly feud with the doves, and had unreconcilable war with them (for how can rakehells° and catchpolls° agree with any man but for gain?), and would in no wise grant so much as any truce, the doves, being tired with their continual affliction in seeking to remedy the matter, leapt out of the frying pan into the fire. For they sought help of the goshawk. And to the intent he should defend them, they craved° him to be their king. He, being hungry, accepted the condition, and used his sovereignty in such sort over the innocent doves that he no more spared their young pigeons than the dams themselves, but devoured them both alike.

The Morals: Against tyrannous princes and the unwieldy government of unruly kings, who, violating their faith at their own lust, and letting themselves loose from all law, execute all manner of cruelty upon their subjects, little considering this most holy saying of the Emperor Justinian (Lib. 6. C. tit. de Testam.): 'Although the law of sovereignty have set the Emperor free from the strictness of the law, yet nothing belongeth to an Emperor more properly than to live according to law.'[62] And therefore, against tyrants the help of tyrants is not to be sought.

---

[62] Emperor Justinian I (*c.* 482–565) significantly revised Roman laws during the sixth century. This saying comes from Book 6, chapter 23, '*De Testamentis: Quemadmodum testimenta ordinantus*' [Concerning wills, and in what way they should be drawn up] of the *Codex Justinianus* [*Code of Justinian*], which is part of the larger *Corpus Juris Civilis* [*Body of Civil Law*].

The end of succour that is sought at tyrants' hands.

Behold, thou trustest to that broken staff of reed, I mean Egypt, whereupon if a man lean, it slivereth° into his hand and pierceth it through. Such a one is Pharaoh, king of Egypt, to all that trust in him. (Isaiah 36:6)

41. Of a Hart and a Horse

Through like hatred to the hart, but in unlike respect and upon better desert, as seeking to cozen others, whereas the doves never imagined any evil, the horse purchased his own undoing by seeking help at man's hand, promising to do him any service in recompense of his succour.[63] When the horse urged the matter, the man accepted it upon condition that he should suffer him to put a bridle on his head, and to ride upon his back with a pair of spurs on his heels, and with other instruments meet for the overcoming of the stag. The horse granted to abide them all and greater, so the stag might be overcome. Thereupon the man, taking the horse's back, chased the red deer, and with a dart overthrew him. For the doing whereof, the horse commended him with singular praises, and, bespeaking him with fair words, desired him to let him go again. But the horse came so far short of obtaining any liberty or redemption for all his kind speeches, that having once yielded his neck to the yoke for the purchasing of another body's destruction, he was compelled to serve even the pleasures of man, and to lead all his life after most miserably oppressed with intolerable toils and labours.

The Morals: Justly do they suffer punishment, and well worthy be they to perish, who to bring other men's lives in danger do yield themselves into shameful and reproachful bondage.

---

[63] This sentence begins by referring back to the previous fable: the horse had a similar hatred for his enemy the hart as the doves did for the kites (in fable 40), but the horse also was more spiteful, because he was seeking to cause harm while the doves never did; for this reason, the horse agreed to pay a man for help in acting against the hart.

Restless is the envy of other men's welfare.

He opened a pit and dug it, and is fallen into the ditch that he himself made. His mischief shall be turned back upon his own head, and his wickedness shall light upon his own pate.°
(Psalms 7:16–17)

42. Of a Fox and a Goat

A goat and a fox, being pressed with dryth° of thirst, leapt down together into a well. The goat, considering the steepness of the descent and the hard getting up again, said he feared lest he should be taken there, and therefore did cast all the ways he could devise to get out. The fox bade him be of good cheer, for he had already devised a way to scape thence. Whereupon he counselled the goat to set up his forefeet as high as he could against the wall, and stooping somewhat° forward with his head, to make himself as a ladder for him to get up. When the goat had so done, and the fox was gotten up upon the brim of the well out of all danger, he taunted the unadvisedness of the goat with these words: 'Had there been as good store of wit in thy head as there is of hair upon thy chin, thou wouldest not have adventured so rashly into the pit without considering how thou mightest have gotten out again.'

The Morals: It is the property of a wise man so to weigh the entrances, consequences, and issues° of things together aforehand, that he fall not into danger through unadvised rashness.

A MORAL FABLETALK

Destruction the end of deceitful light belief.

He that believeth hastily is light-minded, and shall be brought low.
(Ecclesiasticus 19:4)
All deceivers are an abomination to the Lord! (Proverbs 3:32)

43. Of the Lion and the Bear

The lion, for he is known to have sovereignty over all kind of four-footed beasts, commanded them all to come ready furnished for a certain war which he had purposed in his mind. Hereupon the bear, by fortune[64] making mention of the ass and the hare, asked whether the one, being of all living things the most fearful, and the other, being most doltish,° could do any service against the enemy, or stand in any stead for the war? 'Yea, marry,' quoth the lion, 'for the ass may scare the birds with his rude° braying, and peradventure° his noise may have the same force against the fowls which the grunting of swine hath against the elephant;[65] and the hare, by reason of his singular swiftness and good footmanship, may very well perform the charge both of a scout, and of a post° to carry home tidings° what is done in the wars.'

The Morals: It is the part of a vigilant ruler of a commonweal to have such insight in the natures and dispositions of his subjects as he may leave no man's service (be he never so base) unemployed to some good purpose or other.

---

[64] i.e., by chance
[65] Elephants were proverbially afraid of swine: 'The Elephant has a terror of a horned ram and of the squealing of a pig'; see Aelian, *Of the Characteristics of Animals*, vol. 1, trans. by A. F. Scholfield (Cambridge, MA: Harvard University Press, 1958), I.38, p. 57.

Every member yields some profit to a commonweal.

Nay, rather, the members of the body which seem to be of the basest sort, are most necessary. (1 Corinthians 12:22)

44. Of the Housemouse and the Fieldmouse

A certain ranny° or shrew (it is the name of a kind of fieldmouse), bidding the housemouse to dinner, entertained him thriftily with a mess of beans. The housemouse, being desirous to requite his courtesy with like good will, invited him likewise, who went with him to the good cheer that he had at home. When he came within the house, he found great store of delicate meats and of all other things. Howbeit, forasmuch as their mirth was often interrupted by the panter° that came in as they were feeding, insomuch that his scaring of them made their dainty fare unsavory, the fieldmouse said plainly he had no great delight in that unseasonable feasting. 'Nay,' quoth he, 'how much more sweet is it to me to live to myself without fear than to swim here in abundance of dainties,° accompanied with so great fear.'

The Morals: This fable telleth men that the life which is led at liberty void of cares is both more safe and more pleasant than the public is,[66] and that a homely table and spare diet is oftentimes more savoury than a fine table and princely fare.

---

[66] i.e., than the public life is

Dainties are dangerous, but thriftiness is full of safety.

Anon he followed her as an ox led to the slaughter, and as a lamb that waxeth wanton, not knowing that like a fool he was carried to the stocks. (Proverbs 7:22)

45. Of a Fowler° and a Turtledove

As a certain cunning fowler (inferior to no man in his art) watched in a tuft of reeds to catch birds in the harvesttime, and had set his nets for the well-feeding throstles° (as one termeth them), laying wait through covetousness of gain as well for the turtles as for other birds, when he had now wilily allured one into his net, was suddenly stung with a deadly wound by an adder that crept unto him out of the tuft of reeds. And while the fowler was occupied in looking to his present hurt, the turtle scaped out of his net, and, flying away, flouted him with these words: 'Worthily now, O fool, for thy treachery practiced with so great guile and travail[67] against our innocency and unhurtfulness, dost thou by God's vengeance abide the punishment due to thy wickedness, so as thou shalt feel the same death in thyself which thou intendedest against us.'

The Morals: It is agreeable to reason, that such as delight in doing mischief to others should receive the recompense due to their wicked and cruel dealings and be destitute of help at all men's hands.

---

[67] 'Travail' usually means labour or suffering, but in this case, the copia (pairing it with 'guile') suggests that Golding is using the verbal sense of 'travail', meaning affliction, harassing, or vexing.

Treachery treacherous to the treacher.°

The Lord will not grieve the soul of the righteous with hunger, but he will defeat the treacheries of the ungodly. (Proverbs 10:3)

46. Of a Mountain that Travailed with Child

A certain mountain, fisking° to and fro to the great wonderment of the dwellers and passers-by, stayed many travellers and allured others to behold it for the strangeness of the matter. At the last, when throngs of people flocked thither with eager desire to see what end this continual quaking would come unto, 'Get ye hence quickly,' quoth the mountain, 'for anon I shall be delivered of child.' At the which roaring of the mountain, not only men but also even the earth itself (by all likelihood) was put in dread,° expecting the bringing forth of some horrible monster. But in the end, there was yeaned° but a poor mouse, and so all the former fear in expecting some strange and uncouth thing was turned to laughter.

The Morals: Mountains are then said rightly to labour of child when men of Thraso's[68] disposition, despising and disdaining other folks, do gloriously with full mouth make many stout brags of themselves, and yet in very deed do not any act worthy of praise, but rather deal in such sort as they make themselves a laughingstock to all men.

---

[68] Thraso is a stock character from Terence's play *Eunuchus* who is known for being a braggart. Thraso is also mentioned in fable 117.

A MORAL FABLETALK

False pretence of great things.

I saw the wicked man highly advanced, and perking° up above the
Cedars of Libanus.[69] But anon I came by him again, and he was
gone. I sought him, but nowhere could he be found.
(Psalms 36:35–36)[70]

---

[69] Golding's 'Cedars of Libanus', translating Freitag's *cedros libani*, are usually referred to today as 'Cedars of Lebanon'. These cedars were notoriously tall, and are mentioned frequently in the Bible.
[70] In the NRSV this is Psalms 37:35–36.

47. Of the Peacock and the Rest of the Birds Choosing Him King

Lest any man through some foul unskill°[71] should be ignorant that the birds had not a king of their own,[72] I will add here[73] in these fables their careful deliberation in choosing him. Having called a parliament, as they were consulting of diverse matters and considered the stateliness of the peacock and the beautifulness of his feathers, almost all the whole assembly were at the point to have given their voices to the choosing of him. And no doubt but he had out of hand[74] obtained the title of Royal Majesty, but that the woodspeck° alone, encountering the proceedings of the residue,° propounded° to their considerations that if they should happen to be in danger of any enemies, who should be their defender? For the peacock with that glorious array° of his could not be meet for the managing of such matters, because that (setting aside the beauty of his feathers) there was nothing else in him beseeming° a king (to whom it belongeth to punish the bad and to cherish the good), as who had nother strength nor skill of feats of war.

The Morals: The woodspeck proveth by the bravery of the peacock, that princely port° (if ye have no further eye than only to the beauty and proportion of body) deserveth small commendation or none in a king, unless it be matched with the beauty and excellency of virtues.

---

[71] Golding's pun is potentially lost in the modernizing process. The manuscript's spelling 'fowl' is also a generic term for a bird, and the verb 'to skill' means to have knowledge of something. A 'foul unskill' could therefore mean a disgraceful lack of knowledge, or a lack of knowledge about birds. Freitag's Latin has the less punning *turpi* [...] *inscitia* [shameful lack of knowledge].

[72] i.e., lest anyone should incorrectly think that the birds had no king

[73] Field reads 'adhere'.

[74] i.e., immediately

The duty of kings and magistrates.

Woe be to thee thou land whose king is a child. (Ecclesiastes 10:16)
Blessed is that land whose king is a nobleman. (Ecclesiastes 10:17)

48. Of an Ox and a Calf

A certain husbandman,° having an ox and a calf, fed the calf daintily and with ease, and so pulled down the ox with ploughing and daily toil that he needed none other exercise to keep him from growing too fat. Now when the ox came home weary and well-near tired from his labour, the calf was wont to scoff at him and, adding affliction to his affliction, not without scornfulness called him miserable caitiff,° as he was indeed. But anon after, when the ox beheld the calf well fatted to be carried to the slaughterhouse to be killed, then weighing his own state, he greatly commended his toilsome felicity, concluding that that life of his, subject to so many labours, was to be preferred before the voluptuous° life of the calf, and therewith comforted himself forever after.

The Morals: The end of the calf warneth us that pleasure commonly purchaseth sorrow, and that sith it is so easy a matter for us to overshoot ourselves in deeming the ends and felicities of good and evil men, we ought not to envy the happiness which appeareth to be in any man.

Hurtful and unhappy felicity.

He that tilleth his ground shall have store of food, but he that followeth idleness shall be filled with want. (Proverbs 28:18)[75]

---

[75] Both Freitag and Golding give 28:18 as the citation; however, in both the Vulgate and the NRSV this is Proverbs 28:19.

49. Of a Bittern° and a Crow

A bittern, finding an oyster upon the seashore, took great pains to open it and could not. Which thing a crow espying, and hoping that some good might thereby fall to his share, devised a subtle feat, and, coming to the bittern, counselled him to fly up with the oyster and to let it fall down upon some hard stone, whereby the shell would be broken, and so he should easily come by the meat. The bittern, not perceiving the cozenage, but believing the counsel that was given him had been sound, took that way to open the oyster. The crow, waiting the fall of it, flew to it, and, catching up the morsel which he had so eagerly looked for, disappointed the bittern of his hope.

The Morals: Against such as give ear and credit too easily and lightly to deceitful counsel, whose lot for the most part is to be beguiled through their own overpliantness.

Deceitful counsel.

The counsels of the ungodly be deceitful. (Proverbs 12:5)
Their mind imagineth ravin,° and their mouth speaketh guile.
(Proverbs 24:2)

50. Of the Eagle and the Raven

An eagle, catching up a lamb out of a great flock of fat sheep that were feeding in a fine and fruitful pasture, mounted up with it into the air and flew away. Which thing a raven by chance beholding from a tree hard by, and taking hold of the lewd example of the eagle's ravenousness, did through a certain presumptuous trust of his own strength seize upon the back of a very fat ram, and, striking his talons over-deep into his flesh, stuck fast there, for Fortune favoured not his lewd attempt. Whereby he was taught that it was in vain for him to attempt the thing that was above his power. For being so fast entangled in the ram's fleece that he could not fly away, he was caught by the shepherd, and by due punishment was made to rue° his heady rashness.

The Morals: No man ought to attempt anything above his power, but to remember that such as adventure upon everything through rash boldness, do hurt themselves and all that they have. And that I may annex the saying of the wise Epictetus to the former things: 'If thou take upon thee any countenance that exceedeth thy ability, thou shalt both bear it but ill-favouredly, and also thou shalt forgo that which thou mightest maintain.'[76]

---

[76] The saying is from Epictetus' *Encheiridion*, a book of advice about how to conduct oneself according to Stoic principles: 'If you undertake a role which is beyond your powers, you both disgrace yourself in that one, and at the same time neglect the role which you might have filled with success' (Epictetus, *Discourses, Books 3–4. Fragments. The Encheiridion*, trans. by W. A. Oldfather [Cambridge, MA: Harvard University Press, 1928], 37, p. 525).

A MORAL FABLETALK

It is good for a man to know himself.

Seek not for things above thy reach, nor for the things that are beyond thy power. (Ecclesiasticus 3:22)[77]

---

[77] The manuscript is unclear here; it appears as if Golding originally wrote the citation as 3:22, and then either he or a later hand scratched vertical lines over the '2' to change it into a '1'. Freitag gives 3:22, which corresponds to a contemporary Vulgate; in the NRSV this verse is 3:21.

51. Of a Cock that Found a Precious Stone

A cock seeking his food in a dunghill found a very precious diamond. The which when he had diverse times pecked with his bill and saw he could have no good at all by it, as which he could nother break nor convert to his sustenance, he began to scorn it disdainfully and to prefer a grain of wheat or barley far before it. And stomaching° the matter, 'Is there any use,' quoth he, 'of this jewel? Why do men esteem it at such value? Why seek they the farthest parts of the world for it, with so great peril? Truly in mine° opinion they be stark fools, as many of them as have it in such price, and consider not how much one grain of wheat or other corn°[78] is better than it.'

The Morals: Whereas this fable is known even to blinkards° and barbers (as the proverb sayeth),[79] and there is not any other more familiar to the common people, it is a wonder that men perceive not the use of any less than of this.[80] For how many be there to be found, which through a certain heady ignorance are ready to scorn and embase° anything, whereby they show this saying to be most true, which is frequented in common speech, namely that knowledge and skill have no enemy but the ignorant, and that the poet was not overshot° when he said, 'There is no liking of the thing that is unknown.'[81]

---

[78] i.e., or other grain

[79] Field (p. 206, n. 7) identifies the source of the Latin proverb as Horace, *Sermones* I.vii.3. For an English edition, see Horace, *Satires, Epistles, and Ars Poetica*, trans. by H. Rushton Fairclough (London: William Heinemann, 1932), p. 91. Fairclough explains the proverb as follows: 'The shops of apothecaries and barbers were favourite places of gossip' (p. 91, n. b).

[80] i.e., Everyone knows of this fable, and so it is amazing that no one understands it.

[81] The poet in this case is Ovid. Golding here paraphrases or translates the phrase *ignoti nulla cupido* from Ovid's *Ars Armatoria* III.397; for a modern edition, see Ovid, *The Art of Love, and Other Poems*, trans. by J. H. Mozley (Cambridge, MA: Harvard University Press, 1962).

The use of riches not known.

What availeth it a fool to have riches, seeing he cannot buy wisdom? (Proverbs 17:16)

52. Of a Boar and an Ass

A boar, upon a time casting an ass in the teeth with his slowness and sluggishness,[82] told him he thought him to be bred of purpose but to lead his life in laystalls° and among stinking carrions, as unworthy to be in company with other living wights,° or to be admitted of man to his services, be they never so base. And therewithal he chanted out his own daftness° and stoutness with scornful praise, showing by proof how swiftly he could run. The ass, loathing the boar's vainglorious boasting and praising of himself, answered thus: 'I need no such nimbleness of foot, sith no man lies in wait for my life as they do for thine.'

The Morals: We say that for the most part such as are void of guile by reason of the dullness of their nature, or which hunt not greatly for popular° praise because they have abandoned the public functions and dealings in the commonweal, are happier in many respects than those on whom Nature hath bestowed great sageness of wit.

---

[82] i.e., scolding the ass for being slow

Doltish and unprofitable presumption.

What hath our pride booted us? Or what hath the boasting of our riches availed us? (Wisdom 5:8)

53. The Battle between the Birds and the Beasts

At such time as the war was hottest and dangerousest between the birds and the beasts of the earth, whether it were for the enlarging of the bounds° and borders of their empires, or in revenge of harms and wrongs done on either part (for antiquity hath made uncertain and almost quite blotted out the causes of that discord and war), the bat or rearmouse,[83] distrusting the part of the birds (as in his conceit likely to go by the worse), after he had long stood as neuter,° did in the end join himself to the beasts. But when it came to the encounter, fortune gave the victory to the birds, and the bat fled away with the beasts. And daring not to return to the birds because of his unfaithfulness, he doth ever since lie hidden a-daytimes,° and for grief of guilty conscience doth ever fly abroad in the night.

The Morals:[84]

---

[83] The manuscript spells 'bat' as 'backe'. Golding also notes the alternate name of bats in his translation of Ovid's *Metamorphoses*: 'we in English language Backes or Reermice call the same', in Ovid, *Ovid's Metamorphoses: The Arthur Golding Translation of 1567*, ed. by John Frederick Nims (Philadelphia: Paul Dry Books, 2000), IV.513.

[84] Freitag has a moral for this fable, but Golding has not included it. The missing moral reads: *In scelestos ac improbos proditores, quos vtinam etiam hoc tempore pudor ac criminum conscientia ex omnium oculis eximeret, obiter & in mercenarios illos homines, qui nulla aequitatis habita ratione, duarum controuersarum partium hanc tuendam suscipiunt cui fortunam magis comitem, quam ducem virtutem fore sperant*. [[This fable is] against infamous and shameless traitors — whom if only shame and a consciousness of crime would remove from the eyes of all at this time! — and, in passing, against those mercenary men, who, having no regard for fairness, of two opposed sides undertake to support that one to whom they hope Fortune will be a greater friend, rather than [the one to whom] virtue will be a leader.]

Shame accompanieth treachery.

He that is not with me is against me, and he that gathereth not with me scattereth. (Matthew 12:30)
Everyone that evil doth, hateth the light. (John 3:20)

54. Of the Frogs Craving a King

The frogs, being weary, whether of their lawless or of their popular state[85] I dare not affirm, but the one of them is certain, desired Jove[86] to give them a king. He, being tired with their often and importunate suits, granted their desire and cast down a block° out of heaven into the mere.° Now when this block had taken upon him the royalty and government of the kingdom, and had shown himself a mild and merciful prince, the frogs, beholding their king's countenance apparently given to unaccustomed and singular gentleness, said they demanded not such a king as should be without life. Whereupon when they required another, Jupiter for their unthankfulness sent them a curlew,° who became a waster° of their kingdom, which afore was peaceable and quiet.

The Morals: How greatly it is for the behoof of commonweals to have princes of the best sort, and how beneficial they be to their realms. And on the contrary part, how grievous and scareful° the bloody and cruel princes are it appeareth by this fable, which reproveth the servile mind of those that, being weary of the moderate sweetness of the popular government (such as the state of the Israelites was in old time under the government of the judges),[87] cannot be satisfied until they have a king and sole° sovereign.

---

[85] i.e., state governed by the people (or, in this case, frogs)
[86] Jove was the king of the gods; he is also referred to as Jupiter later in the fable.
[87] The judges were leaders thought to have been sent by Yahweh to lead the Israelites in their struggles against oppressors. The 'old time' referred to here is detailed in the Book of Judges of the Hebrew Bible.

A MORAL FABLETALK

The punishment of people that despise a good prince.

Which maketh an hypocrite to reign for the sins of the people.
(Job 34:30)

55. Of a Wolf and a Goat

A shegoat, going abroad to feed, locked her door, and charged her kid very earnestly that he should in no wise open the door to anybody that knocked. A wolf that lay lurking hard by unknown to the goat, by chance overhearing this, and hoping to use the absence of the dam to the performance of his treachery, came speedily to the goathouse as soon as she was gone, and, knocking at the door, required to be let in. But the kid, not forgetting his dam's commandment, asked the wolf at the window who he was and what he would. The wolf, pretending like an hypocrite to be the kid's mother, said she[88] would fain° come in. The kid denied to let anybody in unless he brought his mother's ordinary token. The wolf said he had but forgotten it, but yet nevertheless bade him open him the door without fear. The kid, suspecting that there was some pad° in the straw,[89] refused again, and told him thereto that only that key could open the door, and that, wanting the token, he also had forgotten how to open the door.

The Morals: Hardly° can he be deceived, which followeth and obeyeth the prescript commandment of the law.

---

[88] The pronoun for the wolf changes here, perhaps because 'she' is pretending to be the kid's mother.

[89] A lurking or hidden danger. A 'pad' is a toad, so this phrase is akin to 'a snake in the grass'.

A MORAL FABLETALK

The safety that children are in by obeying their parents.

Honour thy father and thy mother, that thou mayst live long upon the Earth. (Exodus 20:12)
They follow not a stranger but flee from him, because they be not acquainted with the voices of strangers. (John 10:5)

56. Of a Dog Deceived by a Shadow in the Water

A dog, going over a bridge holding a good great lump of flesh in his mouth, and imagining that, because the shadow thereof seemed greater than the gobbet° itself was, by reason of the exceeding great brightness of the sunbeams shining upon the water, it had been a great piece indeed, he let fall the piece that he had in his mouth, and leapt hastily down from the bridge into the water to catch that which he thought he had seen there. Where like a fool, being disappointed of his fat morsel, he bewailed too late his deceiving of himself, imputing his loss to no man, no not even to fortune, but only to his own covetousness, whereby he was bereft of so good a dinner.[90]

The Morals: It is much better to hold still the few things that a man hath in certainty without hazard° than to let go the goods that he hath upon hope of many mo depending upon uncertainty and doubtful chance.

---

[90] Golding originally wrote the phrase 'so good a turne', then crossed out 'turne' and changed it to 'dinner', which more accurately translates Freitag's *prandio*.

It is folly to exchange the certain for the uncertain.

A covetous man will not be satisfied with money, and he that is in love with riches shall take no fruit of them. (Ecclesiastes 5:9)

57. Of a Woodward° and a Wood[91]

A certain woodward, finding an axe without a helve,° and purposing to make it meet for his turn, went by and by to a grove to beg a helve of wood for his hatchet. The grove, harkening to his request, granted him his desire, and yielded him freely that one piece of wood which he required, not knowing that the lewd fellow intended any fraud in his mind, or imagined any deceit in his heart, cloaked under countenance of glozing° and smooth speech. But when the woodward had fastened the steel in the axe, he returned back to the grove, and, like one that had been carried with a frenzy, made utter waste of it within a while after, felling and cutting down all the trees in it.

The Morals: It is the next cousin not only to folly but also to extreme madness to minister weapon[92] to our enemy whereby he may work our destruction, and to undo ourselves through preposterous affection of yielding friendship and courtesy unto others.

---

[91] i.e., a forest or grove
[92] Until the end of the sixteenth century, 'weapon' could be used in the collective sense to mean 'arms' or 'weapons' (*OED*). Barnes emends to 'weapons' (p. 328).

A MORAL FABLETALK

The ministering of weapon to one's enemy.

Do good to the lowly, but give not to the ungodly. Refrain to give him bread, lest thereby he become too mighty for thee. For thou shalt find double mischief in all the good that thou dost unto him.
(Ecclesiasticus 12:5)

58. Of a Jay that Decked Himself with Peacocks' Feathers

A jay, finding peacocks' feathers in a thicket, bore himself on hand[93] that if he graffed° them into his own feathers he should purchase the name and dignity of a peacock. Wherefore, proceeding to the execution of the thing which he had conceived in his imagination, he fitted and fastened them very trimly to him. And fondly believing that being thus disguised he should pass among peacocks for a peacock indeed, he thrust himself boldly into their company. But the peacocks, finding out this counterfeit that had crept into their name and society (whom they discerned even by the haughtiness and arrogancy of his insolent bearing of himself in his unaccustomed state), caught every one of his feathers from him, and with shame enough thrust him out of their fellowship. The jay, returning to his own sort, was welcomed of them with so many scoffs as he had been hissed out from the peacocks with scorns, because that through vain presumption, he had magnified himself above the one, and associated himself to the other, of whose company he was unworthy.

The Morals: Against such as seek glory immoderately, and even without regard of shame do borrow of others, wherewith to set out their own vanity.

---

[93] 'To bear on hand' means to abuse or delude on false pretences. If he is bearing himself on hand, he is deluding himself.

Pride of other men's goods.

What hast thou which thou hast not received? And seeing thou hast received, why boastest thou as if thou hadst not received?
(1 Corinthians 4:7)

59. Of a Stag and of Oxen

Hounds pursuing a certain stag drove him to his shifts,° so as he was fain to flee to a stall where oxen were, and to sue humbly to them for their defence against the ravenousness of the dogs. To which his petition, one of the oxen answered thus: 'Alas poor wretch, dost thou see how weak defenders thou makest choice of? Nevertheless, seeing thou art driven to the last pinch, come hide thyself in this hay, and we will help to cover thee with our bodies as much as we can.' Anon cometh the owner of the stall, and, having found the stag by hot pursuit upon the foot, bebasted° him with stripes and killed him out of hand.[94]

The Morals: A man's neck may then well be said to be come to the halter°, when, being in calamity, he is fain to seek for help to such as are at as great an afterdeal° as himself. And that his unfortunate state is so forlorn, that when he hath laboured never so much to underprop° and stay it up for a time, yet in the end he is driven to sink in his misery, without any possibility to get[95] out of the gulf of calamity by any striving.

---

[94] i.e., immediately
[95] In the manuscript, Golding originally wrote 'wade' before replacing it with 'get'.

A MORAL FABLETALK

Forlorn and hopeless help.

And they said, 'The Lord shall not see it. Understand ye that be unwise among the people; shall not he that made the eye, see?'
(Psalms 93:7)

60. Of a Lion Dividing a Prey among his Attendants

A hungry lion, going a-hunting accompanied with a bloodhound, a wolf, and a fox, chanced upon a stag for his prey, whom he divided in four parts, using this or (that I feign not any untruth of him) such like speech: 'My fellows, I think there is none of you which knoweth not by experience the virtues of the most noble lion, justly king of all beasts, or that, considering the excellent gifts wherewith he is endowed far above all others, will envy him his deserved reward. For as much therefore as I was foremost in the travail, I challenge to myself the first part of the prey now divided. The second part I claim for the excellency of my courage. The third (I dare say, even by your own judgements) is due to me for the strength and force of my body. And the fourth I have earned by taking more pain than you all in catching it. As for the residue, let it be the reward of your travail.'

The Morals: Needs must they wink° at many things and bear many things which live in kings' courts, and not only they, but also the meaner sort which haunt the company of the rich. So as the poet may well seem to have said fitly, 'Let poor men warily deal, and well bethink them what they say, | And look to suffer many things, where rich pass clear away.'[96]

---

[96] Field (p. 224, n. 4) identifies this quotation as coming from Ovid's *Ars Amatoria* II.166–67. Freitag's Latin, which Golding translates, reads *Pauper agat cautè, caueat maledicere pauper: | Multaque diuitibus non patienda feret*. Modern versions of this text read slightly differently: *Pauper amet caute: timeat maledicere pauper, | Multaque divitibus non patienda ferat* [Let the poor man caution; let the poor man fear to speak harshly; let him bear much that the rich would not endure] (text and translation from Ovid, *The Art of Love*, pp. 76–77).

Untrusty° is the society of unequals.

He taketh a burden upon him which accompanieth a more honourable than himself. Therefore be not fellow with a richer than thyself. How may the cauldron and the pitcher agree together?[97]
(Ecclesiasticus 13:2–3)

---

[97] The pitcher is fragile, and therefore if it hits up against the cauldron, it is likely to shatter. Ecclesiasticus 13:3 uses the metaphor as a warning for poor people against associating with rich people. An ancient fable by Avianus about a clay pitcher and an iron cauldron also comes to the same conclusion; this analogy and its lesson cross between biblical and fabulous texts.

61. Of a Wolf and a Sheep

A wolf, arresting a sheep, commenced an action of debt against her. The sheep, on the contrary part, standing upon her right, pleaded in bar[98] that she was not indebted unto him. Upon the pleading of the case in law, the wolf relied himself upon the testimony of witnesses, and suborned° the dog, the kite, and the vulture (all branded with one selfsame mark of ravin) to depose against the silly sheep. The which thing they did, and that in such sort that, like false-forsworn° caitiffs, they not only witnessed the poor wretch to be indebted unto the wolf, but also appeached° her of felony. Whereupon she was not only condemned in the debt, but also was deemed worthy to forfeit all her goods and substance, and also to suffer death. The poor sheep, fearing the cruel and outrageous violence of her enemies, went about to defend her cause; but all was in vain, for she was oppressed by the cruel verdict of those perjured witnesses.

The Morals: The malice of false witnesses, and the corrupt sentences° of wicked judges against guiltless persons, are reproved by this fable. Whereby is also declared how great the force of falsewitnessing is against the lands, goods, yea, and lives of innocents.

---

[98] The phrase 'in bar' means 'as a sufficient reason or plea (against)' (*OED*). In other words, the sheep offered a plea against the wolf to prevent his action of debt.

Innocency oppressed by wrongful judgement.

Thou shalt do no unright, nor give wrong judgement. Thou shalt not pity the person of the poor, nor regard the countenance of the mighty, but judge thy neighbour justly. (Leviticus 19:15)

62. Of Hares Stricken with Great Fear

When certain hares, being suddenly scared out of a very thick wood that was troubled with the violence of very great and tempestuous winds, ran here and there amazed, at last as they ran scattering they lighted upon a pool that was full of frogs, which, being by chance come out of the water, lay in great number sunning of themselves upon the bank. But, being scared at the sudden coming of the hares, they flushed again into the water. Which thing the hares beholding, and perceiving them to flee away with greater haste and noise than they themselves had done afore, restrained their fear, and, taking heart to them, said: 'Let us now stay our flight, sith that even here also we find living things which flee away for fear of us.'

The Morals: Against timorous and fearful soldiers which never take up their swords and targets° again when they have once cast them away until they see their enemies turn their backs, and are always then stoutest when they see themselves furthest from danger.

A MORAL FABLETALK

Shameful boldness.

Fear not them that kill the body, but rather fear him that can throw both body and soul into hellfire. (Matthew 10:28)

63. Of a Fox that Would Eat No Grapes

A fox, beholding certain clusters of very ripe grapes hanging under the vinebranches, gave exceeding great commendation to the fertility and pleasantness of the soil where they grew, insomuch that there could scarce anything be added to the increase of the praise. But when he had taken great pains to come by some of the deepest-coloured and best grapes, sparing no point of policy to get them, and could not, but saw by trial that all his labour was to no purpose, he fell to reviling them as fast as he had sought them afore with such eagerness, calling them hedgegrapes,° and blaming his ill-bestowing of his labour in leaping at the wildgrapes in that wilderness, for so termed he that vineyard in way of disdain.

The Morals: This fable noteth the wiliness of those which, being unable to attain to the things which they have sought with greatest labour and unweariable study, do take occasion at any thing to disgrace them with slanderous speech.

A counterfeit misliking of the thing
that a man would fain° have and cannot.

A fool bewrayeth° his anger by and by, but he that dissembleth
his wrong is wise. (Proverbs 12:16)

64. Of an Ape and a Cat

An ape, marking how a cook had raked up great chestnuts in the embers, and being very desirous of them when they were well roasted, and finding no mean how to get them out, anon did put a cat to the doing thereof, taking her by the foot and therewith scraping them out of the fire. The cat, feeling the heat of the fire, began to chide with the ape, affirming his skin to be as tender as the ape's, and therefore that by his own infirmity he ought to take example of another body's.[99] The ape, jesting out his complaints, said he denied not but the present business had some difficulty in it, but yet the cat ought not therefore to refuse that labour which was the least that could be, because it was unmeet° that anybody should live idle.

The Morals: Those are very like the shrewd and dissembling ape which, by subtle persuasions for their own private profits' sake, use other men's service in most grievous perils, even with the hazard of their lives, nothing regarding other men's harms so they themselves may live out of gunshot[100] and make their gain of other folk's losses.[101]

---

[99] i.e., of somebody else's (infirmity)

[100] Freitag reads *dummodo ipsi extra fortunae aleam constituti sint* [provided that they themselves are set up outside the risk of fortune]. The idea of fortune as gunshot is Golding's addition.

[101] i.e., Those who put other men's lives in danger for their own benefit are like the ape of this fable.

Gain gotten by other men's losses.

These are spots in their feastings,¹⁰² making cheer with you without fear, feeding themselves, and being as clouds without rain carried here and there by the winds. (Jude 12)

---

¹⁰² The biblical quotation is properly 'your feastings'; the letter from Jude warns against those who sponge off others. The word 'their' comes from Golding literally translating the Latin *suis*. No equivalent for 'with you' appears in Freitag, which has only *conuiuantes* [banqueting with].

65. Of a Horse and an Ass

A horsecolt, being occupied in daily and continual labour, but yet under a mild and gentle master, bemoaned his own state, imagining none in his judgement to be more sorrowful. Now when this opinion did sore vex his mind, and make his life the more tedious, by chance he fell into the company of an old forworn ass, to whom, although (besides the loss of his beauty and of the liveliness of his body) even age itself was a burden, yet notwithstanding he was made to draw a wagon loaded, and the churlish wagoner sitting upon the forepart thereof besides and driving him forward with main[103] strokes. Which thing when the colt beheld, then, comparing his lot with the ass's, he by and by so banished all grief out of his mind that he both seemed to himself to be discharged of his accustomed labours and toils, and also bore his condition the willinger ever after.

The Morals: It is no small comfort of adversity, not only to have partners of our pains, but also to see other men sometime° more grievously pressed than ourselves.

---

[103] This word appears as 'mayne' in the manuscript. The Latin word it translates is *immaniter* [extreme, savage, brutal]. We have therefore modernized this as 'main', meaning strong or powerful.

Calamity the lighter for the greater calamity of our neighbour.

Christ hath suffered for us, leaving us an example to follow His footsteps. (1 Peter 2:21)

66. Of a Smith and his Dog

A certain smith, living sparely and hardly upon the painful and continual labour of his hands, insomuch that he sustained himself with bare bread and water, had used his dog to crave his dinner and supper at certain ordinary times.[104] At length, becoming somewhat unpatient through the burden of age growing upon him, and through continuance of labour, and through the slenderness of his fare, he bespake his dog with these words: 'I kill myself daily with endless toil to get me a poor living, insomuch that my flesh and blood are forspent, and I do but martyr my[105] wretched soul within my skin and bones as it were in a prison. But thou farest well with idleness, pampering thy belly, so as thou becometh unwieldy with fatness.' His dog, moiling° at it, gave him none other answer but this: that there was no reason that he which had been accustomed to pleasure and ease, and by means thereof had led a delicate life, should now be put to labour and toil.

The Morals: Even such are the kind of eatwells[106] and gluttons which are not ashamed to live on the sweat of other men's brows, and are always belching out this saying: 'God hath given us this time of ease.'

---

[104] The manuscript is very muddled here, but it appears that Golding initially wrote this as 'howses', perhaps thinking of 'ordinary houses' or taverns, but then corrected to 'tymes' to correspond to Freitag's *statis horis interdiu* [at appointed hours in the daytime].

[105] Golding initially wrote 'myself', and then crossed out 'self' to write the phrase 'my wretched soul'.

[106] The manuscript reads either 'Eatuelles' or 'Eatnelles'; in secretary hand the letters 'u' and 'n' are written the same way. 'Eatuelle', if the 'u' represents a 'w' sound, makes sense as 'Eatwell' (a glutton or person who eats well). 'Eatnell' is listed in the *OED* as an obscure word based on the evidence of a single printed text, Randle Cotgrave's *Dictionary of French and English Tongues* (London, 1611), where two French words (s.v. *Croqueteur*, *Friand*) list the English 'eatnell' as a definition. However, the compositor setting the type would also have seen the ambiguous u/n and would have had to make a decision, so while the evidence from the dictionary is compelling we do not necessarily regard it as absolute. Field reads 'Eatnelles'; Barnes reads 'Eatnells'; Freitag has *glutonum ac lurconum* [gluttons and gluttons].

It is unmeet to live idly of other men's labour.

When I was with you I told you of this, that if there be any that will not labour, he must not eat. (2 Thessalonians 3:10)

67. Of a Fox that Had Lost his Tail

A fox, hunting for some prey, entered by chance into a farmer's house, and cast himself into so manifest peril that the farmer, pursuing him, cut off his tail. Wherewith he was both afraid to remember the danger that he was in, and also no less glad that without any more harm he had escaped into safety unlooked for. When he came again like an ugly monster to his own kindred, considering with himself that he had forgone a great part of his beauty, and was marked° alone among all the rest with a singular note of infamy, he told them he had often desired to see the time that it might be a shame for foxes to wear tails, and therefore had cut off his own, counselling all the residue to do the like. But another of the company as foxish as he, smelling his fox-like fraud, replied thus: 'Indeed the time is come to thee wherein thou mayst teach the rest of us by thy example that if thy tail do grow again, that goodly bum of thine which now stands glaring open to all folks' eyes shall no more be seen afterward.'

The Morals: So wicked and corrupt is the nature of man's mind, that into what misery soever any misfortune do thrust them, they can find in their hearts to have all other men in the same plight.

Lewd is the counsel of selflove.

It is a grief unto us to see [the righteous][107] because his life is unlike other men's and his ways are of another hue. (Wisdom 2:15)

---

[107] These square brackets are in Golding's manuscript and in Freitag's Latin text.

68. Of the Falcon and of Other Birds

The falcon, intending to celebrate his birthday, proclaimed it solemnly to all the other birds, entreating them all very earnestly to the feast lest he might seem to have bestowed his cost in vain in preparing good cheer for his guests. They, being as it were waked out of a dead sleep with the gladtidings, not only refused not the falcon's liberality,° but also thought they should deal very unkindly with him if they did not willingly accept of his courtesy in offering them so good a turn. Hereupon the birds (alas too light of belief) came flocking to his house, in hope to have found all full of joy and gladness. But they were no sooner entered within his doors but the butcherly cozener most cruelly killed them and rent them in pieces every one.

The Morals: The pleasures and delights of the flesh are commonly accompanied with sorrow, as the body is with a shadow. And with that bait of all mischiefs (as Cicero rehearseth° out of Plato)[108] are men caught as fishes with an angle.°

---

[108] The text here refers to Cicero's *De Senectute* [Of Old Age]: 'But if some concession must be made to pleasure, since her allurements are difficult to resist, and she is, as Plato happily says, "the bait of sin," — evidently because men are caught therewith like fish — then I admit that old age, though it lacks immoderate banquets, may find delight in temperate repasts.' See Cicero, *De Senectute*, trans. by Falconer, xiii.44, p. 55. Falconer notes that the passage cites Plato's *Timaeus*, 69D (p. 54, n. 1).

Poisoned honey.

Their throat is an open grave; with their tongues have they wrought deceit; their mouth is full of cursing and bitterness; their feet are swift to shed blood. (Psalms 14:5–6)[109]

---

[109] Freitag cites Psalms 13:3, which corresponds to contemporary editions of the Vulgate. In the NRSV these verses can be found in Romans 3:13–15.

69. Of a Lion that Was Spent with Age

A certain lion had done many mischiefs in his green and flourishing years, and had been terrible to everybody. By which trade of life he had purchased to himself the malice and hatred of all beasts. Insomuch that when he was old and destitute of strength, they all scorned him at their pleasure, and scarcely any did yield him the service and obedience due to a prince as they had done afore. But sometime even the swine all bemired,° sometime the slick and short-haired ass, and erewhiles° the boistous-bodied° bull did him all manner of spite and reproach. Wherefore, perceiving plainly that this state of his was a just reward of his former misdemeanour, 'Woe worth me wretch,' quoth he, 'which have dealt so ill for myself heretofore by purchasing the hatred of so many against me, and by arming so many foes against me by my cruelty.'

The Morals: Let princes and such as are in authority bear in mind that their state is subject to alteration and change, and that nothing is so forcible to the weakening of their power as the unwieldy lust of overruling, and of holding their subjects in awe with terror. And that tyranny and luck[110] are but of one day's continuance, and that the wheel[111] rolleth continually about, now hoising° up the things that were lowest, and anon casting down the things that were highest.

---

[110] There is a blank space in the manuscript where a word is missing. Freitag reads, in a composite Greek and Latin sentence: καὶ τύχας ἐφημέρους καὶ ἐφήμερον τυράννιδα *esse, & fortunae rotam perpetuo versatilem* [both luck and tyranny are short lived, and the wheel of Fortune perpetually turns]. We have therefore supplied the word 'luck', as a translation of the Greek τύχας (*tychas*, luck or fortune), for the blank in the manuscript.

[111] i.e., the wheel of Fortune

A MORAL FABLETALK

Cruelty purchaseth hatred.

They that see thee shall peer and toot° at thee, [saying,]¹¹² 'Is this he that troubled all the earth? And made all kingdoms to quake?'
(Isaiah 14:16)

---

¹¹² These square brackets are in Golding's manuscript, but not in Freitag's Latin, which reads *Qui te viderint, ad te inclinabuntur, teque prospicient: nunquid iste est vir qui conturbauit terram*. Golding likely puts this word in brackets to indicate that it is something he has added to the biblical quotation.

70. Of the Goat, the Lamb, and the Wolf

As the goat and the lamb, having bound themselves by oath of friendship one to another, were travelling by the way, they found a wolf in a most dainty meadow. Who, beholding a while their mutual society, attempted with sweet and enticing words to withdraw the lamb from the goat, saying, 'My boykin,° forsake this stinking goat and keep company with me. For besides that he is loathsome to everybody by reason of the rank and rammish° scent that steameth from him, behold, he is also horned, and if but a fly do chance to sting him, he will one day cruelly kill thee.' As the wolf was thus inveigling° the lamb, the goat, being mindful of the league that he was entered into, came running quickly to them, and bade the wolf get him away with his lewd practices, or else he would make him feel presently in that place that he should not so easily deceive them with those lewd devices and colourable words of his, which had more gall° and bitterness in them than they had sweetness.

The Morals: That man indeed saileth as in a haven° which, despising the vain suggestions of lewd persons, doth join himself continually to the company of good men. And well may he rejoice which, having at length wasted out of the stormy and tempestuous waves of the world, and overpassed° the dangerous quicksands thereof, hath cast anchor in safe harbour.

A MORAL FABLETALK

Fellowship warely and wisely chosen.

My son, if sinners entice thee, hearken not unto them.
(Proverbs 1:10)
Be conversant continually with a holy man, whom thou knowest to
hold fast the fear of God, and whose heart is according to thine
own. (Ecclesiasticus 37:12)[113]

---

[113] Golding's biblical citation modifies Freitag's, which reads 'Eccles. 37,15' and corresponds to contemporary Vulgate copies. Golding's citation corresponds to contemporary Geneva Bibles, and to the NRSV.

71. Of a Fly and an Emmet°

At such time as the fly commended her dwellingplace and fare to the emmet to be so excellent that it was in manner princelike, the ant answered with a soft and low voice that for her part she was fain to endure many labours for the sustaining of her life, and that there grew no good in an idle and resty° house. The fly, urging the matter further with high words, replied that the ant's life was like the horse's, which is subject to endless toil. But the emmet paid her trimly home[114] after this manner: 'Nay,' quoth she, 'thy doggish° life is like the sluggish swine's in devouring shamelessly other folk's labours without doing good to any creature living. But go to[115] — whether of our two states of life is the better, the issue itself will bewray.' Anon, after this brawl betwixt them, the winter came on, wherein the fly died for want of food, but the ant sustained himself[116] with the thrifty fare that she had gotten in the cornfields and of the seeds which she had diligently provided and laid up in store in the summertime.

The Morals: Forasmuch as in man's life nothing is more shameful than sloth and idleness, the provident diligence of the ant warneth every man rather to live honestly even of small traffic° according to his trade of life, rather than to perish through slothfulness, the mother of mischief.

---

[114] i.e., paid her back properly
[115] an interjection expressing (playful) impatience or dismissiveness
[116] The otherwise female emmet in this fable takes on a male pronoun here.

It is ill to prefer pleasure before profit.

Go to the ant, thou sluggard, and consider her ways and learn wisdom. For she, having no guide, teacher, or prince, prepareth food for herself in summer, and gathereth in harvesttime whereon to live afterward. (Proverbs 6:6)

72. Of the Dragon and the Elephant

It is registered to remembrance that dragons of so huge and uncouth bigness are bred in Africa that they dare encounter with the elephants. One of this kind, grappling with an elephant and purposing to kill him, wound his tail with many writhes° about his legs, from whom the elephant did rid himself with his trunk. Anon the dragon leapt into his neck, thinking that to be the fittest place of all other to staunch his thirsty desire of blood, and there so tired the elephant with sucking his blood that he himself, being over-swollen and strutted out therewith, fell first to the ground and was crushed to death[117] by the elephant falling down upon him for faintness, being weakened with the loss of the blood drawn from him, and with the force of the dragon's venom, so as the dragon purchased more harm to himself than he had done to the elephant.

The Morals: Although tyrants do feed excessively upon the flesh and blood of their subjects, yet notwithstanding they perish in the end with much grievouser cruelty than they had used unto other men.

---

[117] The first three letters of this word are badly blotted in the manuscript.

Rightful is the punishment of tyrants.

But thou, O God, shalt bring them into the pit of destruction. The bloodthirsty and deceitful men shall not live out half their days.
(Psalms 54:24)

73. Of a Bear and of Bees

A bear, being stung of some bees as he was licking the honey out of their hives, overthrew their hives for impatiency of anger. By doing whereof, he provoked against himself not the stings of some few, but of all the bees that were there. Insomuch that he was stung much more grievously than afore, but yet he bore the pain of his grief the more quietly, notwithstanding that his snout, his brows, his ears, his eyes, and all his whole head were so sore wounded as he might well say he had purchased his over-short pleasure with too great pain. 'How much better had it been for me,' quoth he, 'and more for my safety in avoiding the mischief wherewith I am now tormented, to have abidden° the pricking of one little bee provoked by my naughtiness and wrong dealing than through desire of revenge to have procured to myself so grievous punishment?'

The Morals: Although there be opportunity of revenge and that the gods of vengeance do pursue our wrongs, yet is it better sometime to forbear a little than to be too hasty to revenge.

A MORAL FABLETALK

Mischief purchased to a man's self.

Who can proceed to utter forth His mercy? (Ecclesiasticus 18:3)[118]

---

[118] Freitag also gives this citation as Ecclesiasticus 18:3; contemporary copies of the Vulgate give 18:4; the NRSV gives 18:5.

74. Of a Raven and a Scorpion

Likewise, the untimely desire of revenge taught the raven, howbeit too late, that grief is now and then to be dissembled. For, being by chance stung of a scorpion, and stomaching the grief thereof more than was meet, he caught up the scorpion and flew away with him, of purpose belike to requite the harm he had done him. But as the scorpion was thus carried, he stung the raven again and wounded him so sore with his venomous tail that the force of the piercing poison shedding° itself into all the raven's limbs bereft him of his life.

The Morals: It is dangerous even for a lewd person to assault a shrewder than himself. And it falleth out oftentimes that such as intend mischief to other folks procure mischief to themselves, and are overwrought even by those whom they meant to have overcome.

Hurtful is the desire of revenge.

Say not I will do to him as he hath done to me. I will yield to every man according to his work. For only unto God doth revenge belong.
(Proverbs 24:29)

75. Of a Wolf Clad in a Sheep's Skin

A wolf, clothing himself subtly in a sheep's skin, and playing the crafty mate under the change of his habit, joined himself to a flock of sheep, and of long time escaped undescried° of the shepherd, going out with the sheep to feed, and returning home with them again to the fold° as if he had been one of them. By which policy, when he had at divers° times bereft many of them of their lives, and yet nevertheless had beguiled the shepherd a good while by his dissimulation, at length his craft was detected, and being found what he was, he prevailed no more by his cunning conveyance, but was hanged up upon a tree in the same habit wherein he had wrought his deceit, and by the verdict of all that passed by (who at the first, taking him for a sheep, found him indeed[119] to be a wolf) was deemed worthy of that kind of punishment, as who had deserved it in due reward of his deeds.

The Morals: Many be endued with a certain glozed° and glittering virtue, whom if ye look into throughly, ye will say they be the wickedest of all men living. Which kind of men is so much the more hurtful as they be the later found out, and do deceive the mo under pretense of honesty.

---

[119] Found him indeed, but also found him, as Golding writes it, 'in deed' (in his actions) to be a wolf.

The tree is known by his fruit.

Beware of false prophets, which come unto you in sheep's clothing but inwardly be ravening wolves. (Matthew 7:15)

76. Of a Wolf and a Hedgehog

A certain wolf, almost mad for hunger, being greedily desirous to devour a hedgehog, and finding no mean or way how to bring it to pass, because he saw him throughly fenced over all his body with rough pricks against all violence and assaults of enemies, devised another trick how to beguile him. He bore him on hand that the enmity which had been betwixt them of former time was clean laid a-water,[120] and all things were quiet, and that it were a matter against conscience to break the peace. Wherefore he desired him to put away his weapons, and to surcease° from the feats of cruel war and battle, and to lay aside his deadly weapons, whereof there was no need in so quiet and flourishing a state of government, adding that he needed not to fear him though he was a wolf, for his coming thither was not of intent to hurt him, but rather to do him good. The urchin,° who had learned rather to be afraid than presumptuously to be bold, refused to lay away his weapons. The which he affirmed himself to wear not of purpose to hurt other folk but to defend himself against cutthroats.

The Morals: We be taught by the hedgehog's discreet obstinacy° that we ought not to give ear overhastily to workers of wiles and layers of baits, nor rashly believe enticing words.

---

[120] To 'lay a-water' is to make of no effect or value, or to dissipate.

The falsehood of a flattering foe eluded.

Be sober and watch, for your adversary the Devil goeth about like a roaring lion, seeking whom he may devour. (1 Peter 5:8)

77. Of a Serpent and an Urchin

A hedgehog, obtaining by entreatance to sojourn the wintertime with a serpent, and being taken into his company as one of his household, was not restrained from any of the commodities which the serpent himself enjoyed. Nevertheless, the urchin, unmindful of the benefit bestowed upon him so kindly in the sorest and hardest time of the year, not only became very troublesome to his host by rolling hither and thither at such times as he gathered himself round into a bowl,[121] but also wounded his thin and smooth skin with the often pricking of his bristles.° Wherefore, the serpent, upbraiding him with the benefit bestowed upon him being such a churl,[122] desired him to depart thence and to get him to some other place. Whereat the hedgehog did shamelessly burst out into these words: 'If thou canst not endure my company, get thee hence thyself.' And so the serpent, being fain to fleet° away, was compelled to give over the right of his habitation to the hedgehog.

The Morals: Into this kind of men's danger (which being driven to extreme beggary, do nevertheless, through I wot not what a kind of haughtiness, usurp to themselves a kind of lordly superiority) do they commonly fall which give ear too easily to flattering words, and are lavish of their benefits to such as are unworthy.

---

[121] i.e., a ball used in a game of bowls, similar to a modern bowling ball
[122] The serpent scolded the hedgehog for being ungrateful by reminding him of the benefit the serpent had given him (housing in winter).

Cumbersome is the company of a lewd guest.

Bring not every man into thy house, for many be the treacheries of the deceitful. (Ecclesiasticus 11:31)[123]

---

[123] Both Golding and Freitag record this citation as Ecclesiasticus 11:31, which corresponds with contemporary copies of the Vulgate; in the NRSV the verse is 11:29.

78. Of the Chameleon[124]

It is reported that the chameleon liveth off the air, and hath his eyes continually open, and is armed with sharp claws, and changeth his colour continually according to the hue of the thing that he leaneth unto, and that whereas he admitteth all other kind of dyes,[125] he refuseth only the red and the white.

The Morals: The disposition of the cormorantly° parasites (that I may use Horace's epitheton)°[126] and of flatterers is in manner all one. For whereas they seem to live off nothing, haunting for a time the houses of great men and the courts of princes, they tickle the ears of such as delight in vanity and novelty with forged flying tales,[127] and sell the smoke of their naughtiness to the richer sort, and so get their living by their covert° and disguised begging. Which scum of naughtypacks, tempering themselves to the pleasing of their hearers, being more mutable than a weathercock° or a chameleon, ought of right to be banished out of all good men's company. For inasmuch as they have put on brazen faces, they be nother ashamed nor afraid of anything. And therefore it is to be greatly lamented that men which have been trained up in the better sort of learning do singularly delight in such trifling mates. For as for the ruder sort, which are blind in all things and are nuzzled in the flatteries of the court, they be somewhat to be borne withal.

---

[124] All of the 'facts' reported about the chameleon in this fable are from Pliny's *Natural History*, book 8, chapter 51; see Pliny, *Natural History*, vol. 3, p. 87.

[125] This word appears as the Greek word χρωμάτων [*chromaton*, colour] in Freitag, but Golding translates everything uniformly into English.

[126] Field (p. 259, n. 3) identifies this quotation as coming from Horace's *Epistles* II.i.173: *edacibus* [...] *parasitis* [greedy or rapacious parasites], p. 410.

[127] Flying tales are tales circulating without definite authority, or rumours.

The unconstancy of fraudulent conversation.

They that say to the ungodly, 'Thou art righteous,' them shall the people curse, and kindreds shall abhor them. (Proverbs 24:24)

79. Of a Ram and a Bull

A certain goodly ram in a flock of sheep, being armed with huger horns than his fellows, challenged so proud and severe authority over the rest of the sheep that he made them either to feed aloof from him, or else to give him the first and chief place in feeding. Through which fear and reverence of the sheep towards him, he, becoming the more insolent, proceeded into so outrageous presumption that he imagined that all other cattle ought to stoop unto him. By means whereof, rashness so far overran his discretion, that by chance espying a bull, he challenged him to the combat. But the bull (even at the first encounter) struck him down dead to the ground.

The Morals: The most part of men, yea, even of them that are not endowed with any note of dignity, do so forget themselves and their ability when they see themselves excel other men in any small thing, or have obtained any office of charge, that they not only become intolerable to their equals, but also, being puffed up with pride, do offer to mate° their superiors, to their own harm.

Great safety in knowing a man's self.

Thine own overweening and the pride of thy heart have deceived thee which dwellest in the caves of rocks and labourest to attain to the top of the hill. (Jeremiah 49:16)

80. Of a Hen and Her Chickens

How earnest zeal to defend her chickens Nature hath bred in the hen we know very well both by Christ's testimony[128] and by daily experience. And therefore it were a token of extreme negligence to forget this so fruitful creature and careful mother in this theatre of fablespeeches.[129] Ye see with how great chariness° she watcheth about the coop to defend them from three fowls of the kind of hawks[130] that lie hovering over them, and how stoutly she keepeth them both from the coop and from seizing upon her birds, and how great earnestness she useth in protecting her dear chicks without regard of her own safety, insomuch that she alone (which is almost uncredible)° riddeth them from the beaks and talons of three most mighty enemies at once.

The Morals: The hen beareth the type of a magistrate,[131] and by her example showeth more clearly than the noonlight[132] that such as are in authority are bound of duty to defend the lives and goods of innocents from the assaults of such as would prey upon them, and by all means to uphold such as are borne down.

---

[128] This is likely a reference to Matthew 23:37: 'Jerusalem, Jerusalem, the city that kills the prophets and stones those who are sent to it! How often have I desired to gather your children together as a hen gathers her brood under her wings, and you were not willing!' (NRSV). Field notes (p. 263, n. 1) that these verses can also be found in Luke 13:34.

[129] The word 'fablespeeches', an alternative translation of the titular 'fabletalk', translates Freitag's *mythologiarum*.

[130] i.e., three birds that are different kinds of hawks. The 'ye see' reminds the reader to incorporate the image especially into the reading of this fable.

[131] i.e., The hen carries the symbolic representation of a magistrate.

[132] Golding originally wrote one word and then corrected it to another; the ink of the two words 'moonlight' and 'noonlight' is equally dark and so it is impossible to determine which is the correction for which. However, because Freitag reads *luce meridiana* [light of midday] we have assumed Golding was correcting to the more accurate translation 'noonlight.'

The defence of innocency.

Learn to do well; seek judgement; succour the oppressed; do justice to the fatherless; defend the widows. (Isaiah 1:17)

81. Of a Ploughman and a Mouse

A certain tippling° ploughman that had been accustomed to full cups from his childhood, fortunating° to celebrate his birthday, and being well stuffed with wine, as he was stirring up the bonfire at his door, being drunken himself and furthered also with a great gale of wind, did set his house on fire. The which the flame did so devour that, for want of help to beat it down, it burned up whatsoever living thing was in the house, saving one poor mouse that, escaping the danger and being gotten out of the doors, took her to flight. But the ploughman (who by that time had digested his surfeit° and was come to himself again), being grieved with the present loss, began to bestir him and, catching up the mouse, threw him[133] into the fire with this check:° 'Ah, thou churl, hast thou been a continual guest with me in my prosperity, and wilt thou now forsake me in my adversity?'

The Morals: So long as the world laugheth upon a man with cheerful countenance, all men seek his friendship. But in adversity when things are forlorn he shall scarcely find one of all his huge heap of friends that will show himself a kindly and unfeigned friend indeed. And alas, too true is this saying of the poet:

> So long as Fortune favoureth thee,
>   Thou shalt have friends good store,
> But let her once upon thee frown,
>   They know thee then no more.[134]

---

[133] The mouse, referred to as a 'her' earlier, seems to have changed genders.
[134] This quotation comes from Ovid's *Tristia*, I.ix.5–6. Freitag's Latin reads *Dum fueris felix, multos numerabis amicos; | Tempora si fuerint nubila, solus eris*. Modern versions of this text read slightly differently: *donec eris sospes, multos numerabis amicos: | tempora si fuerint nubila, solus eris* [So long as you are secure you will count many friends; if your life becomes clouded you will be alone] (text and translation from Ovid, *Tristia*, trans. by Arthur Leslie Wheeler, rev. by G. P. Goold [Cambridge, MA: Harvard University Press, 1988], pp. 44–45).

Adversity trieth friendship.

There is a friend that is but for a time, and he will not abide with thee in the day of tribulation. And there is a friend that will be a companion at thy table, but will not continue in the time of need.
(Ecclesiasticus 6:8, 10)

82. Of a Fowler and a Ruddock°

As a certain birdcatcher, having laid his sheer nets (as one termeth them)[135] to beguile the great-feeding thrushes,° and having cast baits not only for them, but also for all other sorts of birds, stood gaping greedily for his prey, there came divers birds thither to feed, sometimes one, sometimes two, and sometimes mo at once, but not to the full number that his covetous mind conceived. Whereby it came to pass that, not esteeming them worth his labour in taking them, when they had well fed they flew away again, commending the fowler for his negligence. When he had thus spent the whole day strewing new meat very often from time to time in vain hope of a greater prey, at the length blaming his lossful° covetousness lest he might seem to have profited nothing at all, in the end in recompense of all his whole day's labour, he took one poor robin redbreast° that by chance fell into his net.

The Morals: Against the blind greediness of covetous folk which, despising the gain of a small thing, seek heaps of riches with unbridled desire, whereby they both lose that which they had in their hands, and also forgo that which they might have obtained, and hunt after greater things in vain.

---

[135] Freitag reads *Dvm Auceps quidam rara, ut inquit ille, tetendisset retia* [While a certain birdcatcher, having stretched (*tetendisset*) [his] loose-knit (*rara*) — as one says that (*ut inquit ille*) — nets (*retia*)]. Freitag notes that the Latin word *rara* is being used in an unusual sense here, not to mean rare but to mean thin or loosely knit.

Over-late repentance for commodities refused.

Remember thy maker in the days of thy youth, afore the time of adversity come, and afore the years approach wherein thou shalt say, 'I like them not.' (Ecclesiastes 12:1)

83. Of a Clown° and a Satyr°

A certain clown, finding a satyr in a wood curling together[136] and almost dead for cold, was moved with compassion and led him with him to his house to revive his frorne° limbs. Now as they were going homeward, the clown by chance blew upon his fingers' ends to warm them, which doing of his the satyr marked,° not greatly regarding it. Anon after when they were in the clown's cottage, a porringer° or (which is more likely in respect of the clown's hungry stomach) a platter of hot porridge was set before each of them, and the clown to cool his broth blew upon it with the breath of his mouth. When the satyr saw that, by and by wondering how so contrary effects could issue from one fountain,

(The Morals:)[137] 'I must utterly henceforth,' quoth he, 'shun such folk as carry fire in the one hand and water in the other. For by pretending friendship in their countenance and concealing lewdness and cozenage in their hearts, they beguile such as are not ware° of them.'

---

[136] i.e., curled up

[137] These parentheses are original to Golding's manuscript, presumably because the character speaks the moral; they do not appear in Freitag's translation, where the fable ends in a period, and the moral is formatted as it usually is.

The image of a disguised and mutable mind.

Doth a fountain send forth both sweet and bitter water at one hole? My brethren, can a fig-tree yield grapes, or a vine figs? So also cannot a brackish spring send forth sweet water. (James 3:11)

84. Of the Greater Mouse[138] and an Oyster

The great mouse (which some suppose to be the dormouse, but how rightly let themselves look to it), living lordlike at home with dainty fare, and wanting nothing that might be for the exquisite cherishing of his body, fell to misliking the delicates° of his own house, and seeking for foreign and far-fet° cates,° and being allured with a certain longing for shellfish, went down apace to the sea; on the shore whereof anon he espied an oyster lie gaping, which he, thinking to be a fit morsel for his tooth, did eagerly and greedily thrust his head into the shell to get it out. But as soon as the oyster felt him, he nipped his shells together. And so the mouse, purposing to have caught the oyster, was caught himself to his own undoing.

The Morals: A competent state of life is not to be changed for an uncertain. But it is better to live contentedly with a mean lot than in reaching after a gallanter to lose both, and by leaving a state of life that is tolerable, to fall into such a one as not only may not satisfy our desire, but also may turn to our destruction. Which thing cometh even then to pass when we be entangled unawares in the pleasures which we sought with most eager desire.

---

[138] It is possible that the phrases 'greater mouse' and 'great mouse' (in Freitag, *mus maior*) refer to a rat. In *The Historie of Serpents* (London, 1608), Edward Topsell refers to 'a Rat or great Mouse' as if they are synonymous (p. 115, line 23).

Dreary is the desire of over-delicate life.

The flesh was yet between their teeth, and their meat was not yet put down, when suddenly the Lord's wrath, being stirred up against the people, did strike them with an exceeding great plague.
(Numbers 11:33)

85. Of an Eagle and a Snail

Also,[139] the snail, waxing weary of his state, inveighed against his base and abject life with continual reproaches, aspiring to a more high and glorious. Whereupon he entreated the eagle to carry him up aloft into the air, saying he had crept long enough like an abject upon the ground, and it was now high time for him to mount out of the mire. And that he might the easilier obtain his request, he promised the eagle a very rich precious stone. The eagle, in hope of gain, granted the snail's petition, and, taking him up in his talons, soared up with him, where, not forgetting the condition, he demanded the precious stone. Which when the snail had not to pay, the eagle, being angry, nipped him with his talons, and taught him with a mischief that no man ought to promise more than he can perform.

The Morals: The drift of this present fable differeth not much from the former. For it showeth how safe a thing it is for every man to make account of the gifts of his own wit and nature, and not to covet things too high for him, warning us further not to promise that which is not in our power to perform.

---

[139] The 'Also' here signals that this fable is related to the one that comes before it. It appears in Freitag as well.

Unadvised promising.

Be not too curious in seeking after things superfluous.
(Ecclesiasticus 3:24)

86. Of a Kite and a Cuckoo

The kite, oftentimes mocking the cuckoo for that he lived by worms and filled his belly with so base food, did also ride upon him with railings,° telling him that his so doing was for laziness and lack of courage, and not for thriftiness and sparing, declaring with stately port° of words that it behooved him to strain the power of his mind to the doing of some high things, and not to rest in the base things, for the adventurous were furthered by Fortune, but the cowards were put back. The cuckoo, being nothing moved with these speeches, held himself still within the bounds of his own nature, contented with his accustomed food though it was most vile and contemptible. Not long after, the kite, laying wait for a stockdove,° fell into a farmer's net, who hung him up in a cage upon the top of a tower, to the terror of all other fowls that live upon prey, and to be scorned of his enemies. Which thing the cuckoo perceiving, and thinking himself to have gotten a fit occasion to be even with him, 'Haddest thou learned,' quoth he, 'to live of worms as I do, surely thou haddest escaped this imprisonment.'

The Morals: The example of the kite and the cuckoo and the reproach that fell upon the kite warn us to be thrifty and temperate in our diet.

The reward of a scorner is to be scorned himself.

Many have died of surfeiting, but he that abstaineth prolongeth his life. (Ecclesiasticus 37:34)[140]

---

[140] In the NRSV this is Ecclesiasticus 37:31.

87. Of the Puttock and the Nightingale

When on a time a puttock, being led by the evil counsel of hunger, had caught a nightingale, she besought him to have compassion upon her and to spare her for that she was harmless and unarmed, promising that if he would turn rigour into clemency,° and vouchsafe her that great benefit, she would be bound to do him any service ever after. He, restraining his rage a while at the nightingale's speech, asked wherein she would do him service. 'I will,' quoth she, 'delight thine ears with the music of my singing, for Nature hath graced me with the skill of that art, and other than that know I none.' 'But I, being hungry,' quoth the kite, 'have no need of musical harmony. For sith the belly hath no ears, it will not be pacified with that. Not music, but meat is the remedy of hunger.'

The Morals: It behooveth us to leave the things that do but only tickle the organs of the senses with delight, and are to be tasted of us but, as it were, by starts, and to get us the things which needful use requireth.[141] Whereunto we must so apply ourselves, as that the things which do but only besprinkle our minds with a kind of pleasantness, yielding small or no commodity to the common life, may be the last and least that we deal with.

---

[141] i.e., We would do well to leave behind those things which merely please our senses intermittently, and to focus instead on those things we need.

The barbarousness of untamed hunger.

But He said unto them, have ye not read what David did when he was a-hungered, and those that were with him? (Matthew 12:3)

88. Of a Countryman° and an Adder°

As a labouringman returned home from his work in the dead of winter, by hap he found an adder in his way frozen and half-dead in the snow. At the sight whereof it came by and by into his head how good was to be done to others, specially upon so just occasion of one's misery. Therefore, taking up the adder, he carried him home with him and cherished him by a good fire. As soon as the adder had gathered strength again by warmth, suddenly he began to wax proud of the good turn, and no whit therewith meekened, ran about all the house infecting it with his poison. The labouring man, being justly moved to anger at the unworthiness of the matter and at the maliciousness of the adder that still vomited up his venom, did cut him asunder with a hatchet, saying, 'Is this the thank wherewith thou requitest the good that I have done thee? Is this the reward of my pity?'

The Morals: The adder's lewdness bewrayeth the foulness and shamefulness of ingratitude, declaring sufficiently that forasmuch as there is not a greater wickedness than to recompense evil for good, such lewd dealing is of right to be paid home with punishment.

A good turn requited with a bad.

Whosoever requiteth evil for good, evil shall not depart from his house. (Proverbs 17:13)

89. Of a Lion and a Man

As a lion and a man went talking on the way together of divers things after the manner of travellers to pass the time and ease their weariness with sundry communications, they fell from their former talk to altercation about the beauty and strength of body which consisteth in the force of the sinews. For either of them extolled his own strength to the uttermost, with as great commendation as he could. The lion, according to the nobleness of courage bred in him by kind,° maintained his part stoutly. The man, on the other side, according to the ability of his wit, left nothing that might sound to his own praise. When they had thus overpassed a good piece of their journey, coming by chance to a pillar wherein was engraven the heroical deed of a man that had wrestled with a lion and killed him, the man, boasting intolerably of this deed, began to embase the virtue of the lion; whereupon the controversy proceeded so far that the lion, bursting out in heat of choler,° tore the vainglorious fellow in pieces, and with sorrowful example made proof of his strength upon the wretch himself for his immoderate boasting.

The Morals: Great damage and dishonour do commonly follow the unseasonable vaunting of a man's self, with the contempt of others.

Bragging the bane of the bragger.

He hath wrought mightily with his arm; he hath scattered the proud in the imagination of their hearts. (Luke 1:51)

90. Of the Lion, the Fox, and the Ass

Upon a time, the lion, the fox, and the ass agreed to go a-hunting together. The which thing they did lustily, and every of them performed his part stoutly. When they had caught a fat booty, the slow ass, being so much the more saucy as he was most gross-witted, took upon him to divide to everyone his share. In doing whereof, he took the best part to himself, serving himself first. At which malapertness of the ass in neglecting him, the lion, being offended, rent him in pieces, and appointed the fox to the laying out of the parts. The fox, being wily by nature, and now made more circumspect by the present example, allotted the greatest part to the lion, reserving very little to himself. The lion, smiling thereat, asked him who had made him so well advised? 'Other men's harms,' quoth he, 'for fear lest I should drink of the same cup that this ass hath done.'

The Morals: 'Get thee far from Jove and thunder,' sayeth the old proverb,[142] wherewith agreeth this present place. For inasmuch as the fellowship of unequals is untrusty, there is great safety in shunning their company. For commonly full dangerous unto us is the friendship of such as outgo us in wealth and strength, specially if they be endowed with any notable fierceness of mind.

---

[142] Erasmus gives the proverb as follows: *Porro a Iove atque fulmine* [Away from Jove and from the thunderbolt], in Erasmus, *Adages, I.i.1 to I.v.100*, I.iii.96, p. 314.

Wisdom procured by fear of punishment.

How can the pitcher have fellowship with the cauldron?
For if they hap to jostle together, the pitcher goes to wreck.
(Ecclesiasticus 13:3)[143]

---

[143] On the relationship between this biblical quotation and fables see the footnote on the biblical quotation in Fable 60.

91. Of the Lion and the Fox

The fox, espying the lion afar off, fled from him. But when he had looked upon him again, he began to take a little heart to him, howbeit in such wise as he durst not yet come too near him nor trust his talons. But when he had met him the third time, then shaking off all fear, he put himself familiarly into the lion's company, making himself thenceforth so ordinary a guest with him that he seemed now to be one of his kin, whose fierce countenance he had so feared afore. Thus ye see how by little and little there groweth a certain union of mind, even between unknown persons, for all things are not done at once. Troy[144] was not destroyed in one year. The majesty of the Roman Empire was not of one year's growth, nother was Rome itself built in one year.

The Morals: Therefore it is the part of a wise man to take leisure in purchasing the favour of great personages, and to knit their minds to him by long continuance of time, for company engendereth love.

---

[144] Troy was an ancient city that was famously destroyed over the course of the Trojan War, waged against the city by the Greeks.

Prudent and ware conversation.

Behave yourselves circumspectly during the time of your being here. (1 Peter 1:17)
Dear beloved, I beseech you as strangers and wayfarers, abstain from fleshly lusts, which make war against the soul, so as ye may be of good conversation among the heathen. (1 Peter 2:11–12)

92. Of the Lion, the Boar, and the Vulture

As the lion and the boar, the strongest of all beasts, going one the one way and the other the other, met together, the lion first with great fierceness did set upon the boar and fought lustily with him. The boar, gnashing his teeth at the violence of the lion unprovoked or unstirred thereunto, withstood his fierceness with courageous stoutness. This conflict was beheld with singular gladness by a vulture sitting on the next tree, waiting with great desire to see the end thereof, verily in hope that which way soever the victory of that combat inclined, the same would fall out to his gain, as who by the slaughter of the one of them should be sure to prey upon the carcass of him that were slain. But when either of them had to the uttermost of his power maintained his part a long while, at length, being both weary of the battle, they departed on even hand. By reason whereof, the vulture, perceiving himself to have been fed but with vain hope and to have triumphed hitherto with fruitless joy, flew sad away to wreak° the rage of his hunger somewhere else.

The Morals: Oftentimes they be deceived which upon dark and blind hope do linger for uncertain goods. Therefore, putting our trust alonely in God (who disappointeth not our hope so it be agreeable to reason), let us not hope overmuch for anything, lest perchance being disappointed, we may rather have[145] cause to fear.

---

[145] Golding initially wrote 'have', and then crossed it out and wrote 'rather have' instead.

Overhasty and unsatiable hope.

The hope of the hypocrite shall perish. (Job 8:13)
The eyes of the wicked shall fail; they shall not be able to scape,
and their hope shall be loathsome to their soul. (Job 11:20)

93. Of the Wolf and the Fox

Like as it is most certain (even as it were of necessity and by the law of virtue) that no good man ever wisheth evil to a good man, so we find that the friendship of wicked men (as which is knit together by evil means and standeth upon weak foundation) is easily overthrown, and that it is not always true that evil men do not lay wait to deceive such of their own coat as they can. Which thing the present envy of the wolf and the fox does set before our eyes. For a fox, visiting oftentimes a wolf that lay lurking in his den, unpinched of any penury, asked him what was the cause that he spent his time so at home, and wherefore he ran not abroad sometimes in the fields. When the wolf, smelling the fox's fraud, bade him get him away, the fox, stomaching the matter, bewrayed the wolf's kennel to a husbandman, who, coming thither with speed, killed the wolf. The fox, being glad thereof, ran thither in all haste and fed lustily upon the wolf's store. But as he returned thence again, always like a crafty jack, howbeit unaware of the mischief that was towards him, he was torn in pieces of hounds.[146]

The Morals: It is the peculiar reward of envy to perish by envying other men's felicity.

---

[146] i.e., by hounds

Hurtful is the envying of another man's prosperity.

The man that hasteth to be rich and envieth other men is not aware that penury shall come upon him. (Proverbs 28:22)

94. Of a Fox Commending Hare's Flesh

A fox, lighting by chance upon a hound, and seeing no way to scape from him, fell to devising very carefully by what means he might save his life. After he had beaten his brains about many shifts,[147] when he perceived that he was cut off from all opportunity of flight, then putting away all trust in his strength, and taking hold of that which is the last refuge of them that are at an afterdeal, and whereunto they be wont to flee as to their last anchorhold, he submitted himself humbly to the hound, and yielded himself to his mercy. But when he saw plainly that he could not redeem himself with any other ransom than his body, he fell to persuading with orator-like speeches — whereof (as it happed)° he could better skill than the hound that hunted but for his prey — that his flesh was too gross and[148] unsavoury for the hound's delicate taste, and that the hare's flesh was most dainty. And therewithal, showing the hound a hare far off, he gave him the slip.[149] But the hare disappointed the hound by reason he was so far afore him, and, coming again to himself, blamed the fox for his malice in accusing him without his desert.° 'Nay,' quoth the fox, 'it is nothing so, but rather I commended thee in saying that thy flesh is daintier than mine.'

The Morals: Against such as bring the lives and goods of other men in danger to save their own.

---

[147] i.e., after he had racked his brains thinking of many possible ways to get away
[148] Golding originally wrote 'for' before deciding to pair 'gross' with a synonym.
[149] i.e., got away

A MORAL FABLETALK

Treacherous is the commendation of the wicked.

He that speaketh upon knowledge is a just judge, but he that lieth is a deceitful witness. (Proverbs 12:17)

95. Of a Bull and a Dormouse

Here a man may well demand, 'What hath the dormouse to do with the bull? What should the jay do with a viol?° What should the swine do with marjoram?[150] To what end doth the stage show us beasts so far unlike? Is it to the intent to match an elephant with a gnat? Or to compare the husk of a bean with the greatest thing that can be? Or to present here also something more unseemly than the doing of Tityrus whom Virgil speaks of, who was wont to match great things and small together?'[151] No, surely. For justly doth the dormouse obtain some place among the residue of the brute beasts, which was able to vex so huge a body as a bull. For when a certain fierce and strong bull boasted so greatly of his own strength that he despised all others, the dormouse bit him by the foot, and by and by whipped again into his cabin, whom the bull pursued in vain. For the mouse had retired himself into safety and left the bull standing to cool his choler before his door, the which he could not come in at because of the narrowness thereof.

The Morals: This fable betokeneth that even the most despised persons may do harm when they bend their wits to mischief, and therefore that even the feeblest enemy is not to be esteemed lightly.

---

[150] The answer to each question is 'nothing'. That a swine disliked the herb marjoram and a jay had nothing to do with a musical instrument were both proverbial. On the pig, see Erasmus: *Nihil cum amaracino sui* [A pig has nothing to do with marjoram], in Erasmus, *Adages, I.i.1 to I.v.100*, I.iv.38, p. 347; see also Lucretius: *amaracinum fugitat sus* [a pig or swine flees marjoram], from Lucretius, *De Rerum Natura*, trans. by W. H. D. Rouse [London: William Heinemann, 1924], VI.973, p. 512. On the jay, see Erasmus: *Nihil graculo cum fidibus* [A jackdaw has no business with a lute], in Erasmus, *Adages, I.i.1 to I.v.100*, I.iv.37, p. 346. A sixteenth century Latin and English dictionary includes the following entry: '*Graculo cum fidibus nihil*, The Jaye hath nought to do with the harpe. whyche is spoken of theym, whyche lackynge eloquence or good letters, doo scorne theym that haue it,' in Sir Thomas Elyot, *The Dictionary of Syr Thomas Eliot Knyght* (London, 1538), sig. I3v.

[151] Tityrus, a shepherd in Virgil's first Eclogue, discusses how he used to foolishly compare his small town to the great city of Rome. See Virgil, *Eclogues. Georgics. Aeneid: Books 1–6*, trans. by H. Rushton Fairclough, rev. by G. P. Goold (Cambridge, MA: Harvard University Press, 1916), I.19–25, p. 27.

A MORAL FABLETALK

The strength of the weaker, despised to the hurt of the despiser.

Come to me, and I will give thy flesh to the fowls of the air.[152]
(1 Kings 17:44)[153]

---

[152] Field (p. 294, n. 9) notes that Golding omits the phrase *& bestiis terrae* [and to the beasts of the land] from Freitag.
[153] This citation, which also appears in Freitag, corresponds to 1 Samuel 17:44 in NRSV. The NRSV's 1 and 2 Samuel are called 1 and 2 Kings in the Vulgate.

96. Of the Ape and the Fox

The ape, being mocked of all men for his bare buttocks, when he could nowhere borrow wherewith to hide his nakedness, at length after long seeking, spying a fox with a notable bushtail, desired him to lend him a piece of it. And to obtain it the sooner, and to move the fox to pity, he used chiefly two means. The one was the showing forth of his nakedness, and the other was the benefit that the fox should have by granting his petition, namely that he should be the lighter when he had cut off a piece of his tail. But the fox, answering that his tail cumbered° him not, gave deaf ear to the ape's suit, and would not be persuaded by his reasons.

The Morals: There is a kind of men of a foxish disposition, who though they have superfluity,° wherewith they may do good to such as are pinched with penury, yet, through a filthy kind of niggardship,° they ever seek means to pluck their heads out of the collar.[154]

---

[154] a proverbial expression, meaning to draw back from a job or obligation

The relief of the needy and naked.

Let your abundance supply° their want at this present, that their abundance may at another time supply your want again, and so equality be maintained. (2 Corinthians 8:14)

97. Of a Wolf and a Man's Head Carved

A wolf, being either become familiar among men, or sneaking to seek somewhat after his sly manner, entered into the workhouse of a certain excellent carver, where, beholding a man's head so cunningly and artificially wrought that it allured not only men but also brute beasts to look upon it, did in the end burst out into these words: 'O dainty head, in good sooth there are very many things in thee that invite all men to praise thee. Thy incomparable shape and beauty, derived out of some heavenly proportion, wherethrough thou easily surmountest all things, cannot be matched by the work of any craftsman. Nevertheless, forasmuch as thou wantest the most excellent gift of wit, which is the chiefest point of beauty, although thou resemblest man, yet hast thou nothing of man in thee.'

The Morals: The reverendness and sweetness of beauty drawn in the lineaments of our bodies by the hand of the sovereign workmaster that hath adorned us, even in such sort as is to be wondered at, do ennoble no man unless his mind be decked with discretion and virtue. For these are immortal, but the other, either by sickness or by age, or by some other light mischance, do wither and perish.

A body without a soul is but a visor° of beauty.

Vain are all men in whom is not the knowledge of God, which by the good things that are seen, could not understand Him that is, nor discern the workmaster by considering His works. (Wisdom 13:1)

98. Of a Stag and a Sheep

Upon a time, a stag commenced an action against a sheep for a bushel° of rye, and arrested him to appear before the wolf as judge. Now although the sheep was stricken with fear for the notable wickedness of the judge, who was both unjust and also lay in wait for him with continual hatred, yet, notwithstanding, he stood to the denial of the debt unduly claimed by his accuser. For so great is the force of innocency, that it giveth courage to the afflicted, even before the cruellest tyrants.[155] But yet for all that, the sheep was cast,°[156] and by the wolf's judgement condemned as guilty to pay the debt that was not owing, and a day was appointed for satisfaction.° The stag, coming to the sheep at the day limited, demanded payment of the adjudged debt. But the sheep finely gave him the gleek° for the thing which he was forced to by violence and fear.

The Morals: Such as upon trust of their own wealth and power oppress the weaker and inferior sort are oftentimes (and not unworthily) deceived by the wisdom and discreet dealing of the same parties, with no small shame to themselves.

---

[155] This sentence is in parentheses in Freitag's text.

[156] There is a possible play on words here, as 'cast' can mean beaten in the court of law, but is also used to describe a sheep that has been turned onto its back and cannot get up. (*OED*, s.v. 'cast, adj.', 1b'; 'cast, v.', 12). Freitag reads *damnata* [condemned].

Promises extorted.

Lying is a foul fault in a man, and it will be continually in the mouth of the unnurtured. (Ecclesiasticus 20:26)

99. Of a Shegoat and a Wolf's Whelp

A shegoat, adventuring to feed alone out of the goatherd because she was prettily° well armed with horns and mistrusted not that there was any wild beast near at hand of whom she should greatly need to be afraid, did light upon a wolf whelp. Who, commending her greatly for his own commodity's sake, and flattering her because he was not able to hurt her by force by reason of the weakness of his own body, made his way by that policy, and besought her that she would give him a dug,° for he longed greatly for goat's milk, which thing he said she might do to his great good without any hurt to herself, and therefore he desired her not to deny it him. The goat gently granted it. Oftentimes did the goat thus give suck to the crafty imp of a crafty sire. But when he grew somewhat big, she began to be afraid of him, and courteously refused to do the thing anymore which she perceived she had done to her own peril in nursing her own destruction.

The Morals: It is a point of singular wisdom so to pleasure one's enemy, as a man hurt not himself.[157]

---

[157] i.e., It is fine to help your enemy as long as you do not hurt yourself.

A benefit wisely afforded to an enemy.

The highest hateth sinners and will render vengeance to the ungodly. (Ecclesiasticus 12:7)[158]

---

[158] In the NRSV this is Ecclesiasticus 12:6.

100. Of a Cat and a Cockerel°

A cat, seizing upon a cockerel and gripping him cruelly in his ravenous paws, said he had deserved to die, which thing he endeavoured like a lewd losel° to prove by two reasons. The first was that with his own eyes he had seen the cockerel scorn[159] his mother and his sister, and the other was that he made the night irksome and tedious to all men with his untimely outcries. The cockerel, perceiving himself to be charged with feigned faults, and that there was no way of defence left him, answered mildly in excuse of himself that he nother scorned his mother nor any of his, nor yet crowed of any ill intent to break anybody's rest, but only did those things of a certain natural instinct, as all other living wights did. But the cat, admitting not any reason to bear sway, killed him with devouring teeth.

The Morals: When men begin to wax so dim-sighted in the duties of this life that they prefer profit before honesty, they easily take occasion to hurt other men, putting things in execution by force and unright which they cannot do by right.

---

[159] In other versions of this fable, the cat accuses the cock of incest. This does not seem to be the case here; with the word 'scorn', Golding translates Freitag's *ridentem* [ridicule].

The lewd person hunteth for occasion to do mischief.

The words of the wicked lay wait for blood, but the mouth of the righteous will deliver men. (Proverbs 12:6)

101. Of an Old Lame Cat and of the Mice

An old forworn cat, loaden° with age and years, being unable to hunt for mice as she had done aforetimes, and perceiving them to be grown so bold that they would in manner leap in her face, and the breed of them to be so increased that they annoyed the whole house with deadly infection, thought it meet to prevent the imminent danger in due time. Whereupon, weighing with herself that policy oft availeth those that are destitute of strength and nimbleness of body, she devised this notable shift. She hid herself in a kneadingtrough,° a place fit both to sleep in and to watch in, and also to dwell in and to catch mice. To which place the mice, resorting often and mistrusting nothing less than that the cat had watched there for them, or that the meal had been infected with ratsbane,° were caught up every one by the cat, and by that kind of mousehunting which was not the painfullest though the speediest of all other.

The Morals: Commonly that man excelleth in wit to whom Nature hath denied strength. And necessity, the mother of wisdom, doth put the means into our hands when we be destitute of strength. For here we see that need, the schoolmistress of cunning (which teacheth the parrot to greet us in Greek, and the pie[160] to prate° our words), prompted the cat with this device against the mice.

---

[160] i.e., the magpie, proverbial for being chatty or gossipy

Want of strength recompensed with wiliness of wit.

The wily person, foreseeing a mischief, hideth himself from it, but the simple ones, going on still, sustain hurt. (Proverbs 27:12)

102. Of a Lame Dog and his Master

A very old and far forworn dog, being oft beaten of his master[161] because he was not so forward in hunting as when he was young and lusty, sighed in himself. And in bethinking himself somewhat deeply of his flourishing youth forepast, wherein his master had made account and estimation of him, he perceived plainly the cause of his calamity and of his master's dealing so roughly with him every day more than often. Whereupon he besought him by entreatance to mitigate his unmercifulness towards him. But when he saw he did but lose his labour, and that there was no hope to alter his master's mind, he burst out freely into such speeches as this: 'Now I see that all the good which thou hast done me heretofore was for love of thyself and not of me, and that the bitterness wherewith thou now oppressest me is all the recompense that I shall have at thy hand for the service that I have done thee.'

The Morals: This fable taunteth hard-hearted masters which use their servants courteously and feed them with vain hope so long as they be able to take pains and to do them service, but set not a straw by them when their bodies be once weakened and their strength so abated by sickness or old age, as they be no more able to do them service.

---

[161] i.e., by his master

Love limited by profit.

Joas, the king, remembered not the mercy that Joiadas,[162] the father of Zacharias, had done unto him. (2 Chronicles 24:22)

---

[162] The 'o' in Joiadas is badly blotted in the manuscript. Freitag spells this name 'Ioiada', and the Geneva Bible spelling is 'Jehoiada'. We have preserved Golding's spelling, a less common but alternate way of spelling the name in the early modern period.

103. Of a Husbandman and his Dogs

But yet a greater cruelty doth it seem to be when we wrongfully work their destruction to whom we be beholden for our life and welfare. Of which sort this is that I am about to rehearse here. For a certain husbandman, being driven thereto by scarcity of victual in wintertime, killed all his cattle, yea, even those also which he kept to till his ground. Which thing when his dogs beheld, they, being amazed thereat, cried out on him in this wise: 'Alas, if our master be so cruel as to kill those that ministered the things unto him without which he cannot live, will he not show greater cruelty to us? Therefore why provide we not for ourselves in time, and disappoint his cruelty by getting us hence?'

The Morals: Who can think that that man will ever be pitiful and compassionable to strangers which is fell° and cruel to his own? Or that he will spare those to whom he is not bound by any duty?

Inhumanity towards a man's own householdfolk.

The pitiful man doth good to his own soul. But he that is cruel shaketh off even his own near friends. (Proverbs 11:17)

104. Of an Ass and his Three Masters

A certain ass, more worthy to be pitied of all men than to be laughed at (the which notwithstanding is most customably° done), served a gardener. This ass, being beaten one time by his master, besought Jove with continual prayers to give him another master. Being granted his request, he obtained a brickmaker, who, besides his loading of the good ass with peds,° did also lay on load of stripes upon him like a butcher. The ass, cursing and banning him for his labour (yet daring not to blame Jupiter), desired eftsoon° an exchange of that kind of life, and was delivered to a third master, which was a tanner.° This man, omitting no kind of cruelty, passed both the other in outrageous dealing. Then the ass, bewailing his forlorn state with too late repentance of changing his masters, preferred the first far before the other two.

The Morals: Against nicelings,° specially such as are fain to serve for their living, who through impatiency, for every light vexation, by fleeting oftentimes from some trade of life not very inconvenient, are forced in the end to like best of that which they misliked afore.

A MORAL FABLETALK

The change of state from better to worse.

Let every man walk as God hath called him, and as I teach in all churches. (Corinthians 7:17)[163]

---
[163] In the NRSV this is 1 Corinthians 7:17.

105. Of an Ox, an Ass, a Mule, and a Camel

That like do easily sort themselves with their like, and company together without encumbrance, it is known by the old adage,[164] and likewise taught us here by the complaint of the ass, the mule, the ox, and the camel. For these beasts, being the most laboursome of all other, do utter their griefs one to another and comfort one another, not seeking any other help, which they were past hope to find at the hands of their betters, and certainly knew they could not have of their inferiors. Now therefore, while having some respite from their labours, they after this manner, to comfort their sorrows, bewailed their toilsome life subject to stripes. The ass, being more impudent than the rest, leapt upon the mule, saying: 'I will henceforth cast off my fardels,° and, betaking myself to a more easy life, will of a packcarrier become a horseman.' The camel and the ox, looking more advisedly into the gifts wherewith Nature had endowed them, said thus: 'Forasmuch as we be unmeet for any other functions, justly be we put to labour and sweat for the sustenance wherewith we be to be maintained.'

The Morals: Let no man greatly wonder at the ass, sith he hath so many brothers among men so given to sloth and laziness, that whereas they be destitute of all helps of wit to the doing of great things, and are born but only to labour, yet notwithstanding, forgetting themselves, they shun all painstaking, hunting after fine fare and delicate dishes.

---

[164] Erasmus gives the adage *Simile gaudet simili* [Like rejoices in like] in Erasmus, *Adages, I.i.1 to I.v.100*, I.ii.21, pp. 167–68.

Most honest is the living that is gotten by painstaking.

All these (that is to say handicraftsmen)° have their hope tied to their hands, and every of them is wise in his own trade. But upon the seat of judgement they do not sit. (Ecclesiasticus 38:35, 37)[165]

---

[165] In the NRSV this corresponds to Ecclesiasticus 38:31, 33.

106. Of a Handicraftsman, an Ape, and a Monkey

A certain handicraftsman, having taught an ape and a monkey to dance the measures called pyrrhics[166] and some other dances, brought them forth into a theatre to be seen of the people. Now as the whole company and multitude of people stood gazing round about them with great delight to see the variety of their tricks, the ape, by chance espying a young wench taking nuts out of her bosom and cracking them, forgot his dancing and all that he had to do, and, flying to her as fast as he could run, searched her bosom and her apron that was tucked up, and took away as many nuts as he listed. The wench was abashed at the sudden coming of the monstrous ape unto her with so great force, and all the theatre fell a-laughing and giggling at the matter.

The Morals: Look what befell to the ape, and the like is wont to befall to such as, leaving the art which they have gotten most perfectly, and wherein they have long exercised themselves, had rather to follow the inclination and guidance of their nature, and thereby to make themselves a laughingstock to all men, not considering how skilfully it is given for a warning that every man should exercise himself in that art whereof he can best skill.

---

[166] an ancient Greek war dance simulating the movements of combat and performed in full armour

Nature the schoolmistress of cunning.

If an Ethiopian can change his skin, or a leopard his spots, then may you also do good which be nuzzled in evil. (Jeremiah 13:23)[167]

---

[167] Proverbially, the Ethiop not being able to 'wash' off his skin colour and the leopard not changing his spots referred to the fact that some people were incapable of change; the citation therefore says that a person nuzzled in evil will not be able to become good. The impossibility of washing an Ethiop (or black person) is a fable from the Aesopian tradition; see Ben Edwin Perry's Index of fables, the 'Analytical Survey of Greek and Latin Fables in the Aesopic Tradition', in *Babrius and Phaedrus*, ed. by Ben Edwin Perry (Cambridge, MA: Harvard University Press, 1956), number 393, p. 494. In this case, then, we see the biblical and Aesopian traditions feeding reciprocally into one another.

107. Of a Young Unthrift° and a Swallow

A certain prodigal young man, having almost spent all to his very shirt and having nothing[168] left him but one threadbare coat, became somewhat the thriftier by reason of the sharpness of the winter, and with much ado kept it for a while. But as soon as he had conceived in his imagination that he could forbear that also, he fell again to his old bias.° For spying by chance a swallow, and thereupon misconjecturing like an unskilful birdspeller°[169] that summer was at hand, he forgot the proverb that is common in every man's mouth, namely that one swallow maketh not the springtime,[170] and sold away that rag also, so as he had nothing to cover his skin but only his shirt. By reason whereof, when the winter, putting forth his sting again, began to nip his body with the fierceness of his cold unlooked for, beholding the swallow almost starven for cold, 'Woe worth thee thou treacherous bird,' quoth he. 'Thou art the cause of both our sorrows: first of thine own by coming oversoon into this coast, and also of mine by thine overhasty forhighting° of summer.'

The Morals: Timely advisement and deliberation are behooveful° in all things, and nothing is to be attempted upon rash imagination.

---

[168] This word is difficult to read in the manuscript, perhaps because Golding tried to correct an error.

[169] In using the word 'birdspeller' to translate *aruspex* [soothsayer], Golding happens upon an avian pun. Golding also uses 'birdspeller' in John Calvin, *The Psalmes of Dauid and others. With M. Iohn Caluins commentaries*, trans. by Arthur Golding (London, 1571), Psalms 15:4, sig. F6v.

[170] This phrase, from 'he forgot' to 'springtime', is in parentheses in Freitag's text. The phrase in Latin begins with the word *oblitus*, that is, 'having forgotten'. Golding removed the parentheses, presumably because his translation makes this phrase more essential to the grammar of the sentence. Erasmus gives the proverb as *Una hirundo non facit ver* [One swallow does not make a summer], in Erasmus, *Adages, I.vi.1 to I.x.100*, I.vii.94, p. 124.

Overhasty hope of alteration.

Mischief shall not depart from the house of him that requiteth evil for good. (Proverbs 17:13)

108. Of a Drunken Servant[171]

A certain drunken servant, having caught an habit of drinking wine by long custom, did then most chiefly glut himself with it when his master entertained his friends most frankly.° Now as this fellow on a time served his master's guests on a feastday, and had after his manner emptied many full cups, his overliberal taking in of his liquor so bereft him of his wits that, doing all things more unbridledly than at other times, he fell to galping° disorderly and unsavourly after the manner of drunken men, and ran gadding° here and there with frisking and leaping, which was uncomely most of all. Insomuch that, stumbling at a block, he broke his leg with a foul fall. Whereupon, when he had slept away his surfeit, he fell into such a hatred of his intemperance that, utterly forswearing to drink any more wine, he abstained from it and drank nothing but water ever after.

The Morals: The use of wine is to be taken warely and moderately. For it flattereth so long till° the unmeasurable gulling° in of it do thrust wit out of his place. But when it hath once overcome the brain and fettered° the mind, then, leaving his venomous stings in it, it tormenteth a man very sharply. Forasmuch therefore as drunkenness is most shameful, and very noisome° to either part of man, a wise man will flee far from it.

---

[171] Freitag's fable involves a stag (*ceruus*), not a servant (*seruus*); the change could indicate that Golding was translating the text divorced from the accompanying images (see Barnes pp. 338–39).

Sin, hurt, and shame be the followers of drunkenness.

The courage of drunkenness maketh wise men to stumble, weakeneth strength, and causeth wounds. (Ecclesiasticus 31:39)

109. Of a Fowler and a Partridge

A partridge, being caught of a fowler and perceiving her life to be in danger, both humbly and wisely besought him to let her go again, as who served but only for gluttony, and, forgetting her own credit and estimation, she treacherously promised to allure many other of her own kind into his nets. The fowler was so covetous of greater gain that he had almost granted her desire, but that he bethought himself that she which bore so treacherous a mind to her own kindred would not keep touch[172] with her enemy longer than was for her own profit, and therefore things certain were not to be let go for uncertain hope. Whereupon in disdainful manner, 'Art thou so shameless,' quoth he, 'as to presume to crave liberty for bringing others into the same danger which thou thyself dost most abhor? And by entangling them in the nets wherein thou wouldest not be entangled thyself? I therefore for this thy notable wickedness of mind will presently amerce° thee with the penalty of death.'

The Morals: Extreme punishment and shameful death are the kindly reward of treachery and treason.

---

[172] i.e., keep true. This is a reference to the touchstone used to test the integrity of gold.

Treachery returned upon the traitor's head.

If thou have a friend, try him while thou hast him, and be not too hasty in trusting him. (Ecclesiasticus 6:7)

110. Of Cocks and of a Partridge

A husbandman, having bought a partridge, brought him home and put him in his henyard with his poultry. The cocks, perceiving him to be a strange bird, pecked and jobbed° him shrewdly with their bills through envy, which is a natural error that groweth between such as are unknown and unlike one another. The partridge, remembering his former freedom, and how he had led his life aforetimes among the copses° and young shrubs without fear, did at the first take grievously to heart the churlish entertainment of his new companions and the filthiness of the place. But afterward, when he had somewhat more advisedly considered that, being brought into bondage, he was to obey the hard pinch of necessity, and that the cocks themselves, being birds of one feather, agreed not among themselves, but oftentimes fought one with another, and that so fiercely that they departed all bloody from the battle, he took comfort and became the more encouraged, concluding with himself that he, being but a stranger, ought of right to take in good worth the despites° done to him by strangers, seeing that they themselves, being of one kindred and company, did the like injury one to another.

The Morals: We shall comfort ourselves the better by this place if we settle this saying of a certain wise man well and deeply in our minds: that we be not hurt in very deed, but only imagine ourselves to be hurt.[173] And we shall the more easily bear the misbehaviours of wicked folk if we think that such as are as wicked as they (and much more good men) may be free from the things wherewith they reproach them.

---

[173] The wise man is Lucius Annaeus Seneca, who writes in his *Epistles*, *Plura sunt* […] *quae nos terrent, quam quae premunt, et saepius opinione quam re laboramus* [There are more things […] likely to frighten us than there are to crush us; we suffer more often in imagination than in reality]. See Seneca, *Epistles 1–65*, trans. by Richard M. Gummere (Cambridge, MA: Harvard University Press, 1917), XIII.4, pp. 74–75.

It is in vain to find fault with unavoidable injury.

When thou sittest at meat[174] with a great man, consider advisedly what is set afore thee. (Proverbs 23:1)

---

[174] i.e., sit down to eat a meal ('meat' in this case refers to nourishment more generally)

111. Of a Husbandman and a Stork

A husbandman, having singularly well tilled and husbanded his ground with great labour and toil, hoped for a very plentiful wheat harvest. But while the corn was in the blade,[175] such a multitude of wild geese and cranes fed it off that ye would have said no stormy tempest could have done it more harm. The husbandman, therefore, having tried in vain to fray° them away with diverse scarebugs,° in the end laid nets for them, and by chance caught a stork flying in among them. She, trusting in her innocency, declared that she came thither by mistaking the place only to rest her there, being weary of flying, and that she alighted not there of any purpose to feed of his corn, and therefore besought him to let her go. The husbandman not only refused to set her free, seeing she was fallen into his net, but also said he would kill her as well as the others that daily did him so much harm.

The Morals: We be warned by the stork's example to eschew the company of naughtypacks, lest peradventure, being taken with them, we be driven to abide the punishment of other men's misdeeds.

---

[175] i.e., still on the stalk

A MORAL FABLETALK

The good punished for being in company with the bad.

Let not mercy and truth depart from thee, but put them as a chain about thy neck, and engrave them in the tables of thy heart.
(Proverbs 3:3)

112. Of a Sheep and a Wolf

A sheep, being pursued by a wolf, and driven almost to the last pinch, bestirred her stumps[176] so swiftly for fear of the present peril that the wolf could not overtake her. Nevertheless, the wolf, chasing her still, distressed her on every side. At length the sheep, perceiving herself beset round about with his fraud, and that there was scarce any way for her to scape, fled into a chapel that was nearhand. The wolf, seeing that, followed the sheep as fast as he could, and rushed into the place after her,[177] thinking undoubtedly to have obtained his prey. But as eager as he was, he was disappointed of his hoped desire. And whereas he triumphed that he had gotten the sheep cooped up as it were in a pinfold,° he shut up himself in prison. For by his overhasty rushing into the chapel, he clapped to the door after him unawares. By reason whereof he was stricken with such a fear of his own peril before his eyes that he utterly abstained from touching the sheep.

The Morals: This fable is devised against the unstaunchable hunger of such as, being not satisfied with the fleecing°[178] of innocents unless they may also wholly devour them, be manacled° in the same fetters° which they had prepared for the feet of the innocents.

---

[176] i.e., ran

[177] Golding initially wrote 'him' and then wrote 'her' over it as a correction.

[178] Here the moral reminds us of the sheep-shearing origins of the verb 'to fleece', which means to obtain goods unfairly, to strip of money, to victimize.

Craftiness eluded by innocency.

And he beheld her with silence, desirous to know whether that God had made his journey prosperous or no. (Genesis 24:21)

113. Of Jupiter and the Watersnake

Jupiter had prepared a most sumptuous feast and banquet beseeming his majesty for all the rest of the gods. When the brute beasts understood thereof, thinking that the preparature° of the heavenly feast belonged unto them, every of them brought his present and gift, both to honour the feast and to show their thankful goodwills. Insomuch that the very watersnake was not behindhand with his duty, but, forgetting the wrath of God towards him, presented the most gracious and almighty Jove with a most dainty damask° rose of Milet, which with the gloss thereof dazzled the eyes of all that beheld it.[179] But as soon as the snake came in Jove's presence, Jove, disdaining both the gift and the giver thereof, whereas he most graciously and benignly accepted the presents of all the residue, refused the snake's gift, and in the open assembly of all the gods said that gifts were not to be received at the hands of the wicked, because they savoured of fraud and deceit.

The Morals: God (sayeth the scripture) heareth not sinners, nother delighteth He in the gifts of the ungodly, nother requireth He sacrifices and oblations,° but a broken and lowly heart. And that is the thing which this tale teacheth by the example of the watersnake, which of all snakes hath the most present poison and desperate malice.

---

[179] In Book 21, chapter 10 of his *Natural History*, Pliny describes the Milesian rose as having a 'brilliant fiery colour' (Pliny, *Natural History*, vol. 6, trans. by W. H. S. Jones [Cambridge, MA: Harvard University Press, 1961], p. 173). Miletus is an ancient city on the western coast of Anatolia, a region in modern day Turkey.

A refusal of the gifts of the wicked.

Give to the highest according as He hath bestowed upon thee, and let the fruit of thy hand be with a good eye. Offer not evil gifts, for He will not receive them, nother have thou an eye unto unrighteous sacrifices. (Ecclesiasticus 35:12, 14–15)

114. Of Jupiter and the Bee

And no less doth God mislike the suits and gifts of the ungodly, or hear such as desire unlawful things to their own destruction. Which thing is manifestly here shown in the bee, which is more behooveful for mankind than can be expressed. For when she, offering a honeycomb to Jupiter, sued to have this prerogative, that she might sting all those to death which should rob her hives, Jupiter received her gift most graciously; howbeit, being also a most gracious preserver of man, he disallowed her request, saying, 'Far otherwise shall it come to pass, O bee, than thou hast required. For whomsoever thou prickest with thy sting, leaving thy sting in the wound, he shall be thy bane and not thou his. For I will put such a seed of the spirit of life in thy sting, that with the loss thereof thou thyself also must needs lose thy life.'

The Morals: Injury is done to the majesty of the most holy and gracious godhead by wicked prayers, and he returneth them back again upon the heads of them that so pray.

A MORAL FABLETALK

Wicked petitions are hateful to God.

When His disciples James and John saw that, they said, 'Lord, wilt thou have us to command fire to come down from Heaven, and to consume them?' (Luke 9:52)[180]

---

[180] In the NRSV this verse is Luke 9:54.

115. Of a Horse of War and Swine

A certain horse, being gallantly furnished with trappers,° saddle, bridle, and a plume of feathers, was going forth a warfare,[181] either there to receive a glorious and speedy death, or else to bring home victory with gladness. Now as he passed by a swine all bemired, she stayed him with these words: 'Art thou such a wretch,' quoth she, 'as to cast thyself headlong through ignorance into doubtful war and manifest danger of death? Why goest thou, thou madbrain,° to destroy thyself?' 'Thinkest thou,' quoth the horse, beating back the swine's taunt, 'that thou shalt attain to immortality by this thy wallowing in the mire? Knowest thou not that when thou hast fed thyself fat, thou must forgo and yield up thy life by a shameful death void of all glory? But as for me, I, by dying in my master's quarrel, shall obtain immortal glory of fame and renown, which is much better than this dark and dusky life.'

The Morals: Cowardly and haskardly° men do commonly make no regard of coming to a reproachful end of their life, so they may live in the meanwhile in pleasure. But the gentlemanlike and heroical mind despiseth and disdaineth pleasures, seeking the praise and perpetuity of name and fame for life well spent.

---

[181] i.e., going forth to warfare. Using 'a' to mean 'to' is a Latinate construction.

The comparison of glorious and unglorious death.

I heard a voice saying from Heaven, 'write: "Blessed are the dead that die in the Lord."' 'So is it,' sayeth the Spirit, 'for they rest from their labours, and their works follow them.' (Apocalypse 14:13)[182]

---

[182] Apocalypse is now commonly known as The Book of Revelation.

116. Of an Ass and a Horse

A wretched ass that was loaden with a great bundle of wood, espying by him a goodly horse decked with brave furniture,[183] did by and by deem him to be happy and (in his opinion) blessed. And on the contrary part, bewailing his own lot, he condemned himself as born under an unlucky planet, and (as folk say) fallen between the change of the moon and the prime,[184] predestined to continual stripes and toils. But ere long after, it befell that he saw the same horse, barded° and overloaden with the heavy weight of armour, sent away to a great and sore war. Then, comparing his own griefs with the dangerful pomp of the horse, 'I had lever° now,' quoth he, 'to be still a vile and rascal ass, and to have my neck borne down with daily labour, than to follow the rattling of armour in warfare, or to try the hazard of bloody Mars, girded° with a soldier's girdle.'°

The Morals: Nother riches nor honour do make a man happy (for care and a hungry desire of having more accompany the increase of money), but the bridling of the burning lusts of the mind. Insomuch that oftentimes it falleth out that he to whom Fortune hath denied most things proveth a happier man than he that wanteth not anything to the fulfilling of his delights and the perfecting of his pleasures.

---

[183] 'brave' in the sense of showy or fine; 'furniture' in the sense of equipment
[184] The prime is the young crescent moon; the time described here is between the appearance of the new moon and the first quarter.

Counterfeit and deceitful is the felicity of the world.

Better is the man that is patient than the man that is strong, and he that overmastereth his own will than he that conquereth cities.
(Proverbs 16:32)

117. Of a Horse and an Ass

The former fable taught us[185] how quietly we from time to time do rest within the bounds of nature, by weighing in indifferent balance as well our own lives as other men's, wherein we think all things to be most glorious. Which thing this present tale confirmeth with very good reason, declaring that the inferior sort are exempted from the peril wherein those live which, through ambition, having overpassed the slippery path of vainglory, be come to the top of vanity. For when on a time a certain proud horse had met an ass newly taken from the yoke, and then carrying a greater burden on his back, by reason of the heaviness whereof he gave him not the way, he was so inflamed with choler that he menaced to trample the ass under his feet if he gave not place unto him. Wherewith the ass, being amazed, brayed out and gave way to the glorious Thraso.[186] But ere many years after were outrun, it befell that when the horse was attached with sorrowful old age, his master took away his trappers, and put him to the carrying out of dung and such other filth. The ass, by chance finding him in that plight, and remembering his former churlish pride, the which he had now opportunity to upbraid him with at his pleasure: 'Art thou the same,' quoth he, 'whom in time past I saw shaking his mane so bravely,° and breathing out so lusty blasts from his proud breast, which insulted so stoutly against me? Tell me, I pray thee, by what means thou art cast down to this reproachful life?'

The Morals: Pride and disdain do carry with them the law of requital.

---

[185] Note that this is one of the moments where Golding, following Freitag, makes an explicit connection between two fables; he does so by pointing out that they have similar lessons, rather than connecting them by narrative.

[186] Thraso is stock character from Terence's play *Eunuchus*, who is known for being a braggart. He is also mentioned in fable 46.

A MORAL FABLETALK

Odious is the pride of prosperity.

He hath wrought mightily with his arm; He hath scattered the proud in the imagination of their hearts. (Luke 1:51)

118. Of a Turkeycock° and a Dunghillcock°

A dunghillcock, being of a proud courage, stood so immoderately in his own conceit that he disdained all fowls of his own kind. Wherefore, perceiving a turkeycock (whom by another name some call an Indian peacock) to haunt the same places that he did, and to be welcome to the hens and young pullen° there for his gentle and quiet behaviour, he took such spite at it that he made cruel and fierce war against him. When the turkeycock saw the contention grow so excessive that it struck a terror even into the cockerels and made them keep aloof for fear, he, loving quietness, and utterly abhorring such continual battle and discord, forsook his accustomed dwellingplace, and chose him another habitation, deeming that body to have lived well which hath lived unknown.

The Morals: Against unkind[187] and barbarous inhospitality, and the churlish disposition of such as can abide no stranger to dwell in rest by them. With which vice, would God that only Pontus could be noted by Apollonius,[188] and that many nations of the Christian profession were not so infected with it that whereas they will needs seem to have put off all barbarousness, yet notwithstanding, in most shameful unhospitality they be far worse than the barbarousest of all.

---

[187] This word appears as an embedded word of Greek in Freitag. The word is ἀξενίαν [*axenian*, inhospitable].

[188] The Black Sea or a region adjacent thereto, proverbially inhospitable. Apollonius Rhodius describes 'inhospitable Pontus' (πόντον ἐς Ἄξεινᾰν) in *Argonautica* 2.984, trans. by R. C. Seaton (London: William Heinemann, 1919), p. 190–91.

The law of hospitality broken.

If a stranger abide by thee in thy land and dwell among you, thou shalt not vex him. But let him be among you as one born in the land and ye shall love him as yourselves. For the time hath been that you yourselves also were strangers in the land of Egypt.
(Leviticus 19:33)

119. Of a Kite that Was Sick

A kite that had run a long race in wickedness and lewd life, being afflicted with sickness by the judgement of God, the just punisher of wicked deeds and the rewarder of welldoing, sent for his mother, and with most earnest entreatance besought her to pray unto God to restore him his health. But she, rebuking him with severity unaccustomed to mothers towards their children, vexed him more and more with these words: 'Yea?' quoth she, 'Thinkest thou that God will so lightly have mercy upon the wicked, which, despising his law and commandments, forget themselves in the time of their prosperity? Knowest thou not that he is a most sharp punisher of naughtypacks? Justly therefore be these things now come upon thee, and think now to feel the force of this disease in thy body for the robberies and murders which thou hast committed.

The Morals: It is good reason that he which in time of his prosperity and health unthankfully despised God's word and was unmindful of him should be overtaken by the just judgement of the gracious God, and forsaken of him in time of adversity.

The punishment of neglecting the worshipping of God.

If I have harboured wickedness in my heart, the Lord will not hear me. (Psalms 65:18)[189]

---
[189] In the NRSV this verse corresponds to Psalms 66:18.

120. Of an Ostrich and a Nightingale

It is now time for the nightingale to come forth upon the stage, which, being no deceitful messenger of the springtime coming on, or rather, abounding in the divers allurements of herbs and flowers, delighteth men's ears like a most sweet mermaid with her divine harmony at that time of the year. Let us extol her with commendation, for that she contendeth onewhile with the vulture and another while with the peacock, which[190] are the excellentest of all birds, and here also with the huge ostrich. For at such time as the ostrich took pride in his feathers, the nightingale with her singing left him no place of commendation. To be short, either of them so praised himself that he challenged the sovereignty of all other fowls as due to himself of right. The nightingale said she assuaged° the storms of lovers with her singing. The ostrich said that diverse nations used his feathers for their ornament and bravery, and that they claimed to them the chief place among merchandise. The nightingale (lest the ostrich, which had challenged the chief pre-eminence of praise, should obtain so much as he meanest of all)[191] defaced his feathers, as serving but only for vain ostentation, and so flew away.

The Morals: This fable reprehendeth the doltishness of those which, by reason of some benefit of Nature, do through a kind of self-soothing° deem themselves worthy and meet for sovereignty.

---

[190] It appears that Golding started writing 'that' and then wrote 'which' over it instead.
[191] i.e., lest the ostrich, who had challenged the nightingale about who was most worthy of praise, should obtain that which he intended (to win the most praise)

Hateful is the vaunting of ordinary virtues.

For who advanceth thee? What hast thou which thou hast not received? And if thou have received, why boastest thou as though thou hadst not received? (1 Corinthians 4:7)

121. Of an Old Impotent° Stork[192]

The stork, alonely of all the birds which the huge circuit of the Earth and the liquid space of the air nourisheth, surmounteth all the residue in care and curiousness of bringing up his young, and findeth a mutual kindness at their hand again, by which notable example of theirs, men are admonished of the loving kindness which they owe one to another when cause and need require. And the wonderful example of the kindness which the young ones yield back again to their dams shameth the unkindness of most men, which, alas, is too foul.[193] For they so religiously obey the law of nature in taking upon them the care of their parents that in their commonweal it is counted a heinous crime, and not to be cleansed away by any punishment, if they should cast off the care of their parents, and not succour them in their need. Whereby it cometh to pass that, forasmuch as the young birds when they be yet callow° and tender of body be not neglected of their dams, nor the dams likewise be neglected of them to whom they imparted life, their government, being administered with diligence of careful kindness, is never attainted with any penury.

The Morals: The stork, being void of the light of reason, admonisheth us to have a care of our parents, and not to forsake them when they be pinched with penury or old age, but to relieve them with kind affection in their decay which have brought us into this world, and with so great care nourished us.

---

[192] In Book 10, chapter 32 of his *Natural History*, Pliny says, 'Storks return to the same nest. They nourish their parents' old age in their turn' (Pliny, *Natural History*, vol. 3, p. 333).

[193] Note the pun on 'fowl' here, in this fable about birds.

Mutual kindness of children towards their parents.

The father of the righteous leapeth for gladness, and he that begetteth a wise son shall have joy of him. (Proverbs 23:24)

122. Of an Ass Loaden with Provision of Meat and Drink[194]

The dizzardly° ass, which, being so often mentioned, sustaineth now one person and now another, and offereth himself last upon the stage to be gazed at, being loaden with choice meats and drinks, beareth and yieldeth sustenance to others; and yet he himself, being in the meanwhile almost killed with carriage,° is fain to satisfy and put away his hunger and thirst by eating vile thistles and drinking cold water, and doth always somewhat undiscreetly, according to his kind, and to none so like as to himself, discovereth the ears of many asses by his example, conveying fabulous matter° to matter of truth, and bewraying base fellows wedded to their own profit, who, going about to increase and enrich their houses by their travail, do with incomparable toil all their life long rake things together to leave them to be wasted by their thankless children, kinfolk, and successors, while they themselves in the meanwhile play the cruel tormentors to their own bodies and minds.

The Morals: This fable doth lively paint out the forlorn slavery of covetousness and the lewd thraldom° of riches.

---

[194] This fable is written as one long run-on sentence, perhaps reflecting its content, which warns against the dangers of superfluity.

Needy wealth.

When God giveth a man riches, and substance, and honour, so as he wanteth not anything that his heart can desire, and yet giveth him not power to enjoy the same, but a stranger shall devour them, it is a great vanity and wretchedness. (Ecclesiasticus 6:2)

123. Of a Swan and a Stork

What is to be done or left undone in our life we have learned already by the example of many living creatures. Now forasmuch as the path of virtue is steep, and one night abideth for all men,[195] so as one time or other they must tread the way of death, let us learn of the swan with what mind to receive this night coming upon us. The swan, foreknowing his death at hand, falleth to singing with a shirl° voice. A certain stork, wondering at his unseasonable joy, asked him what moved him to so great jollity? He told the stork that he ought not to wonder at his comforting of himself, or at his unwonted° gladness. For he saw that his tranquility approached, and that he had attained to the upshot of all his troubles and cares wherewith he had hitherto been entangled.

The Morals: Seeing it is decreed that all of us must once die, and necessity overcasteth all men with like lot, as well the high as the low, let us learn by example of the swan to despise death with a stout and stately courage, and let us run cheerfully, as wagerers do in a gaming for the prize, unto the mark which the destinies have appointed unto us.

---

[195] i.e., Death comes to everyone.

A MORAL FABLETALK

Honourable is the contempt of death.

The ungodly shall be thrust out in his wickedness, but the righteous is full of hope even in his death. (Proverbs 14:32)

124. Of the Phoenix

To the intent that our manner of philosophy, which we have begun at the crabbed labours and toils of man's life, may be seasoned with some sweetness of rest, let us bring forth the sole° phoenix to end the act of this play with a gladsome winding up, such as comedies ought to have. The report goeth that this bird, after he hath lived six hundred and threescore years, chooseth a tree near some fountain in the deserts of Araby the Happy,[196] and therein makes her[197] a nest of sticks and branches of odiferous° trees gathered together, which, being set full against the sun, she kindleth on fire with the vehement flasking°[198] of her wings. Into the mids whereof so kindled, she casteth herself and there is burnt. Out of the ashes of which burnt matter there breedeth a worm which groweth to be a phoenix again.

The Morals: The phoenix beareth the figure of our saviour Christ, offering up Himself in bloody sacrifice to His father by reproachful death for us, and restoring life unto us by the benefit of His glorious and wonderful resurrection. Therefore, sith we have brought our matters to the utmost point, let Him be the end of our labour, even He I say, which, being the alpha and omega, the beginning and end of all things, and the glorious phoenix in mystery of unity, shall convey us all into one sheepfold. In Him must we be bred and born again here in spirit; by Him must the lump of our rotted carcasses be repaired° to the new and uncorruptible life in the wonderful restitution of our bodies.

---

[196] A region in the southern part of the Arabian peninsula that was sometimes called Arabia Felix, or Happy, Flourishing Arabia, because it was particularly fertile, especially when compared with the other regions of the peninsula. Pliny questions the accuracy of applying the name 'happy' to this region in his *Natural History* 12.41 (Pliny, *Natural History*, vol. 4, trans. by H. Rackham [Cambridge, MA: Harvard University Press, 1945], p. 60–63).

[197] The phoenix's gender changes here.

[198] i.e., flapping. There are only two other recorded uses of the verb 'flask' to mean 'flap', both from Golding's translation of Ovid's *Metamorphoses* (*OED*).

Young desires exchanged with elder years.

Put ye off the old man according to the former conversation, which is corrupted through erroneous lusts. (Ephesians 4:22)

125. Of the Stork

The phoenix had almost put me to silence, and the flourishing hope of the blessed and endless life had shut up the doors of my theatre, but that after that last farewell, the religiousness of the stork had willed me to add this short admonition. Namely that by her example, who yearly payeth firstfruits° unto God by offering unto him some one of her young birds, we, spurring ourselves forward to the honouring and obeying of virtue, should offer unto him the frankincense° of pure heart and mind (which thing will be easy to do, if, having overcome the Lernaean Hydra[199] of vices, we make way for virtue). And we shall be the more forward in doing it if we underprop ourselves with assured hope of God's promise, for the righteous shall flourish as the palm tree.[200] And not only by Christ's warrant, but also by the record of the philosophers, we shall accomplish the globe of virtues chiefly by two duties of man's life, to wit, by yielding chief honour to God as we ought to do, and by loving all men as ourselves.

The Morals:[201]

---

[199] The Lernaean Hydra is a serpentine water monster in Greek and Roman mythology, noted for having multiple heads that would regrow and multiply if cut off; killing the Hydra often symbolized the seemingly insurmountable task of eradicating something that multiplied more quickly than it could be defeated. To say a 'Hydra of vices', therefore, implies that vices pose a similar problem.

[200] In the NRSV the idea that 'The righteous [will] flourish like the palm tree' can be found in Psalms 92:12.

[201] Neither Freitag nor Golding include a moral for this final fable.

Righteousness perfected in all points.

Fear God and keep his commandments, for that belongeth unto all men. (Ecclesiastes 12:13)

WILLIAM CAXTON

from *The Subtle Histories and Fables of Aesop, which were translated out of French into English by William Caxton at Westminster* (1484)

THE SUBTLE HISTORIES AND FABLES OF AESOP

Book 1 Prologue.[1] **Here beginneth the preface or prologue of the first book of Aesop.**

I, Romulus, son of Tiber of the City of Attica: greeting.[2] Aesop, man of Greece, subtle and ingenious, teacheth in his fables how men ought to keep and rule them[3] well. And to the end that[4] he should show the life and customs of all manner of men, he induceth the birds, the trees, and the beasts speaking, to the end that[5] the men may know wherefore° the fables were found. In the which he hath written the malice of the evil people and the argument of the improbes.° He teacheth also to be humble and for to use words. And many other fair ensamples° rehearsed° and declared hereafter, the which I, Romulus, have translated out of Greeks'[6] tongue into Latin tongue, the which, if thou read them, they shall aiguise°[7] and sharp thy wit and shall give to thee cause of joy.

---

[1] The title 'Book 1 Prologue' is an editorial addition.
[2] Though Caxton translates his source accurately, the Latin text from which this fable eventually comes reads, *Romulus tyberino filio. De ciuitate attica aesopus* [Romulus to his son Tiberius. Aesop, of the city of Athens, ...] (*Romulus: Die paraphrasen des Phaedrus und die Aesopische fabel im mittelalter*, ed. by Hermann Oesterley [Berlin: Weidmannsche Buchhandlung, 1870], p. 38). To see how the meaning gradually changed, see Caxton, ed. by Lenaghan, p. 243, n. 142.
[3] i.e., themselves
[4] i.e., in order that
[5] i.e., he induces the birds, trees, and beasts to speak, so that ...
[6] There are no possessive apostrophes in the original text, so this could also be modernized as 'Greek's tongue' (i.e., *the* Greek's tongue, i.e., Aesop's tongue). We think, however, that 'Greeks' tongue' is more likely (i.e., the text was translated out of the tongue or language of the Greeks and into Latin).
[7] Caxton here uses a French word (in his spelling, 'aguyse') as a synonym for its English counterpart 'sharpen'. Because he treats them as continuous in his prose, we have left it out of italics.

1. Of the Cock and of the Precious Stone[8]

As a cock once sought his pasture° in the dunghill, he found a precious stone, to whom the cock said, 'Ha a,[9] fair° stone and precious, thou art here in the filth. And if he that desireth thee had found thee as I have, he should have taken thee up and set thee again in thy first estate.° But in vain I have found thee, for nothing I have to do with thee, ne° no good I may do to thee, ne thou to me.' And this fable said Aesop to them that read this book. For by the cock is to understand[10] the fool which reacheth° not of sapience° ne of wisdom, as the cock reacheth and setteth not by[11] the precious stone. And by the stone is to understand this fair and pleasant book.[12]

---

[8] In 1484, I.1.

[9] An antiquated interjection, meaning either 'ha ha' or 'aha!'

[10] i.e., by the cock is to be understood

[11] i.e., does not understand, and does not set or assign any value to

[12] i.e., And by the stone is to be understood this fair and pleasant book. Note that the stone, which usually stands in for wisdom in general, in this version stands in specifically for the wisdom that this book of fables has to offer.

2. Of the Rat and of the Frog[13]

Now it be so, that as the rat went in pilgrimage, he came by a river, and demanded help of a frog for to pass and go over the water. And then the frog bound the rat's foot to her foot, and thus swam unto the mids° over the river. And as they were there, the frog stood still to the end that the rat should be drowned. And in the meanwhile came a kite° upon them, and both bore them with him.[14] This fable made Aesop for a similitude° which is profitable to many folks. For he that thinketh evil against good, the evil which he thinketh shall once fall upon himself.

---

[13] In 1484, I.3.

[14] i.e., carried both of them away with him (presumably to eat them)

3. Of the Lion and of the Rat[15]

The mighty and puissant° must pardon and forgive to the little and feeble, and ought to keep him fro° all evil. For oft-time° the little may well give aid and help to the great. Whereof Aesop rehearseth to us such a fable of a lion which slept in a forest, and the rats disported and played about him. It happed° that the rat went upon the lion, wherefore the lion awoke, and within his claws or ongles° he took the rat. And when the rat saw him[16] thus taken and held, he said thus to the lion: 'My lord pardon me, for of my death nought ye shall win,° for I supposed not to have done to you any harm ne displeasure.' Then thought the lion in himself that no worship ne glory it were to put it to death. Wherefore, he granted his pardon and let him go within a little while.

After this it happed so that the same lion was taken at[17] a great trap, and as he saw him[18] thus caught and taken, he began to cry and make sorrow. And then, when the rat heard him cry, he approached him and demanded of him wherefore he cried. And the lion answered to him, 'Seest thou not how I am taken and bound with this gin?'° Then said the rat to him, 'My lord, I will not be unkind, but ever I shall remember the grace° which thou hast done to me. And if I can I shall

---

[15] In 1484, I.18.
[16] i.e., himself
[17] i.e., in
[18] i.e., himself

now help thee.' The rat began then to bite the lace or cord, and so long he gnawed it that the lace broke, and thus the lion escaped. Therefore this fable teacheth us how that a man mighty and puissant ought not to dispraise the little. For sometime° he that can nobody hurt ne let° may at a need give help and aid to the great.[19]

---

[19] i.e., Even someone who is not capable of hurting or inconveniencing others may, if needed, be able to help those above him- or herself.

Book 2 Proem.°[20] **Here followeth the proem of the second book of the fables of Aesop, man wise, subtle, and ingenious.**

All manner of fables be found for to show[21] all manner of folk what manner of thing they ought to ensue° and follow, and also what manner of thing they must and ought to leave and flee, for fable is as much to say in poetry as words in theology.[22] And therefore I shall write fables for to show the good conditions of the good men, for the law hath been given for the trespassers or misdoers,° and because the good and just be not subject to the law, as we find and read of all the Athenians, the which lived after the law of kind.°[23] And also they lived at their liberty, but by their will would have demanded a king for to punish all the evil.[24] But because they were not customed° to be reformed ne chastised, when any of them was corrected and punished they were greatly troubled when their new king made justice. For because that[25] before that time they had never been under no man's subjection,[26] and was great charge to them to be in servitude. Wherefore they were sorrowful that ever they had demanded anything, against the which[27] Aesop rehearseth such a fable which is the first and foremost of this second book.

---

[20] The title 'Book 2 Proem' is an editorial addition.

[21] i.e., in order to show. This formulation was common in Middle English.

[22] i.e., a fable says as much by means of poetry as theology does with words

[23] i.e., who lived according to the law of nature

[24] The Athenians lived according to the law of nature and at their liberty, but they desired a king to make laws. These details are included to set up the following fable of the frogs demanding a king from Jupiter.

[25] i.e., 'because.' In Middle English and early modern English 'because' was often written as two words (by cause [that]); the closest modern equivalent might be 'for the reason that'.

[26] i.e., had never been under any man's subjection or power. What sounds like a double negative to modern ears was not an issue in Caxton's fifteenth-century English.

[27] i.e., about which

4. Of the Frogs and of Jupiter[28]

Nothing is so good as to live justly and at liberty, for freedom and liberty is better than any gold or silver. Whereof Aesop rehearseth to us such a fable. There were frogs which were in ditches and ponds at their liberty; they all together of one assent° and of one will made a request to Jupiter that he would give them a king. And Jupiter began thereof to marvel. And for their king he cast to them a great piece of wood, which made a great sound and noise in the water, whereof all the frogs had great dread° and feared much. And after they approached to their king for to make obeisance° unto him. And when they perceived that it was but a piece of wood, they turned again to Jupiter, praying him sweetly that he would give to them another king.

And Jupiter gave to them the heron° for to be their king. And then the heron began to enter into the water, and ate them one after other. And when the frogs saw that their king destroyed and ate them thus, they began tenderly to weep, saying in this manner to the god Jupiter: 'Right° high and right mighty god Jupiter, please thee to deliver us fro the throat of this dragon and false tyrant which eateth us the one after another.' And he said to them, 'The king which ye have demanded shall be your master. For when men have that which men ought to have, they ought to be joyful and glad. And he that hath liberty ought to keep it well, for nothing is better than liberty. For liberty should not be well sold for all the gold and silver of all the world.'

---

[28] In 1484, II.1.

5. Of the Colombes° or Doves, of the Kite, and of the Sparhawk°[29]

Who that put and submitteth himself under the safeguard or protection of the evil, thou oughtest to wit° and know that when he asketh and demandeth aid and help, he getteth none.[30] Whereof Aesop rehearseth to us such a fable of the doves which demanded a sparhawk for to be their king for to keep them fro the kite or milan.° And when the sparhawk was made king over them, he began to devour them. The which colombes or doves said among them that better it were to them to suffer of the kite than to be under the subjection of the sparhawk, and to be 'martyred as we be. But thereof we be well worthy, for we ourselves be cause of this mischief.'[31] And therefore when men do anything, men ought well to look and consider the end of it. For he doth prudently and wisely which taketh good heed to the end.

---

[29] In 1484, II.2.

[30] This sentence is an excellent example of Caxton's doublets, containing five pairs of near synonyms. See Part II of the introduction to this volume for more on the significance of these doublets.

[31] Caxton's text, like others from his period, does not mark out direct speech with inverted commas. We have added the inverted commas for ease of reading, but it is unclear where exactly the quotation begins, as Caxton switches from indirect quotation to direct quotation in the middle of the sentence. Where the quotation begins is therefore open for interpretation and might be located as far back as before 'to suffer'.

6. Of the Thief and of the Dog[32]

When that one giveth[33] anything, men ought well to take heed to what end it is given. Whereof Aesop rehearseth such a fable of a thief which came on a night within a man's house for to have robbed him. And the good man's dog began to bark at him. And then the thief cast° at him a piece of bread, and the dog said to him, 'Thou castest not this bread for no good will,[34] but only to the end that I hold my peace, to the end that thou mayest rob my master. And therefore it were not good for me that for a morsel of bread I should lose my life. Wherefore, go fro hence, or else I shall anon° awake my master and all his meinie.'° The dog then began to bark and the thief began to flee. And thus by covetise° many one have oft-time received great gifts, the which have been cause of their death, and to lose their heads. Wherefore it is good to consider and look well to what intention the gift is given, to the end that no one may be betrayed through gifts, ne that by any gifts no one maketh some treason against his master or lord.[35]

---

[32] In 1484, II.3.
[33] i.e., When one giveth, or gives. Using 'when that' to mean 'when', like using 'for that' to mean 'for', was not uncommon in fifteenth-century English.
[34] i.e., you cast this bread with no good will, or you do not cast it with any good intentions
[35] i.e., It is good to consider why a gift is given [to you] so that no one may be betrayed by gifts, and so that no one may make treason against his master because of gifts.

7. Of the Lion and of the Horse[36]

Each one ought to eschew° dissimuling,° for no one ought to wear on him the skin of the wolf but° that he will be like to him.[37] For none ought to feign himself other than such as he is, as to us rehearseth this fable of a lion which saw a horse which ate grass in a meadow, and for to find some subtlety° and manner for to eat and devour him, approached to him and said, 'God keep thee my brother — I am a leech° and withal a good physician. And because that I see that thou hast a sore° foot, I am come hither for to heal thee of it.' And the horse knew well all his evil thought, and said to the lion, 'My brother, I thank thee greatly, and thou art welcome to me. I pray thee that thou wilt make my foot whole.'°[38] And then the lion said to the horse, 'Let see thy foot.'[39] And as the lion looked on it, the horse smote him on the forehead in such wise° that he broke his head and fell out of his mind, and the lion fell to the ground. And so wonderly° he was hurt that almost he might not rise up again. And then said the lion in himself, 'I am well worthy to have had this, for he that searcheth° evil, evil cometh to him. And because that I dissimuled and feigned myself to be a medicine,° whereas I should have shown myself a great enemy, I therefore have received good reward.' And therefore everybody ought to show himself such as he is.

---

[36] In 1484, III.2.

[37] i.e., no one ought to wear the skin of a wolf, unless he is going to be like the wolf

[38] We have modernized 1484's 'hole' to 'whole' (uninjured, unwounded, unhurt), but 'hale' (healthy) is also a possible modernization.

[39] i.e., Let me see your foot.

8. Of the Knight and of the Widow[40]

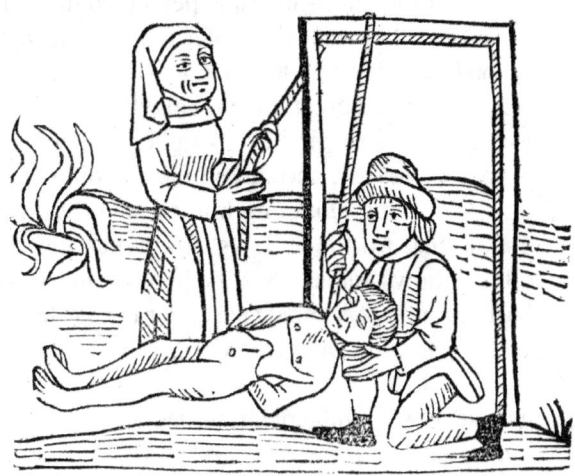

The woman which liveth in this world without reproach or blame is worthily to be greatly praised. Whereof Aesop rehearseth such a fable of a man and of a woman which loved much each other. It happed[41] then by the efforts[42] of Atropos[43] or death — the which we all must suffer — that the said man died. And as men would have borne him into his grave, which was without° the town, there to be buried, his wife made great sorrow and wept piteously. And when he was buried, she would abide[44] still upon the grave, and let do make a little lodge or house thereupon.[45] And out of this lodge she would never depart for no prayer ne fair word, neither for any gifts ne for menaces° of her parents.

Now it befell in the town that a misdoer was condemned to be hanged. And to the end[46] that he should not be taken fro the gallows, it was

---

[40] In 1484, III.9. This fable also appears as the story of the Widow of Ephesus in Petronius' *Satyricon*, a Roman book of satire written in Latin. Later in the Renaissance, the story was also modified and adapted into George Chapman's play *The Widow's Tears* (c. 1605–1606), and into John Ogilby's long poem *The Ephesian Matron*, published with his *Aesopics* (1668, rep. 1673/5).
[41] i.e., happened
[42] In this case, 'efforts' means powers or force, not merely attempts. The *OED* lists Caxton as an example of an author who often uses 'efforts' in this way.
[43] Atropos was one of the three fates, usually described or depicted as holding a pair of scissors to cut the thread of life.
[44] i.e., she did abide or insisted on abiding
[45] i.e., she had a little lodge or house made upon the grave
[46] i.e., for the purpose

then commanded that a knight should keep him.[47] And as the knight kept him, great thirst took him. And as he perceived the lodge of the said woman, he went to her and prayed her to give him some drink. And she with good heart gave him to drink, and the knight drank with great appetite, as he that had great thirst. And when he had drunk, he turned again to the gallows ward.[48] This knight came another time to the woman for to comfort her, and three times he did so. And as he was thus going and coming, doubting him of nobody,[49] his hanged man was taken and had fro the gallows. And when the knight was come again to the gallows and saw that he had lost his dead man, he was greatly abashed, and not without cause. For it was charged to him upon pain to be hanged if he were taken away.

This knight then, seeing his judgement, turned and went again to the said woman, and cast him at her feet, and lay before her as he had been dead.[50] And she demanded of him, 'My friend, what wilt thou that I do for thee?' 'Alas,' said he, 'I pray thee that thou succour° and counsel° me now at my great need. For because I have not kept well my thief, which men have ravished° fro me, the king shall make me to be put to death.' And the woman said, 'Have no dread, my friend, for well I shall find the manner whereby thou shalt be delivered. For we shall take my husband and shall hang him in stead° of thy thief.' Then began she to delve,° and took out of the earth her husband, and at night she hanged him at the gallows in stead of the other, and said to the knight, 'My right dear friend, I pray thee that this be kept well secret, for we do it thiefly.'° And thus the dead men have some which make sorrow for them, but that sorrow is soon gone and passed. And they which be on live[51] have some which dread° them, but their dread wanteth° and faileth when they be dead.

---

[47] i.e., that a knight should guard the body while it hung on the gallows

[48] i.e., toward the gallows

[49] i.e., not worrying about anybody. There is a possible pun in the original, however, which reads 'doubtynge hym of no body', potentially meaning, in addition, not worrying about the body or corpse he was guarding.

[50] i.e., as if he were dead

[51] i.e., they who are alive

9. Of the Hands, of the Feet, and of the Man's Belly[52]

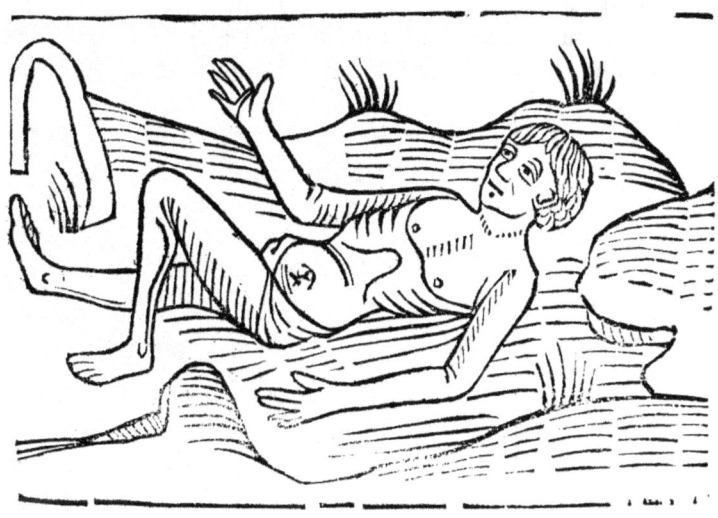

How shall one do any good to another, the which can do no good to his own self? As thou mayest see by this fable of the feet and of the hands, which sometime had great strife with the belly, saying, 'All that we can or may win with great labour, thou eatest it all, and yet thou dost no good. Wherefore thou shalt no more have nothing of us,[53] and we shall let thee die for hunger.' And then when the belly was empty and sore° hungry, she began to cry, and said, 'Alas, I die for hunger! Give me somewhat° to eat.' And the feet and hands said, 'Thou gettest nothing of us!'

And because that the belly might have no meat,° the conduits thorough° the which the meats passeth became small and narrow. And within few days after, the feet and hands for the feebleness which they felt would then have given meat to the belly, but it was too late, for the conduits were joined together. And therefore the limbs might do no good to other, that is to wit,[54] the belly. And he that governeth not

---

[52] In 1484, III.16. This fable was a popular political fable in the early modern period; it is referenced by William Shakespeare in his play *Coriolanus* as a metaphor for the 'body' of the commonwealth (Shakespeare, *The Norton Shakespeare*, ed. by Stephen Greenblatt et al. [New York: W. W. Norton and Co., 2016], I.i), and is taken up in new and different ways by poets during the English Civil War and its aftermath.

[53] i.e., you shall no more have anything of us, or you will not get anything else from us

[54] Literally, this means, that is to know; figuratively, it means, that is to say.

well his belly, with great pain he may hold the other limbs in their strength and virtue. Wherefore a servant ought to serve well his master to the end that his master hold and keep him honestly, and to receive and have good reward of him when his master shall see his faithfulness.

10. Of the Man and of the Lion[55]

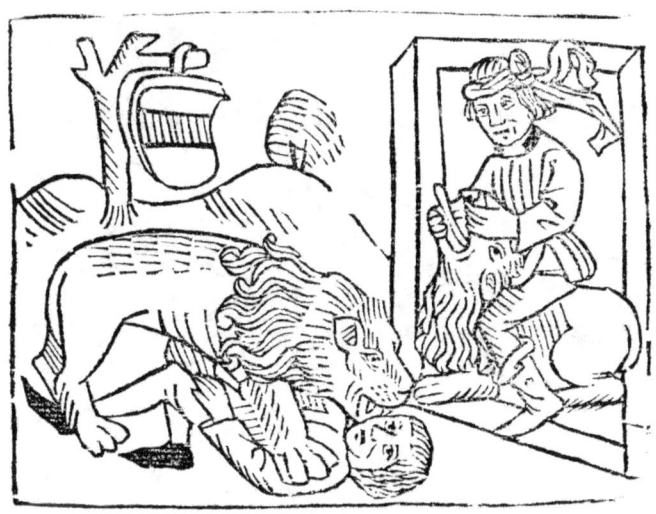

Men ought not to believe the painture° but the truth and the deed, as men may see by this present° fable of a man and of a lion, which had strife together and were in great dissension° for to wit and know which of them both was more stronger.[56] The man said that he was stronger than the lion. And for to have his saying verified he showed to the lion a picture where as a man had victory over a lion, as the picture of Sampson the strong.[57] Then said the lion to the man, 'If the lion could make picture good and true[58] it had been herein painted how the lion had had victory of the man. But now I shall show to thee very and true witness thereof.' The lion then led the man to a great pit, and there they fought together. But the lion cast the man into the pit, and submitted him into his subjection, and said, 'Thou man, now knowest thou all the truth which of us both is stronger.' And therefore at the work is known the best and most subtle worker.

---

[55] In 1484, IV.15. This fable is alluded to, though with a different moral, by Geoffrey Chaucer's Wife of Bath in the *Canterbury Tales*. Her question 'Who peyntede the leon, tel me who?' reminds her husband Jankyn that his book of tales about wicked women cannot be taken as truth because men are inaccurately 'painting' descriptions of women. See Chaucer, *Wife of Bath's Prologue*, in *The Riverside Chaucer*, ed. by Benson, l. 692. Caxton's moral is more general: deeds, not representations of deeds, show the truth.

[56] i.e., which one of them was stronger

[57] This refers to Judges 14:5–6, which tells of Sampson, a man who uses his God-given supernatural strength to tear apart and kill a lion with his bare hands.

[58] i.e., if lions could create high-quality and accurate visual representations

11. Of the Wolf which Made a Fart[59]

It is folly to ween° more than men ought to do. For whatsomever° a fool thinketh, it seemeth to him that it shall be, as it appeareth by this fable of a wolf which sometime rose early in a morning. And after that he was risen up fro his bed, as he reached°[60] himself, made a great fart, and began to say in himself,[61] 'Blessed be God therefore. These be good tidings.° This day I shall be well fortunate and happy, as mine° arse° singeth to me.'

And then he departed from his lodges° and began to walk and go. And as he went on his way, he found a sack full of tallow° which a woman had let fall,[62] and with his foot he turned it upside down, and said to him,[63] 'I shall not eat thee, for thou shouldest hurt my tender stomach, and that more is,[64] I shall this day have better meat and more delicious. For well I know this by mine arse, which did sing it to me.' And, saying these words, went his way.

---

[59] In 1484, V.10.

[60] The word as it appears in 1484 is 'retched'. We have modernized to 'reached', assuming that he is stretching upon getting up from his bed, but it could also possibly be modernized as a version of the modern word 'retch', meaning to clear the throat and lungs by coughing or spitting.

[61] i.e., began to say to himself

[62] i.e., dropped, not necessarily on purpose

[63] i.e., said to the tallow

[64] i.e., and furthermore

And anon after he found a great piece of bacon well salted, the which he turned and re-turned upside down. And when he had turned and re-turned it long, 'Enough,' he said, 'I deign° not to eat of this meat, because that it should cause me for to drink too much, for it is too salty. And as mine arse sang to me last I shall eat this same day better and more delicious meat.'

And then he began to walk farther, and as he entered into a fair meadow, he saw a mare and her young foal° with her, and said to himself alone, 'I render thanks and graces to the gods of the goods[65] that they send me, for well I wist° and was certain that this day I should find some precious meat.' And then he came nigh the mare and said to her, 'Certainly, my sister, I shall eat thy child.' And the mare answered to him, 'My brother, do whatsomever it shall please thee. But first I pray thee that one pleasure thou wilt do to me. I have heard say that thou art a good chirurgeon.° Wherefore I pray thee that thou wilt heal me of my foot.[66] I say to thee, my good brother, that yesterday as I went within the forest, a thorn entered into one of my feet behind,[67] the which grieveth me sore. I pray thee that or° thou eat my foal, thou wilt draw and have it out of my foot.' And the wolf answered to the mare, 'that shall I do gladly, my good sister. Show me thy foot.' And as the mare showed her foot to the wolf, she gave to the wolf such a stroke betwixt both his eyne°[68] that all his head was astonied° and fell down to the ground.[69] And by the same occasion was her foal or colt saved. And a long space[70] was the wolf lying upon the earth as dead. And when he was come to himself again, and that he could speak, he said, 'I care not for this mishap. For well I wot° that yet this day I shall eat and be filled of delicious meat,' and in saying these words, lifted himself up and went away.

And when he had walked and gone a while, he found two rams within a meadow which with their horns launched° each other. And the wolf said in himself, 'Blessed be God that now I shall be well fed.' He then came nigh the two rams, and said, 'Certainly I shall eat the one of

---

[65] i.e., for the goods
[66] i.e., heal my foot
[67] i.e., one of my hind or back feet
[68] a form of the plural 'eyes' common in Middle English
[69] i.e., he fell down to the ground
[70] i.e., a long time

you two.' And one of them said to him, 'My lord, do all that it please you. But first ye must give to us the sentence° of a process° of a plea which is betwixt us both.'[71] And the wolf answered that with right a good will he would do it, and after said to them, 'My lords, tell me your reasons and case, to the end that the better I may give the sentence of your different° and question.'[72] And then one of them began to say, 'My lord, this meadow was belonging to our father. And because that he died without making any ordinance° or testament, we be now in debate° and strife for the parting of it. Wherefore we pray thee that thou vouchsafe° to accord° our different so that peace be made between us.'

And then the wolf demanded of the rams how their question might be accorded.° 'Right well,' said one of them, 'by one manner which I shall tell to thee, if it please to thee to hear me. We two shall be at the two ends of this meadow, and thou shalt be in the mids of it. And fro the end of the meadow, we both at once shall run toward thee. And he that first shall come to thee shall be lord of the meadow. And the last shall be thine.' 'Well then,' said the wolf, 'thine advice is good and well purposed. Let see now who first shall come to me.' Then went the two rams to the two ends of the meadow, and both at once began to run toward the wolf, and with all their might came and gave to him such two strokes both at once against both his sides that almost they broke his heart within his belly.[73] And there fell down the poor wolf all aswooned,° and the rams went their way. And when he was come again to himself,[74] he took courage and departed, saying thus to himself: 'I care not for all this injury and shame. For as mine arse did sing to me, yet shall I this day eat some good and delicious meat.'

He had not long walked when he found a sow and her small pigs with her. And, incontinent° as he saw her, he said, 'Blessed be God of that I shall this day eat and fill my belly with precious meats, and shall have good fortune.' And in that saying, approached to the sow and said to her, 'My sister, I must eat some of thy young pigs.' And the

---

[71] The rams ask the wolf to serve as a judge to settle a legal dispute between the two of them.
[72] The wolf asks the rams to make their individual cases so that he may better resolve their difference or dispute.
[73] i.e., broke his heart within his chest
[74] i.e., when he had recovered himself or regained consciousness

sow went and said to him, 'My lord, I am content of all that which pleaseth to you. But or ye eat them, I pray you that they may be baptized and made clean in pure and fair water.'[75] And the wolf said to the sow, 'Show me then the water, and I shall wash and baptize them well.' And then the sow went and led him at a stank° or pond where as was[76] a fair mill. And as the wolf was upon the little bridge of the said mill, and that he would have taken one pig, the sow threw the wolf into the water with her head, and for the swiftness of the water, he must needs° pass[77] under the wheel of the mill. And God wot if the wings of the mill beat him well or not. And as soon as he might, he ran away, and as he ran, said to himself, 'I care not for so little a shame, ne therefore I shall not be let,° but that I shall yet this day eat my belly full of meats delicious, as mine arse did sing it early to me.'

And as he passed through the street, he saw some sheep. And as the sheep saw him, they entered into a stable. And when the wolf came there, he said to them in this manner: 'God keep you my sisters, I must eat one of you, to the end that I may be filled and rassasied° of my great hunger.' And then one of them said to him, 'Certainly, my lord, ye are welcome to pass. For we be come hither for to hold a great solemnity,° wherefore we all pray you that ye pontifically° will sing. And after the service is complete and done, do what ye will° of the one of us.' And then the wolf for vainglory,° feigning to be a prelate,° began to sing and to howl before the sheep. And when the men of the town heard the voice of the wolf, they came to the stable with great staves° and with great dogs, and wonderly they wounded the wolf, and almost brought him to death, that with great pain he could go.[78]

Nevertheless, he scaped° and went under a great tree, upon the which tree was a man which hewed off the boughs of the tree. The wolf then began to sigh sore, and to make great sorrow of his evil fortune, and said, 'Ha, Jupiter, how many evils have I had and suffered this day. But well I presume and know that it is by me, and by mine own cause,

---

[75] The sow is pretending to accept the death of her babies, but asks that they first be baptized so that they can go to heaven when they die.
[76] i.e., where there was
[77] i.e., he had no choice but to pass
[78] i.e., only with great pain could he manage to walk

and by my proud thought. For the day in the morning I found a sack full of tallow, the which I deigned not but only smell it.[79] And after I found a great piece of bacon, the which I would never eat for dread of great thirst and for my foolish thought. And therefore, if evil is sin° happed to me,[80] it is well bestowed and employed. 'My father was never medicine ne leech, and also I have not studied and learned in the science° of medicine or physic;° therefore if it happeth evil to me when I would draw the thorn out of the mare's foot, it is well employed. *Item*,°[81] my father was never neither patriarch° ne bishop, and also I was never lettered,° and yet I presumed and took on me for to sacrifice and to sing before the gods, feigning myself to be a prelate. But after my desert° I was well rewarded. *Item*, my father was no legist,° ne never knew the laws, ne also man of justice, and to give sentence of a plea I would entermete° me, and feigned myself great justicer.° But I knew neither *a* ne *b*.[82] And if therefore evil is come to me, it is of me[83] as of right it should be. O Jupiter, I am worthy of greater punition° when I have offended° in so many manners. Send thou now to me from thine high throne a sword or other weapon wherewith I may strongly punish and beat me by great penance. For well worthy I am to receive a greater discipline.'

And the good man which was upon the tree hearkened° all these words and devices° and said no word. And when the wolf had finished all his sighs and complaints, the good man took his axe wherewith he had cut away the dead branches fro the tree and cast it upon the wolf, and it fell upon his neck in such manner that the wolf turned upside down, the feet upward, and lay as he had been dead. And when the wolf might relieve and dress himself,[84] he looked and beheld upward to the heaven, and began thus to cry: 'Ha, Jupiter, I see now well that thou hast heard and enhanced° my prayer.' And then he perceived the man which was upon the tree, and well weened that he had been Jupiter.

---

[79] i.e., I deigned only to smell it
[80] i.e., if bad things have since happened to me
[81] The Latin word *Item* [also] was often used roughly as we use bullet points today, to mark individual items on a list.
[82] i.e., I didn't know my ABCs
[83] i.e., it is proper to me, belonging to me; I deserve it
[84] i.e., when the wolf was able to collect himself and stand up

And then with all his might he fled toward the forest sore wounded and rendered himself to humility. And more meek and humble he was afterward than ever before he had been fierce ne proud. And by this fable men may know and see that much resteth to be done of that that a fool thinketh.[85] And it showeth to us that when some good cometh to some it ought not be refused, for it may not be recovered as men will. And also it showeth how no one ought to avaunt° him[86] to do a thing which he cannot do, but therefore every man ought to govern and rule himself after his estate and faculty.°

---

[85] A slightly perplexing phrase, probably meaning either: much remains to be done from what a fool thinks (a fool's thought seldom translates into real action, leaving more action to be done); or, much ceases to be done from that which a fool thinks (a fool's thought does not translate into productive action).

[86] i.e., avaunt himself, advance himself, put himself forward

12. Of the Envious Dog[87]

No one ought not to have envy[88] of the good of other, as it appeareth by this fable of a dog which was envious and that sometime was within a stable of oxen, the which was full of hay. This dog kept the oxen that they should not enter into their stable and that they should not eat of the said hay. And then the oxen said to him, 'Thou art well perverse and evil to have envy of the good the which is to us needful and profitable. And thou hast of it nought to do, for thy kind is not to eat no hay.'[89] And thus he did of a great bone,[90] the which he held at his mouth, and would not leave it because and for envy of another dog which was thereby. And therefore keep thee well fro the company or fellowship of an envious body, for to have to do with him it is much perilous and difficile,[91] as to us is well shown by Lucifer.[92]

---

[87] In 1484, V.11. This is the proverbial 'dog in the manger' fable that serves as the dominant trope of Lope de Vega's 1618 play *El perro del hortelano* (*The Dog in the Manger*) about a jealous person.

[88] i.e., no one ought to be envious

[89] This hay should not concern you; by kind or nature, you are not even capable of eating hay.

[90] i.e., thus (likewise) he (the dog) did with a great bone (namely, kept it from another). This additional example somewhat detracts from the usual purpose of this fable, which is about being envious of others even for things they have that you are not capable of enjoying.

[91] This is a clear example of Caxton's occasional use of French words as if they are English. Because he treats these words as continuous in his prose, we have not italicized them.

[92] Lucifer or Satan's envy of God's power caused the downfall not only of himself but also of his co-conspirators, according to biblical stories.

13. Of Phoebus, of the Avaricious,° and of the Envious[93]

No one ought to do harm or damage to some other for to receive or do his own damage, as it appeareth by this fable of Jupiter, which sent Phoebus into the Earth for to have all the knowledge of the thought of men. This Phoebus then met with two men, of which the one was much envious, and the other right covetous. Phoebus demanded of them what their thought was. 'We think,' said they, 'to demand and ask of thee great gifts.' To the which Phoebus answered, 'Now demand what ye will. For all that that ye shall demand of me, I shall grant it. And of that that the first of you shall ask, the second shall have the double part, or as much more again.' And then the avaricious said, 'I will that my fellow ask what he will first,' whereof the envious was well content, which said to Phoebus, 'Fair sir, I pray thee that I may lose one of mine eyne, to the end that my fellow may lose all both his eyne.'[94] Wherefore Phoebus began to laugh, which departed and went again unto Jupiter and told him the great malice of the envious, which was joyful and glad of the harm and damage of another, and how he was well content to suffer pain for to have a-damaged some other.

---

[93] In 1484, VI.17, from the fables of Avianus. Phoebus was a Greek and Roman god (also called Apollo), variously identified as the god of music or poetry, the sun, healing, and more.

[94] i.e., may lose both his eyes. The redundancy here drives home that the envious man wishes the avaricious man to lose all his eyesight.

14. Of the Disciple and of the Sheep[95]

A disciple was sometime[96] which took his pleasure to rehearse and tell many fables, the which prayed to his master that he would rehearse unto him a long fable. To whom the master answered, 'Keep and beware well that it hap not to us as it happed to a king and to his fabulator.'° And the disciple answered, 'My master, I pray thee to tell to me how it befell.' And then the master said to his disciple, 'Sometime was a king which had a fabulator, the which rehearsed to him, at every time that he would sleep, five fables for to rejoice the king and for to make him fall into a sleep. It befell then on a day that the king was much sorrowful and so heavy that he could in no wise fall asleep. And after that the said fabulator had told and rehearsed his five fables, the king desired to hear more. And then the said fabulator recited unto him three fables well short. And the king then said to him, 'I would fain° hear one well long, and then shall I leve° well the sleep.'[97]

The fabulator then rehearsed unto him such a fable of a rich man which went to the market or fair for to buy sheep. The which man bought a thousand sheep. And as he was returning fro the fair he came

---

[95] In 1484, VII.8, from the fables of Petrus Alphonsus.
[96] i.e., once upon a time there was a disciple
[97] 'Leve' here either means allow (after one more fable, I will allow sleep) or believe (I will believe it possible for me to sleep).

unto a river, and because of the great waws° of the water he could not pass over the bridge. Nevertheless, he went so long to and fro on the rivage° of the said river that at the last he found a narrow way,° upon the which might pass scant enough three sheep at once. And thus he passed and had them over one after another. And hitherto rehearsed of this fable,[98] the fabulator fell on sleep. And anon after, the king awoke the fabulator, and said to him in this manner: 'I pray thee that thou wilt make an end of thy fable.' And the fabulator answered to him in this manner: 'Sire, this river is right great, and the ship is little, wherefore late the merchant do pass over his sheep.[99] And after I shall make an end of my fable.' And then was the king well appeased and pacified. And therefore be thou content of that I have rehearsed unto thee. For there is folk so superstitious or capax° that they may not be contented with few words.

---

[98] i.e., and having recited this fable
[99] i.e., The river is wide, and the ship small, where lately the merchant brought his sheep across the river.

15. Of an Old Harlot° or Bawd[100]

A noble man was sometime[101] which had a wife who was much chaste[102] and was wonder° fair. This noble man would have gone on pilgrimage to Rome and left his wife at home because that he knew her for a chaste and a good woman. It happed on a day, as she went into the town, a fair young man was esprised° of her love, and took on him hardiness,° and required her of love, and promised to her many great gifts. But she which was good had liefer° die than to consent her[103] thereto, wherefore the young man died almost for sorrow. To the which fellow came an old woman, which demanded of him the cause of his sickness. And the young man manifested or discovered unto her all his courage° and heart, asking help and counsel of her. And the old woman, wily and malicious, said to him, 'Be thou glad and joyous, and take good courage, for well I shall do and bring about thy fate, insomuch that thou shalt have thy will fulfilled.'

---

[100] In 1484, VII.11, from the fables of Petrus Alphonsus. The plot of this fable corresponds to that of Fernando de Rojas' fifteenth-century tragicomedy *La Celestina*, which famously features an old bawd as the title character. English versions of this story include *Dame Sirith* (late thirteenth century), John Rastell's interlude *Calisto and Melebea* (c. 1530), and James Mabbe's translation of *La Celestina*, *The Spanish Bawd* (1631).
[101] i.e., once upon a time there was a noble man
[102] A chaste wife was chaste within marriage, or faithful.
[103] i.e., herself

And after this the old bawd went to her house and made a little cat which she had at home to fast three days one after another. And after she took some bread with a great deal or quantity of mustard upon it and gave it to this young cat for to eat it. And when the cat smelled it she began to weep and cry. And the old woman or bawd went unto the house of the said young woman, and bore her little cat with her. The which young and good woman received and welcomed her much honestly, because that all the world held her for a holy woman. And as they were talking together, the young woman had pity of the cat which wept, and demanded of the old woman what the cat ailed.[104] And the old woman said to her, 'Ha a, my fair daughter and my fair friend, renew not my sorrow!' And, saying these words, she began to weep, and said, 'My friend, for no good I will tell the cause why my cat weepeth.'[105] And then the young woman said to her, 'My good mother, I pray you that ye will tell me the cause why and wherefore your cat weepeth.' And then the old woman said to her, 'My friend, I will well, if thou wilt swear that thou shalt never rehearse it to nobody.' To the which promise the good and true young woman accorded herself, supposing that it had been all good, and said, 'I will well.'

And then the old woman said to her in this manner: 'My friend, this same cat which thou seest yonder was my daughter, the which was wonder fair, gracious, and chaste, which a young man loved much, and was so much esprised of her love that because that she refused him he died for her love. Wherefore the gods, having pity on him, have turned my daughter into this cat.' And the young woman, which supposed that the old woman had said truth, said to her in this manner: 'Alas, my fair mother, I ne wot what I shall do. For such a case might well hap to me. For in this town is a young man, which dieth almost for the love of me. But for love of my husband, to whom I ought to keep chastity, I have not will to grant him.[106] Nevertheless, I shall do

---

[104] i.e., what ailed the cat, what was wrong with the cat

[105] i.e., I won't tell you why my cat is weeping for anything you might give me.

[106] 1484 reads for this phrase, 'I haue not wylle graunte hym.' We have emended the statement to read, 'I have not will to grant him', that is, I do not desire (I do not will) to grant him what he is asking, or, I do not have the power/ability (free will, since I'm married) to grant him what he is asking. Another possible emendation would have been, 'I have not *nor* will grant him', that is, I have not granted his request, nor will I. While the 1497 Pynson edition repeats the confusing phrase, Pynson's 1500 edition changes it to 'I haue nat graunted hym' (*In tyme whenne beestes coude speke*

that that thou shalt counsel to me.' And then the old woman said to her, 'My friend, have thou pity on him as soon as thou mayest so that it befall not to thee like as it did to my daughter.' The young woman then answered to her, and said, 'If he require me any more, I shall accord me with him.¹⁰⁷ And if he require me no more, yet shall I proffer° me to him. And to the end that I offend not the gods, I shall do and accomplish it as soon as I may.' The old woman then took leave of her, and went forthwith° to the young man. And to him she rehearsed and told all these tidings,° whereof his heart was filled with joy. The which anon went toward the young woman, and with her he fulfilled his will. And thus ye may know the evils which be done by bawds and old harlots — that would to God that they were all burnt.¹⁰⁸

---

the wolues made warre againest the sheepe [...] [London: Richard Pynson, 1500], sig. R4r). Julien Macho, Caxton's source, reads, *mais pour l'amour de mon mary et de chasteté, i'aymeroye mieulx morir* [but for love of my husband, and of chastity, I would better like to die] (Macho, *Esope. Eingeleitet und herausgegeben nach der Edition von 1486 von Beate Hecker* [Hamburg: Romanisches Seminar der Universitat Hamburg, 1982], p. 256).

[107] i.e., I shall come to an agreement with him.
[108] Thus you know how evil bawds may be — if only they were all burnt.

16. Of a Blind Man and of his Wife[109]

There was sometime[110] a blind man which had a fair wife, of the which he was much jealous. He kept her so that she might not go nowhere,[111] for ever he had her by the hand. And after that she was enamoured of a gentle° fellow, they could not find the manner ne no place for to fulfill their will. But notwithstanding, the woman, which was subtle and ingenious, counselled to her friend that he should come into her house and that he should enter into the garden, and that there he should climb upon a pear tree. And he did as she told him.

And when they had made their enterprise,° the woman came again into the house and said to her husband, 'My friend, I pray you that ye will go into our garden for to disport us a little while there.' Of the which prayer the blind man was well content, and said to his wife, 'Well, my good friend, I will well. Let us go thither.' And as they were under the pear tree, she said to her husband, 'My friend, I pray thee to let me go upon the pear tree, and I shall gather for us both some fair pears.' 'Well, my friend,' said the blind man, 'I will well and grant thereto.' And when she was upon the tree, the young man began to shake the pear tree at one side, and the young woman at the other

---

[109] In 1484, VII.12, from the fables of Petrus Alphonsus. The plot of this fable corresponds roughly to Chaucer's *Merchant's Tale* in his *Canterbury Tales*.
[110] i.e., once upon a time there was
[111] i.e., that she might not go anywhere

side. And as the blind man heard them thus hard shake the pear tree, and the noise which they made, he said to them, 'Ha a, evil woman, howbeit that I see it not, nevertheless I feel and understand it well. But I pray to the gods that they vouchsafe to send me my sight again.' And as soon as he had made his prayer, Jupiter rendered to him his sight again. And when he saw that pageant° upon the pear tree, he said to his wife, 'Ha, unhappy woman! I shall never have no joy with thee.'

And because that the young woman was ready in speech and malicious, she answered forthwith to her husband, 'My friend, thou art well beholden° and bound to me, for by cause and for the love, the gods have restored to thee thy sight, whereof I thank all the gods and goddesses which have enhanced and heard my prayer.[112] For I, desiring much that thou might see me, ceased never day ne night to pray them that they would render to thee thy sight. Wherefore the goddess Venus visibly showed herself to me and said that if I would do some pleasure to the said young man, she should restore to thee thy sight. And thus I am cause of it.' And then the good man said to her, 'My right dear wife and good friend, I remercy° and thank you greatly, for right ye have and I great wrong.'

---

[112] i.e., with reason and for love they restored your sight — and you have me to thank!

17. Of the Recitation of Some Monsters[113]

Poge of Florence reciteth how in his time one named Hugh, prince of the medicines,[114] saw a cat which had two heads, and a calf which also had two heads, and his legs both before and behind were double, as they had been joined all together, as many folk saw.

Item,[115] about the marshes of Italy within a meadow was sometime a cow, the which cow made and delivered her of a serpent of wonder and right marvellous greatness, right hideous and ferdful.° For first, he had the head greater than the head of a calf. Secondly, he had a neck of the length of an ass, and his body made after the likeness of a dog, and his tail was wonder great, thick, and long, without comparison to any other. And when the cow saw that she had made such a birth, and that within her belly she had borne so right horrible

---

[113] In 1484, VIII.5, from the *Facetiae* (1470), a jest-book by Poggio Bracciolini.

[114] This appears to be a reference to Ugo Benzi or Hugh of Sienna, whom Poggio Bracciolini called *Medicorum nostri temporis princeps* [the most eminent doctor of our time] in his *Facetiae* 32 (p. 60). The 'monster' descriptions in this fable are mainly taken from the *Facetiae*: *Facetiae* 32 tells of the two-headed cat; *Facetiae* 33 tells of the two-headed calf; *Facetiae* 31 tells of the cow that gives birth to a snake; and *Facetiae* 34 tells of the sea-monster. For a modern English translation of this Latin text, see *The Facetiae or Jocose Tales of Poggio, now first translated into English with the Latin text, in two volumes* (Paris: Isidore Liseux, 1879).

[115] As above, Caxton uses the Latin word *Item* [also] to mark individual items on a list.

a beast, she was all ferdful, and lifted herself up, and supposed to have fled away. But the serpent with his wonder long tail enlaced° her two hinder° legs, and the serpent then began to suck the cow, and indeed so much and so long he sucked, till° that he found some milk. And when the cow might escape fro him, she fled unto the other kine.° And incontinent her paps° and her behinder° legs and all that the serpent touched was all black a great space of time. And soon after the said cow made a fair calf, the which marvel was announced or said to the said Poge,[116] he being at Ferrara.[117]

And yet again, soon after that, there was found within a great river a monster marine, or of the sea, of the form or likeness which followeth: First, he had from the navel upward the similitude or likeness of a man. And fro the navel downward, he had the form or making of a fish, the which part was jumelle,° that is, to wit, double. Secondly, he had a great beard and he had two wonder great horns above his ears. Also, he had great paps, and a wonder great and horrible mouth, and his hands reached unto his entrails or bowels. And at the both his elbows he had wings right broad and great of fish's mails,° wherewith he swam, and only he had but the head out of the water. It happed then, as many women bucked° and washed at the port or haven° of the said river, that this horrible and ferdful beast was for lack and default° of meat come swimming toward the said women, of the which he took one by the hand, and supposed to have drawn her into the water. But she was strong, and well advised,° and resisted against the said monster. And as she defended herself, she began to cry with a high voice, 'Help, help!' To the which came running five women, which by hurling and drawing° of stones killed and slew° the said monster. For he was come too far within the sound,° wherefore he might not return into the deep water. And after, when he rendered his spirit, he made a right little cry, saying that he was so disformed° and so much cruel, for he was of great corpulence,° more than any man's body.

---

[116] In 1484, the printer here made the typo 'Pope' for 'Poge'. In the copy of 1484 now held at the British Library, the word 'Pope' was violently scratched out, perhaps by a later, sixteenth- or seventeenth-century reader, in the wake of the Protestant Reformation. We have emended to 'Poge', for Poggio Bracciolini, the author of this fable (as he is called at the beginning of the fable).

[117] Ferrara is a city (and municipality) in northern Italy.

And yet sayeth Poge in this manner: that he, being at Ferrara, he saw the said monster, and sayeth yet that the young children were customed for to go bathe and wash them within the said river, but they came not all again. Wherefore the women washed ne bucked no more their clothes at the said port. For the folk presumed and supposed that the monster killed the young children which were drowned.

Item also, within a little while after it befell about the marshes of Italy that there was a child of form human[118] which had two heads and two visages or faces beholding one upon the other, and the arms of each other embraced the body, the which body fro the navel upward was joined save the two heads, and from the navel downward the limbs were all separed° one fro other in such wise that the limbs of generation were showed manifestly. Of the which child the tidings came unto the person of the Pope[119] of Rome.

---

[118] i.e., a child of human form

[119] This is another instance in which the word 'Pope' has been violently scratched out in the copy of 1484 held at the British Library. In this case, there is no typo. The fable refers to the Pope of Rome, the head of the Catholic Church: even the Pope heard of this monster!

RICHARD SMITH

from *The Fabulous Tales of Aesop the Phrygian, Compiled Most Eloquently in Scottish Metre by Master Robert Henryson, and Now Lately Englished* (1577)

The Book's Passport[1]

That man ne'er wrote
    Whose write° pleased all men's minds,
Nor I as now
    Think no such place to find;
5 For find fault he
    Himself that no good can,°
By slanderous tongue
    Doth hinder many a man,
Which else would write
10   To many a one's content;[2]
But bayard I
    Care not for being shent.°[3]

Go, therefore, book,
    To each man's eye to view:
15 To wise and sad,°
    And all the carping° crew.
The wisest sort
    Will well accept my skill;
Sir Momus' mates
20   Take all good things as ill.[4]
And he that likes not
    This as I do say,
Here is the door,
    And there forth right the way.°[5]

        FINIS°

---

[1] This prefatory poem has been added by Smith to the fables of Henryson. The poem, an envoi addressed directly to the book that follows, imitates models such as the end of Geoffrey Chaucer's *Troilus and Criseyde*: 'Go, litel bok, go, litel myn tragedye' (see *The Riverside Chaucer*, ed. by Benson, V.1786).

[2] i.e., For he finds fault who himself is not capable of doing good; [and he] who attacks other men with slanders prevents them from writing what could have made others happy.

[3] A bayard is a proverbial figure for someone blind to the light of knowledge, and self-confident in their ignorance. We emended 1577's 'cares' to 'care' assuming that 'I' was the grammatical antecedent; we understand this phrase to be saying something like, 'But I, blind with self-confidence, don't worry about being disgraced [by those with foul tongues].'

[4] Momus was the personification of satire and mockery; thanks to an Aesopian fable in which Momus judges different species and finds them all wanting, his name was used as shorthand for someone who goes out of their way to find faults.

[5] i.e., If you don't like it, please see yourself out the door.

Epistle[6]

To his worshipful and especial good friend Master Richard Stonley, Esquire, one of the four tellers of the Queen Majesty's receipt of the Exchequer, and Receiver of the first fruits and tenths to her Majesty.[7] R.S.[8] wisheth increase of worship to the glory of God.

Worshipful Sir, calling to my mind that great good will that you have borne° unto me and mine since the time of my first acquaintance with you, except I should be too forgetful and ungrateful, I must remember you, and be as thankful as my poor ability will serve. But the worm of good will still gnawing my mind thereto at last, all dainty meats° and viands° set aside, which are common remembrances, yet vain and soon forgot but while they are a-eating, there came unto my hand a Scottish pamphlet of the *Fabulous° Tales of Esope*,[9] a work, sir, as I think, in that language wherein it was written very eloquent and full of great invention. And no doubt you shall find some smatch° thereof, although very rudely° I have obscured the author, and having two years since turned it into English, I have kept it unpublished, hoping some else[10] of greater skill would not have let it lie dead. But whether most men have that nation[11] in derision for their hollow hearts and ungrateful minds to this country always had (a people very subject to that infection), or, thinking scorn of the author or first inventor,[12] let it pass as frivolous and vain matter, yet in my conceit there is learning

---

[6] This prefatory epistle has been added by Smith to the fables of Henryson. The title 'Epistle' is our editorial addition.

[7] Richard Stonley collected and managed royal revenue for Queen Elizabeth from 1554–1598. During this time, he also engaged in his own personal financial activities that sometimes involved the crown's revenue and eventually landed him in debtors' prison, where he seems to have remained until his death. He is most well known for his diary, where he details, among other activities, his avid book collecting and reading practices. See Felicity Heal, 'Stonley, Richard (1520/21–1600)', in *Oxford Dictionary of National Biography* (Oxford: Oxford University Press, 2016) <http://dx.doi.org/10.1093/ref:odnb/109639>.

[8] i.e., Richard Smith, the author of the epistle.

[9] Though we have normalized the spelling of the fabulist as 'Aesop' elsewhere in the volume, we have maintained 1577's spelling here, as it corresponds to the spelling in the text Smith was translating, Robert Henryson's *Morall Fabillis of Esope the Phrygian, Compylit in Eloquent, and Ornate Scottis Meter, be Maister Robert Henrisone* (hereafter 1570 or 1571).

[10] i.e., someone else

[11] i.e., Scotland

[12] i.e., Aesop

for all sorts of people worthy the memory. Therefore, knowing not how by any means to let you understand my good will toward you but° by this means, at last, putting all fear aside, I boldly present this unto your worship, hoping that at vacant time when other matters of great importance be laid aside, that you will not deign° to recreate° your mind with this trifle,° where you shall find doctrine both pleasant and profitable, and hoping as oft as you look on this book, you will think on me. Accept this poor Persian water or Jew's mite,[13] which in so doing[14] I care not for all the scoffers and taunters, which will do nought themselves nor suffer others to do that may pleasure or profit the posterity. I crave° of God to increase you with worldly worship to his pleasure.

                Yours at commandment,
                Richard Smith

---

[13] i.e., a small offering whose value comes from its good intentions. In Plutarch's life of Artaxerxes, V.1, we are told, 'Once when he was on a journey and various people were presenting him with various things, a labouring man, who could find nothing else at the moment, ran to the river, and, taking some water in his hands, offered it to him; at which Artaxerxes was so pleased that he sent him a goblet of gold and a thousand darics' (Plutarch, *Plutarch's Lives*, trans. by Bernadotte Perrin [Cambridge, MA: Harvard University Press, 1954], p. 135). In Mark 12:41–44, a widow deposits only a small amount of money, and Jesus says, 'Truly I tell you, this poor widow has put in more than all those who are contributing to the treasury. For all of them have contributed out of their abundance; but she out of her poverty has put in everything she had, all she had to live on' (NRSV, Mark 12:43–44). We are grateful to the reviewer of our manuscript for helping us track down these references.

[14] i.e., if you do so

RICHARD SMITH

The Argument between Aesop and the Translator[15]

Late passing thorough° Paul's Churchyard,[16]
    Aside I cast° mine° eye,
And ere° I wist,° to me appeared
    Sir Aesop by and by,[17]

5 Apparellèd both brave and fine,
    After the Scottish guise.°
I stood then still with ardent eyne;°[18]
    I viewed him twice or thrice.

'Behold,' quoth° he, 'now am I here,
10   And fain° would meet someone
To speak English that would me lere.'°
    With that quoth I anon,°

'Why, English, sir, you speak right° well,
    What more would you require?'
15 'Yea,° that's in prose: my tales to tell
    In verse I do desire.'

'Alas, I am not for your turn;°
    Ye must repair° unto
The Inns of Court and Chancery,
20   Where learnèd have to do.[19]

---

[15] This prefatory poem has been added by Smith to the fables of Henryson. In the original printing (1577) of this poem, Smith uses different types to distinguish between Aesop's speech and the translator's speech (see section II of the introduction to this volume). Aesop's speech appears in Roman type, and the translator's appears in black letter. We have chosen to mark out all speech with punctuation instead of typography.

[16] Paul's Churchyard was one of the primary sites of the London book trade. When Aesop laments the fact that 'They do not care for Scottish books' in line 41, he is referring to book consumers who will not even cast a glance at Scottish books, thus giving the translator a reason to 'English' Henryson's translation of Aesop's fables.

[17] i.e., after a while

[18] We have deliberately kept this archaic plural 'eyne' [eyes] to maintain the rhyme. We retain 'eyne' throughout for consistency.

[19] The Inns of Court were places where barristers learned and resided; the Inns of Chancery contained offices and accommodation for solicitors. The Inns of Court and Chancery were therefore the centre of legal activity; in this case, they should be associated with great learning, and perhaps also with the learned literary culture they fostered.

'At Helicon I never came;
    The way I do not know
(God Pan his servant, sir, I am,
    And duty to him owe).[20]

25 'On oaten pipe we still do play;
    That's all that he teach can;
Of other lore he takes no way,
    This groutnoll° rustic Pan.

'Minerva's imps° they Orpheus keep;[21]
30   In music they delight,
To serve your turn before they sleep,
    In verse to make you dite°

'Your fables wise and eloquent,
    With phrases feat° and fine,
35 Enduèd with Apollo gent,°[22]
    That passeth Muse of mine.'

'Content yourself,' quoth Aesop then,[23]
    'Do thus much once for me:
To learn° me verse so as ye can,
40   Myself as plain as ye.

'They[24] do not care for Scottish books,
    They list° not look that way;
But if they would but cast their looks
    Sometime° when they do play,

---

[20] Pan was a Greek god of nature, shepherds, and rustic music. Smith is establishing a contrast between the muses of Mount Helicon (associated here with the Inns and with learning), and the simple, rustic Pan. Aesop, the translator modestly argues, should find a better and more learned translator.

[21] Minerva was the Roman goddess of wisdom; the translator again modestly argues that the sweet music of the mythological figure and famous musician Orpheus would better fit the learning of Minerva (the level, implicitly, that Aesop achieves) than would the rustic 'oaten pipe' of Pan, the translator's comparatively lowly muse.

[22] i.e., putting on the clothes of Apollo, god of poetry, or clothed with Apollo's abilities

[23] The word 'then' is spelled 'than' in Smith's translation; in modernizing we have turned a true rhyme into a slant rhyme. There are many other instances in this text where our modernization has altered a more perfect rhyme from 1577; readers should generally assume that imperfect rhymes are a result of the modernization process.

[24] i.e., English book buyers, especially those passing through St Paul's Churchyard

45 'Somewhat° to see perhaps they might
      That then would like them well,
To teach them tread their way aright,°
      To bliss, from pains of Hell.'

'Farewell, good Phrygian poet,[25] now;
50   I may no more sojourn.'
'If not,' sayeth Aesop, 'then adieu,
      Int' Scotland I'll return.'

'Nay, rather will I venture hard
      And bring your mind to pass,
55 If that I gain to my reward
      King Midas' ears of ass,[26]

'And have a thousand ill reports
      Still tumbling down on me,
Than this to want° unto all sorts
60   And view of every eye.'[27]

Therefore have here, good reader, now,
      My rural skilless skill;
I ask no more but this of you:
      One inch of your good will,
65 Which it to grant as I do crave,
      That's even as much as I would have.

FINIS[28]

---

[25] i.e., Aesop

[26] Apollo gave Midas the ears of an ass for being a bad judge of poetry when Midas ruled against him in a poetry contest.

[27] i.e., I'd rather work to bring your intentions to pass, even if people think I am a fool and say bad things about me, than have this text 'wanting' or lacking, so that no one had a chance to see it.

[28] We have added 'FINIS' at the end of this poem to match other prefatory material.

His Verdict on his Labour[29]

Orpheus once did walk abroad
    'Mong fragrant flowers t'increase his glee,°
To set his harp in one accord,°
    In tune to make his strings agree,
5 Whereby was heard such pleasant sound,
    That all the woods thereof rebound.°

And playing thus in pleasant shade,
    Wild beasts and men to him did come;
With music straight° them stones he made,
10   His gift was such, them to transform;
He fell asleep, and or° he woke,
    In hand a while his harp I took.

This Scottish Orpheus[30] I mean,
    That Aesop's tales hath made to gree°
15 In rhetoric both trim° and clean,°
    That all my wits bereft hath he;
His harp, alas, I make to jar,°
    And both his name and mine do mar.
But since I made them disagree,
20   Leave me the blame, the laurel he.[31]

FINIS

---

[29] This prefatory poem has been added by Smith to the fables of Henryson.
[30] i.e., Henryson
[31] i.e., But since I have made Aesop and Henryson disagree (by taking Henryson's good verse and making it discordant through my Englishing), assign blame to me, and give laurels to Henryson.

RICHARD SMITH

The Argument or Prologue[32]

Though feignèd fables of ancient poetry
Be not all grounded upon truth (what then?),
Their politic terms in sweet rhetory°
Right pleasant are unto the ear of man,
5 And eke° the cause that they first began
Was to reprove the whole° misliving°
Of man, by figure of some other thing.

In like manner thorough the boisterous° earth
(So it be laboured with great diligence)
10 Spring flowers and corn° to our great mirth,
Wholesome and good to man's sustenance.
So doth spring some moral sweet sentence°
Out of the subtle dite°[33] of poetry —
To good purpose, who can it well apply.

15 The nut's shell, though it be hard and tough,
Holds the kernel which is most delectable.
(So lies their doctrine wise enough,
And full of fruit, under a feignèd fable.)
And wise men say it is right profitable
20 Amongst earnest to mingle merry sport,
To recreate the sprite,° and make the time be short.

Further, the bow that is ay° bent
Seems unsmart°[34] and dull on the string;
So doth the mind that is ay diligent
25 In earnest thoughts and great studying;
With sad matters some merriness to ming°

---

[32] This is Henryson's prologue and is the beginning of the text of Henryson's fables, as translated by Smith.

[33] The word 'dite' here means something indited or composed and put in writing, or a composition or piece of writing; after 1500, this word is a Scots form. This is one of many relics of Scots, a variety of English used in Scotland, especially in the Lowlands (*OED*), that survived Smith's Englishing. We note other such relics in later notes.

[34] The *OED* records Henryson's fables as the first instance of this word, meaning the opposite of smart; the lesson is that if you always keep your bow bent, it will become ineffective.

Accordeth well; thus Aesop said iwis:°
Dulcius arrident seria picta iocis.[35]

Of this author, my masters, with your leave,
30   Submitting me to your correction,
In mother tongue, out of Latin, to prove
To make some manner of translation,
Nought° of myself for vain presumption,
But by request and precept of a lord,
35   Of whom the name I need not record.

In homely language and in terms[36] rude
I needs° must write, for why° of eloquence
Nor rhetoric I never understood.
Therefore, meekly I pray your reverence
40   If that ye find it through my negligence
To be lacking, or else superfluous,
Correct it at your wills[37] gracious.

My author in his fables tells[38] how
That brutal beasts spoke and understood,
45   And to good purpose dispute and argue,
And syllogism° propone°[39] and eke conclude,
Put in example, and in similitude,
How many men in operation
Are like to beasts in condition.

50   No marvel, then, though man be like a beast,
Which loves ay carnal and foul delight,
That shame cannot him pluck back nor arrest,°
But takes all his lust and appetite,

---

[35] i.e., The presentation or portrayal of serious things more sweetly smiles than that of jesting things. Edward Wheatley notes that this is a citation of the second line of the prologue to the Romulus collection of fables translated into Latin verse (p. 152); this collection is also often referred to as Walter the Englishman's fables (p. 3).

[36] In Smith's 1577 translation, this is spelled 'termes'. In modernizing the text, we have removed the second syllable, thereby altering the metre.

[37] In the process of modernizing 1577's 'willes' to 'wills', we have altered the metre.

[38] In the process of modernizing 1577's 'telles' to 'tells', we have altered the metre.

[39] i.e., propose. The *OED* notes that this is a Scots form.

55   And that thorough custom and daily rite,
      Sin in their minds is so fast° rooted,
      That they into brutal beasts are transformèd.

      This noble clerk Aesop, as I have told,
      With great invention, as poet laureate,[40]
60   By figure wrote his book, for he nought would
      Lack the disdain of high nor low estate.°[41]
      And to begin, first of a cock he wrote,
      Seeking his meat, which found a precious stone,
      Of whom the fable ye shall hear anon.

      FINIS

---

[40] A poet laureate is distinguished for excellence and bestowed with a crown of laurels by the Muses.

[41] i.e., Aesop wrote it using figuration, literary representation or parable, so that he could give commentary on all levels of society without inviting blame. Smith confusingly seems to say that Aesop would lack nothing of the disdain — i.e., he *would* invite disdain with his parables. Manuscript versions of Henryson read 'nocht wald | Tak the disdane' [would not take disdain] (Kindrick, p. 23); 1570 reads 'nocht wald | Lak the wisedom' [would not lack the wisdome, would have wisdom]; 1571 reads 'nocht wald | Lak the disdane' [would not lack disdain, i.e., would invite disdain]; Smith seems to carry 1571's change forward without modification.

THE FABULOUS TALES OF AESOP THE PHRYGIAN

1. The Tale of the Grosshead° Chanticleer° the Cock[42] and the Precious Stone[43]

A cock sometime with feathers fresh and gay,°
Right cant° and crouse,°[44] albeit he was but poor,
Flew forth on dunghill early on a day;
To get his dinner set was all his cure.°[45]
5   Scraping the muck there, by adventure°[46]
He found a jasper° stone, right precious,
Was casten forth by sweeping of the house.

As damosels° wanton° and insolent,
That fain would play, and on the street be seen,
10   To sweeping of the house they take no tent° —
They care nothing so° the floor be clean —
Jewels are lost, as sometime hath been seen,
Upon the floor, and so swept forth anon;
Peradventure° so was this precious stone.

15   So marveling upon this stone, quoth he,
'O gentle° jasp, O rich and noble thing,
Though I thee find, yet art thou not for me;
Thou art a jewel for a lord or king.
Pity it were thou should lie in this midden,°
20   Be buried thus amongst this muck and mould,°
And thou so fair° and worth so much gold.

---

[42] Chanticleer is the name of the cock or rooster in the *Nun's Priest's Tale* in Chaucer's *Canterbury Tales*; it is also a generic name for a rooster (like Bruin the bear or Tybert the cat).
[43] In 1577, the first fable.
[44] We have modernized the word 'crowes' as 'crouse' here. The words 'cant' and 'crows' are both ways of saying sing or call out. The 1577 spelling 'crowes' suggests that Smith may have intended the verb, but syntactically this can only be the adjective 'crouse', bold, matching the adjectival form of 'cant', also meaning bold.
[45] We have punctuated this line so that it might be paraphrased as follows: 'to get his dinner set (or settled) was his entire concern.' Smith's punctuation also suggests the following possible reading: 'He flew forth to get his dinner; his intention was fixed.'
[46] i.e., by chance

RICHARD SMITH

'It is pity I should thee find, for why?⁴⁷
Thy great virtue nor yet thy colour clear,
It may me nother° extol, nor magnify,⁴⁸
25   And thou to me may make but little cheer,
To great lords though thou be lief° and dear;
I love far better things of less avail,
As draff° or corn to fill my toom° entrail.°

'I had lever° go scrape here with my nails
30   Amongst this muck, and look my life's food,
As draff, or corn, small worms, or snails,
Or any meat would do my stomach good,
Than of jasper stones a mighty multitude.
And thou again upon the same wise,°
35   For less avail thou may me now despise.

'Thou hast no corn, and thereof have I need;
Thy colour doth but comfort to the sight.
And that is not enough my womb° to feed,
For, the wise says, looking things are light.⁴⁹
40   I would have some meat, get it if I might.
For hungry men may not live on looks;
Had I dry bread, I count° not for no cooks.

'Where should thou make thy habitation?
Where should thou dwell but in a royal tower?
45   Where should thou sit but on a king's corone,°
Exalted in worship and in great honour?
Rise, gentle jasp, of all stones the flower,
Out of this dunghill, and pass where thou should be;⁵⁰
Thou cares not for me, nor I for thee.'

---

⁴⁷ In Henryson, 'for why' would be best translated as 'because'; the cock is saying, 'It is a pity I found you, because you do me no good.' However, Smith seems to misunderstand this Middle Scots phrase as a rhetorical question the cock is asking either himself or the jasp.

⁴⁸ i.e., Neither your properties nor your colour do me any good.

⁴⁹ i.e., [good-]looking things are light, or of little value. Henryson reads 'wyfis' (1570, 1571) instead of Smith's 'wise'; this is either an error on Smith's part (reading an 'f' as an 's'; the two letters look very alike in early books), or a deliberate change (changing out the knowledge of wives or women for that of wise people in general).

⁵⁰ The word 'pass', in this context, means go.

50 Leaving this jewel low upon the ground,
   To seek his meat this cock his ways[51] went.
   But when or how, or by whom it was found,
   As now I set to hold no argument.
   But of the inward sentence and intent:
55 Of this (as mine author here doth write)
   I shall rehearse° in rude and homely dite.

   This precious jasp had properties seven:
   The first, of colour it was marvelous,
   Part like the fire, and part like the heaven;
60 It makes a man stout and victorious,
   Preserves also from chances perilous.
   Who hath this stone shall have good hap to speed;[52]
   Nor fire, nor water, he needeth not to dread.°

   Morality[53]

   This gentle jasp, right different of hue,
   Betokeneth perfect prudence and cunning,
65 Ornate with many deeds of virtue,
   More excellent than any earthly thing,
   Which makes men in honour for to ring,
   Happy and stout to win° the victory,
   Of all vices and spiritual enmity.
70

   Who may be hardy, rich, and gracious?
   Who can eschew° peril and adventure?
   Who can govern a realm, city, or house
   Without science?° No man, I you assure!
   It[54] is riches that ever shall endure,
75 Which moth, nor moist, nor other rust° can fret;°
   To man's soul it is eternal meat.

---

[51] In the process of modernizing 1577's 'wayes' to 'ways', we have altered the metre.
[52] i.e., shall have good luck
[53] We have changed 1577's 'The Morall' to 'Morality' to match the other fables in Smith's translation.
[54] i.e., science; note that 'science' means wisdom or knowledge in general (a more old-fashioned meaning that Smith carries over from Henryson).

This cock desireth more the simple corn[55]
Than any jasp (may till° a fool be peer),°[56]
80 Which[57] at science makes a mock or scorn,
And no good can; as little will he lere;
His heart wambles° wise argument to hear,
As doth a sow, to whom men, for the nonce,[58]
Into her draff would throw some precious stones.

85 Who is enemy to science and cunning,
But ignorance, that understandeth nought?
Which[59] is so noble, so precious, and so digne°
That it may not with earthly thing be bought;
Well were that man of all other, that mote°
90 All his life days in perfect study spend,
To get science to keep him 'til his end.

But now (alas) that stone is lost and hid;
We seek it not, nor praise it not to find;
Have we riches, no better life we bide;°[60]
95 Of science, though the soul be bare and blind,
Of this matter to speak, it were but wind.
Therefore I cease, and will no further say.
Go seek the jasp, who will,° for there it lay.[61]

FINIS[62]

---

[55] Smith here either mis-Englishes or changes the verb 'desyrand' [desiring] (1570, 1571), making the first two lines of this stanza into an independent clause rather than a modifying phrase.

[56] The Middle Scots in Henryson is 'peir' [compared] (1570, 1571). However, Smith changes the word to 'peere' (which we have modernized as 'peer'), i.e., in this case, 'equal'. Smith's phrase can therefore be paraphrased as 'may be equal to a fool', instead of Henryson's 'may be compared to a fool'.

[57] The 'which' here refers to the cock.

[58] The phrase 'for the nonce' is a virtually meaningless filler-phrase for verse, meaning indeed.

[59] i.e., which thing (science)

[60] i.e., Even if we have money, it does not make us live a better life.

[61] In Smith's 1577 version, this is both italicized and in parentheses, signalling that it could be used as a motto separate from the rest of the fable.

[62] We have added the 'FINIS' at the end of this fable, to match the other fables in Smith's translation.

2. The Exemplative° Tale of the Lion and the Mouse, with the Author's Prologue before[63]

Prologue[64]

In mids° of June, that sweet season,
When that fair Phoebus[65] with his beams[66] bright
Had dried up the dew fro° dale° and down,°[67]
And all the land made with his beams light,
5   In a morning, betwixt midday and night,
I rose, and put all sloth and sleep aside,
And to a wood I went, alone without guide.

Sweet was the smell of flowers white and red,
The noise of birds[68] right delicious;
10 The boughs hung[69] right above my head,
The ground growing with grass gracious;
Of all pleasance°[70] that place was plenteous,
With sweet odours, and birds' harmony,
The morning mild, my mirth was more for-thy.°

15 The roses red, growing on banks, could rise,[71]
The primrose, violet, purple, and black;
To hear it was a heavenly paradise,
Such mirth the mavis° and the merle° could make;

---

[63] In 1577, the seventh fable.
[64] We have added this subtitle for clarity; this fable contains a long prologue before the tale itself.
[65] Phoebus Apollo, in this case standing in for the sun.
[66] The word 'beams', which appears in the second and fourth lines of this fable, was spelled 'beames' in 1577. In the process of modernizing, we have altered the metre.
[67] i.e., valley and hill (like the modern expression 'hills and dales')
[68] In the process of modernizing 1577's 'byrdes' to 'birds', we have altered the metre.
[69] In 1577 this phrase reads 'Beuis song'; we have emended to 'boughs hung', assuming that 'beuis' meant 'bewes' or 'boughs', and that 'song' was a compositor's error for 'hong' or 'hung'. In 1570 and 1571, the copies from which Smith was presumably translating, the phrase reads 'The bewis braid blomit' [The broad boughs bloomed].
[70] According to the *OED* 'pleasance', meaning a pleasure ground or garden, is a Scots term.
[71] The phrase 'could rise' here, and 'could make' three lines below, are auxiliary intensifiers, rather than a commentary on potential ability. These phrases might be best translated as 'did rise' and 'did make'.

The blossoms brave broke up in bank and brake,°⁷²
20   The smell of herbs and the fowls'⁷³ cry,⁷⁴
     Contending who should have the victory.

     Me to conserve fro the sun's heat,⁷⁵
     Under the shadow of a hawthorn° green
     I laid me down among the flowers sweet,
25   So clad° my head, and closèd both mine eyne;
     On sleep I fell among these birds⁷⁶ fine,
     And in my dream methought came through the field
     The fairest man that ever I beheld.

     His gown was of a cloth as white as milk;
30   His jacket was of camlet° purpure° brown,
     His hood of scarlet broidered° well with silk,
     And hanging wise unto his girdle° down
     His bonnet round of the old fashion;
     His beard was white; his eyne were great and gray,
35   With locks of hairs which on his shoulders lay.

     A roll of paper in his hand he bore,
     A swan's pen sticking under his ear,⁷⁷
     An ink-horn° with a pretty gilt penner,°
     A bag of silk all at his girdle borne;
40   Thus was he goodly° girded° in his gear,
     Of stature large, and with a fearful face.
     Even where I lay, he came a sturdy pace.

     And said, 'God speed my son,' and I was fain°
     Of that good word and of his company;
45   With reverence, I answered him again,

---

⁷² In the process of modernizing the verb 'brake' to 'broke', we have removed the pun on 'brake' in Smith's version: the brave blossoms brake up (broke up) in bank and in brake (in thickets).

⁷³ In the process of modernizing 1577's 'hearbes' and 'fowles' to 'herbs' and 'fowls', we have altered the metre.

⁷⁴ It is clear that Smith attempted to emend Henryson's 'The smell off herbis and off fowlis cry' (1571), which synaesthetically discusses the smells of birdsong. However, Smith merely added the word 'the' without eliminating the second 'of', thereby perpetuating the problem. We have removed the second 'of'.

⁷⁵ In the process of modernizing 1577's 'sunnes' to 'sun's', we have altered the metre.

⁷⁶ In the process of modernizing 1577's 'byrdes' to 'birds', we have altered the metre.

⁷⁷ i.e., a quill made from a swan's feather (not a pen belonging to a swan)

'Welcome father,' and he sat down me by.
'Displease you not, my good master, though I
Demand your birth, your faculty,° and name,⁷⁸
Why ye come here, or where ye dwell at home.'

50 'My son,' said he, 'I am of gentle blood;
My native land is Rome, withouten° nay;
In that town first to the schools I yode.°
In civil° law studied full many a day,
And now my wonning° is in heaven for ay;
55 Aesop I hight;° my writing and my work
Is kend° and known to many a cunning clerk.'

'O master Aesop, poet laureate,
God wot° ye are full dear welcome to me;
Are ye not he that all the fables wrote,
60 Which in effect, suppose they feignèd be,⁷⁹
Are full of prudence and morality?'
'Fair son,' said he, 'I am the selfsame man.'
God wot if that my heart was merry then.

I said, 'Aesop, my master venerable,
65 I you beseech most entirely,
Ye would not deign to tell a pretty fable,⁸⁰
Concluding with a good morality.'
Shaking his head, he said, 'My son, let be;
What doth it profit to tell a feignèd tale
70 When holy preaching may nothing avail?

'Now in this world methinks° right few or none,
Unto God's word that hath devotion;
The ear is deaf, the heart is hard as stone,
Now open sin without any correction,
75 The heart inclining to the earth adown;°

---

⁷⁸ In 1577, this word is spelled 'nome'. 'Nome' can mean social class, but the word is infrequently recorded in the *OED*, and Aesop responds to the question by telling his name. 'Faculty' means profession; the poet is asking to know the stranger's job and his name.
⁷⁹ i.e., which, even if they are feigned, ...
⁸⁰ Smith changes 1570 and 1571's 'disdayne' to 'deyne'. 'Deign' could either be a shortened form or the opposite of 'disdain'.

So rusted is this world with canker° black,
That now my tales may little succour° make.'

'Yes, gentle sir,' said I, 'for my request,
Not to displease your fatherhood,[81] I pray
80 Under the figure of some brutal beast
A moral fable that ye would deign to say;
Who knoweth not, I may learn[82] and bear away
Something thereby, hereafter may avail?'
'I grant,' quoth he, and thus begins his tale.

The end of the prologue, and here begins the tale.

85 A lion at his prey was overrun°
To recreate his limbs[83] and to rest,
Beeking°[84] his breast and belly at the sun,
Under a tree lay in the fair forest;
Then comes there a trip° of mice out of their nest,
90 Right merry and glad, all dancing in their guise,
And over the lion vaulted twice or thrice.

He lay so still the mice were not afeard,
But to and fro o'er him took their trace;°
Some twirled at the mustachios of his beard,
95 And some spared not to claw him on the face;
Merry and glad thus dancèd they a space,
'Til at the last the noble lion woke,
And with his paw the master mouse he took.

She gave a cry, and all the rest, aghast,
100 Their dancing left, and hid them soon elsewhere;
She that was ta'en cried and wept full fast,

---

[81] This is a sign of respect for an elder; Aesop is not literally his father.
[82] The phrase 'Who knoweth not, I may learn' is punctuated in 1577 as follows: 'Who knoweth, not I, may learn'. In 1570 and 1571, there is a 'nor' for the 'not', possibly meant as 'but': 'Who knows, but I may learn'. Smith seems to have struggled with this when translating; we have changed the punctuation to make it more intelligible.
[83] In the process of modernizing 1577's 'limmes' to 'limbs', we have altered the metre.
[84] According to the *OED*, 'beeking' is a word much more commonly used in Scotland than in England. This is one of the relics of Scots that survived Smith's Englishing.

And said, 'Alas the time that I came here!
Now am I ta'en a woeful prisoner,
And for my guilt must bide incontinent,°
105   Of life or death to hear the judgement.'

Then spake the lion to that careful° mouse:
'Thou caitiff° wretch and vile unworthy thing,
Over malapert° and eke presumptuous,
Thou wert to make out over me thy tripping;°
110   Knewest thou not I was both lord and king
Of beasts all?' 'Yes,' quoth the mouse, 'I know,
But I wist not because ye lay so low.

'Lord, I beseech thy kingly royalty,
Hear what I say, and take in patience:
115   Consider first my simple poverty,
And then thy might and high magnificence;
See also how things done of negligence,
Neither of malice, nor of presumption,
The rather should have grace° and remission.°

120   'We were replete,° and had great abundance
Of all things such as to us belonged;
The sweet season provokèd us to dance,
And make such mirth as nature to us learned;
Ye lay so still as though ye had been strangled,
125   That by my soul we wend° ye had been dead,
Else would we not have dancèd o'er your head.'

'Thy false excuse,' the lion said again,
'Shall not avail one whit,° I to thee say;
I put the case[85] I had been dead or slain,
130   And so my skin been stoppèd° full of hay,
Though thou had found my figure in the way,
Because it bore the print° of my person,
Thou shouldst for fear on knees have fallen down.

---

[85] i.e., suppose that

'For thy trespass thou can make no defence,
135   My noble person thus to vilepend,°
Of thy fellows, nor thy own negligence
For to excuse thou can no cause pretend;
Therefore thou suffer shalt a shameful end,
And death, such as to treason is decreed:
140   Upon the gallows all hanged but the head.'

'Nay, mercy, Lord, now at thy grace I ask,
As thou art king of all beasts coronate,°
Assuage° thy wrath and let it overpass,°
And make thy mind to mercy inclinate;°
145   I grant offence is done to thine estate,
Wherefore° I worthy am as now to die,
But if thy kingly mercy pardon me.

'In every judge mercy and ruth° should be,
As assessors and collateral;
150   Without mercy, justice is cruelty,[86]
As said is in the laws[87] special;
When rigour sits in the tribunal,
The equity° of law who may sustain?
Right few or none, lest mercy go between.

155   'Also ye know the honour triumphal
Of all victory upon the strength depends
Of his conquest, which manfully° in battle,
Through jeopardy of war, long defends;
What price or praise, when the battle ends,
160   Is said of him that overcomes one man,
Himself to defend, which neither may nor can.[88]

'A thousand mice to kill and eke devour
Is little manhood to a strong lion;[89]
Full little worship shall ye win therefore,

---

[86] i.e., Every judge should have mercy, which functions to analyze the judge's actions and keep a judge in check, because without mercy, justice is merely cruelty.
[87] In the process of modernizing 1577's 'lawes' to 'laws', we have altered the metre.
[88] i.e., What credit would you get in war for overcoming a man who can't even defend himself?
[89] i.e., Eating a thousand mice does not do much to increase or prove the manhood or bravery of a lion.

165 To whose strength is no comparison:
It will appair° some part of your renown
To slay a mouse which may make no defence,
But asking mercy at your excellence.

'Also, it seems not your selfitude,[90]
170 Which uses daily meats delicious,
To file° your teeth or lips with any blood
Which to your stomach is contagious;
Unwholesome meat, also, is a sorry° mouse,
And that namely° unto a strong lion,
175 Wont° to be fed with gentle[91] venison.

'My life is little worth; my death is less;
Yet and I live,[92] I may, peradventure,
Supply[93] your highness, being in distress,
For oft is seen a man of small stature
180 Rescued hath a lord of great honour
That was beset and in point overthrown;
Through misfortune, such case may be your own.'

When this was said, the lion his language
Paused, and thought according to reason,
185 And made mercy his cruel ire° assuage,
And to the mouse granted remission:
Opened his paw, and she on knees fell down,
And both her hands unto the heaven held,
Crying, 'Almighty God your grace ever shield!'

190 When she was gone, the lion went to hunt,
For he had naught, but livèd by his prey,
And slew° both tame and wild as he was wont,
And in the country made many a great fray,°
'Til at the last the people found the way

---

[90] The word 'selfitude' merely means self; the word appears to have been coined to create a rhyme with 'blood'.
[91] When referring to an animal, 'gentle' means, of excellent breed or spirit. However, the mouse may also be arguing that the noble (gentle, of high birth) lion should only eat noble animals.
[92] i.e., if I live
[93] According to the OED, the word 'supply' could be used to mean assist in Scots.

195 This cruel lion how that they mote take.
     So of hempen° cords strong nets can they make.[94]

     And in a lane where he was wont to run
     With ropes rude fro tree to tree they hung,
     So cast a ring without wood and within,
200 With horns fast blowing, and hounds crying;
     The lion fled, and, through the lane running,
     Fell in the net, and, so caught by chance,
     For all his strength could make no resistance.

     Welt'ring° about with hideous roaring,
205 While to, while fro, while he might succour get,
     But all in vain — it availed him nothing:
     The more he flung, the faster was the net;
     The ropes rude were so fast about him set
     On every side that succour saw he none,
210 But still lying and mourning made his moan:

     'O lamentable lion, lying here so low,
     Where is the might of thy magnificence?
     Of whom all brutal beasts in earth stood awe,
     And dread to look upon thy excellence;
215 Without hope or help, without succour or defence,
     In bands strong here must I lie, alas,
     'Til I be slain; I see no other grace.°

     'There is no wight° that will my harms[95] wreak,°
     Nor creature do comfort[96] to my crown.
220 Who shall me help? Who shall my bands break?
     Who shall me put fro pain of this prison?'
     By that[97] he had made this lamentation,
     Through adventure the little mouse come by,
     And of the lion heard the woeful cry.

---

[94] i.e., they began to make. Smith systematically translates Henryson's 'gan' as 'can'. As in Henryson, this is sometimes an auxiliary (does) and sometimes means began.
[95] In the process of modernizing 1577's 'harmes' to 'harms', we have altered the metre.
[96] i.e., creature to do comfort to my crown
[97] i.e., by the time that

225 And suddenly it came in till her mind
That it should be the lion by his close,[98]
And said, 'Now were I false, and right unkind,
But I quit° of his goodness some part,[99] I suppose,
Thou did to me,' and on her ways she goes
230 To her fellows, and on them fast can cry,[100]
'Come help, come help!' and they came by and by.

'Lo,' quoth the mouse, 'this is the same lion
That grace granted me when I was ta'en anon,
And now is fast here bounden° in prison,
235 Breaking his heart with great mourning and moan;
Without we him help, of succour wots he none;
Come help to quit one good turn for another,
And loose him quickly!' They answered, 'Yea, good brother.'

They took no knife; their teeth were sharp enough.
240 To see that sight, forsooth° it was great wonder,
How that they ran among the ropes tough,
Before, behind, some above, some under,
And shore the ropes of the net in sunder;
Then bade° him rise, and he start[101] up anon,
245 And thankèd them, so on his way is gone.

Now is the lion free from all danger,
Loose and delivered to his liberty
By little beasts, and of simple power,
As ye have heard, because he had pity.
250 Quoth I, 'Master, is there a morality
Of this fable?' 'Yea son,' he said, 'right good.'
'I pray you sir, then,' quoth I, 'conclude.'

---

[98] 1570 and 1571 both read 'did hir grace' for 1577's 'by his close', and 'thy gentrice' (1570) and 'thy gentrace' (1571) for 'I suppose' (two lines below). Smith seems to have changed this rhyme, perhaps to avoid using the word 'gentrice'. The substitution is a bit unclear; 'by his close' may mean in the enclosure (or trap).

[99] i.e., unless I repay at least some part of his goodness (towards me)

[100] i.e., began to cry

[101] i.e., started

Morality

As I suppose, this mighty gay lion
May signify a prince or emperor,
255 Any potestate,° or any king with crown,
Which should be captain, guide, and governor
Of his people, that takes no labour
To rule, and steer the land, and justice keep,
Without lying still in lusts, sloth, and sleep.[102]

260 The fair forest with leaves fresh to see,
With fowls singing, and flowers fair and sweet,
Is but the world and his prosperity,
As false pleasance mingled, and care replete;[103]
Right as the rose with frost and winter wet
265 Fades, so doth the world and them deceive,
Which in their lusts most confidences have.

These little mice are but the commonty,°
Wanton, unwise, without correction;
Their lords and princes when that they see
270 Of justice make no execution,
They dread nothing to make rebellion
And disobey;[104] for why they stand in no awe,
That makes them their sovereign not to know.°

By this fable, ye lords of prudence
275 May consider the virtue of piety,[105]
And to remit sometime a great offence,
And mitigate with mercy cruelty;
Oft-times° is seen a man of small degree
Hath quit a king either with good or ill;
280 As the lord hath done, rigour or grace him till.[106]

---

[102] i.e., The lion is like a prince who should rule diligently, but instead of labouring to steer his country, he wallows in laziness.
[103] In 1571, this reads 'As fals pleasance myngit with cair repleit', or false pleasure mixed with full cares or woes. Smith has changed the 'with' to an 'and', creating two paradoxical pairs: pleasure that is false, and cares that are replete.
[104] i.e., When they see their rulers refuse to prosecute criminals, they don't worry about committing crimes.
[105] i.e., pity
[106] 'Till' in this case means to, so this phrase means: As a ruler has offered either rigorous or merciful justice, so may the same be delivered unto him.

>   Who knoweth not how soon a lord of great renown,
>   Rolling in worldly lust and vain pleasance,
>   May be overthrown, destroyed, and put down
>   Through false Fortune? Which of all variance
> 285   Is whole mistress, and leader of the dance,
>   To unjust men, and blinds[107] them so sore°
>   That they no peril can provide before.
>
>   These rural men that hangèd hath the net
>   In which the lion suddenly was thrown
> 290   Waited alway° amends for to get
>   (For hurt man writes in the marble stone);[108]
>   More to expound, as now I let alone,
>   Both king and lord may well know what I mean;
>   The figure hereof oft-times hath been seen.
>
> 295   When this was said, quoth Aesop, 'My fair child,
>   I thee beseech, and all men, for to pray
>   That treason of this country be exiled,
>   And justice reign, and lords keep their fay°
>   Unto their sovereign prince both night and day,'
> 300   And with that word he vanished, and I woke,
>   So through the wood my journey when I took.[109]

FINIS

---

[107] In the process of modernizing 1577's 'blindes' to 'blinds', we have altered the metre.

[108] i.e., a person remembers wrongs as if they were carved in marble. See Sir Thomas More, *The historie of the pitifull life, and unfortunate death of Edward the Fifth, and the then Duke of Yorke, his brother with the troublesome and tyrannical government of usurping Richard the Third, and his miserable end* (London, 1641), p. 130: 'men use to write an evill turne in marble stone, but a good turne in the dust.'

[109] 1570 and 1571 read for this final line, 'Syne throw the Schaw my Iourney hamewart tuke' [Then through the woods I took my journey homewards]. Smith translates the Scots words 'syne' [then, directly after], and 'shaw' [woods], and changes the final phrase; with the phrase 'when I took' Smith likely means, then I took.

RICHARD SMITH

3. The Merry Tale of the Wolf and the Wether°

Whilom° there was, as Aesop can report,[110]
A shepherd dwelling by a forest near,
Which had a dog that did him great comfort;
Full ware° he was to keep his fold° fro fear,
5   That neither wolf nor wildcat durst° appear,
Nor fox on field, nor yet no other beast,
But he them slew, or chasèd at the least.

So happened it (as every beast must sleep),
This dog of sudden sickness to be dead,
10 But then God wot the keeper of the sheep
For very woe waxed° wanner° than the weed.[111]
'Alas,' quoth he, 'now see I no remeid°
To save these silly° beasts that I now keep,
For why the wolf will worry°[112] all my sheep.'

15 It would have made a man's heart sore to see
The silly shepherd make such lamentation.
'Now is my darling dead, alas,' quoth he,
'For now to beg my bread I may be boun,°[113]
With pikestaff° and with scrip° fro town to town;
20 For all the beasts before that 'bandoned° were
Will now return again, and all my sheep to-tear.'°

With that a wether stoutly° stood on foot:
'Master,' quoth he, 'make merry and be light;°
To break your heart for bale° it is no boot,°[114]
25 For one dead dog ye must not take such flight;[115]

---

[110] i.e., as Aesop did report
[111] The word 'wan' means either dark, or pale and sickly; the line likely means: because of sadness, the shepherd became more sickly than a weed.
[112] The word 'worry' here in line 14, and the word 'worried' in line 60 below, are spelled 'weary' and 'weried', respectively, in 1577. We have changed the spellings, assuming they are early spellings of the verb 'worry', which means to seize by the throat with the teeth, or to kill or injure by biting and shaking.
[113] i.e., Now I will have to set out to beg for my bread; alternatively, Smith's 'bowne' could be read as a rhyme-mutilated 'bound', in which case the line would translate to something like: Now I may be forced to beg for my bread.
[114] i.e., it is no use; there is no point
[115] i.e., flight of fancy, or, in this case, of extreme grief

Go fetch him hither and flay° his skin ere night;
So sew it on me, and look that it be meet,°
Both head and neck, body, tail, and feet.

'Then will the wolf believe that I am he,
30 For I shall follow him fast wheree'er he fare;°
All whole the charge[116] here I take upon me
Your sheep to keep at midday, late, and rare;°
And[117] he pursue, by God, I shall not spare
To follow him as fast as did your dog,
35 So that, I warrant, ye shall not want a hog.'

Then said the shepherd, 'This comes of a good wit;
Thy counsel is both good, faithful, and true;
Who says a sheep's a wretch, they lie of it.'[118]
With that, in haste the dog's skin off he flew,[119]
40 And on the sheep right softly could[120] it sew.
Then was the wether wanton of his weed:°[121]
'Now of the wolf,' quoth he, 'I have no dread.'°

In all things he counterfeit[122] the dog,
For all the night he stood and took no sleep,
45 So that long time there wanted not an hog;
So ware he was, and watchful them to keep,
That Laurence durst not look upon a sheep,[123]
For and he did, he followed him so fast,
That of his life he made him all aghast.

---

[116] i.e., the entire charge or command
[117] i.e., if
[118] i.e., they lie about it
[119] The word 'flew' is being used as the past tense of the verb 'flay' (to remove the skin); though it should be modernized as 'flayed', we have kept this archaic form to preserve the rhyme.
[120] i.e., did
[121] i.e., then the sheep was really excited about his clothing
[122] i.e., counterfeited
[123] In medieval and early modern England, Laurence was a common name for a fox (*OED*, s.v. 'laurence'); the wether keeps the fox from so much as looking at the sheep.

50   Was nother wolf, wildcat, nor yet tod,°
     Durst come within the bounds[124] all about,
     But he would chase them both through rough and snod;°[125]
     These baleful beasts had of their lives such doubt,
     For he was great and seemèd to be stout,
55   That every beast did dread him and eke fear,
     Without the wood that none durst once appear.[126]

     It happened there an hungry wolf to slide
     Out through his sheep where as they did lie.
     'I shall one have,' quoth he, 'whatever betide,
60   Though I be worried, or else I will die.'
     With that a lamb he got by and by;
     The rest start up, for they were all aghast,
     But God wote if the wether followed fast.[127]

     Went never hound more hastily from the hand
65   When he was running most rashly for the roe,°
     Nor went this wether over moss and strand,°
     And stopped neither at bank, bosk,° nor brae,°
     But followed still, ay fiercely on his foe
     With such a drift, while dust and dirt overdrove him,
70   And made a vow to God that he would have him.

     With that the wolf let out his tail[128] at length,
     For he was hungry, and it drew near even,
     And shaped° him for to run with all his strength;
     When he the wether so near coming had seen,
75   He dread[129] his life, and he had taken been;
     Therefore he spared neither bosk nor bog,
     For well he knew the kindness of the dog.

---

[124] In the process of modernizing 1577's 'boundes' to 'bounds', we have altered the metre.

[125] Smith's text reads for this word 'snoe'; we have emended it to 'snod' on the assumption that the change is not deliberate on Smith's part but an error. Both 1570 and 1571 read 'snod', meaning smooth, therefore completing the phrase 'rough and smooth'.

[126] i.e., so that no beast dared to appear outside of the woods (where they lived)

[127] i.e., But God knows that the wether followed quickly.

[128] i.e., ran at full speed

[129] i.e., dreaded

To make him light he cast the lamb him fro,
So leapt o'er leys° and ran through dirt and mire;
80 'Nay,' quoth the wether, 'in faith we part not so;
It is not the lamb but thee that I desire;
I shall come near, for now I see thee tire.'
The wolf ran still and durst not look behind him,
But ay the nearer the wether he could[130] wind° him.

85 Soon after that he followed him so near,
While that the wolf for fear befiled° the field,
And left the way, and ran through bush and briar,
And thought within the woods him for to shield;
He ran still restless, or else he must needs yield;
90 The wether followed him out and in,
While that a briar bush tore rudely off the skin.

The wolf was ware and blinkèd° him behind,
And saw the wether come flinging° through the briar,
So saw the dog skin hanging on the lind.°
95 'Nay,' quoth he, 'is this ye that is so near?
Right now a hound, and now white as a friar;[131]
I fled o'erfar, and I had known the case;
To God I vow that ye shall rue° this race.

'What was the cause ye gave me such a catch?'
100 With that in haste he took him by the horn.
'For all your wiles, you met once with your match;
Suppose ye laughed me all this year to scorn,
For what treason have ye this dog's skin borne?'
'Master,' quoth he, 'but even to play with you;
105 I you require that ye none other trow.'°

'Is this your jesting in earnest then?' quoth he,
'For I am very fearful and also aflocht;°[132]

---

[130] i.e., did

[131] This is perhaps a reference to the Carmelites or White Friars, who wear white habits (*OED*).

[132] Smith writes here, 'and also flote', which seems to be his attempt to English the spelling of his sources, which read 'and on flocht' [and in a flutter] (1570, 1571). Because Smith removes the 'on', we have changed the spelling to the closest *OED*

Come back again and I shall let you see'
(Then where the way was berayed° he him brought)
110 'Whether call ye this fair play or not,[133]
To set your master in so fell° affray,
The which for fear thus filed° hath the way.

'Thrice, by my soul, ye made me look behind,
And upon my haunches my sinews may be seen;
115 For fearedness° full oft I filed the wind;
Now is this ye, nay, but a dog I ween;°
Methinks your teeth o'ershort to be so keen;
Blessed be the bush that wrest°[134] you your array,°[135]
Else flying bursten had I been this day!'[136]

120 'Sir,' quoth the wether, 'suppose I ran in high,[137]
My mind was never to do your person ill;
The fleer° gets the follower commonly,
In play or earnest, prove whosoever will;
Since I but played, be gracious me until,
125 And I shall make my friends to bless your bones,
For sure good servant will help his master once.'

'I have oft times been set in great affray,°
But, by the rood,° so rad° yet was I never
As thou hast made me with thy pretty play;
130 I shat° behind when thou o'ertook me ever,
But certainly now shall we not dissever.'
Then by the neck-bone surely he him took,
Or ever he ceased, and it in sunder shook.[138]

---

headword, 'aflocht' [agitated, aflutter]. In so doing, we have un-Englished Smith's Englishing: 'aflocht' is primarily Scots.

[133] i.e., I am very afraid and agitated; come back with me and see where I shit myself while running! Do you call this fair play?

[134] i.e., wrested

[135] i.e., that tore the dogskin from you (and allowed me to see you were only a sheep)

[136] i.e., otherwise I would have exploded from fleeing from you today!

[137] i.e., at high speeds

[138] i.e., Before he stopped, he had shaken it (the wether's neck) into pieces.

Morality

Aesop that poet, first father of this fable,
135 Wrote this parable which is convenient,
Because the sentence was fruitful and agreeable,
In morality exemplative prudent,
Whose problems be very excellent,
Through similitudes of figures to this day,
140 Gives doctrine to the readers of it for ay.

Here may thou see that riches of array
Will cause poor men presumptuous for to be;
Then think to hold of none, be they as gay,
But counterfeit a lord in every degree;
145 Out of knowledge in pride they climb so high
That they will forbear° their better in no stead,°[139]
'Til some man turn their heels over their head.

Right so in service other some[140] exceeds,
And[141] they have wages, wealth, and cherishing,
150 That they will be lightly lords in deeds,
And look not to their blood and offspring,
But yet none knows how long that rule will ring;
But he was wise that bade his son consider:
Beware in wealth, for the hall bench is right slidder.°[142]

155 Therefore I counsel° men of every state
To know themselves, and whom they should forbear,
And fall not with their better in debate;°
Suppose they be as gallant in their gear,
It cometh° not a servant to hold war,
160 Nor climb so high, while he fall off the ladder,
But think upon the wolf and on the wether.

FINIS

---

[139] i.e., in no way
[140] i.e., some other
[141] i.e., if
[142] 'Slidder' means slippery; Alexander Hislop paraphrases this proverb as 'Great men's favours are uncertain' in *The Proverbs of Scotland* (Edinburgh: Alexander Hislop and Company, 1868), p. 110.

4. The Tale of the Woeful End of the Paddock° and the Mouse, Showing the Mischief of Dissemblers°

Upon a time (as Aesop could[143] report)
A little mouse came to a riverside.
She might not wade, her legs[144] were so short;
Neither could she swim; she had no horse to ride;
5 Of very force behind her to bide;[145]
And to and fro, besides° the river deep,
She ran crying with many piteous peep.°

'Help over, help over,' this silly mouse can cry,[146]
'For God's love, somebody, over the brim!'°[147]
10 With that, a paddock in the water by
Put up her head, and on the bank gan climb,
Which by nature could duck,° and gaily swim;
With voice full rank,° she said in this manner:
'Good morn, sir mouse,[148] what is your errand here?'

15 'Seest thou,' quoth she, 'of corn yond jolly° plat,°
Of ripe oats, of barley, pease,° and wheat?
I am hungry, and fain would be thereat,
But I am stoppèd by this water great,
And on this side I get nothing to eat
20 But hard nuts, which with my teeth I bore;
Were I beyond, my feast were much the more.

'I have no boat; here is no mariner;
And though there were, I have no fraught° to pay.'
Quoth she, 'Sister, let be thy heavy cheer;
25 Do my counsel, and I shall find the way
Without horse, bridge, boat, or else galley

---

[143] i.e., did. In this fable especially, the word 'could' is frequently used as an auxiliary meaning 'did'.
[144] In the process of modernizing 1577's 'legges' to 'legs', we have altered the metre.
[145] i.e., by necessity she was forced to stay behind (on the side of the river she wanted to leave)
[146] i.e., the innocent mouse did cry, or began to cry. In this fable especially, the word 'can' is frequently used as an auxiliary meaning 'began' or 'does'.
[147] i.e., '[I would like] help over the brim [or edge of the water]!'
[148] The mouse is female, but 'sir' seems to work here as a general mode of address.

To bring thee over safely; be not afeard,
And not once to wet the compass° of thy beard.'

'I have great wonder,' quoth the little mouse,
30 'How can thou float without feather or fin?
This river is so deep and dangerous;
Methinks that thou shouldst drownèd be therein;
Tell me, therefore, what faculty or gin°
Thou hast, to bring thee o'er this water wan?'°
35 That to declare, the paddock thus began:

'With my two feet,' quoth she, 'long and broad,
Instead of oars, I row the stream full still,
And though the brim be perilous to wade,
Both to and fro I row at mine own will;
40 I may not drown, for why my open gill
Devoids[149] all the water I receive;
Therefore, to drown forsooth no dread I have.'

The mouse beheld then her frowning face,
Her wrinkled cheeks, and her lips'[150] side,[151]
45 Her hanging brows, and her voice so hoarse,
Her loggering°[152] legs, and her harsky°[153] hide;
She ran aback° and on the paddock cried,
'If I can any skill of phys'nomy,[154]
Thou hast some part of false villainy.

---

[149] In the process of modernizing 1577's 'Deuoydes' to 'Devoids', we have altered the metre.
[150] In the process of modernizing 1577's 'lippes' to 'lips', we have altered the metre.
[151] 'Side' is used here as an adjective meaning large, ample, long, or wide. It can also mean hanging low to the ground. According to the *OED*, it is primarily a Scottish and Northern word and is therefore another relic of Scots that survives Smith's Englishing.
[152] The *OED* notes that the verb 'logger' is a word used in Scots and Northern dialects.
[153] 'Harsky' seems to be a word coined by Henryson, combining an old spelling of 'harsh' with an extra 'y' added at the end (presumably for metrical purposes). It means that the frog has harsh or coarse, rough skin.
[154] Physiognomy, shortened here to preserve metre, is the study of a person's character by a study of their face and body. The word 'can' in this line means know.

50 'For clerks say[155] the inclination
Of man's thought proceeds commonly
After the corporal° complexion,
To good or evil as nature will apply,
A froward° will and crabbèd° phys'nomy;
55 The old proverb is witness of this *lorum*:
Distortum vultum, sequitur distortio morum.'[156]

'Nay,' quoth the frog, 'that proverb is not true,
For fair things oft-times are founden° faken;°[157]
The blaeberries,° though they be sad of hue,
60 Are gathered up when primrose is forsaken;
The face may fail to be the heart's token;
Therefore, I find this written in each place:[158]
Thou shouldst not judge a man after his face.

'Though I be irksome for to look upon,
65 There is no cause why I should lackèd° be;
Were I as fair as jolly Absolon,[159]
I am no causer of that great beauty;
This difference in form and quality

---

[155] In the process of modernizing 1577's 'Clerkes sayes' to 'clerks say', we have significantly altered the metre.

[156] i.e., From distorted faces follows a distortion of mores; bad faces indicate bad morality. This phrase was listed as proverbial in *Carminum proverbialium totius humanae vitae statum breuiter deliniantium, necnon vtilem de moribus doctrinam iucundè proponentium. Loci communes, in gratiam iuuentutis selecti* (London, 1595), p. 36. *Lorum* is a Latin word meaning 'a strap, whip, or thong'; Henryson, and Smith after him, may be using it to mean 'lore' or 'advice' (Kindrick, p. 107), distorted slightly to rhyme with *morum* in the next line.

[157] This phrase is 'found infakin' in 1577, which is either Smith's error or a printer's error for the earlier copies' 'founden fakin'.

[158] Henryson reads for this line 'Thairfoir I find this Scripture in all place' (1570, 1571); Robert Pope tentatively identifies the scripture as John 7:24: 'Do not judge by appearances, but judge with right judgment' (NRSV); see Robert Pope, 'A sly toad, physiognomy, and the problem of deceit: Henryson's *The Paddock and the Mouse*', *Neophililogus* 63 (1979), 461–68 (p. 464). In translating Henryson's 'Scripture' as 'writing', Smith generalizes the idea: everyone writes about this, not just the Bible.

[159] Absolon is a character from Chaucer's *Miller's Tale*. Henryson was one of the Scottish writers in the fifteenth century influenced by Chaucer; Smith carries the reference forward.

Almighty God hath caused Dame Nature
70 To print and set in every his creature.

'Of some the face may be full° flourishing,
With silken tongue, and cheer right amorous,
With mind inconstant, false, and varying,
Full of deceit and means cautelous° —'
75 'Let be thy preaching,' quoth the hungry mouse,
'And by what means now make me understand,
That thou canst help me unto yonder land.'

'Thou knowest,' quoth she, 'a body that hath need,
To help themself, should many ways[160] cast;[161]
80 Therefore, go get a double-twinèd thread,
And bind thy leg to mine with knots[162] fast;
I shall thee learn to swim — be not aghast —
As well as I.' 'As thou?' then quoth the mouse,
'To prove that play, it were right perilous.

85 'Should I be bound and fast, that now am free,
In hope of help? Nay, then beshrew my head,[163]
For I mote lose both life and liberty;
If it were so who should amend the deed?
But if thou wilt swear to help me with speed,
90 Without fraud or guile, to bring me o'er the flood,
And without hurt or harm, in faith,' quoth she, 'good.'

She gowked° up, and to the heaven can cry:
'O Jupiter, of nature god and king,
I make an oath truly to thee, that I
95 This little mouse shall over this water bring.'
This oath was made; the mouse, without perceiving
The false engine° of this foul carping pad,°[164]
Took thread and bound her leg as she her bad.[165]

---

[160] In the process of modernizing 1577's 'wayes' to 'ways', we have altered the metre.
[161] i.e., You know that someone who has need should look for as many ways as possible to help themselves.
[162] In the process of modernizing 1577's 'knottes' to 'knots', we have altered the metre.
[163] i.e., may evil fall upon me
[164] i.e., the deceitful plan of this foul lying frog
[165] Although elsewhere we have modernized this word as 'bade' [commanded], we have retained the alternative form 'bad' here to preserve the rhyme.

Then foot for foot, they leapt both in the brim,
100 But in their minds they were right different:
The mouse thought of nothing but for to swim,
The paddock for to drown set his[166] intent.
When they in midway of the stream near went,
With all her force the paddock pressèd down,
105 And thought° the mouse without mercy to drown.

Perceiving this, the mouse on her can cry,
'Traitor to God, and forsworn° unto me,
Thou tookest upon thy faith, right now, that I
Without hurt or harm, should ferried be and free!'
110 And when she saw there was but do or die,[167]
With all her might she forced herself to swim,
And pressed upon the toad's back for to climb.

The dread of death her strength made increase,
And forcèd her defend with might and main;°[168]
115 The mouse upward, the paddock down can press;
While to, while fro, while duckèd up again,
This silly mouse, plunged into great pain,
Can fight as long as breath was in her breast,
'Til at the last she crièd for the priest.[169]

120 Fighting thus together, the kite° sat on a twist,°
And to this wretched battle took good heed;
And with a whisk, or any of them wist,[170]
He clenched his talons° betwixt them on the thread;
So to the land he flew with them good speed,
125 Glad of that catch, piping with many pew,°[171]
So loosed° them, and without pity slew.

---

[166] The frog, who is elsewhere female, receives a masculine pronoun here.

[167] i.e., There was nothing to do but to get herself out of it, or die.

[168] i.e., Fear of death increased her strength, and forced her to defend herself with great power and force.

[169] i.e., she felt herself dying and therefore called for a priest to administer her last rites

[170] i.e., before either of them knew

[171] The word 'pew' is one of the relics of Scots that survived Smith's Englishing.

Then bowelled° them that butcher with his bill,
And belly drawn full featly,° them he flayed;
But all their flesh would scant be half a fill,
130 And guts also, unto that greedy glede.°
Of their debate thus when I heard the read,°[172]
He took his flight and over the fields flew;
If this be not true,[173] then ask of them that saw.

Morality[174]

My brother, if thou will take advertence,°
135 By this fable thou may perceive and see
It passes far all kind of pestilence,
A wicked mind fraught° with words fair and sly;
Beware therefore with whom thou matchest thee,
For thee were better go to cart and plough,
140 And all thy days to delve° in wet and dry,
Than to be matchèd with a wicked fellow.

A false intent under a fair pretence
Hath caused many an innocent to die;
Great folly it is to give oversoon credence[175]
145 To all that speaks[176] fairly unto thee;
A silken tongue, an heart of cruelty,
Smites more sore than any shot of arrow;
Brother, if thou be wise, I read° thee flee
To match thee with a feignèd° froward fellow.

---

[172] This line strangely seems to make the kite's flight dependent on the narrator's having heard the story; an exact paraphrase would be something like, 'Of the fight/struggle (either between the mouse and frog or between the pair of them and the kite), when I (the narrator) had heard the outcome, then the kite flew away over the fields.' Further, Smith has changed Henryson's 'outred' (meaning outcome) to 'read', which can only mean, here, something like reading or interpretation. We find no way to fix the sense of these lines — if indeed this strangeness is not on some level intentional — without radically changing them.

[173] Smith has added the 'not', while translating the meaning of 1570 and 1571, which read 'Gif this be trew' (1570) and 'Giff this be trew' (1571) [whether this be true].

[174] For some reason, the first three stanzas of the morality change poetic form; instead of rhyme royal, Henryson changes temporarily to an 8-line stanza rhymed ABABBCBC.

[175] i.e., to believe too quickly

[176] In the process of modernizing 1577's 'speakes' to 'speaks', we have altered the metre.

150 I warrant thee also, it is great negligence
To bind thee fast where thou were frank and free;
When thou art bound, thou can make no defence
To save thy life, nor yet thy liberty.
This simple counsel, brother, take of me,
155 And it to con° forth both early and late:
Better without strife to live alone we see,
Than to be matchèd with a wicked mate.

This hold in mind;[177] right more I shall thee tell,
What by these beasts[178] may be figurate:[179]
160 The paddock using in the flood to dwell[180]
Is man's body, swimming rare and late
In this wretched world, with cares implicate,
Now high, now low, whiles° plungèd up, whiles down,
Continually in peril, and ready for to drown.

165 Now dolorous, now glad as bird on breer,°[181]
Now in freedom, now wrapped in distress,
Now whole and sound, now dead and brought on bier,°
Now poor as Job,[182] now rolling in riches,
Now gowns gay, now rags laid in press,[183]
170 Now full as pease,[184] now hungry as the hound,
Now hoist[185] on wheel,[186] now thrown upon the ground.

---

[177] We have used a semi-colon here because the 'this' could refer to what he just said or what he is about to say.

[178] In the process of modernizing 1577's 'beastes' to 'beasts', we have altered the metre.

[179] i.e., what all these different animals stand for in the allegory of the fable (the frog represents the body, the mouse the soul, etc.)

[180] i.e., the paddock, accustomed to living in the water

[181] The word 'breer' is a Scots word meaning the first appearance of grain above ground. To be as happy as a bird on newly sprouted wheat is to be very happy indeed.

[182] In the biblical Book of Job, Job loses his wealth as part of a test of his faith.

[183] In the process of modernizing 1577's 'gownes' to 'gowns' and 'ragges' to 'rags', we have altered the metre.

[184] This phrase, clearly meant to seem proverbial and to mean very full (in contrast to the hungry hounds), is not recorded elsewhere as a phrase. It is Smith's change: 1570 doesn't contain this stanza, while 1571 reads 'full as fitche'. Smith perhaps gets it from extrapolating backwards from the phrase 'pease-fed', which, according to the *OED*, means fed by pease, or peas, and seems to suggest well fed.

[185] i.e., hoisted

[186] i.e., the wheel of Fortune

This little mouse here knit thus by the shin
The soul of man betoken may indeed,
Bounden, and from the body may not win,
175 While cruel death come break of life the thread,
The which to drown should ever stand in dread
Of carnal lust, by the suggestion
Which draws the soul continually a-down.

The water is the world ay weltering
180 With many waves of tribulation,
In which the soul and body be stirring,
Standing right different in their opinion.
The soul upward, the body presses down;
The soul right fain would be brought o'er iwis,
185 Out of this world, into the heavens' bliss.

The kite is death, that cometh suddenly,
As doth a thief, and endeth soon the battle;
Be vigilant therefore, and still ready,
For man's life is brickle° and ay mortal.
190 My friend, therefore, make thee a strong wall
Of faith in Christ, for death will thee assay,°
Thou knowest not when, even morrow or midday.

Adieu, my friend, and if that any ask
Of these fables, so shortly I conclude:
195 Say thou I left the rest unto the learnèd's task,
To make example and some similitude.
Now Christ for us that died on the rood,
Of soul and life as thou art saviour,
Grant us to pass into a blessèd hour.

Finished in the Vale° of Aylesbury the thirteenth
of August, Anno Domini 1574.[187]

---

[187] This colophon (an inscription placed at the end of a book containing information such as a scribe, printer, or author's name; the place where a work was completed; and/or a date) is most likely by Smith, marking the date that he finished his translation. The Vale of Aylesbury is a valley in northern Buckinghamshire, not too far from London.

RICHARD SMITH

The Epilogue[188]

Behold, ye men: Aesop, that noble clerk,
Although of body yformèd° wondrous° ill,
His fables wrote with wisdom deep and dark
To stir our minds (to good which had no will);
5   By beasts and fowls, he spake to warn us still,
As fox, wolf, sheep, dog, cock, and hen,
To stir our minds to live on earth like men.

It's writ of old by authors that are past
That Aesop was crook-backed,° great belly and head,
10   Crook-legged, splay-foot,[189] and like a cow in waist,
Yet virtuous of his life, as it is said,
Whose good examples live,[190] though he be dead,
In each man's mouth, and shall do still for ay.
Lo, virtue brings forth fruit without decay.

15   Thus as ye hear, ill shapen of his body,
Yet of his mind none perfecter than he;
But mark his saws,° and ye find him no noddy,°
But perfect ay, as perfect lo may be,
Who lends you light good virtuous ways to see.
20   Then love this work, and read it at your will;
I but eclipse his tales of so great skill.

FINIS

---

[188] This epilogue is not in 1570 or 1571, and is most likely written by Smith; if it was written by Smith, it is noteworthy that he has adopted the rhyme royal of the fables.

[189] i.e., splay-footed

[190] In 1577, this phrase reads 'whose good examples lives'. We have modernized to conform to the sense that the plural examples refer to Aesop's fables, which live on in each man's mouth (or even, the good examples that stem from Aesop's biography). However, the dangling modifier creates an ambiguity, making it possible that the example of Aesop's life is what lives on (so another possible emendation would be 'whose good example lives').

JOHN BRINSLEY

from *Aesop's Fables Translated Grammatically, and also in propriety of our English phrase; and, every way, in such sort as may be most profitable for the grammar school. The use of it is according to the directions in the prefaces, and more fully set down in* Ludus Literarius, or the Grammar School (1617)

AESOP'S FABLES TRANSLATED GRAMMATICALLY

Epistle Dedicatory[1]

To the right° worshipful Sir John Harper, Knight, all true prosperity:

Right worshipful, I may not be forgetful of the love which you have showed towards the furtherance of my endeavours for *The Grammar School*.[2] Accept therefore this small pledge of my thankful acknowledgement. Though it be little in value and in the esteem of the most, yet the benefit of it will (I trust) help to make amends, and further the perfecting of my desires. By the right use hereof may the little ones from their first years get much profitable understanding and wisdom, yea,° such as whereof they may have very good use all their days, in what place soever they shall be employed, and may moreover have every point and part of the learning in it so imprinted in their memories as they shall never forget them, but have them, as it were, lively before their faces, that so they may learn to embrace the virtues therein taught and to fly the vices, to foresee dangers and how to avoid them, to behave themselves wisely and discreetly in the whole course of their life.

As for example, to give a taste hereof, in the first fable of the cock esteeming a barley corn° above a precious stone, they may see the foolishness of men, and more especially of children preferring play before learning, a little pleasure and folly before the most excellent and divine wisdom, to teach them to follow after and to embrace learning and wisdom, even from their tender years, and to be ashamed of misspending their precious time in play and idle vanities. So in the second fable of the wolf and the lamb they may learn to take heed all their life long how they have to deal with or any way provoke cruel men that are too hard for them, because they, when they list,° can take any occasion to prey upon them, or to do them a mischief, and that

---

[1] The title 'Epistle Dedicatory' is an editorial addition. Brinsley's text, as is explained at greater length below, has a number of explanatory notes, so throughout this text we distinguish our notes from Brinsley's by adding '[Eds]' at the end of each of our notes. [Eds]

[2] This refers to Brinsley's previously published *Ludus literarius: or, the grammar schoole: shewing how to proceede from the first entrance into learning, to the highest perfection required in the grammar schooles, with ease, certainty and delight both to masters and schollers; onely according to our common grammar, and ordinary classicall authours* (London, 1612). [Eds]

this is matter enough if they be not able to resist them. Thus, likewise, the third fable of the mouse and the frog — being at war together about the regiment° of the marish° ground until the kite° snatch them both away and devour them — may teach children in all their time to beware of discord and dissension° with others, especially contention for superiority and preferment,° because such usually as will go to war, as it were, for every trifle° make themselves a prey to others, especially to the common adversary. And but only to name the fourth, the apologue° of the dog swimming over the river — which through overmuch greediness, chopping° at the shadow of the flesh which he saw in the water, lost the flesh itself which he carried in his chaps° — is to teach even children always to take heed of too much greediness, and ever to keep a measure in their desires, lest that, by overmuch earnestness in seeking more than is fit, they come to lose all and to repent when it is too late.

Now beside this sound wisdom, and besides all the other helps concerning the more certain, easy, and speedy means of attaining the Latin tongue (as happy experience hath taught very many, who have given plentiful testimony hereunto, for construing, parsing, making Latin, getting° phrase, and the like, by such translations)[3] they may learn hereby chiefly to make report of a fable, or of any like narration or history, in good sort and fit words, which is no small commendation to any whosoever. For the manner of effecting hereof, I have set it down shortly in the Epistle to the Reader,[4] and more fully in my *Grammar School*. And thus (that you may see my constant desire, in creeping forward by little and little for performing my promise in accomplishing my service[5] for the perpetual benefit of schools and of all posterity, by learning still of the learned to help the unlearned, and by propounding° to all what I have found by experience, that they may find the like and be partakers of all my travails)° have I presumed upon your love to present this little translation unto you. Which you

---

[3] This four-part process entails the following steps: 1) To analyze or trace the grammatical construction of a sentence; 2) to resolve (a sentence, phrase, etc.) into component parts of speech and describe each part syntactically; 3) to turn the English into Latin, and 4) to 'get phrase', perhaps meaning to gather phrases that might be inscribed, for example, in a commonplace book. [Eds]

[4] Brinsley refers here to the letter that follows below, which he addresses 'To the painful schoolmaster'. [Eds]

[5] i.e., performing my promise to accomplish my service [Eds]

accepting accordingly, I shall be more encouraged to strive forward for perfecting of the whole, and to spend my last thoughts for the common good. And thus with all thankful acknowledgement unto yourself, with your worthy lady and all yours, I humbly take my leave, and rest,[6]

>Your worship's in the Lord,
>J. Brinsley

---

[6] i.e., remain [Eds]

Epistle to the Reader[7]

To the painful[8] schoolmaster:

First, cause° your scholar, by reading this translation, to tell you in every fable what the matter° of the fable is. Secondly, to what end and purpose it was invented, what it is to teach, and what wisdom he can learn out of it. Thirdly, how to make a good report of the fable,[9] both in English and Latin, especially in English. Fourthly and lastly, to make right use of it for all matters concerning grammar, as for construing, parsing, making, and proving the Latin,[10] and so for reading forth of English into Latin, according to the directions in my former translations, as, namely,° in *Sententiae*, Cato, Cord. etc.,[11] and principally for observing the best phrases both English and Latin. Thus shall you receive your desire. Those things which are too harsh to be uttered in English word for word, according to the Latin phrase, I have referred to the margent° with an asterisk or little star; and variety of English phrase I have set also in the margent, noted with italic letters in alphabetical order.[12] But for these I refer you to that which I have written in my former translations, and in my *Grammar School*. Vouchsafe° me your better direction,° in love, and what is defective, I shall (God willing) labour to supply in the next edition.[13]

---

[7] The title 'Epistle to the Reader' is an editorial addition. [Eds]

[8] i.e., taking pains, careful [Eds]

[9] i.e., how to give an accurate summary of the fable and its moral [Eds]

[10] See note 3 above for a fuller account of this translation practice; in this case, he seems to have substituted 'proving' or 'testing' the Latin (presumably by turning it back into English) for the 'getting phrase' mentioned in the 'Epistle Dedicatory'. [Eds]

[11] Prior to translating Aesop, Brinsley published *Sententiae pueriles, translated grammatically* (London, 1612), Cato, *Cato translated grammatically* (London, 1612), Mathurin Cordier, *Corderius dialogues translated grammatically* (London, 1614), and Cicero, *The first book of Tullies Offices translated grammatically* (London, 1616). For the full titles of these texts, see the bibliography. [Eds]

[12] For the ease of our modern readers, we have modified Brinsley's system as follows: for Brinsley's marginal notes that indicate something about Latin construction for the purposes of translation, we have given a footnote and ended it with '**B/T**' (Brinsley, translation); for Brinsley's marginal notes that are intended to teach the variety of the English language, we have given a footnote and ended it with '**B/V**' (Brinsley, variety). For any Brinsley notes that are not one of these two varieties, we end the note with a plain '**B**'. To see what Brinsley's page originally looked like, see p. 20 of the introduction. [Eds]

[13] i.e., send me constructive feedback, and I will correct it in the next edition. [Eds]

Aesop's Fables[14,15]

1. Of a Cock[16] [This fable setteth out the foolish contempt of learning and wisdom.][17,18]

When on a time a cock[19] scratched in a dunghill,[20] he found a precious stone, saying, 'What,[21] do I find so gay° a thing?[22] If a jeweller[23] had found [it] none[24] could have been[25] more jocund[26] than he, as who knew the price [of it.][27] [But] in truth[28] it is of no use to me,[29,30]

---

[14] The Fables of Aesop **B/T** This is Brinsley's first note about translation; his rewriting of 'Aesop's Fables' as 'The Fables of Aesop' is intended to communicate to his student translator that the Latin uses the genitive case here. [Eds]

[15] tales or feigned° devices **B/V** This is Brinsley's first note meant to communicate variety of the English language; he supplies two synonyms for 'fables' to enrich the vocabulary of his readers. [Eds]

[16] Of a cock leading hens, or of a dung-hill cock. *Gallinaceus* signifieth belonging to a cock or hen, or hennish, seeming to be added only to distinguish the word from *gallus*, signifying a French man. **B/T** Brinsley here supplies a word from the Latin title of the fable, which reads *De Gallo gallinaceo* [the hennish or cock-like cock] (1518, sig. A1r). The redundancy, as he notes, seems to be to clarify that *Gallo* means cock, not Frenchman. [Eds]

[17] *Foolish contempt of learning* **B** All square brackets that appear in Brinsley's text have been put in by Brinsley. [Eds]

[18] In 1617 and 1624, this is the first fable. Because the number and order of fables is the same in both editions, we cite 1617 henceforth. [Eds]

[19] Whilst a cock, etc., or a cock found, etc., whilst **B/T** Brinsley uses an 'etc.' here as we might use an ellipsis today: 'Whilst a cock ...' or 'A cock found ... whilst.' [Eds]

[20] turned over a dunghill, viz.,° scratching in it, turned it up by little and little **B/T** Brinsley here gives his translators a hint that the original Latin fable contains the word *uertit* [turns over or destroys] (1518, sig. A1r). [Eds]

[21] 'What,' quoth he, or 'Why?' **B/V**

[22] a thing so bright or shining **B/T**

[23] a lapidary, or one that trimmeth and selleth precious stones **B/T**

[24] no thing **B/T**

[25] could be **B/T**

[26] merry or joyful **B/T**

[27] because he knew the worth of it **B/V**

[28] truly **B/T**

[29] it will serve me for no purpose **B/V**

[30] to me, or for me, to no use **B/T**

neither do I greatly esteem it.³¹,³² Yea, I in very deed³³ had rather have³⁴ a grain of barley³⁵ than all precious stones.'³⁶

The Moral:³⁷ Understand³⁸ by the precious stone, art and wisdom.³⁹ By the cock,⁴⁰ a foolish man given to pleasure.⁴¹ Neither fools love⁴² liberal arts,⁴³ sith° they know not the use of them, nor a man given over to pleasure,⁴⁴ as⁴⁵ whom only pleasure doth delight.⁴⁶

2. Of a Wolf and a Lamb [showing the nature of cruel oppressors, that they can easily take any occasion to prey upon and spoil the poor.]⁴⁷,⁴⁸

A wolf, drinking at the head⁴⁹ of a spring,⁵⁰ seeth a lamb drinking far beneath.⁵¹ He runneth to⁵² [and] rateth°⁵³ the lamb, for that⁵⁴ he marred the spring.⁵⁵ The lamb trembled,⁵⁶ besought [him] that he

---

³¹ esteem, or reckon, it of a great [price] or value **B/T**

³² make any reckoning of it **B/V**

³³ I in truth **B/T**

³⁴ *malim, h.e. magis velim*, will, or would, rather have **B/T** The '*h.e.*' in this note most likely stands for *hic est* [that is]. Brinsley here tells his reader that the word *malim*, which appears in the Latin text from which he translates (1518, sig. A1r), is technically an abbreviated or syncopated version of two separate words, *magis velim* [I would rather prefer or want]. [Eds]

³⁵ a barley corn **B/V**

³⁶ all the precious stones in the world **B/V**

³⁷ the moral sense, or the meaning, use, and application of this fable for the framing and ordering of our manners **B/V**

³⁸ you must understand **B/V**

³⁹ learning and knowledge **B/V**

⁴⁰ [understand] by the, etc. **B/T**

⁴¹ sensual, or given over to pleasure **B/V**

⁴² for neither foolish men do love **B/T**

⁴³ good learning **B/V**

⁴⁴ a voluptuous° man **B/V**

⁴⁵ because **B/V**

⁴⁶ to whom one alonely,° pleasure can please or be pleasant **B/T**

⁴⁷ *Tyranny* **B**

⁴⁸ In 1617, fable 2. [Eds]

⁴⁹ top **B/V**

⁵⁰ fountain **B/T**

⁵¹ a far off or a great way beneath **B/V**

⁵² runneth to [him] **B/T**

⁵³ chideth or blameth **B/V**

⁵⁴ because **B/T**

⁵⁵ troubled the fountain, viz., muddied the water **B/T**

⁵⁶ *trepidare* for *trepidabat*. *Enallage*. **B/T** *Enallage* is the substitution of one grammatical form for another (*OED*). In this case, Brinsley's note reads that although

would spare [him], being innocent. That he neither could indeed mar[57] the drink of the wolf, sith he drank far beneath, nor yet would.[58] The wolf contrarily[59] thundereth,[60] [saying,] 'Thou church robber,[61] thou dost nothing;[62] thou always hurtest [me];[63] [thy] father, mother, all thy odious[64] kind[65] is against me by all means.[66] Thou shalt smart° for[67] it this day.'[68]

The Moral: It is an old saying that it is an easy matter to find a staff to beat a dog.[69] A mighty man easily taketh an occasion[70] of hurting if he list[71] to hurt. He hath offended sufficiently[72] who cannot resist.[73]

---

the Latin reads *trepidare* (the infinitive form, meaning to tremble; 1518, sig. A1r), it should be translated as if it were *trepidabat* (the imperfect form, meaning 'trembled') — or, if a student is translating into Latin, they should give *trepidare* as the Latin translation of 'trembled' to have their translation correspond to the original. [Eds]

[57] himself neither indeed to have been able to trouble **B/T**
[58] to have been willing **B/T**
[59] on the other side **B/V**
[60] speaketh terribly or rails against the lamb **B/V**
[61] wicked wretch **B/V**
[62] this is nothing thou sayest **B/V**
[63] hurtest [me] always **B/T**
[64] envied **B/T**
[65] stock or kindred **B/V**
[66] diligently or always **B/T**
[67] abye° **B/V**
[68] Thou shalt give punishment to me today. **B/T** The Latin reads *Tu mihi dabis hodie poenas* (1518, sig. A1r). The expression *poena dare* means to pay the penalty, so the translation should be, literally, 'You will pay the penalty to me', meaning, I will punish you. This note by Brinsley indicates to his translators the structure of sentence; 'punishment' was another translation of *poenas*. [Eds]
[69] a staff to be found easily, that you may beat a dog **B/T**
[70] a cause **B/T**
[71] he please **B/V**
[72] committed fault enough **B/T**
[73] could not resist or withstand **B/T**

3. Of a Mouse and a Frog [setting out the fruit of discord.]⁷⁴,⁷⁵

A mouse made war⁷⁶ with a frog. The contention was⁷⁷ concerning the empire⁷⁸ of the fen.°⁷⁹ The battle⁸⁰ was vehement⁸¹ and doubtful.⁸² The crafty mouse, lurking⁸³ under the weeds,⁸⁴ sets upon the frog by policy.⁸⁵ The frog, being better in strength,⁸⁶ puissant°⁸⁷ in breast and in bouncing,⁸⁸ provokes⁸⁹ the enemy⁹⁰ in open war.⁹¹ A bulrush° was the spear to each of them.⁹² Which battle⁹³ being seen far off, the kite⁹⁴ maketh haste unto [them], and whilst neither [of them] taketh heed to⁹⁵ themselves⁹⁶ for the earnestness⁹⁷ of the battle, the kite snatcheth away and teareth in pieces both the warriors.⁹⁸

The Moral: It is wont° even so to fall out⁹⁹ to factious° citizens, who, being inflamed¹⁰⁰ with a desire¹⁰¹ of bearing rule, whilst they

---

⁷⁴ *Discord* **B**
⁷⁵ In 1617, fable 3. [Eds]
⁷⁶ warred or waged battle **B/V**
⁷⁷ it was striven **B/T**
⁷⁸ government, rule, or sovereignty **B/V**
⁷⁹ marish ground **B/V**
⁸⁰ fight **B/V**
⁸¹ very sore° **B/V**
⁸² i.e., The outcome of the battle was uncertain. [Eds]
⁸³ oft lying hid or hiding himself **B/V**
⁸⁴ herbs, viz., wild herbs, or grass **B/T**
⁸⁵ deceits, or lying in wait **B/T**
⁸⁶ more strong **B/V**
⁸⁷ able **B/T**
⁸⁸ leaping upon **B/T**
⁸⁹ challengeth **B/V**
⁹⁰ mouse **B/V**
⁹¹ by open Mars: Mars, the God of war, for war **B/T** In Latin, the line is *aperto marte hostem lacessit* [he provokes his enemy into open fight or battle] (1518, sig. A1r). Brinsley tells his translators to choose the word for war that derives from the name of Mars (*Mars, Martis*). [Eds]
⁹² They had either of them a bulrush for their spear. **B/V**
⁹³ strift° **B/T**
⁹⁴ glede° or puttock° **B/T**
⁹⁵ bewareth, or looketh to **B/T**
⁹⁶ herself **B/T**
⁹⁷ study **B/T**
⁹⁸ either of the warriors, *al.* either warrior **B/T** The abbreviation '*al.*' is for *alia*, meaning other or another, and suggests that this is another possible translation. [Eds]
⁹⁹ to happen, or betide, after the same manner **B/T**
¹⁰⁰ kindled or set on fire **B/T**
¹⁰¹ lust **B/T**

contend[102] amongst themselves to be made magistrates,[103] do put their wealth[104] and also their life very oft[105] in danger.

4. Of a Dog and a Shadow [warning to beware of too much greediness.][106,107]

A dog swimming over a river carried a piece of flesh[108] in [his] chap.[109] The sun shining, as it fell out,[110] the shadow of the flesh shined in the waters, which being seen, he, greedily catching at it,[111] lost that which was in his jaws.[112] Therefore, being sore° smitten[113] with the loss both of the thing[114] and also of his hope, first he was amazed;[115] afterwards, getting heart again,[116] he howled out[117] thus: 'O wretch, there wanted° a measure to thy greediness.[118,119] There was enough, and more than enough,[120] if thou hadst not doted;[121] now thou hast less than nothing by thy foolishness.'[122]

The Moral: We are put in mind of modesty[123] by this fable; we are put in mind of wisdom, that there be a measure in our desire,[124] lest

---

[102] strive **B/T**
[103] for magistracy,° or to be governors **B/V**
[104] riches **B/T**
[105] for most part also their life **B/T**
[106] *Unsatiable° greediness* **B**
[107] In 1617, fable 4. [Eds]
[108] flesh **B/T** Brinsley is noting that the phrase 'piece of flesh' is his expansion, and that the Latin only contains a single word for flesh; the Latin reads *carnem* [meat, flesh] (1518, sig. A1v). [Eds]
[109] grinning mouth **B/T**
[110] so as it cometh to pass, or happeneth **B/T**
[111] he catching at greedily so soon as he saw **B/V**
[112] cheeks, or chaps **B/V**
[113] astonied° **B/V**
[114] flesh **B/V**
[115] astonished **B/V**
[116] and then receiving again courage **B/T**
[117] barked out **B/T**
[118] a measure was wanting, or thou wast too greedy **B/T**
[119] covetousness **B/T**
[120] thou hadst enough and too much **B/V**
[121] unless thou hadst doted, or but that thou doted **B/T**
[122] less than nothing is now to thee by thy foolishness **B/T** Brinsley is here giving a literal translation of the Latin construction: *minus nihilo tibi est* [less than nothing is to you] (1518, sig. A1v). [Eds]
[123] admonished of modesty, or to be modest **B/T**
[124] to our covetousness **B/T**

we lose certain things for uncertain. Surely that Sannio in Terence[125] [speaks] wittily:[126] 'I,' quoth° he, 'will not buy hope so dear.'[127]

5. Of a City Mouse and a Country Mouse [showing the fears and dangers that rich men are always in. And that therefore a little with safety is better than abundance with continual fear and danger.][128,129]

It pleased a city mouse to walk into the country. A country mouse saw him,[130] inviteth [him;] preparation is made;[131] they go to supper.[132] The country mouse fetcheth forth whatsoever he had laid up against winter, and bringeth[133] out all his store[134] that he might satisfy[135] the daintiness of so great a guest. Yet notwithstanding,[136] the city mouse, frowning,[137] condemneth the scarcity[138] of the country, and then[139] praiseth the plenty[140] of the city. [And,] going back, he leadeth the country mouse with him into the city, that he might approve[141] in deed that which he had bragged of in words. They go to the banquet which the city mouse had gorgeously prepared.[142] As they were at the banquet,[143] the noise of a key is heard in the lock. They trembled and,

---

[125] Terentian Sannio **B/T** Sannio is a character in the Roman playwright Terence's play *Adelphi* [*The Brothers*]; he is a pimp and a slave trader. See Terence, *The Brothers*, in *Phormio. The Mother-In-Law. The Brothers*, trans. by John Barsby (Cambridge, MA: Harvard University Press, 2001). [Eds]

[126] subtly, craftily **B/T**

[127] with a price **B/T**

[128] *Bitterness in riches, or the fears and dangers wherein rich men live* **B**

[129] In 1617, fable 9. [Eds]

[130] this [mouse] **B/T** The Latin reads *hunc* [this] (1518, sig. A2v); Brinsley instructs his translators to choose a demonstrative pronoun, not a personal pronoun, to translate 'him'. [Eds]

[131] it is prepared **B/T**

[132] it is gone to sup **B/T**

[133] draweth out **B/T**

[134] victuals° or provision **B/T**

[135] fulfil or fill **B/T**

[136] nevertheless **B/V**

[137] wrinkling his forehead **B/T**

[138] poverty **B/V**

[139] and afterward **B/V**

[140] abundance **B/V**

[141] give proof and experience of that to him **B/T**

[142] had prepared gaily, or richly, excellently **B/T**

[143] between to feast, or their feasting **B/T** The Latin reads *Inter epulandum* [amidst the banqueting] (1518, sig. A2v). [Eds]

running, fled away.¹⁴⁴ The country mouse, both unaccustomed and ignorant of the place, hardly° saved himself.¹⁴⁵ The servant departing, the city mouse returneth unto the table and calleth the country mouse. He, scarcely at length having put away his fear,¹⁴⁶ creepeth out, [and] asketh the city mouse, drinking unto him,¹⁴⁷ whether this peril¹⁴⁸ be often. He answered that it was daily, that it ought to be contemned.°¹⁴⁹ Then the country mouse:¹⁵⁰ 'Daily?' quoth he. 'In good sooth,°¹⁵¹ your dainties° savour more of gall° than of honey. I, in truth, had rather¹⁵² have my scarcity with security, than this abundance with such fear.'¹⁵³

The Moral: Riches have indeed a show of pleasure,¹⁵⁴ but if you look within [them] they have perils¹⁵⁵ and bitterness. There was one Eutrapelus¹⁵⁶ who, when he would hurt his enemies most of all, made them rich, saying¹⁵⁷ that he would revenge himself of them, for¹⁵⁸ that they should receive¹⁵⁹ with their riches a great pack¹⁶⁰ of cares.¹⁶¹

---

¹⁴⁴ They began to tremble exceedingly, and, in flying, often to fly away. **B/T** The Latin reads *trepidare illi, & fugitare fugitando* (1518, sig. A2v). The verbs *trepidare* and *fugitare* are both in the infinitive form ('to tremble', 'to flee'), rather than being conjugated properly (e.g., *trepidant*, 'they flee'). In his parsed version of these fables, Sturtevant adds in what he assumes is a missing word, *occipiunt* [they begin] to make sense of the infinitive forms (Simon Sturtevant, *The Etymologist of Aesops Fables, containing the construing of his Latin fables into English* [London, 1602], p. 14). Brinsley's note accords with Sturtevant's emendation. [Eds]
¹⁴⁵ to defend himself hardly or grievously **B/T**
¹⁴⁶ he, his fear being scarcely laid away at length **B/T**
¹⁴⁷ inviting him to the pots **B/T** i.e., inviting him to drink [Eds]
¹⁴⁸ danger **B/V**
¹⁴⁹ it to be daily to owe to be contemned **B/T**
¹⁵⁰ country mouse said or replied **B/T**
¹⁵¹ As Hercules shall help me **B/T** Brinsley removes the reference to Hercules in his translation of this mild oath but retains it for the purposes of translating back into Latin. The Latin reads *mehercule* [by Hercules, indeed], a mild oath (1518, sig. A2v). [Eds]
¹⁵² will rather, or desire **B/T**
¹⁵³ anxiety, or care; doubtfulness, or fearfulness **B/T**
¹⁵⁴ indeed do bear before themselves [or make a show of] pleasure **B/T**
¹⁵⁵ dangers **B/V**
¹⁵⁶ P. Volumnius Eutrapelus was a Roman knight and a close friend of Marc Antony. This description of his treatment of his enemies is first recorded in Horace's *Epistles* I.xviii.31–35 (Horace, *Satires, Epistles, and Ars Poetica*, trans. by Fairclough, p. 370). [Eds]
¹⁵⁷ saying oft **B/T**
¹⁵⁸ revenge them [or take vengeance of them] so **B/T**
¹⁵⁹ them to receive **B/T**
¹⁶⁰ a very great, or huge fardle **B/T**
¹⁶¹ troubles **B/V**

6. Of a Lion and a Mouse [teaching great men to deal kindly with the meanest.]°[162,163]

A lion, being weary with heat and with running, rested in the shadow upon green leaves,[164] and,[165] a flock of mice running over his back, he, awaking, catched one of them.[166] The captive beseecheth [him], crieth that he was not worthy that the lion should be angry at him.[167] He, bethinking[168] himself that there was no praise in the death of such a silly° little beast,[169] lets go the prisoner.[170] And not very long after,[171] as the lion by chance runs through the land, he falls into nets; he may roar, but he cannot get forth.[172] The mouse heareth the lion roaring miserably, acknowledgeth [his] voice, creepeth into the holes, seeketh the knots of the nets, findeth [them] being sought, gnaweth [them] being found; the lion escapeth out of the nets.[173]

The Moral: This fable persuadeth clemency° to mighty men.[174] For as human things are unstable, [so] mighty men themselves sometimes need the help of the baser. Wherefore° a wise man, although he may, will be afraid to hurt any man whosoever.[175] But he that feareth not to hurt another doth exceeding foolishly.[176] Why so? Because although, trusting in his own power,[177] he feareth no man, it will peradventure° come to pass in time[178] that he may fear. For it is evident that it hath happened to famous and great kings, that they

---

[162] *Clemency towards inferiors* **B**
[163] In 1617, fable 14. [Eds]
[164] a green leaf **B/T**
[165] but **B/T**
[166] one of many of them **B/T**
[167] him to be unworthy whom the lion should be angry at **B/T**
[168] thinking seriously **B/T**
[169] no praise to be in the death of so very small a little beast **B/T**
[170] captive or [mouse] being taken **B/T**
[171] neither truly so much after **B/T**
[172] it is lawful to roar; it is not lawful to go out **B/T** The Latin reads *Rugire licet, exire non licet* (1518, sig. A4r). Brinsley is explaining that the Latin repeats the word *licet* [one may, it is permitted, it is lawful]. [Eds]
[173] having sought them findeth them, and having found them gnaweth them, whereby the lion escapeth out of the nets **B/V**
[174] great men to be courteous towards the poor **B/V**
[175] even any of men **B/T**
[176] doteth greatly **B/T**
[177] enjoying, or relying upon his own power **B/T**
[178] it will be peradventure in time to come **B/T**

have either needed[179] the favour of base men,[180] or feared their anger.[181]

7. Of a Thief and a Dog [teaching to beware of flatterers.][182,183]

A thief of a time reaching° bread to a dog that he would hold his peace, the dog answered,[184] 'I know thy treachery.[185] Thou givest [me] bread that I should leave off barking.[186] But I hate thy gift, because if I shall take [thy] bread, thou wilt carry away all things out of these houses.'[187]

The Moral: Beware you lose[188] [not] a great [commodity] for a small commodity's sake.[189] Take heed you trust [not] every man.[190] For there are [men] who will not only speak courteously but also deal kindly,[191] only with purpose to deceive.[192]

---

[179] stood in need of **B/V**
[180] vile dwarves, or men of no reputation **B/T**
[181] been afraid of their displeasure **B/V**
[182] *Flattery and deceit* **B**
[183] In 1617, fable 19. [Eds]
[184] A dog answered sometimes, a thief reaching bread [to him] that he may be silent. **B/T**
[185] I have known thy lyings in wait. **B/T**
[186] whereby I may cease to bark **B/T**
[187] from these roofs of the houses, or from under these roofs **B/T**
[188] take heed thou lose **B/T**
[189] for the cause of a little commodity **B/T**
[190] you have trust to everyone whom you please **B/T**
[191] do not speak bountifully, but also do bountifully **B/T**
[192] by deceit, or in craft **B/T**

8. Of a Wolf and a Young Sow[193] [teaching us to beware of them who are too officious.]°[194,195]

A young sow was about to pig.°[196] A wolf promiseth that he will be[197] the keeper[198] of [her] young.[199] The sow[200] answered that she had no need of the service[201] of the wolf. If he would be[202] accounted devout,[203] [and] if he desire to do her a kindness,[204] that he would get him further off.[205] For that the kindness of the wolf should consist[206] not in [his] presence, but in [his] absence.

The Moral: We are not to give credit to all things which everyone saith.[207] Many will promise their help not for the love of you, but of themselves,[208] seeking their own commodity,° not yours.[209]

---

[193] a sow **B/V** In 1617 this note is not marked in the text, nor is it preceded by '*' or 'r' in the margin. In 1624 it is preceded by a lowercase letter in the margin (thereby indicating that it communicates something about the variety of the English language, which we have marked as '**B/V**'). We think, however, it might indicate something about translation, signalling that the translator could use a generic word for pig, and not necessarily 'young pig'. The Latin reads *sucula* [little pig] (1518, sig. B1v). [Eds]
[194] *Too much officiousness* **B**
[195] In 1617, fable 20. [Eds]
[196] farrow° **B/V**
[197] himself to be **B/T**
[198] tender **B/V**
[199] pigs **B/V**
[200] *Puerpera* signifying a woman travailing° or in childbed, here put for a sow pigging **B/T** It is unusual for Brinsley to supply his translators with the necessary Latin word; in this case, the metaphorical use of the word *puerpera* [woman in labour] in the Latin (1518, sig. B1v) caused a wrinkle in the translation practices used in the rest of this text. [Eds]
[201] herself not to need the pliantness [or attendance] **B/T**
[202] will be **B/T**
[203] godly or courteous **B/T**
[204] if he covet to do an acceptable thing or a pleasure **B/T**
[205] that he go away further **B/T**
[206] for the office or service of the wolf to consist **B/T**
[207] All things are not to be credited to all men. **B/T**
[208] Many do promise their diligence not by or for the love of you, but of themselves. **B/T**
[209] not your [commodity] **B/T**

AESOP'S FABLES TRANSLATED GRAMMATICALLY

9. Of a Horse and an Ass [showing how it commonly falls out with them who are too insolent in their prosperity.][210,211]

A horse [of a time], adorned[212] with trappings and with a saddle, ran by the way with a very great neighing.[213] But, by chance, a loaden° ass hindered him as he was running.[214] The horse, raging[215] with anger, and fiercely chewing [his] foaming bridle:[216] 'What,' quoth he, 'thou slow, thou sluggish [ass,] dost thou hinder the horse?[217] Give place,[218] I say, or I will trample thee[219] with my feet.' The ass contrarily, not daring to bray, gives place quietly.[220] But as the horse was swiftly flying forward[221] and speeding his pace, [his] groin[222] burst. Then, being unfit[223] for running and show, he is stripped[224] of [his] furniture,[225] and afterwards is sold to a carman.°[226] Afterwards, the ass[227] seeth him coming with a car,[228] and speaks unto him: 'Ho, good sir, what fine furniture is there? Where is your golden saddle, [your] studded[229] girth? Where [is] your glittering[230] bridle? Oh, friend, it must needs° so fall out to [you] being [so] proud.'[231]

The Moral: Most men are lifted up in prosperity, neither mindful[232] of themselves nor of modesty. But because they wax° insolent in

---

[210] *Insolency° of proud men in their prosperity* **B**
[211] In 1617 this fable is misnumbered as 32, following another fable 32 and preceding fable 34. In 1624 it is corrected to fable 33. [Eds]
[212] trimmed, or set out **B/T**
[213] whinnying **B/V**
[214] a little ass, being loaden, stood against [him] [or in his way] running **B/T**
[215] fuming or storming **B/V**
[216] being fierce biting on the frothing bridles **B/T**
[217] stand against the horse, or stand in the horse's way **B/T**
[218] depart **B/V**
[219] I do tread upon thee **B/T**
[220] departs, or yields stilly, or being still gives place **B/T**
[221] the horse flying forward **B/T**
[222] the part of the belly about the sheath **B/T**
[223] unprofitable **B/T**
[224] spoiled **B/T**
[225] ornaments **B/T**
[226] carter **B/V**
[227] little ass **B/T**
[228] drawing° in a car or a cart **B/V**
[229] bossed° **B/T**
[230] shining or fine **B/T**
[231] i.e., It was necessary that this would happen to you because you were so proud. [Eds]
[232] remembering **B/V**

prosperity, they run into adversity. I would admonish[233] them to be wary[234] who seem [to themselves] to be in prosperity.[235] For if the wheel of Fortune shall be turned about, they shall perceive it[236] a most miserable kind of misfortune to have been in prosperity.[237] That mischief also is added[238] unto the heap of their unhappiness, that they shall be contemned of those whom they[239] have contemned, and those will mock them whom they themselves have laughed at.[240]

10. Of a Wood and a Countryman° [teaching us to beware wherein and how we gratify our enemies.][241,242]

At what time the trees spake,[243] a countryman came unto a wood, desiring that he might take[244] a helve°[245] for his hatchet. The wood assenteth unto [him].[246] The countryman, having fitted his hatchet,[247] began to cut down the trees. Then, and[248] indeed too late, it repented the wood[249] of her facility.[250] It grieved her to have been[251] the cause of her own destruction.

The Moral: See[252] of whom you deserve well. There have been many who, having received a benefit,[253] have abused it to[254] the destruction of the author.[255]

---

[233] would have admonished **B/T**
[234] heedy° **B/V**
[235] happy **B/T**
[236] feel it **B/T**
[237] happy **B/T**
[238] cometh **B/T**
[239] they themselves **B/T**
[240] mocked **B/V**
[241] *Gratifying our enemies to our hurt* **B**
[242] In 1617, fable 39. [Eds]
[243] their own [or proper] speech was to the trees **B/T**
[244] that it may be lawful to take **B/T**
[245] halm° or stool° **B/V**
[246] noddeth unto it **B/T**
[247] his hatchet being fitted **B/T**
[248] but **B/V**
[249] i.e., the wood repented [Eds]
[250] readiness to yield or be entreated **B/V**
[251] be **B/T**
[252] take heed **B/V**
[253] a benefit being received **B/T**
[254] unto **B/T**
[255] giver **B/V**

11. Of the Limbs[256] **and the Belly** [declaring the necessity of gratifying others.][257,258]

The foot and hand of a time accused the belly, for that their gains were devoured by it living in idleness.[259] They command that it labour or that it seek[260] not to be nourished. It beseecheth them once or twice,[261] yet, notwithstanding, the hands deny to relieve it.[262] The belly being consumed[263] thorough° lack of food,[264] when all the limbs began to faint,[265] then at length the hands would be kind,[266] but that too late.[267] For the belly, being feeble[268] thorough lack of use,[269] repelled[270] [all] meat;° so whilst all the limbs envy the belly, they perish together with the belly.[271]

The Moral: It is even so in human society like as in the society of the members.[272] One member needs another,[273] [and] a friend needeth a friend. Wherefore we must use mutual kindnesses,[274] [and] mutual works,[275] [for] neither riches nor the highest dignities[276] can sufficiently defend a man.[277] The only and chief stay[278] is the friendship of very many.[279]

---

[256] members or parts of the body, or joints **B/T**
[257] *Necessity of friendship and gratifying others* **B**
[258] In 1617, fable 40. [Eds]
[259] being idle **B/T**
[260] require **B/T**
[261] once and again **B/T**
[262] nourishment [or relief] unto it **B/T**
[263] spent **B/T**
[264] by famine or hunger **B/V**
[265] fail **B/T**
[266] dutiful or officious **B/T**
[267] i.e., then at length the hands were willing to cooperate, but it was too late [Eds]
[268] weak **B/T**
[269] disuse **B/T**
[270] beat or put back, or refused **B/T**
[271] with the belly perishing **B/T**
[272] human society hath itself so, even as it is in the society of, etc. **B/T**
[273] A member needeth a member. **B/T**
[274] duties of one another **B/V**
[275] good turns **B/V** an idiom meaning good deeds or friendly acts [Eds]
[276] tops of dignities, honours, or preferments **B/T**
[277] do defend a man sufficiently **B/T**
[278] garrison,° or aid **B/T**
[279] very many men **B/T**

12. Of an Ape and a Fox-Cub [teaching that the rich had rather hurt themselves with too much than to part with aught° to the poor.]²⁸⁰,²⁸¹

An ape entreats a fox-cub that she would give her a part of her tail to cover [her] buttocks, for that that was a burden to her, which would be of use and an honour to herself.²⁸² The cub answereth²⁸³ that she had nothing too much,²⁸⁴ and that she had rather²⁸⁵ have the ground to be swept²⁸⁶ with her tail, than the buttocks of the ape to be covered.²⁸⁷

The Moral: There are which need;²⁸⁸ there are others who have too much,²⁸⁹ yet, notwithstanding, it is not the manner of any of the rich to bless the needy with their superfluity.°²⁹⁰

---

²⁸⁰ *Miserableness in the rich, who cannot part with aught to the poor* **B**
²⁸¹ In 1617, fable 41. [Eds]
²⁸² for [that thing] to be a burden to her [viz. the cub] which would be a use and an honour to herself **B/T** Here, the ape argues that the part of the tail that she is asking for is just a burden to the fox-cub anyway and would be put to better use by the ape, who would be honoured to use it to cover her buttocks. Brinsley's note is a close, literal translation of the Latin: *Illi enim esse oneri, quod sibi foret usui, & honori* (1518, sig. B6r). [Eds]
²⁸³ she answereth **B/T**
²⁸⁴ there to be nothing too much **B/T** In other words, the fox-cub responds that she does not have too much or spare tail. [Eds]
²⁸⁵ herself to will rather **B/T**
²⁸⁶ brushed **B/V** The phrase 'ground to be swept' indicates that the Latin verb is the passive infinitive (*uerri*) (1518, sig. B6r). [Eds]
²⁸⁷ than to cover the ape's buttocks with it **B/V**
²⁸⁸ i.e., There are some (people) who need. [Eds]
²⁸⁹ to whom it doth abound **B/T**
²⁹⁰ That fashion is to none of the rich, that he may bless the needy with his superfluous matter [or goods]. **B/T** The Latin reads *Nulli tamen diuitum id moris est, ut re superflua beet egenos* (1518, sig. B6r). Brinsley's paraphrase alerts his reader to certain features of the Latin, such as the fact that the Latin uses the dative of possession ('to none of the rich', *nulli*, dative singular; *diuitum*, genitive plural masculine), and the fact that the second part of the sentence requires a subjunctive verb ('that he may bless', *beet*, third-person singular present active subjunctive). [Eds]

JOHN OGILBY

from *The Fables of Aesop, paraphrased in verse, adorned with sculpture, and illustrated with annotations* (1651)

and *Aesopics, or a second collection of fables, paraphrased in verse, adorned with sculpture, and illustrated with annotations* (1668)

Examples are best Precepts; And a Tale
Adorn'd with Sculpture better may prevaile,
To make Men lesser Beasts, than all the store
Of tedious Volumes vext the World before.

JOHN OGILBY

THE FABLES OF AESOP AND AESOPICS

To the Right° Honourable Heneage Finch, Earl of Winchilsea and Viscount Maidstone, and the Right Honourable Henry Seymour, Lord Beauchamp

My lords,

After the felicity my first labour, the translation of Virgil,[1] received in the protection of so learned and so honourable a patron as your noble father, my very good lord, I could not, nor did, resist — being charged home with gratitude, duty, and the harmony of order — to entitle my second piece to the same renowned family by this humble dedication to your lordships.

Nor is it (may it please your honours) without something of design, by which this my last work, whate'er it be, may in such a grove of honour, with your names inscribed, and influenced by your virtues, last until the truest test of books shall sign its commission for milder ages, and perhaps more clear from prejudice, barbarity, and, the most cruel of all enemies, ignorance.

If any, my good lords, shall accuse my judgement and choice, who had the honour of conversation with Virgil, that I have descended to Aesop — whose apologues° this day are read and familiar° with children in their first schools, and in these latter times dishonoured by unworthy translators — though the dictates of my own reason deny I should make answer to such men, it shall not be impertinent to say, this ancient mythologist hath through all and the most learned times been highly esteemed by the wisest, and studied to the great advantage of human life. Macrobius, of most eminent judgement, allowed his book a place in the temple of wisdom, and Socrates, who was judged by the oracle the wisest man then living, followed him in all his ways of persuasive oratory, not disdaining to translate him into verse.[2]

---

[1] Ogilby refers to Virgil, *The Works of Publius Virgilius Maro*, trans. by John Ogilby (London, 1649), which was dedicated to Henry Seymour's father, William.

[2] Ambrosius Theodosius Macrobius was a fifth-century Latin grammarian and philosopher who divided fables, meaning fiction more generally, into two categories in his *Saturnalia*: that which only serves to bring pleasure to its audience and that which inspires its audience to perform virtuous deeds. Aesop's fables were considered to fall into the latter category, though they do not meet Macrobius's ideal, which is those fables that rest 'on a solid foundation of truth, which is treated in a fictitious style' (Macrobius, *Commentary on the Dream of Scipio*, trans. by William Harris Stahl [New York: Columbia University Press, 1952], p. 85). According to Plato in

But I fear I have troubled your lordships with this vindication, and now be pleased to receive your own, the old philosopher in a modern and poetical dress; if he find entertainment from you, it shall be an honour to him, and the greatest engagement upon,

My lords,
Your must humble and obedient servant,
John Ogilby

---

his *Phaedo*, the Greek philosopher Socrates translated Aesop's fables into verse while he was imprisoned (60B–61B); for more on this, see Sections I and II of the introduction to this volume.

To my Friend Mr. Ogilby[3]

In empire's childhood, and the dawn of arts,
When God in temples dwelt not, but in hearts,
When men might teachers by their deeds believe,
When pow'r robbed none, nor science did deceive,
5 Nor soaring thought wildly to Heaven did fly,
Searching records which in God's closet lie,
To know (since none like God eternal were)
How His dominion could at first appear,
Presuming He, nor honour had, nor sway,
10 Before some were to worship and obey—[4]
    Vain thought! Could man doubt God was e'er alone,
Whose several beings to Himself were known,[5]
Who if He pow'r could want,° it must but be
Because He could not make fit company
15 To tend His own perfections, which were more
Than now best souls can perfectly adore;
Or could He, if alone, feel want° of sway,
Who worlds could make, and make those worlds obey?
For what He since created argues more
20 His love of doing good, than love of pow'r;
Nor so could God mistake, as to believe
That to be honour which His creatures give;
Nor could He then, since honour is respect,
Want honour 'til Himself He did neglect;
25 For if it might be said He was alone,
Yet to Himself His excellence was known,
Which was so great, that if Himself could raise
His honour higher with His own just praise,
He was Himself His own abundant theme,
30 And only could Himself enough esteem.[6]
But these vexed thoughts, which schools unquiet make,

---

[3] This commendatory poem is signed at the end by William Davenant, a poet and dramatist of the seventeenth century.
[4] i.e., At that time (unlike now), thought did not fly up to Heaven attempting to figure out God's secrets, assuming that God had no power before people existed to worship Him. The first ten lines are not technically a sentence: they are a series of introductory dependent clauses that get interrupted by the tangent on God's (lack of) solitude.
[5] i.e., How could anyone believe that God, who has several selves, could be alone?
[6] i.e., Even if God were alone, He would be aware of His own excellence, which was so superior that only God would be excellent enough to praise it.

And like to madness keep their souls awake,
Took rest and slept in th'infancy of time,
And with sealed eyes did never upward climb.
35   To study God, God's student, man, was made,
To read Him as in nature's text conveyed,
Not as in Heaven, but as He did descend
To Earth, His easier book, where, to suspend
And save His miracles, each little flower
40 And lesser fly shows His familiar power.
Then usefully the studious world was wise,
Not learned as now in useless subtleties.
Truth naked then, not armed with eloquence,
Walked safe, because all rose in her defence.
45 But now the gravest schools through pride contend,
And truth awhile, at last, themselves defend.
So vexed is now the world with mysteries,
Since prouder minds dressed truth in art's disguise,
And so serene and calm was empire then,
50 Whilst statesmen studied beasts to govern men.
    Accursed be Egypt's priests, who first through pride
And avarice° this common light did hide,
To temples did this moral text confine,
And made it hard to make it seem divine;
55 In creatures' forms a fancied° deity
They drew, and raised the mystery so high,
As all to reach° it did require their aid,
For which they were, as hired expounders, paid.
This clouded text, which but to few was known,
60 In time grew darker, and was read by none;
So weak of wing is soaring mystery,
And learning's light goes out when held too high.
    But blessed be Aesop, whom the wise adore,
Who this dark science° did to light restore,
65 Which though obscured when raised and made divine,
Yet soon did in his humble morals shine.
For that which was by art for profit hid,
And to the laity,° as to spies, forbid,
He, as the hireless°[7] priest of nature, brought

---

[7] The word 'hireless' here means without hire or pay, unpaid; Aesop's only thanks, we are told, was knowledge in itself, unlike the priests, who hid knowledge for their own profit.

70   From temples, and her doctrine freely taught,
Whilst even to beasts, men, blushing, seemed ashamed
That men by beasts he counselled° and reclaimed.
    Blessed be our poet too! whose fire hath made
Grave Aesop warm in death's detested shade;
75   Though verses are but fetters° deemed by those
Who endless journeys make in wand'ring prose,
Yet in thy verse, methinks° I Aesop see
Less bound than when his master made him free;
So well thou fitt'st the measure of his mind,
80   Which, though the slave, his body, were confined,
Seemed, as thy wit, still unconstrained and young,
And like thy numbers easy and as strong.[8]
Or as thy muse in her satiric strain
Doth spare the person, whilst the vice is slain,
85   So his rebukes, though sharp, were kind and grave,
Like judges chiding those whom they would save.
Thus since your equal souls so well agree,
I needs° must paint his mind in drawing thee.
Be both renowned! And whilst you nature preach,
90   May art ne'er raise your text above our reach.
Your morals will (they are so subtly plain)
Convince the subtle, and the simple gain,
So pleasant too, that we more pleasure take
(Though only pleasure doth our vices make)
95   To hear our sins rebuked with so much wit,
Than e'er we took when those we did commit.
Laws do in vain with force our wills invade,
Since you can conquer when you but persuade.

    W. Davenant
    From the Tower
    Sept. 30, 1651[9]

---

[8] Aesop was supposedly deformed, and therefore his hunchbacked body did not reflect his agile and able mind. Davenant flatters Ogilby by saying that Ogilby's verse matches, or measures up to, Aesop's mind rather than his body.

[9] In 1651, Davenant was in prison in the Tower of London for supporting the Royalist cause during the English Civil War. This signature not only identifies his location but also aligns him with Ogilby's own Royalist sympathies and the political nature of this translation.

JOHN OGILBY

To my Worthy Friend Mr. John Ogilby[10]

In what part of our hemisphere could spread
A cloud so long t'obscure thy radiant head?
Shine forth, prodigious star, and make us know
What to thy welcome beams our age must owe.
5   As thou appear'st, how doth each trembling light
Retreat? Whilst thou, emergent from the night,
Like day's new sovereign, hast discovered more
Than all their revolutions showed before.
    At this a marble heaves! Methinks I see
10 The learnèd shade of Virgil rise to thee,
Taught our own language, with that soul and sense
As hath not shamed his Roman eloquence,
And kissing his fresh shroud, smile that he must
Confess himself thy debtor in his dust,
15 Whilst we admire both thy bold hand and fate,
Who hast performed the next thing to create.
    Yet here thou leav'st us not, as if thy fame
Were narrow, and too stooping for thy name;
Aesop the great mythologist, thy pen
20 Hath raised, and more than made alive again
(When rhymers vexed his ghost, and men to see't,
Staining fair° paper with their cloven feet).[11]
Thou hast new° made him, for (as if by thee,
Shuffled into his antique dust) we see
25 Him rise, but visible in some earthy part;
His soul is the new creature of thy art.
This could thy great converse with Virgil do,
To make old Aesop rise a poet too.
    What in thy method must our wits amaze
30 Next thy translation, and this paraphrase:
Awake that poem, born from thy own flame,
And at least second in heroic name;
This, only this, remains then: thou may'st try,
And thy muse tell thee 'tis too late to die.

    James Shirley

---

[10] This poem is signed at the end by James Shirley, a poet and dramatist of the seventeenth century.

[11] i.e., You resurrected Aesop's spirit at a time when other poets, who were staining paper with their poor poetry, were vexing both Aesop's ghost and other men.

THE FABLES OF AESOP AND AESOPICS

1. Of the Cock and Precious Stone[12]

Stout Chanticleer° three times aloud proclaims
Day's signal victory o'er night's vanquished flames;[13]
As oft the mighty lions are affrighted[14]

---

[12] In the first book of fables, *The Fables of Aesop*, fable 1.
[13] Ausonius:

>   —*ter clara instantis Eoi*
> *Signa canit serus deprenso Marte satelles.*

> Mars' tardy sentinel° three times aloud proclaimed
> Th'approaching day.

The fable is thus related by Lucian: There was a young man named Alector, very intimate with Mars, insomuch that whensoever Mars went to Venus, he took Alector with him (fearing the sun might betray him to Vulcan) and left him to watch at the door and to give notice when the sun approached. On a time, Alector fell asleep and unwillingly betrayed his trust. The sun discovered the two lovers to Vulcan, who caught them in a net. Mars, as soon as he was got loose, in anger turned the young man to a cock. For this reason, before the sun riseth, the cock crows to give notice of his approach. Chaeremon the Stoic, and Proclus and Porphyrius, Pythagorean philosophers, ascribe the crowing of the cock before day to a sympathy betwixt that bird and the sun, affirming that the sun contributes something celestial to it, for which it gratefully riseth up and clappeth its wings, and celebrates the approach of its patron. Hence perhaps is the cock called the Persian bird (Hesychius, Περσικὸς ὄρνις, ὁ ἀλεκτρυών·) because, as the Persians, he worships the rising sun. But the common reason is taken from the fable related by Aristophanes, in *Avibus*, that on a time the cock was emperor of Persia, and reigned tyrannically, insomuch that still all persons as soon as he crows betake themselves to labour, as if fearing punishment for negligence. [Ogilby's note.] The two lines quoted are from Ausonius' 'A Riddle of the Number Three,' *Ausonius, in Two Volumes*, vol. 1, trans. by Hugh G. Evelyn White (London: William Heinemann, 1919), ll. 26–27, p. 360. The translation that immediately follows, here and throughout, is Ogilby's own. Lucian's story about Alector is in his 'The Dream, or the Cock,' in Lucian, *Lucian, in Seven Volumes*, vol. 2, trans. by A. M. Harmon (London: William Heinemann, 1915), pp. 177–79. Hesychius was a fifth- or sixth-century CE Greek grammarian who compiled a Greek lexicon. The lexicon defines περσικὸς ὄρνις [Persian bird] as ὁ ἀλεκτρυών [the cock]; see Hesychius, *Hesychii Alexandrini Lexicon*, ed. by Mauricius Schmidt (Jenae: Sumpibus Hermanni Dufftii, 1867), s.v. περσικὸς ὄρνις. In Aristophanes' play *The Birds*, a character claims, 'Time was that the Persians were ruled by the Cock, a King autocratic, alone; | [...] | And the 'Persian' [Περσικὸς ὄρνις] he still by the people is called from the Empire that once was his own' (Aristophanes, *Aristophanes, in Three Volumes*, vol. 2, trans. by Benjamin Bickley Rogers [London: William Heinemann, 1924]; quotation from *The Birds* ll. 483, 485, pp. 174–75).

[14] The reason why the lion is afraid of the cock, Proclus saith, is because the cock hath a much greater share of the sun's influence than the lion, though they both derive their natures from him. But Lucretius otherwise:

With his shrill notes, while others are delighted.
5   In a short coat of feathers warm as furs,
       In boots drawn up and gilded spurs
   (Of old the valiant cock the eagle knighted),
   He from proud roosts, high as the thatch descends,
   His wives, his concubines, and fair race attends.

10 Scaling a sordid mountain, straight° he found
    A star in dust, a sparkling diamond.
    Then spake the cock: 'Stone of the whitest water,[15]
    Whom time, nor fire can waste,° nor anvil batter,[16]

Nimirum, quia sunt gallorum in corpore quaedam
Semina, quae cum sunt oculis immissa leonum
Pupillas interfodiunt, acremque dolorem
Praebent, ut nequeant contra durare feroces.

Because a seed in the cock's body lies,
Whose effluent atoms hurt the lion's eyes,
And through the balls with horrid anguish goes,
That they their courage and all fierceness lose.

There are not any sects of philosophy more opposite than these two: the Pythagoreans and Academics endeavouring to bring up all things to immateriality, the Epicureans to bring down all to materiality. And if I may freely give my opinion of the reasons which both allege for this, (*absit verba invidia*) they seem equally extravagant. [Ogilby's note.] The poetry is from Lucretius' poem about Epicurean atomism, *De Rerum Natura* [*On the Nature of Things*], IV.714–17. The phrase *absit verba invidia* means: let the words not be from hatred or envy, or let these words not be taken amiss. The phrase may be a citation of Livy's phrase *absit invidia verbo* from his *Ab Urbe Condita Libri*; see Livy, *Livy, in Thirteen Volumes*, vol. 4, trans. by B. O. Foster (London: William Heinemann, 1926) IX.xix.15; p. 240.

[15] The diamond plays four waters, which are four colours: white, brown, blue, and green. White the best, brown the second best, blue the third, green the worst. Yet the white table diamond, if it be thick, will play black, but if it play white it is much better. [Ogilby's note.] A 'table diamond' is a diamond with a large flat upper surface, and a diamond's 'water' is its transparency or lustre: 'The three highest grades of quality in diamonds were formerly known as the *first water*, *second water*, and *third water*' (*OED*, s.v. 'water, n.' 28; see also P1e(a)). To 'play' coloured waters seems to mean to show different colours.

[16] Pliny, lib. 37, cap. 6: *Duritia inenarrabilis est, simulque ignium victrix natura, et nunquam incalescens; unde et nomen 'indomita' vis Graeca interpretatione accepit.* Its hardness is unexpressible; its nature conquers fire, never taking heat, whence named ἄδαμας by the Greeks. By the Arabians, *diamah*, from *dim*, to endure, whence our word *diamond*. [Ogilby's note.] In modern editions, the Pliny quotation can be found in book 37, chapter 15; see Pliny, *Natural History*, vol. 10, trans. by D. E. Eichholz (Cambridge, MA: Harvard University Press, 1967), p. 208. F. Corriente notes that a sixteenth-century Arabic-Spanish lexicon based heavily in Andalusi

If thee some skilful jeweller had sold,
15   Adornèd thus with purest gold,
To a fond lover, he, his love to flatter,
Would swear his lady's eyes outshine thy rays
(Brightest of gems), although she look nine ways.[17]

'Thou emblem of vain learning[18] may'st adorn
20 The wisest, but give me a barley corn.°

---

dialect includes an entry for the Arabic noun *diáma* [diamond]. The early lexicon also lists forms of the Arabic verb **dām yudūm dāyim** [to last or continue], including the forms *deguém*, *déim*, and *deymín* (F. Corriente, *A Dictionary of Andalusi Arabic* [Leiden: Brill, 1997], s.v. DYM, DWM). Although Ogilby states that the two words are etymologically linked, Corriente treats the word *diáma* not as a verbal noun (**diyāma**) derived from **dām yudūm dāyim**, but as an independent borrowing from Spanish (in Spanish the word for diamond was *diamante*). The more common term for diamond in Arabic is **al-mās**, which is well attested in Andalusi Arabic.

[17] i.e., even if she were cross-eyed

[18] Amongst other properties for which the diamond is compared to and made the emblem of learning, receive these from Pliny, lib. 37, cap. 6: *Venena irrita facit, et lymphationes abigit, et metus vanos expellit:* It nulls the force of poison, it expels frenzy and vain fears.

This fable was elegantly translated by Phaedrus, one of the Liberti of Augustus.

   Lib. 3, Fab. 11.
In sterquilinio pullus gallinaceus
Dum quaerit escam, margaritam repperit;
Iaces indigno quanta res, inquit, loco!
Hoc si quis pretii cupidus vidisset tui,
Olim redisses ad splendorem maximum.
Ego qui te inveni, potior cui multo est cibus.
Nec tibi prodesse, nec mihi quicquam potes.
   Hoc illis narro qui me non intelligunt.

The young cock, ransacking a dunghill, found,
In quest of softer fare, a diamond;
'Bright gem, how ill,' said he, 'thou here art set;
If one with thee who knew thy worth had met,
Thou hadst ere this in all thy glory shined.
But give me food; such gewgaws° I not mind;
Here's no preferment° for your fairer looks.'
   Know this all you who value not good books. [Ogilby's note.]

As in the note immediately preceding this one, this quotation from Pliny can be found in book 37, chapter 15 in modern editions. The modern Loeb edition (op. cit.) renders this moment in Pliny slightly differently: *adamas et venena vincit atque inrita facit et lymphationes abigit metusque vanos expellit a mente* (p. 210). In modern editions, these lines of poetry from Phaedrus, who was one of Augustus' *liberti* [freed slaves], can be found in Phaedrus's fables, book III, fable 12, in *Babrius and Phaedrus*, trans. by Ben Edwin Perry (Cambridge, MA: Harvard University Press, 1965), pp. 189–369. The Latin version of this fable in Perry's Loeb edition (p. 278) differs slightly from Ogilby's Latin.

Let meagre scholars waste their brains and tapers°
In quest of thee, while they turn anxious papers;
Let me have pleasure, and my belly full;
Far better is an empty skull
25 Than a head stuffed with melancholy vapours.
Lie still obscure; *I'll be to nature kind;*
My body I'll not starve to feed my mind.'[19]

Moral

Voluptuous° men philosophy despise;
'Down with all learning!' the armed soldier cries;
30 On glebe° and cattle greedy farmers look;
And merchants only prize their counting book.

---

[19] Occasionally, Ogilby will italicize whole lines or couplets, presumably to call attention to concise lessons, or to mark lines as proverbial. These lines are italicized in every edition. We have kept these lines in italics throughout.

2. The Battle of the Frog and Mouse[20]

    Frogland to save, and Micean realms to spare
    From war and ruin, two bold kings prepare
    The empire of the marshes to decide
    In single fight; from all parts far and wide,
5   Both nations flock to see the great event,
    And load with vows and prayers the firmament.
    Opposed petitions grant Heaven's court no rest,
    While hopes and fears thus struggle in their breast.
        Up to the fatal lists° and measured banks
10 Both armies drew; bold yellowcoats in ranks
    And black-furred Mouscovites the circle man,[21]
    Which the six-fingered giant could not span.[22]
    The rising hills each where the vulgar crowned,
    Nor long expect they, when the warlike sound
15 Of spirit-stirring hornets, gnats, and bees
    (Such trumpeters would blood turned ice unfreeze)
    Told the approach of two no petty kings,
    While the long vale° with big-voiced croakers rings.
        First King Frogmorton[23] with the freckled face
20 Enters the list (for they by lot° took place)
    Riding a crayfish, armed from head to heel
    In shell, Dame Nature's gift, instead of steel.
     Although the many-footed could not run
    With the great Crab, which yearly feasts the sun,
25 Nor with the golden Scorpion could set forth[24]
    And measure daily the tun-bellied° Earth,
    Yet such his speed, he ne'er was overtook
    By any shell-backed monster of the brook.

---

[20] In the first book of fables, *The Fables of Aesop*, fable 6.
[21] The yellowcoats are the frogs, and the black-furred mouscovites are the mice, with a pun on 'Muscovite', or an inhabitant of Russia.
[22] The hill is so large that even the biblical Goliath (described in 2 Samuel 21:20 as a six-fingered giant) could not span or step across it in one stride.
[23] In 1651, the frog king is named 'Frogpaddock'; as 'paddock' was another word for frog, the king's name originally meant 'Frogfrog'. Mark Loveridge explains that the name was 'topically altered' to 'Frogmorton' in later editions (Loveridge, *A History of Augustan Fable*, p. 113); the reference may be to William Morton, a prominent Royalist active during the English Civil War.
[24] The crab and the scorpion mentioned in these lines represent the Cancer and Scorpio constellations, respectively.

    The arms he wore once were a water snake's,
30 Which, in the battle when the springs and lakes
    Decided were, a conqueror he brought
    From the deep floods, with gold and purple wrought;
    O'er these a water rat's black fur he cast,°
    Dreadful with teeth and claws. Thus as he passed,
35 The vulgar shout to see their six-inched king
    Like great Alcides in his lion's skin.[25]
    A whole house armed his head, had been a snail's;[26]
    Though ostrich plumes it wants, and peacocks' tails,
    Yet every colour the great rainbow dyes
40 Shone on his crest, the wings of butterflies,
    Sent him of old a present from Queen Mab.[27]
    His targe,° the shell of a deserted crab,
    Where in the Frogian[28] tongue this verse was writ:
    'The manlike swimming king unvanquished yet.'
45 Six sprightly tadpoles his rush javelins bore;
    His sword — a sharp, long, two-edged flag — he wore
    Girt to his thigh, a wand'ring snail the hilt,
    With a bright varnish in meanders gilt.[29]

---

[25] Hercules, being about sixteen or eighteen years of age, slew the Nemaean lion (whose skin Juno had caused to be impenetrable, intending thereby the destruction of Hercules), and bore it ever after for his target. Euripides in his *Hercules Furens*:

Στολήν τε θηρὸς ἀμφέβαλλε σῷ κάρα
Λέοντος, ἧπερ αὐτὸς ἐξωπλίζετο.

Upon your head you put the lion's case,
Which both his cask, back-piece, and breast-plate was.

Whence we seldom see any statue of Hercules without it. [Ogilby's note.] Alcides was another name for the mythological hero Hercules. Ogilby's Greek comes from Euripides's *Hercules Furens* ll. 465–66.

[26] i.e., a snail's house (its shell) served as his helmet

[27] Queen Mab is the fairy described by Mercutio in William Shakespeare's *Romeo and Juliet* I.iv.51–93 (Shakespeare, *The Norton Shakespeare*, ed. by Greenblatt et al.). According to Mercutio, this miniature fairy was said to go into the noses and brains of people and compel them to have wishful dreams. In this fable, she is the deity that oversees the battle between the two warriors.

[28] In 1651 and 1665 this word was spelled 'Phrogian'. We have regularized the adjective with respect to the rest of the fable, but the spelling might suggest a pun on 'Phrygian', and therefore a nod to Aesop's supposed birthplace.

[29] A river of Lydia that had so many windings and turnings that it became a proverb among the Grecians, all obliquities° being called by them meanders. [Ogilby's note.] Because, as Ogilby notes, the Meander was a winding river, 'in meanders gilt' means a hilt with a meandering or wavy pattern of gilt or gold.

Appointed thus, about the lists he rode,[30]
50 While all admire the champion's arms and steed.
   Soon as the pleased spectators settled were,
   Glad acclamations melting into air,
   Voices were heard through echoing valleys ring,
   Th'approach foretelling of the Micean king.
55   A subdued mousetrap, his sedan° in peace,
   His chariot now, from man's high palaces
   Moustapha brought; ne'er through the scorching plain
   Did sweating kings draw such a Tamburlaine.[31]
   Six princes, captive ferrets, through deep tracts,°
60 Fearing the lash, oft fired his thund'ring axe,
   And though a heavy mortal was their load,
   King Oberon they o'er hill and dale° outrode.
   Entered the lists, he lights,° then mounted on
   A dappled° weasel, the bold Micedon[32]
65 Appeared (may we great things compare with small)
   Like the world's conqueror, though not so tall.
      His arms were not of steel, nor gold, nor brass,
   Nor sweating Cyclopes°[33] turned the yielding mass
   With griping° tongs, nor bull-skin bellows roar
70 To purge electrum° from the frothy ore,
   But the black coat of a Westphalia swine,[34]

---

[30] The word 'rode' is spelled 'rid' in *The Fables of Aesop*, to come closer to rhyming with 'steed'.

[31] Thanks to the plays of Christopher Marlowe, Tamburlaine was a well-known figure in early modern England; in Marlowe's play *Tamburlaine the Great, Part 2*, Tamburlaine forces conquered kings to pull his chariot.

[32] i.e., the bold mouse-leader

[33] The Cyclopes were the sons of Coelum and Tellus, released by Jupiter out of Hell, and employed to forge his fearful artillery, thunderbolts, for him; of whom thus Virgil, *Aeneid* 8:

Ferrum exercebant vasto Cyclopes in antro
Brontesque, Steropesque, et nudus membra Pyracmon,
His informatum manibus iam parte polita
Fulmen erat.

The Cyclopes in vast caves their anvils beat:
Steropes, Brontes, naked Pyracmon sweat
In forging thunder.

The names of these three express their faculties: thunder, lightning, and fire. [Ogilby's note.] These lines are from Virgil's *Aeneid*, VIII.424–27.

[34] i.e., black swine or pigs from Westphalia, a region in north-western Germany

JOHN OGILBY

    Long hung in smoke, which now like jet did shine.
       Fame says (and she tells truth as oft as lies)
    The seasoned gammon° Miceans did surprise,
75   Spoiled the red flesh before 'twas well served up
    After full boards, to relish a full cup.
    This their king's right his captains did present
    To him for safety, and an ornament;
    Such was black Moustapha's habergeon.°
80   The ancient heroes had but steel upon
    The heads of cruel spears, but this did wield
    A lance, whose body was all over steeled;°
    It was a knitting-needle, strong and bright;
    His helm, a thimble, dazed the en'mies' sight,
85   O'er which a thick-falled plume[35] wagged with each gale,
    Of tiffany,° gnawn from a lady's veil,
    In it a sprig which made his own afeard:
    The stiff mustachios of a dead cat's beard.
       His solid shield, which he so much did trust,
90   Was biscuit, though some write 'twas manchet° crust.
    Historians oft, as poets, do mistake,
    But I affirm 'twas biscuit, for the cake,
    They all agree, by navigation
    Four times was seasoned in the torrid zone.[36]
95   The story thus is told: the rattish prince,
    A great diviner, had intelligence
    From occult causes that the dangerous seas
    Must be forsa'en,[37] and floating palaces:
    The ship next voyage would by storms be lost.
100 Therefore his black bands swam to the next coast
    On biscuit safe, but Tybert[38] by the way
    (The prince of cats) made him and it a prey,
    Slew° on the shore, and feasted on his head;

---

[35] i.e., a thickly falling or full feather

[36] i.e., the tropics; the biscuit has been seasoned (and, presumably, hardened) over the course of four sea-voyages through the tropics. The word 'biscuit' means twice cooked (*bis cuit*), so Ogilby distinguishes the hardened biscuit from a softer manchet crust or cake.

[37] *The Fables of Aesop* reads 'forsook' where we have 'forsa'en'; we attempted to preserve the metre in this line even as we modernized Ogilby's verb form.

[38] Tybert became a typical name for a cat after it was popularized by the medieval tales about Reynard the Fox.

>   He, with blood sated, leaves neglected bread,
> 105 Of which black Moustapha after made his targe,
>   Like Ajax's sevenfold shield,[39] but not so large.
>   His motto was his title and his name,
>   Transposed into no costive anagram,[40]
>   Which from the Micean tongue we thus translate:
> 110 'The parmesan affecter,° strong, and great.'
>   Both champions searched, found free from fraud or charms,[41]
>   They take their stands, and peise° their mighty arms.
>   At once loud hornets sound, at once they start,
>   At once couched° spears; with equal force and art
> 115 Closed beavers° met, struck fire; at once they both
>   Did backward kiss their mother Earth, though loath.
>   But first his nimble foot the Micean found,

---

[39] Ajax's shield deserved a peculiar description by the Prince of Poets, *Iliad* 7:

Αἴας δ'ἐγγύθεν ἦλθε φέρων σάκος ἠΰτε πύργον,
Χάλκεον ἑπταβόειον, ὅ οἱ Τυχίος κάμε τεύχων, etc.

Ajax drew nigh, bearing a tower-like shield
Of brass, with seven hides lined, by Tychius dressed,
Of all the curriers in rich Hyle the best.
He with seven skins of bullocks fed at grass
Covered his shield, o'er all a plate of brass;
Defended with this breastwork, Ajax made
Straight up to Hector, and thus threat'ning, said: [Ogilby's note.]

Ogilby quotes the Greek of Homer's *Iliad* VII.219–20, but his translation is of VII.219–25.

[40] i.e., his motto was very clear, and was not mysterious or uncommunicative

[41] It seems to have been the opinion of the ancients that it was in the power of magic to preserve men invulnerable, for Chrysermus in his history of Peloponnesus tells how Juno by magical arts caused the moon to descend from Heaven, which filled a chest with froth, out of which was brought forth a lion, whose skin was impenetrable. Another story there is to the same purpose recorded by Aelian, thus: where Silenus tells the king of Lydia that there was a certain city whose inhabitants were not fewer than two hundred myriads° who died sometimes of sickness, but most commonly in the wars killed either by stones or wood, for they were invulnerable by steel. [Ogilby's note.] Chrysermus was a Greek historian whose work only survives in fragments. The myth that Ogilby describes is referenced in a text called 'Of the Names of Rivers and Mountains, and of Such Things as Are to Be Found Therein' (Plutarch, *Plutarch's Essays and Miscellanies, in Five Volumes*, vol. 5, ed. by A. H. Clough and William W. Goodwin [New York: The Colonial Company, Ltd., 1905], p. 499). This text used to be ascribed to Plutarch, though it is now commonly rejected from the canon of his works as pseudonymous. The story of Silenus is recounted in Aelian, *Historical Miscellany*, trans. by N. G. Wilson (Cambridge, MA: Harvard University Press, 1997), III.18, pp. 145–49.

When King Frogmorton, as loathed Irish ground[42]
His limbs had touched, lay on his back upright.
120   Yet, soon recovering, never Frogian knight
Made such a charge, for with strange fury led,
At the first blow he leaps quite o'er his head,
Bearing his pond'rous arms, his sword and targe.
    Nor was black Moustapha wanting in the charge
125   To show his wond'rous courage, strength, and skill,
For by th'advantage of a rising hill
A mole had wrought, he strikes, and though the stroke
Would not have felled° an ox, or cleft an oak,
Yet such it was, that had it ta'en, in blood
130   His soul had wandered through the Stygian flood,[43]
But missing, the soft air receives the wound,
And o'er and o'er he tumbles to the ground.
    Nor at th'advantage was Frogmorton slack,
But at one jump° bestrides° the Micean's back;
135   Then grasping him 'twixt his cold knees, he said,
'Robber of man, who now shall give thee aid?'
'Foul toad, so° Oberon please, I fear not thee,'
Stout Moustapha replied; then actively
He backward caught the short-armed king by th'wrists,
140   And bore him on his shoulders round the lists.
Loud croaks scale Heaven, then maugre° all his strength
Regained his sword, and threw him thrice his length.
    On equal terms again they battle joined,
Heroic souls in narrow breasts confined!
145   For these in Trojan wars, once champions fierce
With gallant acts adorned great Homer's verse,
After became testy philosophers,
And fought in hot disputes and learnèd jars,°
Then lions, bears, cocks, bulls, and brisly hogs,
150   Last transmigrated schismatics, or dogs.[44]

---

[42] It is observed that no venomous creature lives in Ireland, neither frogs which are not venomous, which, being brought over in ballast° from England and laid upon Irish ground, they gasp ready to expire, but being returned, recover presently, of which I have been an eyewitness. [Ogilby's note.]

[43] i.e., through the River Styx, the river of the underworld

[44] The Pythagoreans taught not only the transmigration of the soul from one man to another, but from man into beasts, and from beasts into man again. This is clearly delivered by Ovid, speaking in the person of Pythagoras:

>   Where'er they meet, the war is still renewed,
>   With lasting hatred and immortal feud.
>   The king — whose grandsire,° when it thundered loud,
>   'Mongst fire and hail dropped from a broken cloud,
> 155   And with an host of tadpoles from the sky[45]
>   In those vast fens° a Frogian colony
>   At first did plant — though icy was his skin,
>   With rage and shame an Etna felt within,[46]
>   Raised his broad flag to make a mighty blow,
> 160   Thinking at once in two to cleave the foe,
>   Who nimbly traversing with skill his ground,
>   On th'cerealian[47] shield received the wound;
>   Yet from the orbèd biscuit fell a slice,
>   Which near the list was snapped up in a trice.°
> 165   Here the crumb-picking king puts in a stuck°
>   With a bright needle, his stiff Spanish tuck,°
>   Which pierced Frogmorton's skin through's dragon's mail;[48]
>   Rage doubles, then the flag becomes a flail,
>   And on his thimble cask° struck such a heat,
> 170   That Moustapha was forcèd to retreat,

Ipse ego (nam memini) Trojani tempore belli
Panthoides Euphorbus eram, cui pectore quondam
Haesit in adverso gravis hasta minoris Atridae, etc.

I'th'Trojan wars (which I remember well)
Euphorbus was, Panthous' son, and fell
By Menelaus' lance; my shield again
At Argos late I saw in Juno's fane.°
All alter, nothing finally decays,
Hither and thither still the spirit strays,
Guest to all bodies; out of beasts it flies
To men, from men to beasts, and never dies. [Ogilby's note.]

Ogilby quotes the Latin of Ovid's *Metamorphoses* XV.160–63, but his translation is of XV.160–68.

[45] Amongst the rest of the prodigies, the ancients accounted the raining of frogs, mice, blood, stones; of which he will find many instances in the history of the Romans, that will peruse Julius Obsequens, *De Prodigiis*. [Ogilby's note.] Julius Obsequens was a Roman writer who most likely lived during the fourth century CE. Ogilby refers to his *Liber de prodigiis* [*Book of Prodigies*], which is an account of the wonders and prodigies that occurred in ancient Rome.

[46] Etna is an active volcano on the island of Sicily; King Frogmorton feels hot with rage and shame.

[47] Ogilby is reminding us here that the shield is a biscuit, or made of cereal.

[48] i.e., through his dragon-like armour

Not struck with fear, but from his hole to fling
Assurèd vengeance on the diving king.
Seven times he sallies forth, as oft retired,
But now both champions, with like fury fired,
175 Lay off all cunning, scorning to defend;
Strength, rage, and fortune must the battle end.
There was no interim; so the Cyclopes beat
When Mars his arms require a second heat,
Though louder the Etnean cavern roars;[49]
180 Blows had for death now made a thousand doors,
As many more for life to issue out.
    But here among our authors springs a doubt:
Some, in this mighty combat, dare aver°
Both champions, fainting, symptoms showed of fear:
185 In a cold sweat, Frogmorton, almost choked
With heat and dust, gasped thrice, and three times croaked.
And Moustapha, bestewed in blood and sweat,
As oft cried peep,° and made no slow retreat.
To these detractors, since I am provoked,
190 I say 'tis false: this peeped not, nor that croaked.
Historians feign, but truth the poet sings;
Some writers will asperse° the best of kings.
    While thus the battle stood, the Kitish prince
Had from loud croaks and cries intelligence
195 Of this great fight, then to himself did say:
'*What mighty matter's in the marsh today!*'
Then mounted high on labouring wings he glides,
And the vast region of the air divides.
    The woeful fairy Mab did this foresee,
200 Whom grief transformed now to a humble-bee;°
She flies about them, buzzing in their ear,
For both the champions she esteemèd dear.
The black prince did with captive Frogians come,
And at her altars paid a hecatomb°
205 That day, and King Frogmorton in her house
With reared-up hands offered a high-born mouse,
And when th'immortal mortal cates° did wish,
The fattest sacrifice was made her dish.

---

[49] In Roman mythology, the volcano Mount Etna was thought to be the place where the Cyclopes forged instruments of war for Mars, the god of war.

Therefore she hums, 'Desist! No more! Be friends!
210 Behold, the common enemy attends!
In vain 'gainst him are your united pow'rs.
O stay your rage; see, o'er your head he tow'rs.'
But they, engaged in cruel fight, not heard
The queen's admonishments, nor did regard
215 Approaching fates, but suddenly they bind
In grapple fierce, their targets° cast behind.
When the plumed prince down like swift lightning stoops,°
And seized both champions maugre all their troops;
Their arms drop down; upon them both he feasts,
220 And reconciles their doubtful interests.
    Amazed spectators fly; hunt-crumbs and vaulters
    Run to their holes and leap into the waters.

          Moral

Thus petty princes strive with mortal hate,
Till both are swallowed by a neighb'ring state;
225 Thus factions with a civil° war imbrued°
By some unseen aspirer are subdued.

3. Of the Lion and the Mouse[50]

'What's this that troubles us we cannot sleep?
Something is in our furs; we feel it creep
    Betwixt our neck and shoulders; 'twill invade
    Our throat anon,'° the weary lion said,
5   New come from hunting, stretched in a cool shade.

'Peace, and we'll catch a mouse.' His word is kept:
His great paw seized the straggler as he crept.
    Who trembling thus began: 'King of the grove,
    Whom when thou thunder'st beasts more fear than Jove,
10   Let no small crime thy high displeasure move.

'Hither I strayed by chance; think not, great sir,
I came to pick a hole in royal fur,
    Nor with the wolf and fox did I contrive
    'Gainst you, nor questioned your prerogative.°
15   If so, then justly me of life deprive.

'Should I relate for what great act my name
Through Micean realms resounded is by fame,
    It would too much my modesty invade;
    But when at stake life is, and fortune laid,
20   To speak bold truths why should I be afraid?

'Pyrrhus, who now is through the world renowned,
The Roman soldier no barbarian found.[51]
    In complete steel he saw their armies shine;
    Full squadrons stand exacter than a line,
25   Beyond the Cinean[52] tactics' discipline.

---

[50] In the first book of fables, *The Fables of Aesop*, fable 9.
[51] Pyrrhus was a Greek general who later became the King of Epirus. The devastation that his army suffered when they defeated the Romans in 279–280 BC inspired the phrase 'Pyrrhic victory', which now refers to any victory that takes a devastating toll on the victor. Ogilby includes more information about Pyrrhus in the footnotes below.
[52] Cineas was a commander under Pyrrhus, King of Epirus, who wrote a book of military affairs. Cicero in his *Epistles*: *Summum me ducem literae tuae reddiderunt. Plane nesciebam te tam peritum esse rei militaris. Pyrrhi te libros et Cineae video lectitasse.* Thy letters have made me an excellent commander. I knew not thou wert so expert in military affairs. Now I see thou hast read the works of Pyrrhus and Cineas. [Ogilby's note.] The Latin quotation is from Cicero's *Letters to Friends*,

'Mountains of flesh, he mighty land-whales brought,
That tow'rs supported with armed soldiers fraught,°⁵³
    Supposing by the castle-carriers' might
    To break the brazen ranks, and to affright
30   Ausonian° squadrons with th'unusual fight.

'But the great warrior failed in this design:
The subtle Roman herds of filthy swine
    On th'elephants drove;⁵⁴ straight at their dismal cry
    Citadels clash, ranged castles routed fly,
35   And tow'rs unsaddled in their ruin lie.⁵⁵

'Yet one maintained the field against all odds,
For which his king him with new honour loads,⁵⁶
    And to paternal scutcheons,° charged before
    With sable° castles, in a field of or,°
40   Cantoned in gules,° he adds an argent° boar.⁵⁷

'This mighty elephant I, in dead of night,
With these small arms, though sharp, challenged to fight,
    And said, "Your castle and your guard are gone:
    On equal terms encounter me alone."
45   *True valour best is without witness shown.*⁵⁸

---

book IX, letter 25; see Cicero, *The Letters to his Friends, in Three Volumes*, vol. 2, trans. by W. Glynn Williams (London: William Heinemann, 1928), p. 278.

⁵³ i.e., Pyrrhus brought to the battle elephants carrying structures on their back that were loaded with soldiers

⁵⁴ So Aelian tells the story of the overthrow of King Pyrrhus his elephants, and the loss of his army thereby, though Plutarch mentions them not. However, it is generally observed by the physiologists° that elephants are affrighted at the gruntings of swine. [Ogilby's note.] Aelian describes this overthrow in his *Of the Characteristics of Animals* I.38: 'The Elephant has a terror of a horned ram and of the squealing of a pig. It was by these means, they say, that the Romans turned to flight the elephants of Pyrrhus of Epirus, and that the Romans won a glorious victory' (Aelian, *Of the Characteristics of Animals*, vol. 1, trans. by Scholfield, p. 57).

⁵⁵ As the elephants flee from the pigs, of whom they were proverbially afraid, the towers on top of the elephants are destroyed or come crashing down.

⁵⁶ i.e., Yet one elephant held the line against all odds, for which action the king greatly honours him.

⁵⁷ i.e., To his father's coat of arms — which before consisted of black castles on a gold background, perhaps with a red square or canton in the upper left corner — he [the king] added a silver boar.

⁵⁸ We ended the mouse's speech to the elephant before the proverb, assuming it was not spoken to the elephant, but delivered as a commentary (to the lion) of what he

'Strange! from a mouse this mountain trembling ran,
And prayers in vain to the high moon began,⁵⁹
   But when in clouds she hid her silver wain,°
   I through his trunk like lightning pierced his brain,
50   And till° the dawn triumphed o'er the slain.

'But now my fortune's changed; I captive lie,
Imploring quarter° from your majesty.
   Make me your friend; to sentence° not proceed;
   If fickle chance should frown (which Jove forbid),
55   The lion of my aid may stand in need.'

This said, the king, admiring that a mouse
Should such a monster's mighty soul unhouse,
   Seizing the pia mater° of his brain,
   And there with death and sullen darkness reign,
60   Signs his dismiss, then seeks repose again.

Soon as to th'East tall shades began to creep,
The lion rose, and shakes off drowsy sleep;
   Feasts for his pregnant queen must now be sought
   In fields remote; far fetched as dear was bought.⁶⁰
65   The roaring king in a strong net is caught,

---

had said to the elephant. However, it would also be possible to read this line as still part of the mouse's self-reported speech.

⁵⁹ That elephants worship the moon was a common tradition among the ancients. So Pliny in his *Natural History*, lib. 8: *Imò vero (quae etiam in homine rara) probitas, prudentia, aequitas, religio quoque siderum, solisque ac lunae veneratio*, etc. The elephants embrace too honesty, prudence, and equity° (rare qualities to be found in men), and withal have in religious reverence the stars and planets, and worship the sun and moon. Writers there be who report thus much of them: that when the new moon begins to appear fresh and bright, they come down by herds to a certain river in the deserts of Mauritania, where, having purified and sprinkled themselves over with water and adored the planet, they return into the woods again. The same is delivered by Aelian in the *History of Animals*, lib. 3. [Ogilby's note.] In modern editions, the Pliny quotation can be found in book 8, chapter 1; see Pliny, *Natural History*, vol. 3, trans. by Rackham, p. 2. Aelian describes the elephants as worshipping the moon in his *Of the Characteristics of Animals*, IV.10, p. 225. Ogilby's reference to Aelian's Book III could be either an error or an indication that he was working with a different version of this text.

⁶⁰ i.e., The pregnant queen values things more that have been fetched from farther distances. The phrase 'Far-fetched and dear bought (is good for ladies)' was proverbial; see *Proverbs, Sentences, and Proverbial Phrases from English Writings Mainly before 1500*, ed. by Bartlett Jere Whiting and Helen Wescott Whiting (Cambridge, MA: Harvard University Press, 1968), F58, p. 173.

Laid by a subtle sunburnt African;
While he his great strength used, and strove in vain,
   Twisted grates gnawing of his hempen° cage,[61]
   The Micean heard th'indulgent lion rage,
70   And, grateful, straight to free him did engage.

First hunts out busily to find the cord
Which closed the snare, which found, as with a sword,
   His teeth (before well on an old cheese set)
   Clears all the meshes of the tangling net.
75   When thus the lion spake, at freedom set:

'Kings be to subjects mild; and when you move
In highest spheres, with mercy purchase love.
   From private grudges oft great princes have,
   'Midst triumphs, met with an untimely grave,
80   And swains° have power sometimes their lords to save.'

Moral

Mercy makes princes gods, but mildest thrones
Are often shook with huge rebellions;
Small help may bring great aid, and better far
Is policy than strength in peace or war.

---

[61] i.e., gnawing the twisted ropes that made up the net

4. Of the Dog and Thief[62]

'*Bow-wow*, Who's there? *Bow-wow*, Who's that dares break
Into my master's house? First stand, then speak,
Or else I'll have you by the throat — ne'er start![63] —
You sir, I'll know your business ere° we part.'
5 Thus in the Cynic language,[64] loud and brief,
A true dog barked, discov'ring a false thief.
  When softly thus night's pilfering minion[65] said,
'This sacred silence, and the holy shade
Of night, dear friend, disturb not. I am sent
10 (Because thy master keeps a stricter Lent[66]
Than wiser mortals) with a sop to thee
From Cerberus;[67] at such fond° piety
From triple jaws exclaiming, he bids eat.
Wise sects, who Nature serve, forsake no meat.°
15 Then take this morsel and lie down to rest;
Let not fleas nor others thee molest.'
When thus the faithful dog replied again:
'Hast thou thy habitation among men,
And know'st not me? Hast thou not heard how I

---

[62] In the first book of fables, *The Fables of Aesop*, fable 21.
[63] i.e., don't start back, or jump back!
[64] Ogilby makes a Greek pun here: the word 'Cynic' comes from the Greek word κύνικος (*kynikos*), meaning 'dog-like'.
[65] i.e., the thief
[66] i.e., closely observes the fasting rituals during the Christian Lenten season
[67] Cerberus is the door-keeper of Hell, feigned° by the poets to have three heads, representing that triple-natured devil that haunts the air, earth, and water. So Virgil describes him, *Aeneid* 6:

Cerberus haec ingens latratu regna trifauci
Personat, adverso recubans immanis in antro.
Cui vates horrere videns iam colla colubris,
Melle soporatam, etc.

Stretched on his kennel, monstrous Cerberus round
From triple jaws makes all these realms resound,
But when the priestess on his neck espied
The serpent's bristle,° she a morsel, fried
With drugs and honey, cast; he swallows straight
With three devouring mouths the drowsy bait. [Ogilby's note.]

Ogilby quotes these lines about the canine guardian of Hell from Virgil's *Aeneid* VI.417–20, but translates VI.417–22.

JOHN OGILBY

20 Six winter days and stormy nights did lie
　　Watching my murdered lord? His bleeding head
　　Three spring-tides° washed on a cold osier° bed;
　　At last with extreme hunger overcome,
　　I to this house through the broad river swam,
25 Where, well recruited with warm viands,° then
　　From hospitable boards and living men
　　I crossed rough mountains with a silver head,
　　To wait in open mansions of the dead.
　　At last, they following me with swifter oars,
30 Where by the smell were found polluted shores,
　　They made a search, and ere I took my place,
　　Kissed his pale lips, or licked his woeful face,
　　My person they secured, then him interred,
　　And I for faithfulness was thus preferred.
35 　'Nay, more than that: 'twas I the murd'rer found,
　　And with my forces first beleaguered round;
　　Loud vollies spent with foam, with tooth and nail
　　Fell in on's quarters,° all parts did assail;
　　No man durst° rate° me off, no not the frown
40 Of my dread lord, until I plucked him down.
　　And he cried out, "'Twas I thy master slew!"
　　Then fiercer dogs upon him, sergeants,° flew.
　　And think'st thou I'll be treacherous for a crust?
　　Dogs are than men more faithful to their trust.
45 Not our penates°68 keep a stricter watch
　　Over these seats than I, such rogues to catch.

---

68 The Romans had not only tutelar° gods for their cities and towns, but peculiar gods for every particular household, which they called *lares* and *penates*, to whom they attributed the protection of the house and family; so Plautus:

Ne qui miretur qui sim, paucis eloquar;
Ego Lar sum familiaris, ex hac familia;
Vnde exeuntem me aspexistis; hanc domum
Iam multos annos est cum possideo et colo.

Lest any should admire who I may be,
Know I the lar° am of this family;
I many years from whence you see me come,
Dwell and possession held of every room. [Ogilby's note.]

These lines come from the Roman playwright Plautus's *Aulularia* [usually translated as *The Pot of Gold*], Prologue, ll. 1–4.

Erre, erre, bow-wow, thieves, thieves, with speed awake!'[69]
He frighted flies; the trusty dog then spake,
  But what he said is dangerous now to tell:[70]
50 What tortures Cerberus told him were in Hell
For servants that are false, but they that sold
Their country, or their native king for gold,
To them Judge Minos[71] deepest seats allots,
Where molten gold they quaff° in iron pots,
55 And when their blood with burning liquor fries,
They get° on snakes the worm which never dies.

    Moral

Servants that sentinels to princes are,
When close conspirers plotting civil war
Do send them gold, if they prove faithful, then
60 They are the best; if false, the worst of men.

---

[69] Ogilby mixes animal sounds with animal language in this line; the second half of the line could be a 'translation' of the sounds in the first half, or it could simply be a continuation of his speech.

[70] i.e., The thief, frightened by the dog's barking, flees. The trusty (trustworthy) dog then spake — but what he said is too dangerous to tell.

[71] Judge Minos was one of the three judges in the underworld.

5. Of the Fox and Ape[72]

The French ape gives the fox of Spain *bonjour*,
Three congees,° and *très humble serviture*,[73]
Then thus begins: 'In France we not endure
    To see long cloaks; all there
5   Go in the shortest wear,
But your large fashion is the statelier sure.

'*Pardonnez-moi*, as we are all too short,
In curtailed garments, à la modes o'th'court;[74]
So with th'other extreme, yours, sir, doth sort.
10   Be pleased to wear your fur
      A little shorter, sir;
'Twill be as grave, and suit well with your port.°

'*Seigneur*, I know your tailor is not here;
My apeship's° workman quickly with his shear
15 Shall cut you shorter, and myself will wear
    The remnant of your train,
      Conformable to Spain,
And then Don° Diegoes both we shall appear.'

'*Sí, señor*,' said the fox, 'we dons of Spain
20 Are constant to our fashion; such a train
My father's father wore, and to be plain,
    This long wear I will keep,
      Though it the kennel° sweep,
Rather than give an inch to Monsieur Vain.'

Moral

25 Heaven to each nation several[75] genius gave:
The French too airy, Spaniards seem too grave;
City, the country, courtiers both despise;
Civil, and rude,° most their own manners prize.

---

[72] In the first book of fables, *The Fables of Aesop*, fable 34.
[73] i.e., 'very humble servitude'; the ape, being courtly, announces himself the humble servant of the fox
[74] i.e., according to the fashions of the court
[75] i.e., separate or distinct

6. Of the Bear and the Bees[76]

Bruin the bear,[77] receiving a slight wound
   From a too waspish bee,
Joyful to raise a war on any ground
(It was their wealth had done the injury),
5   Did now propound,°
     And to himself decree
Ne'er to return, till he had overthrown
Twelve waxen cities of that nation,
And seiz'd their honey-treasure as his own.

10 This being resolv'd, he to the garden goes
     Where stood the stately hives;
One after one, the barbarous[78] overthrows,
And many citizens of life deprives.
     A few survive,
15   Who in a body close:[79]
'For your everted tow'rs, your slaughter'd race,
For your great losses, and your high disgrace,
Fix all your venomed weapons in his face!'
     This said, the trumpet sounds, the vulgar rage,
20   And all at once in mighty war engage.

Now Bruin's ugly visage did not freeze,
     Nor his foul hands want gloves;[80]
The monstrous bear you could not see for bees;
No bacon gammon was so stuck with cloves.
25   Who honey loves
     Not with sharp sauce agrees.
O'erpow'rd by multitude, and almost slain,
He draws his shatter'd forces off again,
Then said, 'I better had endured the pain
30   Of one sharp sting, than thus to suffer all,
     Making a private quarrel national.'

---

[76] In the first book of fables, *The Fables of Aesop*, fable 44. The events in this fable will precipitate the events in fable 10; see fable 10, line 27.
[77] Bruin is a proper name frequently applied to the common or brown bear.
[78] i.e., the bear
[79] i.e., who together, as one body, close ranks
[80] i.e., The bear was covered in so many bees that they were like clothing that kept him warm.

Moral

Great kings that petty princes did despise
Have oft by war's experience grown wise;
Who whipped the sea and threatened floods to chain[81]
35   Brought back for millions but a slender train.

---

[81] The insolence of the Persian emperor, here alluded to, in his expedition against Greece, we shall deliver in the words of Herodotus, who lived, though but a child, at the same time. From Abydus to the opposite continent is a strait of only seven furlongs over, which when Xerxes had caused a bridge to be laid, a violent tempest on a sudden destroyed it, which when he heard, highly incensed, he commanded that they should inflict three hundred stripes° on the Hellespont, and drop a couple of chains into the bottom of it, charging them to say these impious and barbarous words: 'O bitter and salt water, thy master inflicts this punishment on thee because thou hast injured him, being not provoked by any precedent wrong. King Xerxes shall pass over thee whether thou wilt or no.' Thus he commanded them to punish the sea, and to strike off the heads of the overseers of the work. [Ogilby's note.] The story of Xerxes commanding a body of water to be beaten is told in Herodotus' *The Histories*, in VII.35. See Herodotus, *Herodotus, in Four Volumes*, vol. 3, trans. by A. D. Godley (London: William Heinemann, 1922), pp. 346–49.

7. Of the Rebellion of the Hands and Feet[82]

Reason, once king in man, deposed and dead,
The Purple Isle[83] was ruled without a head.
The stomach, a devouring state, swayed all,
At which the hands did burn, the feet did gall;°
5 Swift to shed blood, and prone to civil stirs
These members were, who now turn Levellers.[84]
The vast revenue of the little world
Is in the exchequer of the belly hurled,
And toil on them imposed by eternal laws;
10 With a drawn sword, the hands thus plead the cause:
   'Freeborn as you, here we demand our right!
Reason being vanquished, the proud appetite
In microcosmos[85] must no tyrant be;
The idle paunch shall work as well as we.
15   'The stomach promised — and so gained our loves —
Our king dethroned, we should in kid-skin gloves
Grow soft again, and free from corns, the feet
In cordovan° at leisure walk the street,
Who now toil more than when that monarch swayed.
20 Then we did works of wonder; then we made
Egyptian pyramids, Mausolus' Tomb,[86]

---

[82] In the first book of fables, *The Fables of Aesop*, fable 47. This fable was a popular political fable in the early modern period; it was alluded to by William Shakespeare in his play *Coriolanus* as a metaphor for the 'body' of the commonwealth (Shakespeare, *The Norton Shakespeare*, ed. by Greenblatt et al., I.i), and was taken up in new and different ways by poets during the English Civil War and its aftermath. Ogilby's version is unusual in that the fable begins after King Reason has been defeated. King Charles I was beheaded in 1649, two years before the first edition of *The Fables of Aesop*.
[83] i.e., the body; blood was often described as purple in the early modern period
[84] During the English Civil War and until the Restoration (1641–1660) a number of political groups sprang up advocating for a more free and even distribution of goods and sovereignty. The Levellers argued for 'levelling' or eliminating differences in positions and rank among men.
[85] i.e., the body; describing the body as a microcosm or 'little world' was a commonplace in the early modern period
[86] The Mausoleum at Halicarnassus was a tomb built between 353 and 350 BC for Mausolus, a provincial governor in the Persian Empire. It was considered one of the Seven Wonders of the Ancient World.

Built the Gran Caire,[87] great Ninive,[88] and Rome,
Heaven-threat'ning Babel;[89] those sky-kissing tow'rs
Proud boast themselves a mighty work of ours;
25 We Daedalus[90] winged to fly from spire to spire,
And, thunder framed, outranted Jove's loud fire.
These were our works, which are by fame enrolled;
Now we dress meat, change it some god to gold.[91]
Skies, seas, we spread with nets, vast earth with gins,°

---

[87] i.e., Cairo, the Egyptian city associated with architectural wonders such as the pyramids of Giza
[88] i.e., Nineveh, an ancient Assyrian city, which was the capital of the Neo-Assyrian Empire
[89] i.e., the tower of Babel, a tower described in the Bible; see Genesis 11
[90] Daedalus, with his son Icarus, being imprisoned by Minos, and seeing no possibility of escape either by sea or land, makes himself and his son artificial wings, and saves himself by flight through the air, but his son, having the cement of his wings melted by his too near approach to the sun, dropped into the sea, from him called the Icarian Sea. The moral of this fable Seneca the tragedian delivers thus:

Male pensantur magna minis,
Felix alius magnusque volet;
Me nulla vocet turba potentem, etc.

Great heights, great downfalls balance still;
Be great and glorious they that will;
Let none for potent me adore.
May my small bark° coast by the shore,
Unforc'd to sea by lofty winds;
Calm bays proud Fortune never minds,
But ships on high-wrought seas assails,
Whose topsails swell with cloudy gales.

The history contained in it is this: Daedalus, imprisoned by Minos in the labyrinth, escaped by a wile, and put to sea in two small vessels, the one guided by himself, the other by his son Icarus, when by the help of their sails invented by Daedalus, they outstripped their pursuers. Which because they were displayed like wings, and carried them with so strange a celerity,° they were feigned to fly. But Icarus by bearing too great sail overset his bark, and perished in the sea. [Ogilby's note.] Ogilby quotes Seneca, *Hercules Oetaeus*, ll. 690–93, but his translation is of ll. 690–99. The Latin in Miller's edition (Seneca, *Seneca's Tragedies*, vol. 2, trans. by Frank Justus Miller [London: William Heinemann, 1929], p. 240) differs from Ogilby's Latin; where Ogilby has *minis* Miller gives *ruinis*, and where Ogilby has *volet* Miller gives *sonet*.
[91] 'Now we dress meat' means, roughly: now (instead of building great monuments and cities) we (merely) prepare food for you. The second half of the line is a bit perplexing; though 'gold' is not listed as a verb in the *OED*, we understand this line to say something like: now we prepare food, changing it as if in order to reward some god, as if with gold.

30   To banquet you, who feast seven deadly sins.
       'Did we for this storm the bold breast, and raze°
    Jove's image in the heaven-advanced face,
    Where our sharp nails a rubric° penned in gore,[92]
    And curled roofs from King Reason's palace tore?
35   'For such rewards the feet in cooling streams
    Sweating did rush, who by such stratagems
    Did at strange distance disaffect with pain
    The head, hurt Reason, and disturb the brain.
    In brief, or work or fast,[93] take up your staff;
40   Gird thy loins, belly, and leave banquets off.'
    This said, the stomach, with sharp choler° stirr'd,
    Cast forth such things, belching at every word:
       'Rebellious members, you that be so far
    From peace, that rather 'mong yourselves you'll war,
45   What acts did you to those that we have done?
    Who was it carried the great business on,
    The senses took, the Cinque Ports of the realm,[94]
    With a fair shade and a deluding dream?
    Was't you, or we, full with Egyptian gods[95]
50   The brainish monarch[96] drove from his abodes,
    Beat up all quarters of the heart by night,
    And did that fort with its own trembling fright?
    Who swelled the spleen, and made the gall° o'erflow?
    The feet and hands? Who made the liver glow,
55   Till all those purple atoms in the blood,
    Which make the soul, swam in a burning flood,
    From whence inflamed, they seized upon the head,
    And o'er the face their blushing ensigns° spread?
       'All that you boast of since this war began

---

[92] The word 'rubric' refers to the parts of legal or religious documents typically written in red, which include titles, chapter headings, or rules, so this line suggests that the scratches caused by the sharp nails are akin to writing in red ink.

[93] i.e., either get to work, or go hungry!

[94] The Cinque Ports are a collection of sea-ports in the south of England (*OED*). Ogilby uses them to represent the five senses of the body.

[95] garlic and onions [Ogilby's note.] According to Pliny in book 19, chapter 23, 'In Egypt people swear by garlic and onions as deities in taking an oath' (Pliny, *Natural History*, vol. 5, trans. by H. Rackham [Cambridge, MA: Harvard University Press, 1950], p. 487). The stomach asks rhetorically, who was it that used the fumes from garlic and onions to drive Reason, living in the brain, to distraction?

[96] i.e., the monarch Reason (who both is intelligent and resides in the brain)

60 Are but light skirmishes with th'outward man;[97]
    Leave threat'ning — must we keep perpetual Lent?
    The members shall, as soon as we, repent.'
       Trembling with rage, the feet and hands depart;
    The stomach swells; high goes th'incensèd heart.
65 Three days in pockets closeted, the hands
    Refuse to put on gloves; the vexed foot stands.
    Meanwhile the stomach was come down, and cries,
    'What once a hollow tooth served, would suffice
    The straightened maw;°[98] one bit, one crumb bestow!'
70 But still the moody members answer, 'No.'
       At last an extreme feebleness they felt,
    Saw all but skin and their hard bones to melt,
    A pale consumption° lording over all,
    At which a counsel the faint brethren call;
75 The stomach must be fed, which now was so
    Contracted, that, like them, it answered, 'No.'
    At which, pale Death her cold approaches made,
    When to the dying feet the weak hands said,
       'Brethren in evil, since we did deny
80 The belly food, we must together die.
    All that are members in a commonwealth
    Should, more than private, aim at public health.
    The rich the poor, and poor the rich must aid;
    None can protect themselves with their own shade.
85 *None for themselves are born.* We brought in food,
    Which the kind stomach did prepare for blood;
    The liver gave it tincture; the great vein
    Sends it in thousand several streams again
    To feed the parts, which there assimilates.°
90 *Concord builds high, when discord ruins states.*
    But the chief cause did our destruction bring
    Was we rebelled 'gainst Reason, our true king.'

---

[97] i.e., merely superficial, unimportant battles
[98] A 'hollow tooth' here most likely means a tooth greatly decayed; the belly tells its limbs, 'I would be willing to eat even the meagre, probably liquid, sustenance that one eats when one has a bad tooth!'

Moral

Civil commotions strongly carried on
Seldom bring quiet when the war is done;
95   Then thousand interests in strange shapes appear,
And through all ways to certain ruin steer.

8. Of the Lion and the Forester[99]

Vast forests and great cities opened, when
    Betwixt wild beasts and men
    A long cessation was.
    And it was then
5   That citizens and rustics viewed the lion's den,
    At his vast courts amazed,
Where now fat bulls, colts, and tame asses grazed;
  Through deserts travellers took the nearest way,°
  Where with their spaniels wanton° tigers play,
10 Foxes 'mong geese, wolves 'mong fat wethers° lay.

At skinners' shops the bear unmuzzled calls,
    Cheap'ning on furnished stalls
    His friend or cousin's fur;
    In common halls
15 Panthers behold themselves on stately pedestals.
    And now no yeoman° cur,°
Nor sergeant mastiff,° beasts indebted, stir;[100]
  The woods' inhabitants wander everywhere,
  And bristly boars walk safe, with untouched ear,
20 After the proclamation they did hear.

When the great lion met a forester
    (With whom he oft in war
    Had striv'n with various chance:
    This with a spear
25 The lion galled, that would his strong-spun ambush tear,
    Then boldly up advance,
And with his teeth in sunder bite the lance),
  To whom the lion said, 'Sir, you and I
  Could ne'er decide our strength by victory.
30 Let us dispute and it by logic try.'

---

[99] In the first book of fables, *The Fables of Aesop*, this is fable 50, which marks the beginning of a three-fable sequence.
[100] i.e., The dogs are no longer indebted to humans, and are no longer working for them.

Then said the woodman, 'Let us wave dispute;
    Antiquity shall do't:
    Behold Mausolus' Tomb,[101]
        And then be mute;
35 If the world's wonder by example thee confute,
        There let us take our doom.'[102]
This said, they to the monument did come,
    Where straight he showed him, by rare artists made,
    A lion's head in a man's bosom laid.
40   This no sufficient proof the lion said:

'Could we, as well as you, our stories cut,[103]
    We might, and justly, put
    Your lying heads beneath
        Our conquering foot:
45 *From partial pens all truth hath been forever shut.*
        Where first I drew my breath,
I heard a Carthaginian at his death
    The Roman nation most perfidious° call,
    Crying out by treason they contrived the fall
50   Of them, and their great captain Hannibal.'[104]

Moral

Through a gross medium by refracted beams,
Historians friends appear still in extremes;
The wrong end of the perspective must show
In little the great actions of their foe.[105]

---

[101] Mausolus' Tomb was considered one of the Seven Wonders of the Ancient World. This tomb is also mentioned in fable 7.
[102] i.e., there let us judge the dispute between us
[103] i.e., if we were able to carve (or write) our own stories
[104] Over the course of three wars known as the Punic Wars (264–146 BC), Rome laid siege to and destroyed Carthage, despite the Carthaginian leader Hannibal's notorious crossing of the Alps and invasion of Italy.
[105] Ogilby claims here that reading biased history is like looking into the wrong end of a telescope, which makes great things seem smaller.

9. Of the Lion, the Forester, and his Daughter[106]

When they had viewed the wonder and the strife
Admired of artists working to the life,
Then drew the forester's fair daughter near,
And whispered in her swarthy° father's ear.
5   The lion starts, and feels a sudden wound,
As when at first his lioness he found,
And made her pregnant in a shady wood,
High with man's flesh and draughts of human blood.
To whom the woodman said, 'Sir, since the sun
10 Mounts our meridian,° half his business done,
And your own court so far, be pleased to share
Part of what's mine, though mean, yet wholesome fare;°
Oft human princes in poor lodges° have
Gladly reposed, and low roofs honour gave.'
15   The king the proffer° takes; to lowly rooms,
Yet daily visited with cleansing brooms,
The lion is conveyed, where he in state
At a full board in ancient maple sat.
Where, whom the father never overcame,
20 The daughter did;[107] scorched with love's cruel flame,
The lion burns; the valiant, strong, and wise,
Who javelins did, dogs, men, and nets despise,
Trammels° of bright hair took; a slender dart
Shot from a virgin's eye transpierced his heart.
25 The amorous lion lays his dreadful jaws
Now in her lap; gently with dangerous paws
Her fair hand seizeth, shrinketh up his nails,
Fain° would, but cannot tell her what he ails.
Then, staring in her face, offers to rise,
30 Ambitious of her lip; she, frighted, flies,
Whom with a groan he draws by th'garments back,
And, troubled, to the trembling virgin spake:

---

[106] In the first book of fables, *The Fables of Aesop*, fable 51. This is a continuation of the previous fable.
[107] i.e., the lion, whom the father was never able to defeat, was defeated by the daughter (because he fell in love)

'Sweet creature, fear not me; a Roman slave,[108]
Who cured my festered foot, once in my cave
35   I feasted forty days, and when that I
Was pris'ner took, and he condemned to die
In a sad° theatre, where men sat and laughed
To see how beasts the blood of wretches quaffed,
I mocked their expectations, and did grace
40   My trembling surgeon with a dear embrace.
The story known, to him they pardon gave,
And, honouring me, sent to my royal cave.
    'Dear, if you knew me, I not dreadful am;
How many ladies have made lions tame?
45   My grandsires Berecynthia's chariot drove,[109]

---

[108] Ogilby tells this story at much greater length in the long poem *Androcleus*, which appears at the end of his second volume of fables *Aesopics*.

[109] That the chariot of Berecynthia, or Cybele, the mother of the gods, was drawn by lions, we find in the third of Virgil's *Aeneid*:

> *Hinc mater cultrix Cybele, Corybantiaque aera*
> *Idaeumque nemus: hinc fida silentia sacris,*
> *Et juncti currum Dominae subiere leones.*

> Corybantian sounds for Cybele he ordained,
> And silent rites in Ida's grove maintained.
> The lady's chariot is with lions drawn.

By their heat and rapacity representing the heavens, wherein the air, in which the earth, or Cybele, is moved, is contained. Ovid feigns that Hippomenes and Atalanta, having polluted a sacred grot° with their unseasonable lusts, were by Cybele transformed into lions and forced to draw her chariot.

> *Turritaque mater*
> *An Stygia sontes dubitavit mergeret unda.*
> *Poena levis visa est. Ergo modo levia fulvae*
> *Colla jubae velant*, etc.

> Cybele, crowned
> With tow'rs, had struck them to the Stygian sound°
> But that she thought that punishment too small.
> When yellow manes on their smooth shoulders fall;
> Their arms to legs, their fingers turn to nails,
> Their breasts of wondrous strength; their tufted tails
> Whisk up the dust; their looks are full of dread;°
> For speech they roar; the woods become their bed.
> These lions, feared by others, Cybele checks
> With curbing bits, and yokes their stubborn necks. [Ogilby's note.]

The lines quoted from Virgil's *Aeneid* are from III.111–13. Ogilby quotes Ovid's *Metamorphoses* X.696–99, but translates X.696–704.

Not by force coupled, but almighty love.
We with your smiles are raised, and when you frown
The greatest monarch values not his crown.'
    Then to her father turning, thus he said,
50 Still holding in his armèd foot the maid:
'Lo! I, the king of beasts, a suitor stand,
And this thy daughter for our queen demand.
We need not tell you what our interests are
In this great forest, and my power in war
55 To you is known, but joined with such a bride,
Our race deriving from the father's side
Such active spirits, strength, and valiant hearts,
From her womb taking human form, and arts,
How may we be advanced? Where shall our sons
60 Find limits for their vast dominions?
The Cybele's man-lion, styled° the wondrous° birth,
Must rule the conquered nations of the Earth.[110]
The Macedonian[111] was a type of this,
Who sent the spoils of Persia to Greece,
65 Which to his father was in sleep revealed,
When his queen's womb he with a lion sealed.'
    Then said the man, 'I know, great prince, you are
In deserts king; I know your force in war.
But all the laws of men and gods forbid
70 That human creatures should with savage wed.'
    The lion then, ready to lash his side,
Rousing up anger, with grim looks replied,
'Did not a queen match with an ugly bear,
And in dark caverns live with him a year?
75 Was not the pregnant lady, he being slain,
By hunters brought to her own courts again?
Did not his son prove a most valiant king,
And slew all those were at the murdering

---

[110] i.e., When your daughter and I marry and have a half-man, half-lion child, that baby will be considered wondrous, and will be destined to conquer the whole world. Because Cybele was a goddess associated with lions, she is perhaps imagined here as the ideal goddess to oversee the child's well-being.

[111] Alexander the Great [Ogilby's note.]

Of his dear father? Orson was no beast,
Though like his sire he had a hairy breast.'[112]
   Thus having said, he cruel weapons draws;
Sharp teeth appear, and needle-pointed claws.
Now wit assist: against the lion's rage
Inflamed with love, what madman would engage?
Then said the forester, 'Great sir, sheath your arms;
If you vast realms will join to humble farms,
My daughter's yours; my error I confess.
For many savage beasts in marriages
With women have conjoined; the golden ass
As fair a lady hath as ever was;[113]
Mastiffs and pious virgins wed so rife,°
Ballads in streets have sung them dog and wife.
Take, sir, my daughter to your royal seat,
Yet one thing for the damsel I entreat;
For sweet love grant her this. See how she stands
Trembling to view your teeth and armèd hands!
Meet her with equal arms, that face to face
She may as boldly charge with strict embrace.
Then pare,° and draw them out. The lion said,
'Whate'er thou ask'st, I freely give, O maid;
I will devest° myself of all my pow'r,
And make my teeth and claws thy virgin dow'r.'°
   No sooner said, but done: with bleeding jaws
On tender feet he stands; the woodman draws
Then a bright falchion° hanging by his side,
Which to the hilts he in his bosom dyed.
The lion's slain, and the cessation broke,
When to the dying king the woodman spoke:
'They that give up their power to foe or friend,
Let them for love expect a woeful end;

---

[112] In a popular romance in late medieval and early modern Europe, Orson is the name of a twin brother who was taken away from his mother and raised by a bear. His kidnapping is described (among other versions) in Henry Watson, *The hystory of the two valyaunte brethren Valentyne and Orson, sonnes vnto the Emperour of Grece* (London, *c.* 1555), sig. E2v. Here the lion uses (or attempts to use) Orson to prove that being raised by a wild animal does not make a child a beast.

[113] The tenth book of Apuleius' *The Golden Ass*, a novel composed in Latin during the second century CE, includes the tale of a woman leading the golden ass to her bedroom in order to have sex with him.

They that undo themselves to purchase wives,
Like Indians, part with gold for beads and knives.[114]
Love is a child, and such as love obey
Like kingdoms fare that infant sceptres sway.'[115]

Moral

115 The powdered gallant, and the dusty clown,°
The horrid soldier, and the subtle gown,
Old, young, strong, weak, rich, poor, both fools and wise
Suffer, when they with frantic love advise.

---

[114] The 'Indians' referred to here are Native Americans; it was a common belief in the early modern period that the natives of the New World did not understand the value of objects, and would trade away gold for trifles.

[115] i.e., Anyone who obeys love fares as well as a kingdom that is ruled by a baby or child.

10. Of the Forester, the Skinner, and a Bear[116]

The lion slain, the greedy forester
Soon strips him of his robe and royal fur;
The crown and sceptre, old regalities°
Of many former princes, now are his;
5   He takes possession of the palace, which
Trophies made proud, and spoils of enemies rich,
Where at an outcry precious things are sold
At small rates, dear to potentates° of old.
When the same man that bought the lion's skin
10   Thus to th'insulting victor did begin:
    'Sir, since the groves are yours, and you have won
Dark haunts, impenetrable by the sun,
The lion dead, go, and th'ambitious bear
Destroy, who now aspires his master's chair.
15   A heathen king sent to my shop this morn
To have a Libyan bearskin to adorn
His spreading shoulders with at annual feasts,
When barbarous cups must raise his savage guests.
Call forth thy dogs, and a fresh war begin,
20   Then gold receive for slaughtered Bruin's skin.'
Then said the woodman, 'Wilt thou buy? I'll sell
The devil's hide, and bring it thee from Hell
For ready money; come, and give me coin,
And the bear's skin, though now he lives, is thine.
25   And thou shalt go along and see the sport,
And how I'll rouse him from his shady court;
I'll make him pay now for my slaughtered bees.'[117]
Here they strike hands, and gold the earnest is.
    Then in vast woods to hunt they both prepare.
30   The valiant for'ster trusts his new-ground spear;
The citizen, more wary, takes a tree
Near Bruin's cave, where he might safely see.
The dogs are straight sent in; such ranting guest

---

[116] In the first book of fables, *The Fables of Aesop*, fable 52. This is a continuation of the previous fable.
[117] The slaughter of the bees is recounted in fable 6, above; this is a prime example of how Ogilby sees the fables not just as discrete narratives but also as events in a larger narrative.

So troubled Bruin, newly gone to rest,
35 That to the terriers he resigns his cave,
At whose dire gates the woodman with a glaive°
Did ready stand, thinking to give the blow
Should his staff crimson in the dying foe,
When his foot slipped, his sure hand fails, his spear
40 Leaves him to mercy of the cruel bear;
Fainting, or feigning, to the ground he fell
As one struck dead. Then, with a hideous yell
Came the incensed, and arrested° him
With his great paw, to tear him limb from limb
45 Fully resolved: he broke the peace, he slew
The king his guest, and watched° to kill him too.
   But when he, nuzzling, laid his nose to ground,
And from his mouth nor lips no passage found
For vital breath, nor saw his breast and sides
50 To ebb and flow with life-respiring tides,[118]
Scorning to wreak° vain anger on the dead,
To man more cruel he this lecture read:
'Let wolvish monsters rip up putrid graves[119]
Of buried foes, and be old malice slaves.
55 Although thou sought'st my life when thou didst live,
Thy friends shall thee due rites of funeral give;
I war not with the dead.' Thus having said,
He coverts° in the wood's protecting shade.
When from the tree the skinner did descend,
60 And having roused almost from death his friend,
He thus began: 'Good sir, what was't the bear
Spake, when so long he whispered in your ear?'
Who answered, 'Bruin said I did not well
Before the bear was slain his skin to sell.'

---

[118] i.e., the bear didn't see his breast moving in and out with the breath that sustains life

[119] Wolves were known in the early modern period for digging up dead bodies out of graves.

Moral

65　Fortune assists the bold; the valiant man
　　Oft conqueror proves, because he thinks he can;
　　But who too much flattering successes trust
　　Have failed, and found their honour in the dust.

11. Of the Young Man and the Cat[120]

Grimalkin's grandchild, Tybert's noble race,[121]
For beauty gave no cattish damsel place.
    Round was her face;
Her eyes were grey° as Germans', or the Gaul;[122]
5   The stars that fall
Through gloomy shade cast no such dazzling light,
Nor glow-worms that most glorious are by night;
    Her bosom soft and white
Like down of silver swans; her head was small,
10   And round as any ball;
Daily she wore a particoloured° gown,
Curiously mixed with white, black, grey, and brown.

Stol'n from her mother's teat, a young man bred
This female up, and laid her in his bed;
15   Each morning fed,
And evening, with warm strokings from the cow;
    Would fish allow,
But not to wet her tender feet afford;
She may in pleasant gardens catch a bird,
20   Or make afeared.
Scorched with love's cruel flames, this youth did now
    At Venus' altars bow,
That she his love would change into a maid,
When thus with reared-up hands to Heaven he prayed:

25 'O Citherea,[123] since the cruel dart
Of thy dear son hath strangely pierced my heart,
    Some aid impart.
Thou at the prayer of sad Pygmalion[124]

---

[120] In the first book of fables, *The Fables of Aesop*, this is fable 73, which marks the beginning of another three-fable sequence.
[121] Grimalkin and Tybert were typical names for a cat.
[122] i.e., the French
[123] Citherea is another name for Venus, the goddess of love; her 'dear son' mentioned in the next line is Cupid.
[124] Pygmalion, the son of Cilax the Cypriot, deterred by the beastly life of the Propetides, and the vices generally incident to women, resolved to live a single life; who, carving the image of a virgin in ivory, fell in love with his own workmanship;

       Mad'st flesh of stone,
30 Formed a soft woman from obdurate° flint;
    That had no soul, this hath a spirit in't;
    This hath her passions, hath affection shown,
       And loves or me, or none.
    Make her for marriage fit, and she and I
35 Will day and night adore thy deity.'

    The goddess heard; first on her hairy face
    Did lilies of untainted beauty place,
       Which roses grace,
    And now her grey eyes sparkle more by day;
40   A Milky Way
    'Twixt hills of snow, which coral fountains shows,
    And her clear neck like silver dawn arose;
       Her white foot grows
    Now a fair palm, whence fingers long display,
45   Where azure° rivers stray.
    A virgin then appeared, so fair and sweet

---

at whose prayers Venus converted the statue into a woman, of whom he begot Paphus. Thus Ovid relates the fable:

Sit Conjux opto, non ausus, eburnea virgo,
Dicere Pygmalion, similis mea dixit eburnae, etc.

'Give me a wife, one like,' Pygmalion said,
But durst not say, 'Give me my ivory maid.'
The golden Venus, present at her feast,
Conceives his wish, and friendly signs expressed;
The fire thrice flaming, thrice in flames aspires.°
To his admired image he retires,
Lies down besides° her, raised her with his arm,
Then kissed her tempting lips, and found them warm.
That lesson oft repeats; her bosom oft
With amorous touches feels, and felt it soft;
Th'ivory, dimpled with his fingers, lacks
Accustomed hardness, as Hymettian° wax
Relents with heat, which chafing thumbs reduce
To pliant forms, by handling framed for use.
Amazed with doubtful joy and hope that reels,
Again the lover what he wishes feels;
The veins beneath his thumbs' impression beat,
A perfect virgin full of juice and heat, etc. [Ogilby's note.]

Ogilby quotes Ovid's *Metamorphoses* X.275–76, but (loosely) translates X.275–89.

She seemed a heaven all o'er, from head to feet.

Nor could the ravished youth admire too much,
Nor could believe, till by enduring touch
50   He found her such,
But when she spake, sweet love was in his breast
            With joy oppressed,
And loud he cries, 'Come all my friends, and see
The gods' great gift, what Heaven hath done for me;
55   I shall too happy be!
Bring silk and gold; with gems let her be dressed;
            Prepare the marriage feast!'
All came, and wonder; women's envious eye,
Surveying her, could not one blemish spy.

60   All rites performed, and Hymen's torch put out,[125]
Who of the joys of marriage bed could doubt,
            Or fear a flout?°
The Cyprian goddess then desired to find
            If that her mind
65   Was with her form improved; a little mouse
Straight she presents on th'eaves°[126] of the house.
            The bride leaps from her spouse,
And leaves the young man to embrace the wind.
            The cat will after kind.°
70   Just when he thought to reap the joy of joys,
'A mouse!' she cries, and all his hope destroys.

When Venus thus, highly incensed, stormed:
'A hateful cat t'a virgin we transformed,
            But still deformed,
75   And bestial thoughts within her breast remain;
            The task was vain:
No power can stave off nature. Though our art
Gave fair dimensions to the outward part,
            We could not change the heart.'
80   Here she transformed her to a cat again;

---

[125] i.e., the marriage ceremony having been completed; Hymen is the god of marriage
[126] In modernizing *The Fables of Aesop*'s 'Evins' as 'eaves', we have altered the metre of this line.

Then did the youth complain:
'Thy pity, Venus, thou hast turned to spite.
Wouldst thou not let me have her one short night?'

Moral

No punishment, no penalty, nor hire
85   Can repulse nature led by strong desire.
So barbarous people civilized with care,
The least occasion turns to what they were.

JOHN OGILBY

12. Of the Cat and the Cock[127]

She that so lately was the young man's spouse,
And left the joys of marriage bed to mouse,
Now conscious of her crime, and hooted at
    By all the house,
5   Grew more and more a cat.
    And after that,
By day she haunts sad rocks and shady groves;
When dark, through gutters o'er housetops she roves,
    And seeks night-walking loves,
10   Who couple not like doves,[128]
Where round about her cattish youngsters throng
(For she was fair), and with a hideous song,
    A dismal note and long,
The haughty rivals challenge, meet, and fight,
15 And terrify the silence of the night.

'Mongst these she proves; her pregnant womb being laid,
The ravenous beast in neighbouring houses preyed,
That milky breasts her tender young might breed.
    Once thus she strayed,
20   And not supplied her need,
    Nurses must feed.[129]
When thus she spake: 'Each passage, door, and lock
In my lord's house I know; there dwells a cock,
    Chief of a feathered flock,
25   Which once my hopes did mock,
But now he shall not scape.° Hark how he crows!
What, boast thou, fool, ere thou subdu'st thy foes?'
    This said, on straight she goes,
Through ways unknown, and mischievously bent,
30 Down boldly leaps, and seized the innocent.

---

[127] In the first book of fables, *The Fables of Aesop*, fable 74. This is a continuation of the previous fable.
[128] i.e., who have one-night stands
[129] i.e., She needed to eat regularly, because if she ran out of milk even once she would not be able to breastfeed, and her children would have to breastfeed from a nurse.

With her sad prisoners Puss was used to play —
Though he must die, she'll do't by legal way —
And thus attainders° formally began:
    'Thou before day
35   Awaken'st drowsy man,
    Who curse and ban,
Vexed with thy minstrelsy's° unwelcome airs,
At such a time when Heaven should hear their prayers
    To prosper them and theirs.'
40   This said, the cock declares,
'I am the husbandman's° alarm and watch;
Those sons of toil that live in smoke and thatch,
    Raised by my voice, dispatch
(Buckling on leather, frieze,° and clouted shoon)°
45 A long day's labour, often before noon.'

Then said the cat, 'Is thy impiety
(O wicked bird) and incest hid from me?
Thou hast against all laws of men and God,
    Which I did see,
50   Thy virgin daughter trod;
    Nay, thy hot blood
Thy sister, mother, grandam did not spare.'
Then he replied, 'Thy last charge less I fear,
    Since 'tis my master's care
55   For him, and for his fair
Lady, I should get eggs, who now is wed.'
'Shalt thou a strumpet feed enjoys the bed
    From whence I'm banishèd?
Accumulative crimes have no retreat;
60 'Tis treason: thou must die, and I must eat,'
Said angry Puss, and sharp-set° with a growl
She eats his flesh, and drinks in blood his soul.

    Moral

When tyrants would their empty coffers fill,
Against some wealthy peer they draw a bill;
65 The trial's fair: charge, answer, and reply;
But riches is your crime, and you must die.

13. Of the Cat and the Mice[130]

And now our cat, which once had been a wife,
    The iron tooth of time
    Had altered from her prime;
Old, she with nuns led a monastic life,
5 Free from rough lovers and proud rivals' strife,

And with those pious virgins went to prayer,
    Who, while they number beads,
    About them softly treads,[131]
Disturbing none that at devotion were,
10 Contented with long fasts and Lenten° fare.

Settled for strength, convenience, and health
    Near to the larder° door,
    Some Miceans had a poor
Plantation raised from sacrilege and stealth,
15 Almost from nothing to a commonwealth.

These hogen mogens,[132] when their cruel foe
    The cat they heard drew near,
    Were struck with mighty fear,
And at the tidings° straight to counsel go;
20 Till then these people knew no face of woe.

When some informed, and they of no mean place,
    They Tybert's issue° saw;
    Her countenance struck no awe,
But full of meekness, heavy was her pace,
25 And sadness much dejected had her face.

---

[130] In the first book of fables, *The Fables of Aesop*, fable 75. This is a continuation of the previous fable.

[131] The antecedent of 'who' is the cat: while the nuns count their rosary beads in prayer, the cat softly treads around them.

[132] The phrase 'hogen mogens' is an ironic way of saying 'high and powerful people'; it can also mean people from the Netherlands, who serve as a target for satire in other fables in this first volume.

They saw how oft she contemplating sat,
    Nor in that holy house,
    They thought, she'll touch a mouse,
Nor view with jealous eye their rising state;
30 This was a saint, a most religious cat.

When they this character had understood,
    Commissioners they chose
    (No time they careful lose)
That should bear gifts, and kiss great Puss' hand,
35 And leagues confirming lasting peace demand.

Soon they admitted were, and audience had;
    The subtle cat in state[133]
    Heard what they could relate
With mild aspect, her visage pale and sad,
40 And thus to them a friendly answer made:

'Bold Miceans, know (if you ne'er heard the same):
    I have been once a wife;
    Seeking one Micean's life,
I was transformed to what you see I am,
45 For which bold crime to penance here I came.

'Your suit we grant, but as our custom, nine
    Potentates I invite
    To sup with me this night,
So intimate, but you with us shall dine;
50 Then in their presence lasting peace I'll sign.'

This known, nine chosen march through narrow ports
    And winding passes forth
    With many mice of worth;
There the fond vulgar in great troops resorts,
55 Expecting banquets in the cattish courts.

---

[133] i.e., the cat, receiving them with great pomp and ceremony

No sooner in, but stern Puss shuts the door,
    Stops all the chinks and holes;
    Then terror strikes their souls,
And to a fury she transformed once more,
60   Bestrews the room with mangled limbs and gore.

Which to the senate° a new lesson reads:
    Fair words and simpering looks
    Are still deceivers' hooks;
None that is wise outward comportment heeds;
65   *Mortals their face declares not, but their deeds.*[134]

Moral

Treaties are full of fraud; if rising states
Would join with princes and make kings their mates,
Let them beware how they confirm the league;
Monarchs still jealous for small cause renege.

---

[134] In 1673/5 the last four lines of this stanza are italicized.

14. Of the Sheep and the Butcher[135]

Wethers a dozen, all of special note,
Each in a golden fleece or silver coat,
Fed in one stall, rich in their numerous flocks,
Free from incursions of the wolf and fox,
5 Where they, long prospering, securely dwelt,
And never frown of fickle Fortune felt,
Whom from their golden dream a butcher wakes,
And a fat brother from Sheep College[136] takes.
    Much at this unexpected chance dismayed,
10 In frequent counsel, thus Bell-Wether[137] said:
    'How are we fall'n whom pride and riches swelled?
Who such a consternation e'er beheld?
We, in gold tunics and striped silver vests,
For nuptials fitted, look like funeral guests;
15 With our surprisal° struck, each face did show
A map of misery and ensuing woe.
Where's former strength and courage, where our vaunt?°
No fortune could the Sheepish nation daunt.
But now our business mind; no time neglect;
20 We must be sudden stout, and circumspect;
Apparent danger's near; by one consent
Our ruin by defensive arms prevent.
What fool on us embodied once dares fall,[138]
Whose heads may batter down a brazen wall?
25 But if you suffer thus the subtle foe
To seize us single, and unquestioned go,
Thus unarrayed° let him the fattest cull,°
And at once strip us both of skin and wool,
We inch by inch shall like a taper melt,
30 Lost in destruction ere one blow be dealt.
Wars are begun, and yet no war proclaimed;
No trumpet sounding, why should we be blamed

---

[135] In the second book of fables, *Aesopics*, fable 20.
[136] Ogilby imagines the flock of sheep as an organized body of members, a college; this may be ironic, given the action that will follow.
[137] A bell-wether is a sheep who leads the flock; Ogilby is using it as a proper name. The word is used figuratively for a leader, often contemptuously (*OED*).
[138] i.e., What fool would attack us if we have come together into one unified body?

To take up arms, and so revenge our wrong?
Surprisal makes us forty thousand strong;
35 In Belin's name,[139] next ent'ring, him arrest,
And beat the breath out of his wicked breast;
This bloody butcher kill, and then sit down
In peace, and once more masters of your own.'
    This said, a biased brother rising spoke,
40 And thus in pieces his grave counsel took:
    'We may your courage, not your prudence praise,
Would us persuade a dangerous war to raise
Upon such slender grounds, before we know
If this invasion be, or he a foe;
45 Under attainder and to prison led,
Must we him rescue, private quarrels wed?
Engage republic on so slight a score,
Be all undone rather than one grow poor?
A province seized, the fact will never reach
50 To make upon the empire's peace a breach;
Whilst you enjoy whate'er makes mortals blessed,
To help a neighbour ne'er yourselves molest;
Some with their blood may water fleur-de-lis,°
Others regild pale-growing golden fleece.
55 But whoe'er takes up arms, the die once thrown,
May call their proper goods no more their own;
Let their allies and friends the better get;
United states may in a province set.
    'But to the point, the foe you would surprise,
60 He watches with his own, not others' eyes;
His preparations he will never slack,
But still be ready at the first attack;
Not sloth nor avarice shall e'er abuse,
Being a master of his own reviews.
65 So fall on when you please; you soon shall feel,
'Gainst your unpractis'd arms, his ready steel;
Though twelve to one, he in prepared bowls
Will cool this fever in your purple souls;[140]

---

[139] Belin became a typical name for a ram after it was popularized by the medieval tales about Reynard the Fox. Here the sheep swears by Belin as a kind of god or king of rams.

[140] i.e., the odds are that he will cool or diminish your passion for rebellion by killing you and bleeding you out, collecting the blood in bowls

So in one action we shall perish all.
70 The worst that may betide, fall what may fall,
We shall have time, whilst us he singly takes;
Each posting minute alterations makes.
Whilst present° junctures° may our cause advance,
Wonders the bosom fill, of time and chance,
75 And this encroaching tyrant may, perhaps,
On false pretensions levying war, relapse.
Therefore be patient; live whilst live we may,
Nor to a desperate hazard° all betray.'
    This counsel taking, they despise the first,
80 And, none there contradicting, chose the worst.
When in the slaughterer comes, just as before,
And their full dozen shrunk to half a score,
So daily picks and culls, making no noise,
Till of twice six, remains not any choice.
85 Only his orator, whom forth he draws,
Last to reward who so preached up his cause,
Who not suspected cutting of his throat,
But to be duke and peer made of the coat.
'False and ambitious counsellors,' then said he,
90 *'May they be paid their punishment like me.'*

Moral

Few public spirits common counsels find;
These fathom wants, those private interest blind;[141]
Most for the present, and their own affairs,
Sudden calamities seizeth unawares.

---

[141] i.e., some enquire into desires or things lacking [in a kingdom]; private interests blind others [to the common good]

15. Of the Wolf and the Fox[142]

A river by a thunder-tempest swelled
Would not in bounds° of modesty be held,
But with an inroad° o'erruns bordering strands;°
Retreat then sounding, plashes° leaves, and ponds.
5 'Mongst which a tardy salmon Reynard[143] spies,
And without net or angle° makes his prize.
   The wolf hard by observed the lucky hit,
And thus puts in to share the dainty bit:[144]
   'Halves, half I cry! What you seized, first I saw,
10 And claim the moiety° by Partners' Law.[145]
In happy time this creature comfort came;
My queasy stomach checks° at kid or lamb;
Tasteless seems human blood; I from a drab°
Last night made seizure of a tender squab,
15 Thought on the infant, warm, myself to treat,
And scarce the liver and the heart could eat.
   'Come, let's to breakfast, and at night with me
You shall co-partner of my fortune be;
I at Hogs Norton[146] twinkling of a jig
20 On profane organs took a popish pig;
I'll only feast you with that single dish;
By that time well we shall digest our fish.'
   Then Reynard thus: 'Whate'er this Lenten fare,
For a small purchase I release my share;
25 My peevish madam ready to cry out,

---

[142] In the second book of fables, *Aesopics*, fable 21, which marks the beginning of another three-fable sequence.

[143] Reynard became a typical name for a fox after it was popularized by the medieval tales about Reynard the Fox; Isgrim, named below, was a wolf from the same set of narratives.

[144] i.e., puts himself up to share in the fish

[145] Despite the wolf's use of legal terms ('seized', 'moiety', etc.), there doesn't seem to have been a law in early modern England called 'Partners' Law'. The wolf is most likely offering to enter into some sort of partnership with the fox, where, as if in a business, all partners would share equally in any 'profits' of any ventures: the wolf gets some of the fox's fish, and will share his own takings later in the day.

[146] The phrase 'Hogs Norton, where pigs play the organ' was proverbial (*OED*). Hogs Norton was the name of a fictional town, sometimes associated with having boorish inhabitants; in short, the wolf tells the fox that he has captured a pig which he will trade later for some fish now.

Nothing will serve her but a salmon-trout,
Which brought not when expected, she will rise,
Bedung my face, and urine in my eyes.
  'But learn to fish, I'll soon your wolfship teach,
30 Both for yourself and friends enough to catch;
Bring yonder basket tackled to that rope,
Which you shall satisfy beyond your hope;
That wicker laden will be such a heap,
Shall markets make, so much now risen, cheap.'
35   This said, Isgrim, though surly, draws the tools,
Which, tying to his stern, thus Reynard fools:
'Now to the river bring the fastened pail,
Which I'll so settle that you shall not fail;
But you by no means, till I give the word,
40 Must not look back, nor your drag-net be stirred.'
  The greedy wolf, this said, obeys command,
And as the fox directed, takes his stand,
Whilst he the wicker with huge pebbles thwacks,
Until the circling sallow belly cracks.[147]
45 This done, he calls, 'Now please your wolfship pull!
Well you are handselled:°[148] your new engine's° full;
The river's drained; what fish, how fat and fair!
Now I demand with you a partner's share.
Put all your strength; your cordage° strong and dock,
50 So well united, may remove a rock.'[149]
  This said, glad Isgrim gives a lusty hale,°
Until he tentered° out both rope and tail;
But fast° the work stood fixed, nor more would jog
Than stubborn rock, or a perverser log.
55   When Reynard calls, 'I see we need some help;
I'll fetch my eldest son, an able whelp,°
Who, joined with you, the task shall undertake;
But till we come, by no means, sir, look back.'
The wolf persuaded, fox bears home his trout,
60 Then mustering thus the villages about:

---

[147] This perhaps means, until the circular, yellow-brown 'belly' or bottom of the basket was so full of rocks that it cracked.
[148] i.e., you're in a lot of luck
[149] i.e., The ropes and cords tied to your dock (the fleshy part of a tail in an animal) can work together so well that they could move a rock.

'Swains, come away, and arm with speed! The wolf,
Your flocks' devourer, that all-swallowing gulf,
Now drains your river, and what havoc there
May sheepskin doublets make that never swear,
65 Pure zeal pretenders, to your grief you know;[150]
Now, now avenged be on the common foe!'
    Straight from the neighbouring dorps° bold rustics throng,
And like a gathered tempest, old and young,
Upon his quarters falling, him assail,
70 With bats, and staves,° and stones as thick as hail;
No way to save himself, of life no hope,
He quits his rudder fastened to the rope;
To nearest coverts° bare-breeched° Isgrim flies,
Whilst mingled shouts and clamours scale the skies.

Moral

75 Those that at private or at public feasts
Use to invite themselves[151] 'mongst bidden guests,
Often upon them such affronts are put,
They had been better at the threepenny cut.[152]

---

[150] i.e., Much to your sadness, you know what kind of damage those who wear sheep's clothing — those who only pretend to be genuine — can do.
[151] i.e., frequently invite themselves
[152] A threepenny cut is either a very small or poor cut of meat, worth only three pennies, or a cut of meat so small it is only the size of a threepenny piece.

16. Of the Same Wolf and Fox[153]

Glad of the mercy and escape so fair,
Though with no little smart° and gaskins° bare,
Whilst he lay licking whole his scarce no stump,
Rustics in triumph bearing round the rump,
5   Thus Isgrim did his bosom disembogue:°
    'How shall I be revenged upon this rogue,
Who me in danger put, and utter shame,
To be thus despicable as I am?
Where shall I wander now? Where show my face,
10 Bearing about the brand of my disgrace?
How shall I be disguised, or which way dressed,
Unless I wear a tunic and a vest?
I that abhorred all fashions whate'er, new°
Must bid to those my dogging modes adieu.[154]
15 I'll lay my vizard° by, a Hector turn,[155]
And my too formal sanctity adjourn,
Fall on this subtle fox where'er we meet —
No, 'twill not do; wit must encounter wit.
Thus clad,° I'll to the court; the lion's sick;
20 Mint on, my brains, and show him trick for trick.'[156]
    This said, he lays aside his formal shape,
His sheepskin cloak and mutton-velvet cape,[157]
Puts on a vest that covered his disgrace,
And with a peruke° owled his wolfish face;[158]
25 Low-crowned his hat, not the same beast he showed;
So forth he walks, a new old à la mode.[159]
    Ent'ring the court, he in the royal hall
The king and queen saw, sitting at a ball,

---

[153] In the second book of fables, *Aesopics*, this is fable 22. Ogilby calls this '2. Of the Same Wolf and Fox', thereby doubly indicating that this is a continuation of the same characters.
[154] To 'dog' is to continue at a thing consistently or doggedly; the wolf announces that he must give up his previous stubborn refusal of fashion, perhaps with a slight pun, since the wolf is somewhat dog-like.
[155] i.e., I'll become or act like a valiant warrior, like the Trojan hero Hector in Homer's *Iliad*
[156] i.e., Get started minting or producing ideas, brains — it's time to get even.
[157] i.e., a cape sewn out of velvet, perhaps made from an adult sheep's wool
[158] i.e., perhaps, he used a wig to make his head more rounded and owl-like
[159] i.e., a new version of his old self, now fashionable

Dancing baboons, and singing parakeets;[160]
30 The lion eased in melancholy sits;
Up in a bower his cats and fiddles stood;
The band twice twelve made galliards° in the blood.
    The pastime over, Isgrim did appear,
And going forth, desired his royal ear;
35 He his old counsellor, though disguised, not balks,
But a turn with him in the gallery walks;
Then he himself applying, from his forge
New-anviled° spleen and malice did disgorge:°
    'I from a populous city came of late,
40 Where all diseases sell at any rate,
Who golden showers pour in a Danaë's lap,
Only to purchase a sufficient clap;[161]
Smallpox is little valued, lesser swine
All seek the best they barter may for coin.
45   'About your health inquisitive, I found
Those that keep patients sick, could make them sound;
At spring and fall their bloods did so ferment,
To pay them twice a year their constant rent.
I 'mongst those doctors met a reverend sage,
50 And told him your distemper, sir, and age;
Not only trusting practice, down he took
From shelves with learning loaden° an old book,
The text and stuffed-up margents° long surveyed,
And thus from Galen's observations,[162] said:
55   '"The person disaffected, vexed with fumes,
Vertiginous° vapours, and distilling rheums°
Must purge, must diet, and must issues° make;
But old, take care lest any cold he take.
Get him warm furs; his garments line and face;

---

[160] In *Aesopics* this word is spelled 'Parachitts', to rhyme with 'sits'.
[161] In Greek mythology, Jove, the king of the gods, visits the woman Danaë in the form of a shower of gold and impregnates her. In this case, the wolf seems to be describing the busy life of prostitutes in a city: 'golden showers' of money are poured into their laps, but in return the women's 'customers' receive only the clap, a venereal disease.
[162] Galenic medicine, named after the doctor Galen (129–c. 200 CE), assumed that illness was caused by the imbalance of bodily humours or fluids; here the doctor advises that a person who is ill must purge the body of excess humours by a variety of methods.

60 Nothing more sovereign than a fox's case,
That only will, if rich, solder° all flaws
Of wintry age, and quite remove the cause.'"
  Then said the lion, 'A fox skin so good
Youth to renew, and circulate the blood!
65 King-craft[163] and gravest counsellors allege
That foxes' tails best royal ermine° edge.'
  Then Isgrim said, 'Sir Reynard,[164] now gone down,
That in late turmoils fought against your crown,
And knighted since by you, get him to court,
70 And your dear life to lengthen, cut his short.'
  The lion likes th'advice, and orders straight
That on emergencies, affairs of state,
He should attend the king, whom more to blind,
His gracious letter he both seal'd and sign'd;
75 No common messenger nor usual post°
Were sent, by which the business might be lost,
But a swift tiger that like lightning flew.
  The work thus perfected, the king withdrew,
And Isgrim, joyful of his well played part,
80 Goes to his lodgings with a merry heart.

Moral

He that receives a wrong should bear it too;
Are they too subtle or too strong for you?
Better sit down, loss and affronts digest,
Than, rising, tread upon a serpents' nest.

---

[163] We have modernized this as 'king-craft', or the art of ruling as a king, but it is also possible that King Craft is a particularly crafty character.
[164] i.e., the fox

17. Of the Same Wolf and Fox[165]

This closet-secret,[166] the whole junto° two,
Early next morning sly Sir Reynard knew;
His pensioners,° intelligencers° there,
Picked out each whisper from the king's own ear;
5 Such as their prince and country, such as would
Their wives — their wives! — and children sell for gold,
Who public spirits count both weak and base,
Let private interest, self-concern take place;
What care they if whole kingdoms sink or swim,
10 So they buoy up and float above the brim?°
    Startled at first, a consternating cold
Agu'd° his joints, attacked life's warmer hold;
Soon as his better spirits cleared the damp,
And sparks of courage lightened reason's lamp,
15 Then Reynard spake: 'Be circumspect, and quick;
Mischief prevent, and show him trick for trick;
To cure the lion, must I be uncased?°
You may be met with, wolf, for all your haste.'
    This said, he all bemires° his back and head,
20 In carrion° rolls where rooks° and ravens fed,
So to court goes, so armed with this disguise
And noisome° stench, to play his master-prize,
And soon he came where the old lion sat,
Bemelancholied° and disconsolate.°
25   But when he saw Sir Reynard there, he said,
'Cousin! Draw near; to see you I am glad!
You must for me a business undertake,
Concerns my life and crown. Why draw'st thou back?
Come near, and me, your king, advice afford;
30 The work's too knotty for our council-board.
They only follow sport, eat, drink, and droll,
Scarce one a learnèd or a knowing soul.'

---

[165] In the second book of fables, *Aesopics*, this is fable 23. Ogilby calls it '3. Of the Same Wolf and Fox', once again doubly indicating that it is part of a series with the same characters.
[166] Ogilby seems to have invented this hyphenated word. A closet meant, generally, a private room or inner chamber, so a closet-secret should be especially private; that it is quickly made known to the fox is a sign of his great power in the court.

Then Reynard said, 'Ah, my most gracious liege!
I thus bespattered with foul dung and siege,°
35 Sir, ought not in your royal presence stand,
But that I bring you from a foreign land
Fair overtures of health, nay, certain cure
For ling'ring sickness worse than calenture.°
What comfort boasts the emperor of the world,
40 Whose cheeks bear pale distempers, flags unfurled?
When hypochondric fumes, more strong than spells,
Or pulpits conjure up ten thousand hells,
Legions of devils, and as many saints,
Breathing rebellion, oaths, and covenants,
45 Tortured with fancy worse than his disease,
He lives or dies as court physicians please.
    'Observing, sir, that all in physic° dealt,
Oft'ner our purses than our pulses felt,
And whensoever double fees not drop,
50 They leave their patient then in little hope.
Galenic this, chymistry that pretends,
Their chiefest learning Greek and Latin ends.[167]
'So I at last a great magician found,
That only dealt with spirits underground;
55 By me importuned much, he called from rest
Old Aesop, that renowned mythologist,
Who first to business found the nearest way —
What in long sermons orators could say
Of state affairs, of moral or divine,
60 His cock and bull contracts all in a line[168] —
Whose pale shade told me vain were med'cines all;
You might perhaps linger a spring, and fall,
But you your course must finish ere the sun
Could through the ecliptic° annual periods run.
65   'I, grieving much, straight made this sad reply:
"Ah! Must my dear and royal master die?"

---

[167] Galenism, as described in the previous fable, promised a humoral cure, while chymistry, or alchemy, promised a transformative chemical cure. Neither, the fox goes on, can deliver on their promise. The point is that both of these methods for healing were more interested in ancient learning than in modern cures.

[168] i.e., What it would take others a very long time to say, Aesop can contract into a short line.

When thus he spake in few and pithy words:
"One only med'cine the whole world affords
Whose sovereign power can o'er his fits prevail,
70 And that's a wolf, a wolf without a tail,
Whose bristly skin must gird him back and side;
This in seven days will cure, if well applied."
'This said, the vision fled the dazzling light,
Since when I neither rested day nor night
75 To bring from shadows and the gates of Hell
What us must happy make, and you, sir, well.
My haste, and your necessity, hath made
Me venture in your presence thus berayed.'°
'Who's there?' the king said. 'On your lives not fail,
80 But fetch me straight a wolf without a tail.'
When one replied, 'Isgrim, late come to court,
A rudder wants,[169] or else 'tis wondrous short;
To hide his wants, thus he himself hath dressed,
His sheepskin cloak turned to a coat and vest.'
85 'Ha!' said the monarch, 'Bid him hither straight';
No sooner entered, but he met his fate.
The lion throws him back upon the floor,
And off his skin, and out his bowels tore.
No sooner Reynard saw thus Isgrim stripped,
90 But to Fox Hall[170] the sly insulter slipped.

Moral

Not he who first, but last, the king's ear gets,
At subtle plots and counterminings° beats;
Yet they who foremost charge, cry traitor first,
Play a fore-game,° and seldom get the worst.

---

[169] i.e., is lacking a tail

[170] This place name, presumably the proper name of the fox's dwelling, also appears to be a pun on the noun 'foxhole', which literally means a fox's burrow and figuratively means 'a hiding place' or 'place of refuge' (*OED*).

TEXTUAL NOTES

A full discussion of the status of each text and our editorial guidelines can be found at the end of our introduction; in short, we have modernized the texts of each of our five authors, including updating spelling, punctuation, and in most cases typography (including the use of italic and other fonts) to conform to modern practice. Below are more detailed textual notes.

These textual notes include, for each author, a list of all substantive emendations we have made in the process of modernizing and editing the texts. For our earlier authors especially we have frequently had to alter verb forms to bring them in line with modern practice; if we merely changed a vowel (e.g., changing 'spake' to 'spoke') we have not counted that as an emendation, but if we have changed the form of the verb (e.g., changing 'spake' to 'spoken'; or changing 'been' to 'be') we have listed it among the emendations. Each of our authors frequently gives as two words what we would give as one (e.g., 'any body' for 'anybody'; 'in deed' for 'indeed'; 'where ever' for 'wherever'); we have not counted combining these words as emendations, but have done so regularly throughout.

For two of our authors (Golding and Smith), only one surviving copy of their texts survive (Golding's manuscript, and Smith's edition from 1577). For Caxton, only one edition survives (three copies of his 1484 edition). For our other two authors, multiple versions survive: Brinsley has two editions, one from 1617, and one from 1624 (which survive in one copy each); and Ogilby has four editions of *The Fables of Aesop* (1651, 1665, 1668, 1673/5) and two editions of *Aesopics* (1668, 1673/5). For these last two authors we have therefore included, in addition to the list of emendations, a list of significant variants between (or among) the editions. We define as 'significant' anything that would have survived modernization; that is, we do not include differences in spelling or punctuation, but do include entirely different words and what we consider to be compositorial errors (as they indicate, in some cases, interesting things about the relationships among editions). Because Ogilby's fables are poetic, we also note differences in elision (when they occur in his poetry, though not in his prose) that would affect the metre (e.g., we note among the variants if one edition has 'the advantage' and another has 'th'advantage'). Since, as is discussed at greater length in the introduction, Ogilby seems to deliberately italicize entire lines, we have noted where those italics differ across editions, and marked them with a note in square brackets.

I. ARTHUR GOLDING, *A MORAL FABLETALK*

Below is a list of all emendations made to Arthur Golding's *A Moral Fabletalk*. To the left of the square bracket is the word or phrase as it appears in our edited text; to the right of the square bracket is the word as it appears in Golding's manuscript held in the Columbia University Rare Book and Manuscript Library (Western Manuscript 16). Preceding each entry is the fable number from this volume.

We have not counted expanding Golding's biblical citations as emendations, but we have counted as an emendation the addition or modification of a missing or obviously incorrect citation.

Golding: Emendations

Fable 2 be entrapped] bin intrapped
Fable 3 but also with reasons] (but also with reasons
Fable 4 stream. (Ecclesiasticus 4:32)] streame.
Fable 11 worried] wirryed
Fable 12 striven] strived
Fable 12 woke] waked
Fable 12 thanks] thanke
Fable 14 so much] smuch
Fable 15 stuck] sticked
Fable 15 (Sapience 16:29)] Sap: 10.29
Fable 16 When the reed regarded the ash fallen] When the Reede the Asshe falne
Fable 23 quickly] quitly
Fable 25 as] as as
Fable 29 vixen] Fixen
Fable 31 hypocrisy] Hyporisy
Fable 35 Of a Horse and an Ass] Of a Horse an Asse
Fable 35 with a store] with store
Fable 36 feet. (Proverbs 29:5)] feete.
Fable 37 renowned] renowmed
Fable 37 strove] stryved
Fable 38 (Proverbs 29:23)] Pro: 20.23.
Fable 39 (Jeremiah 49:16)] Jerem. 40.10.
Fable 41 as] as as
Fable 41 When the horse] Whe the horse

TEXTUAL NOTES

Fable 41 dug] digged
Fable 42 (Proverbs 3:32)] Pro: 3.23.
Fable 46 (Psalms 36:35–36)] Psalm: 30.35.36.
Fable 47 beseeming] beseening
Fable 48 deeming] deening
Fable 51 disdainfully] disdeyfully
Fable 51 farthest] furthest
Fable 51 (Proverbs 17:16)] Pro: 17.10.
Fable 52 hunt] hant
Fable 54 shown] shewed
Fable 55 he had but forgotten] he but forgotten
Fable 55 (Exodus 20:12)] Exod. 10.12.
Fable 57 returned] retured
Fable 58 every one of his feathers] every one his feathers
Fable 65 loaded] Loden
Fable 69 and luck are] and   are
Fable 77 Of a Serpent] Of Serpent
Fable 79 aloof] afoofe
Fable 81 again)] again
Fable 83 more likely in respect] more likely in in respect
Fable 91 built] bwilded
Fable 91 Prudent] Pruden
Fable 93 does] doo
Fable 94 the hound that hunted] the Hound) that hunted
Fable 95 greatest] greateth
Fable 95 by and by] by and
Fable 97 wondered] windered
Fable 100 begin] bogin
Fable 102 which] with
Fable 108 unmeasurable] vnneasurable
Fable 109 forgetting] fogetting
Fable 110 considered] consired
Fable 114 shown] shewed
Fable 115 renown] renowme
Fable 117 from time to time] from tyme
Fable 118 forsook] for-forsooke
Fable 119 harboured] harber
Fable 121 when they be yet callow] (when they be yet callow
Fable 122 mentioned] metioned
Fable 122 and doth always somewhat undiscreetly] dooeth alwayes somewhat vn-discreetly

503

Fable 124 end of all things] end of all all things
Fable 124 restitution] restititution

II. WILLIAM CAXTON, *THE SUBTLE HISTORIES AND FABLES OF AESOP*

Below is a list of all emendations made to William Caxton's *The Subtle Histories and Fables of Aesop*. To the left of the square bracket is the word or phrase as it appears in our edited text; to the right of the square bracket is the word as it appears in Caxton's 1484 edition held in the British Library (Shelfmark C.11.c.17). Preceding each entry is the fable number from this volume. In those instances where the word may be too isolated to be located (for example, the word 'thou' may appear several times in one fable), we have included the larger phrase in which the emended word or phrase appears for context (for example, ['which thou hast done']).

Caxton: Emendations

Fable 1 pasture] pastnure
Fable 1 he should have] he shold hane
Fable 1 taken] take
Fable 2 swam] swymed
Fable 3 taken and held] taken and hold
Fable 3 he said thus to the lion] sayd thus to the lyon
Fable 3 taken] take ['taken at a great trap']
Fable 3 taken] take ['I am taken and bound']
Fable 3 thou] thon ['which thou hast done']
Book 2 Proem second book of the fables of Aesop] second book booke of eso fables of esope
Book 2 Proem be found] ben found ['all manner of fables be found']
Book 2 Proem write] wryten
Book 2 Proem been] be ['hath been given']
Book 2 Proem been] be ['had never been under no man's']
Fable 4 cast] casted
Fable 4 into] m to ['began to enter into the water']
Fable 4 ate] ete ['and ate them one after other']
Fable 4 ate] ete ['destroyed and ate them']
Fable 4 your] yonr
Fable 5 demandeth] demanded
Fable 5 to] do ['to suffer from the kite']

TEXTUAL NOTES

Fable 5 ourselves] our self
Fable 5 be] ben ['we be cause of this mischief']
Fable 5 do] done
Fable 6 cast] casted
Fable 6 no one] none
Fable 7 no one] none
Fable 7 ate] ete ['a horse which ate grass']
Fable 7 shown] shewed
Fable 7 myself] my sel
Fable 8 never] nener
Fable 8 taken] take ['if he were taken away']
Fable 8 been] be ['as he had been dead']
Fable 8 be] ben ['they which be on live']
Fable 8 be] ben ['when they be dead']
Fable 9 great] grede
Fable 10 stronger than the lion] stronger than the loyn
Fable 10 it had been] it had be
Fable 10 then] thenue
Fable 10 into] m to ['into the pit']
Fable 11 of] df ['this fable of a wolf']
Fable 11 be] ben ['These be good tidings']
Fable 11 and] aud ['better and more delicious meat']
Fable 11 lifted] lyft
Fable 11 taken] take
Fable 11 be come] ben comen
Fable 11 the service is complete and done] the seruyse complete and done
Fable 11 town] touue
Fable 11 hewed] hewe
Fable 11 be] ben ['may not be recovered']
Fable 11 no one] none
Fable 12 No one] None
Fable 12 envious] ennyous
Fable 13 No one] None
Fable 14 merchant] marrhaunt
Fable 15 a wife who was much chaste] a wyf moche chaste
Fable 15 gone] go ['would have gone on pilgrimage']
Fable 15 I have not will to grant him] I haue not wylle graunte hym
Fable 15 be] ben ['which be done by bawds']
Fable 16 began] begannn
Fable 16 And as the blind man] And And as the blynd man

505

Fable 16 heard them thus hard shake] herd thus hard shake
Fable 16 bound] bounden
Fable 17 been] be ['as they had been joyned']
Fable 17 lifted] lyfte
Fable 17 Poge] Pope
Fable 17 swam] swimmed
Fable 17 but] bnt ['he had but the head']
Fable 17 come] came
Fable 17 drawn] drawe
Fable 17 that there was a child] that a child

III. RICHARD SMITH, *THE FABULOUS TALES OF AESOP THE PHRYGIAN*

Below is a list of all emendations made to Richard Smith's *The Fabulous Tales of Aesop the Phrygian*. To the left of the square bracket is the word or phrase as it appears in our edited text; to the right of the square bracket is the word as it appears in Smith's 1577 edition held in the National Library of Scotland (Shelfmark Ry.III.h.38). Preceding each entry is the fable number from this volume (or the title of the prefatory matter), followed by the line number in which the emendation appears.

Smith: Emendations

The Book's Passport.2 minds] mind
The Book's Passport.12 care] cares
The Book's Passport.40 Take] takes
Epistle let it lie dead] let it lyen dead
Prologue.10 Spring] Springs
Prologue.19 wise men say] wise men says
Prologue.20 If that ye find it] If that ye find
Fable 1.0 (title) the Precious Stone] precious Stone
Fable 1.20 buried thus amongst] buried this amongs
Fable 1.63.1 (heading) Morality] The Morall
Fable 2.10 boughs hung] Beuis song
Fable 2.13 harmony] hatmony
Fable 2.20 the fowls' cry] of the fowles cry
Fable 2.39 borne] beare
Fable 2.71 in this world me think] in this worlde my thinke
Fable 2.135 thus] this
Fable 2.291 hurt man writes] hurt men, writes

Fable 3.11 waxed] woxe
Fable 3.52 snod] snoe
Fable 3.73 shaped] shope
Fable 3.107 aflocht] flote
Fable 3.117 Methinks] My thinkes
Fable 3.138 be] bene
Fable 3.156 themselves] them selfe
Fable 4.13 in this manner] on this manier
Fable 4.50 clerks say] Clerkes sayes
Fable 4.58 founden faken] found infakin
Fable 4.99 leapt] lap
Epilogue.12 good examples live] good examples liues
Epilogue.20 work, and read] worke, and and reade

IV. JOHN BRINSLEY, *AESOP'S FABLES TRANSLATED GRAMMATICALLY*

Below is a list of all emendations made to John Brinsley's *Aesop's Fables Translated Grammatically*; under that is a list of all significant textual variants among the editions. To the left of the square bracket is the word or phrase as it appears in our edited text; to the right of the square bracket is the word as it appears in the original printings of Brinsley's fables, with the edition(s) in which it appears in that form. Preceding each entry is the fable number from this volume; if the emendation or variant is in one of Brinsley's notes, the fable number will have an 'n' after it (so, for example, 'Fable 1n' indicates that the emendation or variant occurs in one of Brinsley's marginal notes to Fable 1 in this volume). Brinsley uses a large number of square brackets in his texts, so below, any text enclosed in square brackets that has not been signed 'Eds' belongs to Brinsley.

Brinsley: Emendations

Title Ludus Literarius] Ludus Lit 1617, 1624
Fable 1n *Gallinaceus*] *Gallinaceus*] 1617, 1624 [both editions include a closing square bracket after the word [Eds]]
Fable 5 returneth unto the table and calleth] returneth vnto the table, calleth 1617, 1624
Fable 5n *or the fears and dangers*] *and the feares and dangers* 1617; *or feares and dangers* 1624
Fable 9 Most men are lifted up] Most men are lift vp 1617, 1624

Fable 11n beat or put back] bet or put backe 1617; bet, or put back 1624

Brinsley: Variants

Title *Aesop's Fables*] ESOPS EABLES 1617
Title *Translated Grammatically*] Translated both Grammatically 1624
Title *directions*] directionrs 1624
Epistle Dedicatory have very good use] haue worthie vse 1617
Ep. Ded. to fly the vices] to flee the vices 1617
Ep. Ded. they may see] to see 1617
Ep. Ded. the foolishness of men] the foolish- of men 1617
Ep. Ded. and more especially of children] especially of children 1617
Ep. Ded. they may learn] to teach them 1617
Ep. Ded. likewise the third fable] likewise in the third fable 1617
Ep. Ded. may teach children in all their time] to teach children in all their time 1617
Ep. Ded. the fourth, the apologue] the fourth, In the Apologue 1617
Ep. Ded. his chaps — is to teach even children] his chops, to teach children 1617
Ep. Ded. by learning still of the learned] by learning still of all the learned 1617
Epistle to the Reader Italic letters in alphabetical order] *a little r* 1617
Ep. Read. in my former translations, and in my *Grammar School*] *in my* Grammar-School 1624
Fable 1 learning and wisdom.]] learning and wisedome. 1624 [no closing square bracket in 1624 [Eds]]
Fable 1 When on a time] As on a time 1624
Fable 1n belonging to a cock or hen] belonging to a cock or a hen 1617
Fable 1n *Foolish contempt of learning*] *Contempt of learning* 1624
Fable 1n Whilst a cock, etc., or a cock found, etc., whilst] Whilst a cock &c. 1617
Fable 1n in it,] init, 1624
Fable 1n 'What,' quoth he, or 'Why?'] what quoth he 1617
Fable 1n to me, or for me, to no use] [no note in 1624 [Eds]]
Fable 1n [understand] by the, etc.] understand by the 1617

TEXTUAL NOTES

Fable 1n for neither foolish men do love] Neither foolish men doe loue 1617

Fable 1n voluptuous] volpptuous 1624

Fable 1n to whom one alonely, pleasure can please or be pleasant] to whom alone, or one, pleasure can please 1617

Fable 2 He runneth to [and] rateth] He runneth [and] rateth 1624

Fable 2n a far off or a great way beneath] far off or a great way beneath 1624

Fable 2n himself neither indeed to have] himself not indeed to haue 1624

Fable 2n speaketh terribly] speaketh vehemently 1617

Fable 2n wicked wretch] wretch 1617

Fable 3 a Mouse and a Frog] a Mouse and n Frog 1624

Fable 3 the spear to each of them] the speare to either of them 1617

Fable 4 waters, which being seen] waters: which seene 1624

Fable 4 greedily catching at it] greedily catching at 1617

Fable 4n cheeks, or chaps] chaps 1624

Fable 5 your dainties savour more] youth dainties savour more 1624

Fable 5 A country mouse saw] A counlry mouse saw 1624

Fable 5n *Bitterness in riches*] *The bitternesse in riches* 1624

Fable 5n this [mouse]] this mouse 1617

Fable 5n had prepared gaily, or richly, excellently] had prepared richly or excellently 1624

Fable 5n between to feast, or their feasting] Betweene to feast, or [their] feasting 1617

Fable 5n They began to tremble] They [began] to tremble 1617

Fable 5n exceedingly] exceedling 1624

Fable 5n it to be daily to owe to be contemned] it to be daily to one to be contemned 1617

Fable 5n oft] eft 1617

Fable 5n revenge] rerevenge 1617

Fable 6 The captive beseecheth [him]] The captiue beseecheth him 1617

Fable 6 And not very long after] And not very to long after 1617

Fable 6 the lion by chance] the lion bechance 1617

Fable 6 findeth [them] being sought] findeth them being sought 1617

Fable 6 gnaweth [them] being found] gnaweth them being found 1617

509

Fable 6 mighty men themselves sometimes] mighty men sometimes 1617
Fable 6n captive or [mouse] being taken] captiue or mouse being taken 1617
Fable 6n it is not lawful to go out] it is not lawfull to get out 1624
Fable 7 you lose [not] a great [commodity]] you lose [not] a great commodity 1617
Fable 7 you trust [not] every man] you trust not euery man 1617
Fable 7 For there are [men]] For there are men 1617
Fable 9 the horse was swiftly flying forward] the horse was swiftly fleeing forward 1617
Fable 9n a little ass] a iittle ass 1624
Fable 11n honours, or preferments] hononrs, or preferments 1624
Fable 12n would be a use] would be an vse 1624

V. JOHN OGIBLY, *THE FABLES OF AESOP* AND *AESOPICS*

Below is a list of all emendations made to John Ogilby's *Fables of Aesop* and *Aesopics*; under that is a list of all significant textual variants among the editions. To the left of the square bracket is the word or phrase as it appears in our edited text; to the right of the square bracket is the word as it appears in the original printings of Ogilby's fables, with the edition(s) in which it appears in that form. Preceding each entry is the fable number from this volume (or the title of the prefatory matter), followed by the line number in which the emendation or variant appears. Emendations or variants that occur in one of Ogilby's footnotes are marked with an 'n' (so, for example, 'Fable 1.2n' means an emendation or variant that occurs in a note to the second line of the first fable in this volume).

The Fables of Aesop went through four editions: 1651, 1665, 1668, and 1673/5; *Aesopics* went through two editions, 1668 and 1673/5. As discussed in the introduction, 1673/5 is treated as one printing throughout this volume. 1651 contained no marginal notes. The prefatory letter and prefatory poems appear only in the 1651 edition of *The Fables of Aesop*; Fables 1–13 in this volume come from *The Fables of Aesop*; and Fables 14–17 come from *Aesopics*.

Ogilby: Emendations

To My Worthy Friend.10 learned] *Learued* 1651 [this poem only exists in 1651]

TEXTUAL NOTES

Fable 1.2n Ausonius:] Auson. 1665, 1668, 1673/5
Fable 2.36n ἀμφέβαλλε] ἀμφέβαλλεε 1665, 1668, 1673/5
Fable 2.84 the en'mies'] th'enemies 1651; th'Enemies 1665, 1668, 1673/5
Fable 2.98 forsa'en] forsook 1651, 1665, 1668, 1673/5
Fable 2.106 Ajax's] *Ajax* 1651, 1665, 1668, 1673/5
Fable 2.129 ta'en] took 1651, 1665, 1668, 1673/5
Fable 4.16 nor others thee molest] thee nor others thou molest 1651, 1665, 1668, 1673/5
Fable 5.7 *Pardonnez-moi*] *Pardonne moy* 1651, 1665, 1668, 1673/5
Fable 6.14 survive] survives 1651, 1665, 1668, 1673/5
Fable 8.23 striv'n] strove 1651, 1665, 1668, 1673/5
Fable 12.27 boast] boasts 1651, 1665, 1668, 1673/5

Ogilby: Variants

Title *adorned with sculpture, and illustrated with annotations*] and adorn'd with Sculpture 1651
Fable 1.1 three] four 1651
Fable 1.2n tyrannically] Tyranically,: 1673/5
Fable 1.3n they both derive] they borh derive 1673/5
Fable 1.3n all things] all hings 1668
Fable 1.3n *verba*] *verbis* 1668, 1673/5
Fable 1.12 whitest] blackest 1651
Fable 1.19n Know this [...] good books.] *Know this [...] good Books.* 1673/5 [italics]
Fable 2.8 hopes and fears] Hope aud Feare 1651
Fable 2.19 Frogmorton] *Frogpadock* 1651
Fable 2.36n and bore it] which he bore 1668, 1673/5
Fable 2.36n κάρᾳ] κάρᾷ 1673/5
Fable 2.63 lists] list 1651
Fable 2.69 tongs] tongues 1651, 1665, 1668
Fable 2.75 well served up] once serv'd up 1651, 1665, 1668
Fable 2.76 full cup] fresh cup 1651, 1665, 1668
Fable 2.99 The ship] His ship 1651, 1665
Fable 2.112 peise] poise 1673/5
Fable 2.118 Frogmorton] *Frogpadock* 1651
Fable 2.126 th'advantage] the advantage 1651, 1665
Fable 2.130 through] to 1673/5
Fable 2.133 Frogmorton] *Frogpadock* 1651
Fable 2.142 Regained] Regaines 1651; Regains 1665

511

Fable 2.150n I'th'Trojan wars (which I remember well)] In Trojan wars I (I remember well) 1665
Fable 2.162 th'cerealian] the *Ceralian* 1651
Fable 2.164 snapped up] eaten 1651
Fable 2.167 Frogmorton's] *Frogpadocks* 1651
Fable 2.185 Frogmorton] *Frogpadock* 1651
Fable 2.188 slow] small 1673/5
Fable 2.192 will] still 1651, 1665, 1668
Fable 2.196 *What mighty matter's in the marsh today!*] What mighty matters in the Marsh to day! 1651 [italics]
Fable 2.200 a] an Humble-Bee 1651, 1673/5; an humble-Bee 1668
Fable 2.205 Frogmorton] *Frogpadock* 1651
Fable 2.207 th'immortal mortal cates] th'Immortal Cates 1673/5
Fable 2.211 pow'rs] powers 1651
Fable 2.212 head] heads 1651, 1673/5
Fable 2.212 tow'rs] towers 1668
Fable 2.224 neighb'ring] *neighbouring* 1651, 1665; Neighbouring 1668
Fable 3.2 furs] fur 1665
Fable 3.5 New come] Now come 1665, 1668
Fable 3.5 a cool shade] a coal shade 1665
Fable 3.8 began] begun 1651, 1665, 1668
Fable 3.25 Cinean] *Aelian* 1651
Fable 3.43 guard] Arms 1673/5
Fable 3.47n lib. 8] l.8 1665, 1668
Fable 3.47n begins] beginneth 1651, 1665
Fable 3.47n lib. 3] l.3 1665, 1668
Fable 3.58 piamater] *Pericranium* 1651
Fable 3.79 triumphs] Triumph 1673/5
Fable 4.1 dares] dare 1651, 1665, 1668
Fable 4.5 Thus] This 1673/5
Fable 4.6 discov'ring a false thief] discovering a *Thief* 1651, 1665, 1668
Fable 4.12n triplenat.ured 1665
Fable 4.12n *autro* 1668
Fable 4.35 murd'rer] Murtherer 1651, 1665, 1668
Fable 4.38 in on's] on his 1651
Fable 4.45n [Ogilby's footnote about penates is not included in all copies of 1665]
Fable 5.16 remnant] remant 1651
Fable 6.34 threatened] threatned 1665, 1668, 1673/5

TEXTUAL NOTES

Fable 7.10 plead] pleads 1651
Fable 7.17 corns] corn 1651 ['corns' in some copies of 1651]
Fable 7.22 Ninive] *Ninevie* 1651
Fable 7.23 tow'rs] Towres 1651
Fable 7.25n *Felix*] *Foelix* 1668, 1673/5
Fable 7.25n them with] with them 1668, 1673/5
Fable 7.27 These were our works] These were our Work 1665, 1668
Fable 8.21 When the great lion] When a great lion 1673/5
Fable 8.22 whom] home 1673/5
Fable 8.46 first I] I first 1651, 1665
Fable 8.54 their foe] the foe 1673/5
Fable 9.27 shrinketh] shrinking 1651
Fable 9.28 but cannot tell her] but could not tell her 1651, 1665, 1668
Fable 9.39 expectations] expectation 1651, 1665, 1668
Fable 9.45n *dubitavit mergeret unda*] *dubitavit mergerit undâ* 1673/5
Fable 9.45n *Ergo modo levia*] *Ergò modo livia* 1673/5
Fable 9.45n *Colla jubae velant*] *Colla juba velant* 1668, 1673/5
Fable 9.53 need not tell you] need tell you 1665
Fable 9.74 live] liv'd 1651, 1665, 1668
Fable 9.83–84 Against […] engage] *Against […] engage* 1673/5 [italics]
Fable 9.101 pow'r] Power 1651, 1665, 1673/5
Fable 9.102 dow'r] dowre 1651; Dower 1673/5
Fable 10.10 th'insulting] the insulting 1651, 1665, 1668
Fable 10.24 skin] Skiu 1673/5
Fable 10.48 lips] Lip 1651
Fable 11.28 prayer] prayers 1651
Fable 11.28n Hymettian] *Hymetitian* 1668
Fable 11.69 The cat will after kind.] *The Cat will after Kind.* 1673/5 [italics]
Fable 11.73 t'a virgin] to a virgin 1651, 1665, 1668
Fable 11.74 But still deformed] But the deformed 1651
Fable 11.75 within her breast] still in her breast 1651
Fable 11.77 No power can stave off nature] *No Power can stave off Nature* 1673/5 [italics]
Fable 12.16 'Mongst] 'Mong 1673/5
Fable 12.17 ravenous] ravenons 1651
Fable 12.23 there dwells a cock] where dwells a cock 1665, 1668, 1673/5

Fable 12.35 Awaken'st] Awakenest 1651, 1665, 1668
Fable 12.60 Though must die] Though shalt die 1651, 1665, 1668
Fable 13.4 led] lead 1651, 1665
Fable 13.13 Miceans] *Miceaus* 1651
Fable 13.41 you ne'er] nere you 1651
Fable 13.59 To a fury she transformed] To a fury she's transformed 1651
Fable 13.60 Bestrews] Best strews 1651
Fable 13.62–63 Fair words […] deceivers hooks] *Fair words […] Deceivers Hooks* 1673/5 [italics]
Fable 14.45 led] lead 1668
Fable 14.46 Must we him rescue] Must him we rescue 1668
Fable 14.72 Each posting […] makes] *Each posting […] makes* 1673/5 [italics]
Fable 16.18 wit must encounter wit] *Wit must encounter Wit* 1673/5 [italics]
Fable 16.26 So forth] Lo forth 1673/5
Fable 16.30 sits] Fits 1673/5
Fable 16.38 disgorge] discharge 1668
Fable 16.46 keep patients sick] kept patients sick 1668
Fable 16.75 No common messenger] Nor Common Messenger 1673/5
Fable 17.41 hypochondric] *Hypochondriack* 1673/5
Fable 17.56 mythologist] Methologist 1668
Fable 17.72 will cure] shall Cure 1668

GLOSSARY

Most definitions below are taken from the *Oxford English Dictionary*. In some instances a word is used in very different ways by our different authors; in those cases, we have included the different definitions and noted which use corresponds to which author. Where a word is used as multiple parts of speech, we have included separate definitions, and marked them with (n) for noun; (v) for verb; (adj) for adjective; (adv) for adverb; and (conj) for conjunction.

We have, for the most part, added definitions that might be unexpected to modern readers; for example, we have listed the word 'needs' as an adverb, meaning 'necessarily', or 'or' as a preposition meaning 'before', but we have not listed more common and well-known definitions. The first time a word appears in the fables of *each author*, in the sense that appears in the glossary, we have marked it in the text with the following symbol: °

A

aback	backwards
abidden	abided, endured
abject	a degraded or downtrodden person
abye	to pay a price for
accord (n)	agreement
accord (v)	to settle, come to an agreement
accorded	agreed; how the question might be ~, how the question might be resolved
a-daytimes	on or in the daytime
adder	a snake, serpent
adown	down; to the earth ~, down onto the earth
adventure	chance; by ~, by chance
advertence	attention, heed, consideration
advised	prudent, cautious, circumspect
affecter	lover
affray	fright, fear
aflocht	agitated, in a flutter
aforetimes	in the past, previously
afterdeal	a disadvantage
agu'd	agued; caused to shake
aiguise	to sharpen

alonely	alone
alway	always
amerce	to punish with a penalty or fine determined in a legal context
angle	a fish hook
anon	immediately, instantly; in a little while
anvil	to fashion, as on an anvil
apeship	an honorific, or mock honorific, for the ape
apologue	an allegorical story intended to convey a useful lesson; a moral fable
appair	to damage, impair
appeach	to charge with a crime, accuse, inform against
argent	silver
aright	correctly
array	clothing
arrest	to stop
arse	the buttocks
ash	a kind of tree, with a close-grained wood that is valuable for instruments
asperse	to slander
aspire	to breathe out; to breathe desire towards
assay	to try or test
assent	agreement
assimulate	to simulate, feign, counterfeit
assuage	to appease
astonied	stunned, astonished
aswooned	in a swoon or faint, unconscious
attainder	condemnation, accusation; sentence
attainted	tainted, corrupted
aught	anything
Ausonian	of or pertaining to Ausonia; Italian
avarice	greed
avaricious	greedy; as a noun, a greedy person
avaunt	to brag; advance; ~ himself, advance himself or put himself forward
aver	to assert the truth of a statement
ay	still; constantly
azure	bright blue

GLOSSARY

B

bade	commanded
bairn	a child
bale	misery, sorrow
ballast	heavy material, such as gravel, sand, or metal, used to weigh a ship down
'bandon	to abandon; drive out or banish
barded	armed or covered with bards, protective coverings for a war-horse
bare-breeched	bare-arsed
bark	a small ship or sailing vessel
beaver	the moveable faceguard of a helmet used in jousting or combat
bebaste	to beat all around, as with a cudgel
beek	to expose (oneself, one's limbs, etc.) to the pleasurable warmth of sun, fire, etc.
befile	to defile, render foul or filthy
behinder	hind, back; ~ legs, back legs
beholden	obliged
behoof	a use, benefit, advantage
behooveful	beneficial
bemelancholied	completely melancholy or sad
bemire	to cover or befoul with mire
berayed	dirtied, fouled, made filthy
beseem	to befit, be in accordance with the character of
besides	beside
bestride	to mount and straddle
bias	a tendency
bide	to endure, suffer, put up with, undergo
bier	the movable stand on which a corpse, whether in a coffin or not, is placed before burial; that on which it is carried to the grave
birdspeller	one who casts spells or charms; soothsayer
bittern	a bird that lives primarily in marshes, similar to herons, but smaller
blaeberries	bilberries, a dark-coloured berry found in northern England and Scotland
blinkard	one with imperfect sight; one who lacks intellectual perception
blinked	glanced

block	a log of wood; part of the trunk of a tree
boisterous	roughly massive, bulky, big and cumbrous
boistous	rough, rude; untaught; rustic, unpolished
boistous-bodied	roughly massive in body, bulky
boot (n)	help
boot (v)	to do good, to avail, to help; it ~s not, it doesn't help
borne	carried; delivered
bosk	a bush
bossed	studded, ornamented, embossed
boun	headed [to]
bounden	bound
bounds	boundaries
bowelled	disembowelled
boykin	an affectionate term for a little boy
brae	a slope or hillside, esp. the steep bank bounding a river valley; usually in the phrase 'banks and braes'
brake	a clump of bushes; a thicket
bravely	in a showy manner; gaily, splendidly, finely, handsomely
breer	a sprout or shoot
brickle	brittle
brim	a body of water
bristle	a short, stiff, pointed or prickly hair on animals
broidered	embroidered
buck	to steep or boil in an alkaline lye as a first process in buck-washing, or bleaching
bulrush	a cat's tail (the reed)
bushel	a measure of capacity, approximately eight gallons
but	sometimes, except

C

caitiff	a captive, prisoner
calenture	a disease that typically inflicts sailors in the tropics and causes delirium
callow	hairless; of birds, unfledged, without feathers
camlet	originally, a beautiful and costly Eastern fabric; afterwards, imitations and substitutes

GLOSSARY

can	to know; no good ~, knows no good
canker	a chronic, non-healing sore or ulcer [Golding]; a destructive influence that corrodes or corrupts [Smith]
cant	bold, brisk, hearty, lusty; in Scots, lively, merry
cantle	a thick slice or broken off piece of food (bread, cheese, etc.)
capax	able or ready to receive; susceptible
careful	full of cares
carle	a man of low birth or rude manners
carman	a man who drives a cart
carping	speaking, talking
carriage	the action of carrying
carrier	one who carries or transports things, as by cart or wagon
carrion	a corpse, dead meat
cask	a helmet
cast (v)	to throw; threw
cast (adj)	condemned, beaten in a lawsuit
casualty	causality, chance
catchpoll	technically, a debt-collector; sometimes, a word of contempt
cates	provisions purchased, usually fancier than ones made at home
cause	to induce, make
cautelous	wily, crafty
celerity	speed
chafe	state of anger or frustration
chafed	angry, irritated
challenged	claimed
Chanticleer	a standard name for a cock
chariness	wariness, caution, care
check (n)	a reproof, reprimand, rebuke
check (v)	to reprove [Golding]; to rein in; to recoil [Ogilby]
chirurgeon	a surgeon
choler	a bodily humour or fluid, supposed to cause anger or temper
chopping	attacking, pouncing
chops	jaws
churl	a base or low-born fellow

civil	pertaining to the city or state; ~ law, law pertaining to the city or state, as opposed to international law; of war or conflict, taking place between inhabitants of the same country or state
clad	covered
clean	clear
clemency	mercy
clew	a ball of thread, clue
clown	a countryman, rustic, or peasant
cockered	indulged, pampered, coddled
cockerel	a young cock
colombe	a dove
cometh	becomes, suits
commodious	advantageous, beneficial, of use
commodity	the quality of being commodious, suitable; comfort
commons	the common people, as distinguished from those of noble, knightly, or gentle rank
commonty	the body of the common people, the commons
compass	a limit; ~ of thy beard, outer edges of your beard
con	to know or learn, especially by memory
congee	a bow, for taking one's leave or for salutation
consternate	to amaze, fill with terror
consumption	a disease that consumes the body and causes extreme weight loss
contemn	to treat with contempt
copse	a thicket of small trees or underwood periodically cut for economic purposes
cordage	cords, especially those used in the rigging of a ship
cordovan	a leather made in Cordova (Córdoba), Spain
cormorantly	like the cormorant, a notoriously greedy and voracious sea-bird
corn	grain(s)
coronate	crowned
corone	a crown
corporal	bodily
corpulence	fatness
couch	to lower (a spear, lance, etc.) to the position of attack
counsel	to advise

GLOSSARY

count	to esteem, consider; I ~ not, I account it not, I give it no notice
counterminings	counter-plots
countryman	a man of rural birth, occupation, appearance, or manner
courage	what is in one's heart or mind; what one is thinking or intending
covenanted	entered into a covenant; agreed upon
covert (n)	a place to conceal oneself
covert (v)	to conceal (oneself), hide
covert (adj)	hidden
covetise	covetousness, greed
coy	to stroke or touch soothingly, pat, caress
cozen	to cheat, dupe, beguile
cozenage	cheating, deception, fraud
crabbed	harsh or unpleasant; crooked; perversely intricate; difficult to unravel; disagreeable, contrarious [Golding]; expressing a harsh or disagreeable disposition [Smith]
crack	a sharp blow
craftsmaster	one who is a master of his craft
crave	to beg for; to ~ a dinner, to beg for a dinner
crook-backed	hunchbacked
crouse	bold, audacious, cocky; vivacious
cudgeled	beaten
cull	to pick out or select; to gather the choice things or parts of
cumber	to harass, distress, trouble, annoy
cur	a dog
cure	care, concern
curlew	a long-legged wading bird with a long, slender, curved bill
customably	usually, customarily
customed	accustomed
cutfowl	an insect
Cyclopes	the plural of Cyclops; a race of one-eyed giants in ancient Greek mythology who forged thunderbolts for Zeus

D

daftness	madness
dainty	a choice item of food, delicacy
dale	a valley
dam	a mother
damask	of Damascus; ~ rose, a species of rose
damosel	a lady, usually young and unmarried
dappled	marked with spots or round patches
debate	a fight, struggle; strife, contention
default	a lack
deign	to condescend [Caxton]; to disdain [Smith]
delicate	a luxury item, choice viand or delicacy
delve	to dig
desert	recompense; reward or punishment
despite	scorn, contempt, disdain
devest	to strip or rid (oneself of)
device	a trick [Golding]; talk, chat [Caxton]
dewlap	the loose skin that hangs under the throat of cattle
different	a difference, dispute
difficile	difficult
digne	of high worth
direction	guidance, advice
disappointed	thwarted
discommend	to find fault with
disconsolate	forlorn, despondent
discreet	prudent, exhibiting sound judgement
disembogue	to discharge or empty
disformed	deformed
disgorge	to expel, discharge
dissembler	a liar, deceiver
dissension	dissent, disagreement, contention
dissimule	to dissemble, deceive, disguise
dite (n)	a piece of writing
dite (v)	to write or compose
divers	various
dizzardly	like a dizzard, silly, idiotic
doggish	having a doglike disposition or character
doltish	stupid, foolish
don	a Spanish title; a Spanish man; ~ Diego, a stereotypical name for a Spanish man

GLOSSARY

dorp	a (Dutch) village
dower	the money or property a wife brings to marriage
down	a hill
drab	an untidy woman; a slut; a prostitute
draff	refuse, dregs, lees
draw	to pull, haul
dread (n)	fear
dread (v)	to fear
dryth	drought, dryness
duck	to dip the head rapidly under water
dug	the pap or udder of an animal; a woman's breast (usually contemptuous)
dunghillcock	a common fowl, as distinguished from the game-cock
durst	dared
durstest	(you) dare

E

eaves	the edge of a roof that overhangs a house
ecliptic	the great circle of the celestial sphere which is the apparent orbit of the sun
eftsoon	a second time, again; afterwards, soon afterwards
eke	also
electrum	an alloy of gold and silver which was used in ancient times to make jewelry and the earliest metal coins
embase	to devalue, debase, discredit
emmet	an ant
endued	endowed; outwardly clothed [Golding]; educated; clothed [Smith]
engine	a device
enhance	to elevate spiritually or morally
enlace	to lace about, encircle
ensample	an example
ensign	a banner or flag
ensue	to follow
entermete	to put oneself between, intermeddle, concern oneself
enterprise	a design of which the execution is attempted; a piece of work taken in hand, an undertaking

entrail	the intestines and internal parts generally
entreatance	entreaty; demand
epitheton	an epithet; that which is ascribed to a person; attribute
equity	the quality of being fair
ere	before
erewhiles	a while ago, formerly
ermine	an animal of the weasel tribe known for its white fur and black-tipped tail
eschew	to avoid
esprised	enflamed, set on fire
estate	one's status, standing, position in the world
exaction	the action of demanding and enforcing payment
exemplative	furnishing an example
eyne	eyes

F

fabulator	one who relates fables; a story-teller
fabulous	like or resembling a fable
factious	inclined to form factions or dissent
faculty	an ability
fain (adj)	obliged [Golding]; pleased, willing [Golding, Smith, Ogilby]
fain (adv)	gladly, with pleasure
fair	beautiful
faken	deceitful, fraudulent
falchion	a sword, sometimes with a curved edge
familiar	friendly, informal; inappropriately informal, casual; intimate, close
fancied	imagined
fane	a temple
fardel	a bundle, package
fare (n)	a litter (of a sow); food
fare (v)	to journey, travel
far-fet	far-fetched
faring time	a time to give birth to a litter (of a sow)
farrow	to bring forth a litter (of a sow)
fast	firmly attached; not able to escape
faulteth	lacks, has faults
fay	faith; a promise

GLOSSARY

fearedness	the condition of being frightened or afraid
feat	neat, elegant
featly	cleverly, deftly, skilfully
feigned	false, deceptive
fell (v)	to cut, knock, strike down
fell (adj)	cruel, savage, brutal [Golding]; fierce, excessive [Smith]
fen	a low land covered with shallow water; marsh
ferdful	fearful, inspiring fear
fetter	to restrict, limit
fetters	chains, shackles
file	to defile, render foul or filthy
filed	defiled, filthy, unclean; polished, smooth (of speech or language)
finely	properly
finis	the end
firstfruits	the earliest products or results of anything, often given as an offering
fisk	to move briskly, scamper about
fitly	aptly, appropriately
fitteth	pertains to
flask	to flap (as wings)
flay	to strip or pull the skin off of
fleecing	robbing; tricking; stripping of fleece
fleer	one who flees
fleet	to flit, fly, slip away
fleur-de-lis	an iris-like plant; a heraldic lily
fling	to go or run violently or hastily
flout (n)	a mock, jeer, insult
flout (v)	to mock, jeer, insult
foal	a young horse, colt (usually male)
fold	a pen or enclosure for animals
fond	foolish
forbear	to tolerate, bear with
fore-game	a first game; first plan
forhight	to promise; literally, to hight, hope, or anticipate in advance
forsooth	truly
forspent	exhausted completely
forsworn	falsely sworn, perjured
forthwith	immediately

for-thy	for this reason, therefore
fortunating	being fortunate, happening; ~ to celebrate, happening to celebrate
for why	because
forworn	worn out, exhausted, grown old
founden	found
fowler	a birdcatcher
frankincense	an aromatic tree resin frequently burned as incense
frankly	liberally, generously
fraught (n)	money paid for transport (across water)
fraught (adj)	laden
fray	to frighten
frayeth	defrays; frightens
fret	to eat, devour
frieze	a kind of coarse woollen cloth
frisk	a caper, jig
frisking	moving briskly and sportively
fro	from
frorne	frozen
froward	difficult to deal with; perverse; evilly disposed
full	entirely

G

gad	to go from one place to another, wander; esp. to wander about with no serious object, stopping here and there; to rove idly
gall (n)	bile (an extremely bitter substance)
gall (v)	to injure; to harass or annoy in warfare
galliard	a quick and lively dance
gallowclapper	one who deserves to be hanged
galping	gaping
gambol	a leap; caper; playful or high-spirited movement or gesture
gammon	a ham; haunch of a pig
garrison	defence
gaskins	the muscular part of the hind leg of an animal
gay	noble, excellent
gent	noble, of high birth
gentle	noble, of high birth

GLOSSARY

gently	kindly
get	to produce, beget
gewgaws	trifles, ornaments; things of little value
gibing	mocking, taunting
gin	a trap, device, trick
girded	encircled, as with a belt
girdle	a belt worn around the waist to secure garments
glaive	a lance; halbert; sword
glebe	a piece of cultivated land; field
glede	a kite
glee	play, sport; mirth, pleasure
gleek	a sneer or flout; to give the ~, play a trick or make a jest
glozed	speciously adorned, specious
glozing	flattery, cajolery; deceitful blandishment; specious talk or representation
gobbet	a piece of raw flesh
goodly	handsome, beautiful, good-looking
goshawk	a large short-winged hawk
gourd	a long, hollow vessel
gowked	stared foolishly
grace	salvation; benevolence; favour
graffed	grafted
grandsire	a grandfather
gree	to agree; to be in accord or harmonious
grey	(of eyes) bright pale iris
griping	grasping or clutching tightly
grosshead	a thick-headed person, a dullard
gross-witted	ignorant; deficient in common sense
grot	a grotto, cave, cavern
groutnoll	a blockhead, dunce
guise	fashion, style
gules	in heraldic terms, red
gulling	swallowing or guzzling (with gluttonous implications)

H

habergeon	a sleeveless coat or jacket of mail or armour
hackneyman	a keeper of hackney, or horse and carriage, for hire

hale	a pull
halidom	holiness
halm	a stalk or stem
halter	a rope used to lead cattle; noose; the gallows
handicraftsman	a man who exercises a handicraft; one employed in a manual occupation
handsel	to give a gift; confer luck
happed	happened
hardiness	boldness, daring, audacity
hardly	with difficulty
harlot	an unchaste woman
harsky	coarse, rough, rugged
hart	a male deer
haskardly	of low degree, base or vulgar
haven	a sheltered body of water along a coast or shore where boats can moor or anchor, esp. during stormy weather
hawthorn	a thorny shrub, often used for hedges
hazard (n)	a risk
hazard (v)	to risk
headiness	rashness, impetuousness; stubbornness
heady	headlong, precipitate, impetuous; passionate; headstrong
hearken	to listen
hecatomb	a sacrifice
hedgegrapes	grapes that grow in hedges
heedy	attentive, heedful
helve	a handle of weapon or tool, such as an axe
hempen	made of hemp
heron	a long-legged and long-necked wading bird
hight	to call, name; I ~, I am named or called
hinder	hind, back; ~ legs, back legs
hireless	without hire or pay
hoise	to raise aloft
horseleech	a horse doctor; greedy or rapacious person
humble-bee	a large bee that makes a humming sound, bumble-bee
hunger-starven	starved
husbandman	one who tills or cultivates soil, a farmer
Hymettian	of or belonging to Mount Hymettus in Attica

GLOSSARY

I

imbrued	stained or dyed, as with blood
imp	a child, offspring
importunity	the quality of being persistent in making demands, sometimes causing irritation
impotent	powerless
improbe	a wicked person
impute	to assign blame
inclinate	inclined
incontinent	immediately, without delay [Caxton]; not continent, wanting in self-restraint [Smith]
ink-horn	a small portable vessel (originally made of a horn) for holding writing-ink
inroad	a powerful or sudden incursion
insolency	pride
instant	pressing, urgent
intelligencer	a spy
inveigh	to speak vehemently
inveigling	beguiling, deceiving, or cajoling
ire	anger
issue	offspring, children; release, outflow; result
item	also (often used to connect items on a list)
iwis	certainly

J

jack	a man of the common people; lad, fellow, chap; low-bred or ill-mannered fellow, knave
jade	a contemptuous name for a horse
jar	to sound harshly, make musical discord
jasper	a kind of precious stone
jobbed	pecked
jolly	cheerful; having the freshness and lively spirits of youth or good health; fresh, lively, sprightly, spirited
jumelle	twinned or paired; double
jump	to agree
juncture	a union or joining; convergence of events or circumstances
junto	a body of people who have joined for a common purpose

justicer	one who maintains or executes justice
justling	jostling; coming into collision as in a tournament

K

kend	known
kennel	the surface drain of a street; the gutter
kind	nature
kine	cows
kite	a bird of prey
kneadingtrough	a wooden tub in which to knead dough
know	to acknowledge

L

lacked	missing, absent; I should ~ be, I should be avoided
laity	lay people, as distinct from clergy
lar	the tutelary deities of a house; household gods
larder	a room or closet in which meat is stored
launch	to wound or pierce; hurl
laund	an open space among woods, glade; untilled ground, pasture
laystall	a place where refuse and dung is laid
learn	to teach
leech	a doctor
legist	one who is versed in the law
Lenten	such as is appropriate to Lent; meagre (of provisions or diet)
lere	to learn; teach
let (n)	a hindrance
let (v)	to prevent, hinder
lettered	literate, learned
leve	to permit; believe
lever	rather; I had ~, I would rather
lewd	wicked; naughty
ley	land that has remained untilled for some time; arable land under grass
liberality	generosity
lickerousness	strong desire
lief	agreeable, acceptable
liefer	rather; I had (as) ~, I had rather

GLOSSARY

light (v)	to alight
light (adj)	cheerful
lind	a lime or linden tree
list (n)	a catalogue listing a series of names, for a tournament, or for horse racing
list (v)	to like or prefer; as he ~ed, as he liked
loaden	laden, loaded with goods
lobhole	the dwelling of a lob or country bumpkin
lodges	house or housing in a general sense
loggering	bow-legged, loose-jointed, wobbly
loose	to loosen
lope	leaped, jumped
losel	a worthless person; scoundrel; ragamuffin, ne'er-do-well
lossful	productive of loss; detrimental; unprofitable
lot	that which has been given to a person by fate
lumpishness	sluggishness; heaviness, clumsiness

M

madbrain	a hot-headed or uncontrolled person
magistracy	the position or office of a magistrate (member of the executive government)
mails	fish scales
main (n)	strength; might and ~, strength and power
main (adj)	strong, forcible
malapert	a presumptuous or saucy person
malapertness	presumptuousness or impudence
manacled	handcuffed, shackled, fettered
manchet	fine quality wheaten bread; pandemain
manfully	in a manful manner; with manly courage; bravely
margent	a margin
marish	marshy, boggy
marked	noted; distinguished
marry	a mild interjection expressing surprise
mastiff	a large, powerful dog
mate	to rival, equal; to overcome, subdue
matter	content
maugre	despite
mavis	a song thrush
maw	a stomach

meanest	lowest class
meat	food, nourishment, or fodder more generally
medicine	a doctor
meet	proper, fitting
meinie	a household; retinue; servants; company
menace	a threat
mere	a body of water, such as a lake, pond, creek, or marsh
meridian	the position of the sun at midday
merle	a blackbird
methinks	it seems to me
midden	a dunghill, dungheap, refuse heap
mids	middle
milan	a kite (bird of prey)
mine	my
ming	to mix, blend
minstrelsy	the occupation or practice of singing and playing music
misdoer	a wrongdoer, offender, malefactor
misliving	evil or sinful living
mo	more
moiety	a half
moiling	distressing oneself; worrying
mote	might
mought	might
mould	earth
murlimewes	foolish gestures or antics
myriad	ten thousand of something; a unit of ten thousand soldiers

N

namely	particularly, especially; more specifically
naughtypack	an immoral person (sometimes with connotations of sexual promiscuity)
ne (adv)	not; an adverb of negation before a verb
ne (conj)	nor
neatherd	a cowherd, one who herds cows
needs	necessarily, unavoidably
neuter	neutral
new	newly

GLOSSARY

niceling	an effeminate or delicate person
niche	a recess in a wall, usually for the purpose of displaying a statue
niggardship	stinginess, cheapness
noddy	a fool, simpleton
noisome	harmful or injurious
nother	neither
nought	not, not at all, in no way
nuzzled	trained, educated, nurtured, brought up (in a habit, custom, opinion, etc.)

O

obdurate	hard; not responsive
obeisance	obedience; to make ~, to pay homage
oblations	the presentation of money, goods, property, etc. to the Church for use in God's service
obliquities	twists, curves
obstinacy	stubbornness
odiferous	odoriferous, strong-smelling (pleasant or unpleasant)
offensed	offended
officious	annoyingly assertive and authoritative
oft-time	often, frequently
oft-times	often, frequently
ongles	claws, fingernails
opprobrious	shameful; reproachful
or	before [Caxton, Smith]; in heraldic terms, a gold or yellow color [Ogilby]
ordinance	the decision of a judge or referee which settles a disputed matter
osier	a willow tree
overpass	to pass over
overrun	to outrun; overcome or escape by running; run too far or too fast; overflow
overshot	exaggerated, excessive
overweening	excessively self-confident; arrogant, presumptuous

P

pad	a frog
paddock	a frog
pageant	a performance, scene; spectacle
painture	that which is painted; painted matter; a painting
panter	the officer in a household who has charge of the pantry or of food supplies in general
paps	breasts
pare	to cut, trim
particoloured	mixed, varied in colour
pasture	food, sustenance
pate	a head
patriarch	in the context of the Christian church, a bishop
pease	a pea plant; plant with edible seeds
ped	a wicker basket; hamper with a lid
peep	a feeble high-pitched sound; squeak
peer	equal (to)
peise	to weigh, heft
penates	gods that watch over the household in ancient Roman mythology
penner	a writing case
pensioner	a person who receives a pension or payment
penury	the condition of being destitute; poverty; need
peradventure	perhaps, by chance
perfidious	treacherous
perk	to project or rise up; stick out
peruke	a wig
pew	the thin cry of a bird, esp. of the kite
physic	the art or practice of healing, the medical profession
physiologist	a naturalist, natural philosopher
pia mater	the brain
pig	to give birth to piglets
pikestaff	a staff, walking stick
pinch	an instance, occasion, or time of special difficulty; critical juncture; crisis, emergency
pinched	afflicted with pain or trouble, distressed
pinfold	a confined space, trap
pismire	an ant

GLOSSARY

plash	to break the surface, plunge into, splash (water or another liquid)
plat	a plot, patch of land for growing vegetables
pleasance	the action of pleasing; a pleasure ground or garden; pleasure
pontifically	by or as a pontiff, bishop, or other high-ranking cleric, esp. the Pope; in a manner appropriate to a pontiff
popular	(of a state) of, relating to, deriving from, or consisting of ordinary people or the people as a whole; generated by the general public; democratic
porringer	a small bowl or basin, typically with a handle, used for soups and stews
port	bearing, deportment, manner, demeanour
post	messenger, carrier of mail
potentate	a monarch, ruler
potestate	a ruler
prate	to talk idly, chatter
preferment	advantage
prelate	a cleric of high rank and authority
preparature	preparation
prerogative	an inherent advantage or privilege; gift, talent
present	that which is currently being dealt with, written, or discussed [Golding, Caxton, Ogilby]; (of poison or medicine) taking immediate effect, acting speedily [Golding]
prettily	considerably
print	an impression
privy	hidden
process	the whole of the proceedings in any legal action; action; a case, cause, or hearing
proem	an introduction, preface, prologue
proffer	an offer
propone	to propose
propound	to put forward, offer for consideration
provender	food, provisions
puissant	powerful
pullen	poultry, domestic fowl
punition	punishment
purpure	of a purple colour; spec., of the distinguishing colour of royal or imperial dress

puttock	a large bird of prey

Q

quaff	to drink deeply
quarter	mercy, clemency; one of four parts of the body
quit	to requite, repay
quoth	said

R

rad	afraid, alarmed
railing	invective, complaint
rakehell	a dissolute or immoral person
rammish	characteristic of a ram; rank, pungent (of a smell)
rank	haughty, arrogant
ranny	a shrew
rare	early
rassasy	to satisfy (a hungry person) with food; satiate
rate	to berate, scold violently [Brinsley]; drive away with rebukes or scolding [Ogilby]
ratsbane	rat poison
ravening	rapacious, bloodthirsty; voracious
ravin	plunder, booty, spoils; predatoriness; greed, rapacity; gluttony
ravished	stolen
raze	to scratch
reach	to stretch [Caxon]; to understand [Caxton, Ogilby]; to offer [Brinsley]
read (n)	a reading, interpretation
read (v)	to teach, advise
rebound	to reverberate, echo
recreate	to refresh, reinvigorate by means of recreation
redbreast	a robin
redoundeth	rebounds
regalities	lands or territory subject to royal authority
regiment	rule or governance
rehearse	to recite
remeid	a remedy, cure
remercy	thanks
remission	forgiveness of sins

GLOSSARY

rent	tore, pulled apart
repair	to go, return
repine	to feel or express discontent or dissatisfaction
replete	full
reprover	one who disapproves or rebukes
residue	the rest, the remainder
resty	restful, characterized by inactivity
rhetory	rhetoric, eloquence
rheum	a watery or mucous secretion, originally believed to originate in the brain or head and to be capable of causing disease
rife	abundantly; readily; frequently
right	truly; most
rivage	a coast, shore; riverbank
roe	a deer
rood	a (usually Christian) cross
rook	a gregarious Eurasian crow
rubric	something traditionally written in red
ruddock	a European robin
rude	rough, unrefined
rudely	without elegance, coarsely, roughly
rue (n)	a shrub with feathery and bitter leaves, often used for medicinal purposes
rue (v)	to regret
rust	a coating formed on metal by oxidation; any deteriorating or impairing effect or influence on the character, mind, or body
ruth	pity

S

sable	in heraldic terms, black
sad	serious
sanguine	blood-red
sapience	wisdom, knowledge
satisfaction	compensation or amends
satyr	a mythological woodland creature, half human, half bestial
saws	sayings, speeches, tales
scape	to escape
scarebug	a bugbear, an object intended to create fear

scareful	terrifying, alarming
science	knowledge; discipline
scrip	a small bag, wallet, or satchel, esp. one carried by a pilgrim, a shepherd, or a beggar
scutcheon	an escutcheon, a shield on which a coat of arms is depicted
search	to look for, seek out
sedan	a closed vehicle to seat one person, borne on two poles by two bearers, one in front and one behind
selfsoothing	encouraging oneself; flattering oneself
senate	an assembly or council of citizens charged with the highest deliberative functions in the government of a state
sentence	a ruling (as of a court case) [Golding, Caxton, Ogilby]; a way of thinking, opinion [Smith]
sentinel	a guard
separe	to separate
sergeant	a common soldier
shaped	prepared; ~ him, prepared himself
sharp-set	eager or keen for food; very hungry
shat	defecated
shedding	dropping; diffusing; ~ into, diffusing into (of liquids)
shent	disgraced
shift	a contrivance, stratagem; piece of sophistry, evasion, subterfuge
shirl	shrill
shoon	shoes
siege	excrement
silly	innocent
similitude	a sign, symbol; parable; simile
sin	since; then, thereupon; thereafter, afterwards, subsequently
sith	since, because
slew	hit; threw down violently; killed
slidder	slippery
sliver	to split into slivers
smart (n)	an injury
smart (v)	to hurt
smatch	a taste, slight indication

GLOSSARY

snod	smooth
so	as long as
solder	to cause (wounds) to close up and become whole; reunite (tissues or bones)
sole	singular, unique
solemnity	an occasion of ceremony; observance or celebration of special importance; festival or other similar occasion
sometime	at a certain time, at one time
somewhat	something; slightly
sooth	truth
sore (adj)	painful, grievous, distressing, severe
sore (adv)	sorely
sorry	pathetic
sound	a relatively narrow channel or stretch of water, esp. one between the mainland and an island, or connecting two large bodies of water; a strait; an inlet of the sea
sparhawk	a sparrowhawk
spring-tide	springtime
sprite	a spirit
stablishing	establishing
stablishment	an establishment; a means of establishing or strengthening
stank	a pond or pool
starkling	showing signs of fear, quaking
stave	a thin, narrow piece of wood
stead	a place; in ~ of, in the place of
steeled	covered with steel
stith	a stithy, anvil
stithy	an anvil
stockdove	a wild pigeon
stomaching	feeling indignation or bitterness
stool	the stump of a tree that has been felled
stoop	to descend swiftly (on prey); swoop
stopped	stuffed; obstructed
stoutly	vigorously, with might and main, lustily
stoutness	pride, arrogance
straight	immediately
strand	a stream
strift	strife, contention

stripes	lashes
strutted out	puffed or swollen
stuck	a thrust, lunge
styled	designated, called
suborn	to bribe someone to commit a crime or misdeed
subtlety	craftiness, cunning
succour	help, assistance
sue	to appeal, petition
suit	kind, class
superfluity	excess
supply	to assist
surcease	to cease
surfeit	overindulgence in food or drink, gluttony
surprisal	the act of surprising or being surprised
swain	a male servant; man of low degree
swarthy	of a dark hue or complexion
swound	to swoon, faint
syllogism	a logical argument

T

tale	number, sum
tallow	hard animal fat obtained by melting and clarifying, used for making candles and soap, dressing leather, and other purposes
talons	claws of beasts or birds
tanner	one who tans, or converts animal hides into leather
taper	a wax candle
tardy	slow, sluggish
targe	a shield
target	a shield
tent	attention
tentered	stretched, as on a tenter or rack
thiefly	stealthily, like a thief
thorough	through
thought	intended
thraldom	the state of being a thrall; bondage, servitude, captivity
throstle	a thrush, esp. the song-thrush (small or medium-sized songbird)

GLOSSARY

throughly	thoroughly; all the way through
thrush	a songbird
tidings	news, happenings
tiffany	a thin, transparent silk or gauze muslin
till	to; until
tippling	habitually indulging (to excess) in strong drink; given to drinking
tire	to bother, pester, worry (usually by pulling)
tod	a fox
toom	empty, vacant, containing nothing
toot	to peep, peer, look out
to-tear	to tear into pieces
toy	whim, caprice; a foolish or unreasoning dislike or aversion
trace	a course; to take one's ~, to make one's way, proceed
tract	a course, way
traffic	dealings, business
trammel	a net
trappers	a covering for a horse, made of leather or metal for defence, or of cloth for shelter or adornment
travail (n)	labour
travail (v)	to labour
treacher	a traitor
trice	an instant
trifle	a small, insignificant thing
trim	in good order, excellent
trimly	effectively, cleverly; neatly, nicely, elegantly
trip	a troupe or small flock; error; to take in a ~, to catch tripping, to detect in an error
tripping	dancing
trow	to believe (in)
tuck	a slender, pointed, straight, thrusting sword; a rapier
tun-bellied	pot-bellied
turkeycock	the male of the turkey
turn	purpose; for your ~, helpful to you
turncoat	one who changes his principles or party; a renegade
tutelar	tutelary; having the position of protector, guardian, or patron

twist	a branch

U

unarrayed	disordered; unclothed; unarmed
uncased	skinned, flayed
uncredible	incredible, unbelievable
underprop	to support with a prop; to keep upright
undescried	unknown, unannounced
undiscreet	not exhibiting sound judgement
unmeet	improper
unsatiable	insatiable
unskill	a lack of knowledge
unsmart	not sharp; not smart
unthrift	a spendthrift, dissolute person
untrusty	untrustworthy
unwonted	unusual
urchin	a hedgehog

V

vainglory	unwarranted pride
vale	a valley
vaunt (n)	boasting, bragging
vaunt (v)	to brag (about)
vertiginous	giddy, dizzy
viands	food, provisions
victuals	food, provisions
vilepend	to speak of with disparagement or contempt; represent as contemptible or worthless; abuse or vilify
viol	a stringed instrument that was held between the knees and played with a bow
visor	a mask, disguise
vixen	a female fox, she-fox
viz.	namely
vizard	a mask
voluptuous	indulging in sensuous pleasures
vouchsafe	to confer or bestow (a thing, favour, or benefit) on a person

GLOSSARY

W

wain	a chariot
wallowing	a rolling gait or walk
wamble	to totter, waver; move unsteadily, stagger, reel
wan	lacking light, dark, gloomy
wanner	more wan; more pallid, faded, or sickly
want (n)	a lack
want (v)	to be lacking
wanton	undisciplined, unmanageable
ware	aware, alert; wary
warely	warily
waste	to destroy
waster	one who lives in idleness or extravagance; one who wastes; a spendthrift
waw	a wave
wax	to grow or become
way	a path
wayfarer	a traveller by road; one who goes on foot
wayfaring man	a wayfarer
wayfellow	a fellow wayfarer
weathercock	a weathervane; someone who changes constantly
weed	clothing
ween	to expect, anticipate; to think possible or likely; to think or suppose
weltering	writhing or wriggling; sometimes, rolling around in one's own blood, hence drenched in blood
wend	to think, suppose
wether	a male sheep
whatsomever	whatever
whelp	an offspring of an animal
wherefore	because of which
wherethrough	through which
whiles	sometimes
whilom	once upon a time
whit	a very small part, the least amount; no ~, not at all, not in the least
whole	recovered from an injury [Caxton]; entire, complete [Smith]
wight	a living being in general, a creature
will	to wish

win	to gain [Caxton]; gain victory in a battle [Smith]
wind	to go; to go rapidly or forcefully
wink	to close one's eyes; to wink
wise	a way; in such ~, in such a way; in no ~, in no way
wist	knew
wistly	with close attention, intently
wit	to know; that is to ~, that is to say
without	outside
withouten	without
womb	the belly, abdominal area
wonder	wondrously, marvellously
wonderly	wonderfully
wondrous	spectacularly
wonning	a dwelling
wont	accustomed, used (to)
wonted	accustomed, used (to)
woodspeck	a woodpecker
woodward	a keeper of wood, in charge of growing tinder
workmaster	a producer, overseer, creator; fig., God
worry	to seize by the throat with the teeth and tear; kill or injure by biting and shaking
wot	to know
wreak	to gratify; ~ his hunger, satisfy his hunger [Golding]; to deliver or rescue (a person) from or out of woe [Smith]
wrest	to turn, twist; to pluck or drag away with a wrench or twist
write	that which is written, a piece of writing
writhe	a curled or twisted formation, loop

Y

yea	an emphatic interjection, slightly stronger than 'indeed'
yeaned	gave birth to, brought forth
yeoman	a servant or attendant in a royal or noble household
yformed	formed
yode	went

BIBLIOGRAPHY

Acheson, Katherine O., 'The Picture of Nature: Seventeenth-Century English Aesop's Fables', *Journal for Early Modern Cultural Studies* 9 (2009), 25–50

Aelian, *Historical Miscellany*, trans. by N. G. Wilson (Cambridge, MA: Harvard University Press, 1997)

——, *Of the Characteristics of Animals*, vol. 1, trans. by A. F. Scholfield (Cambridge, MA: Harvard University Press, 1958)

Aesopi phrygis fabulae: iam recenter ex collatione optimorum exemplarium emendatius excusae, cum nonnullis eiusdem & Poggij fabulis adiectis: et indice correctiori adiuncto (London: Excusae pro Societatis Stationariorum, 1618)

Aesops fabl'z in tru ort'ography with grammar-nóts He'r-vntoo ar al'so iooined the short sentenc'es of the wýz Cato im-printed with lýk form and order: bóth of which autorz ar transláted out-of Latin intoo E'nglish by William Bullokar, trans. by William Bullokar (London, 1585)

Alciatus, Andreas, *Emblemata V.C. Andreae Alciati Mediolanensis iurisconsulti; cum facili & compendiosa explicatione, qua obscura illustrantur, dubiáque omnia soluuntur* (Antwerp, 1584)

Altman, Joel B., *The Tudor Play of Mind: Rhetorical Inquiry and the Development of Elizabethan Drama* (Berkeley: University of California Press, 1978)

Apollodorus, *Library*, ed. and trans. by Sir James George Frazer, 2 vols (Cambridge, MA: Harvard University Press, 1921)

Apollonius Rhodius [Apollonius of Rhodes], *Argonautica*, trans. by R. C. Seaton (London: William Heinemann, 1919)

Aristophanes, *Aristophanes, in Three Volumes*, vol. 2, trans. by Benjamin Bickley Rogers (London: William Heinemann, 1924)

Ascham, Roger, *The Schoolmaster*, in *English Renaissance Translation Theory*, ed. by Neil Rhodes (London: Modern Humanities Research Association, 2013), pp. 411–25

Ausonius, *Ausonius, in Two Volumes*, vol. 1, trans. by Hugh G. Evelyn White (London: William Heinemann, 1919)

Babrius and Phaedrus, ed. by Ben Edwin Perry (Cambridge, MA: Harvard University Press, 1956)

Bacon, Francis, *The New Organon*, ed. by Lisa Jardine and Michael Silverthorne (Cambridge: Cambridge University Press, 2000)

——, *The Wisedom of the Ancients, written in Latine by the right honourable Sir Francis Bacon Knight, Baron of Verulam, and Lord Chancelor of England*, trans. by Arthur Gorges (London, 1619)

Bracciolini, Poggio, *The Facetiae or Jocose Tales of Poggio, now first translated into English with the Latin text, in two volumes* (Paris: Isidore Liseux, 1879)

Brinsley, John, *Esops Eables [sic] translated grammatically, and also in propriety of our English phrase; and, euery way, in such sort as may bee most profitable for the Grammar-schoole. The vse of it is according to the directions in the prefaces, and more fully set downe in Ludus Lit. or the Grammar-schoole* (London: H. L. for Thomas Man, 1617)

——, *Esops Fables translated both grammatically, and also in propriety of our English phrase; and, euery way, in such sort as may be most profitable for the Grammar-schoole. The vse of it is according to the directionrs [sic] in the prefaces, and more fully set downe in Ludus Lit. or the Grammar-schoole* (London: by I. D. for Thomas Man, 1624)

——, *Ludus Literarius*, in *English Renaissance Translation Theory*, ed. by Neil Rhodes (London: Modern Humanities Research Assocation, 2013), pp. 435–47

——, *Ludus literarius: or, the grammar schoole: shewing how to proceede from the first entrance into learning, to the highest perfection required in the grammar schooles, with ease, certainty and delight both to masters and schollers; onely according to our common grammar, and ordinary classicall authours* (London, 1612)

British Library, London, Harley MS 5923

Calvin, John, *The Psalmes of Dauid and others. With M. Iohn Caluins commentaries*, trans. by Arthur Golding (London, 1571)

Carminum proverbialium totius humanae vitae statum breuiter deliniantium, necnon vtilem de moribus doctrinam iucundè proponentium. Loci communes, in gratiam iuuentutis selecti (London, 1595)

Carnes, Pack, 'Henrich Steinhöwel and the Sixteenth-Century Fable Tradition', *Humanistica Lovaniensia* 35 (1986), 1–29

Carter, Harry, and H. D. L. Vervliet, *Civilité Types* (London: Oxford University Press, 1966)

Cato, *Cato translated grammatically directing for vnderstanding, construing, parsing, making, and proouing the same Latine: and so for continuall practice of the grammaticall analysis and genesis. Done for the good of schooles, and of all desirous to recouer, or keep that which they got in the grammar-schoole, or to increase therein*, trans. by John Brinsley (London, 1612)

——, *The Distichs of Cato: A Famous Medieval Textbook*, trans. by Wayland Johnson Chase (Madison: University of Wisconsin Studies, 1922)

Caxton, William, *Caxton's Aesop*, ed. by R. T. Lenaghan (Cambridge, MA: Harvard University Press, 1967)

——, *The Fables of Aesop, as first printed by William Caxton in 1484 with those of Avian, Alfonso, and Poggio*, ed. by Joseph Jacobs (London: David Nutt in the Strand, 1889)

——, *Here begynneth the book of the subtyl historyes and Fables of Esope whiche were translated out of Frensshe in to Englysshe by Wylham Caxton at Westmynstre in the yere of oure Lorde. M.CCC.lxxxiij* (Westminster: William Caxton, 1484)

Chapman, George, *The crowne of all Homers workes Batrachomyomachia or the battaile of frogs and mise* (London, 1624)

Chaucer, Geoffrey, *The Riverside Chaucer*, ed. by Larry Benson (Boston: Houghton Mifflin, 1987)

Cicero, *The first book of Tullies Offices translated grammatically, and also according to the propriety of our English tongue; for the more speedy and certain attaining of the singular learning contained in the same, to further to a pure Latin stile, and to express the mind more easily, both in English & Latine. Done chiefly for the good of schools; to be vsed according to the directions in the admonition to the reader, and more fully in Ludus lit. or Grammar-schoole*, trans. by John Brinsley (London, 1616)

——, *De Senectute, De Amicitia, De Divinatione*, trans. by William Armistead Falconer (Cambridge, MA: Harvard University Press, 1946)

——, *The Letters to his Friends, in Three Volumes*, vol. 2, trans. by W. Glynn Williams (London: William Heinemann, 1928)

Clark, George, 'Henryson and Aesop: The Fable Transformed', *ELH* 43:1 (1976), 1–18

Coldiron, A. E. B., 'The mediated "medieval" and Shakespeare', in *Medieval Shakespeare: Pasts and Presents*, ed. by Ruth Morse, Helen Cooper, and Peter Holland (Cambridge: Cambridge University Press, 2013), pp. 55–77

——, *Printers Without Borders: Translation and Textuality in the Renaissance* (Cambridge: Cambridge University Press, 2015)

——, 'William Caxton', in *The Oxford History of Literary Translation in English*, Vol. 1: *To 1550*, ed. by Roger Ellis (Oxford: Oxford University Press, 2008), pp. 160–68

Conti, Natale, *Mythologiae*, trans. by John Mulryan and Steven Brown, 2 vols (Tempe: Arizona Center for Medieval and Renaissance Studies, 2006)

——, *Mythologiae sive explicationum fabularum libri X* (Venice, 1581)

Cordier, Mathurin, *Corderius dialogues translated grammatically; for the more speedy attaining to the knowledge of the Latine tongue, for writing and speaking Latine. Done chiefly for the good of schooles, to be vsed according to the direction set downe in the booke, called Ludus literarius, or The grammar-schoole*, trans. by John Brinsley (London, 1614)

Corriente, F., *A Dictionary of Andalusi Arabic* (Leiden: Brill, 1997)

Corrozet, Gilles, *Des fables d'Esope Phrygien, mises en ryme françoyse* (Paris, 1542)

Cotgrave, Randle, *Dictionary of French and English Tongues* (London, 1611)

Cottegnies, Line, 'The Art of Schooling Mankind: The Uses of Fable in Roger L'Estrange's Aesop's Fables (1692)', in *Roger L'Estrange and the Making of Restoration Culture*, ed. by Anne Dunan-Page and Beth Wynn (Aldershot: Ashgate, 2008), pp. 131–48

Daly, Peter M., 'Emblems: An Introduction', in *Companion to Emblem Studies*, ed. by Peter Daly (New York: AMS Press, 2008), pp. 1–24

——, 'Emblem Theory: Modern and Early Modern', in *Companion to Emblem Studies*, ed. by Peter Daly (New York: AMS Press, 2008), pp. 43–78

Dick, Hugh Gilchrist, Hugh Gilchrist Dick Papers, 1937–1974, UCLA Library Special Collections, Charles E. Young Research Library, University of California, Los Angeles

Diehl, Huston, *An Index of Icons in English Emblem Books 1500–1700* (Norman and London: University of Oklahoma Press, 1986)

DuBruck, Edelgard, 'Aesop's Weeping Puppy: Late-Medieval Migrations of a Narrative Motif', *Early Drama, Art, and Music Review* 22 (1999), 1–10

Eames, Marian, 'John Ogilby and his Aesop: The Fortunes and Fables of a Seventeenth-Century Virtuoso', *New York Public Library Bulletin* 65 (1961), 73–88.

Elyot, Sir Thomas, *The Dictionary of Syr Thomas Eliot Knyght* (London, 1538)

Enterline, Lynn, *Shakespeare's Schoolroom: Rhetoric, Discipline, Emotion* (Philadelphia: University of Pennsylvania Press, 2012)

Epictetus, *Discourses, Books 3–4. Fragments. The Encheiridion*, trans. by W. A. Oldfather (Cambridge, MA: Harvard University Press, 1928)

Erasmus, Desiderius, *Adages, I.i.1 to I.v.100*, trans. by Margaret Mann Phillips, vol. 31 of the *Collected Works of Erasmus* (Toronto: University of Toronto Press, 1982)

——, *Adages, I.vi.1 to I.x.100*, trans. by R. A. B. Mynors, vol. 32 of the *Collected Works of Erasmus* (Toronto: University of Toronto Press, 1989)

——, *Adages, II.i.1 to II.vi.100*, trans. by R. A. B. Mynors, vol. 33 of the *Collected Works of Erasmus* (Toronto: University of Toronto Press, 1991)

Fabularum quae hoc libro continentur interpretes, atque authores sunt hi. Guilielmus Goudanus. Hadrianus Barlandus. Erasmus Roterodamus. Aulus Gellius. Angelus Politianus. Petrus Crinitus. Ioannes Antonius Campanus. Plinius Secundus Nouocomensis. Nicolaus Gerbellius Phorcensis. Aesopi Vita ex Max Planude excerpta. & aucta (Strasbourg: Matthias Schürer, 1518)

Finch, Chauncey E., 'The Renaissance adaptation of Aesop's "Fables" by Gregorious Corrius', *Classical Bulletin* 49 (1973), 44–48

Folger Shakespeare Library, Washington, DC, 'Receipt from Arthur Golding of Little Birch, Essex, Esq., to Lady Golding, his sister-in-law' [manuscript], May 20, 1590, X.d.318

Fox, Denton, 'Henryson and Caxton', *Journal of English and Germanic Philology* 67 (1968), 586–93

Freitag, Arnold, *Mythologia Ethica, hoc est, moralis philosophiae per fabulas brutis attributas, traditae, amoenissimum viridarium: in quo humanae vitae labyrintho demonstrato, virtutis semita pulcherrimis praeceptis, veluti Thesei filo docetur. Artificiosissimis nobilissimorum sculptorum iconibus ab Arnoldo Freitagio Embricensi, latin explicatis, aeri incissum* (Antwerp, excudebat Christopher Plantin: Philip Galle, 1579)

Fudge, Erica, *Perceiving Animals: Humans and Beasts in Early Modern English Culture* (Champaign: University of Illinois Press, 2002)

——, ed., *Renaissance Beasts: Of Animals, Humans, and Other Wonderful Creatures* (Champaign: University of Illinois Press, 2004)

Galbraith, Steven K., '"English" Black-Letter Type and Spenser's *Shepheardes Calender*', *Spenser Studies* 23 (2008), 13–40

Geirnaert, Dirk and Paul Smith, 'The Sources of the Emblematic Fable Book *De warachtighe fabulen der dieren* (1567)', in *The Emblematic Tradition in the Southern Netherlands: Selected Papers of the Leuven International Emblem Conference, 18–23 August, 1996*, ed. by Karel Porteman, Marc Van Vaeck, and John Manning (Turnhout: Brepols, 1999), pp. 25–38

Gheeraerts, Marcus, the Elder, and Eduard de Dene, *De warachtighe fabulen der dieren* (Bruges, 1567)

Golding, Arthur, 'Arthur Golding's *A Morall Fabletalke*: An Annotated Edition', ed. by Nora Rooche Field (unpublished doctoral dissertation, Columbia University, 1979; abstract in *Dissertation Abstracts International* 40 (1979), 3314A)

——, 'Epistle to Leicester', in Ovid, *Metamorphoses*, trans. by Arthur Golding, ed. by Madeleine Forey (New York: Penguin Books, 2002), pp. 5–22

——, *A Moral Fable-talk*, ed. by Richard G. Barnes (San Francisco: The Arion Press, 1987)

Golding, Louis Thorn, *An Elizabethan Puritan: Arthur Golding the Translator of Ovid's* Metamorphoses *and also of John Calvin's Sermons* (New York: Richard R. Smith, 1937)

González González, Enrique, 'Martinus Dorpius and Hadrianus Barlandus Editors of Aesop (1509–1513)', *Humanistica Lovaniensia: Journal of Neo-Latin Studies* 47 (1998), 28–41

Gray, Douglas, *Robert Henryson* (Leiden: Brill, 1979)

Green, Ian, *Humanism and Protestantism in Early Modern English Education* (Farnham: Ashgate, 2009)

Hale, David G., 'Aesop in Renaissance England', *Library* s5-XXVII (2) (1972), 116–25

——, 'The Source and Date of Golding's "Fabletalke"', *Modern Philology: A Journal Devoted to Research in Medieval and Modern Literature* 69.4 (1972), 326–27

Heal, Felicity, 'Stonley, Richard (1520/21–1600)', in *Oxford Dictionary of National Biography* (Oxford: Oxford University Press, 2016) <http://dx.doi.org/10.1093/ref:odnb/109639>

Henderson, Arnold Clayton, 'Having Fun with the Moralities: Henryson's *Fables* and Late Medieval Fable Innovation', *Studies in Scottish Literature* 32 (2001), 67–87

Heninger, S. K., Jr., *The Subtext of Form in the English Renaissance: Proportion Poetical* (University Park: The Pennsylvania State Press, 1994)

Henryson, Robert, *The Fabulous Tales of Esope the Phrygian, compiled moste eloquently in Scottishe metre by Master Robert Henrison, and now lately Englished. Euery tale moralized most aptly to this present time, worthy to be read*, trans. by Richard Smith (London: Richard Smith, 1577)

——, *The Morall Fabillis of Esope the Phrygian, compylit in eloquent, and ornate Scottis meter, be Maister Robert Henrisone, scholemaister of Dunfermeling* (Edinburgh: Robert Lekpreuik, 1570)

——, *The Morall Fabillis of Esope the Phrygian, compylit in eloquent, & ornate Scottis meter, be M. Robert Henrisone, scolmaister of Dunfermling. Newlie corectit, and vendicat, fra mony errouris, quhilkis war ouersene in the last prenting, quhair baith lynes, and haill versis war left owt* (Edinburgh: Thomas Bassendyne, 1571)

——, *Morall Fabillis. The Poems of Robert Henryson*, ed. by Denton Fox (Oxford: Clarendon, 1981)

——, *The Poems of Robert Henryson*, ed. by Robert L. Kindrick (Kalamazoo: Medieval Institute Publications, 1997)

——, *Robert Henryson: The Complete Works*, ed. by David J. Parkinson (Kalamazoo: Medieval Institute Publications, 2010)

Herodotus, *Herodotus, in Four Volumes*, vol. 3, trans. by A. D. Godley (London: William Heinemann, 1922)

Hesychius, *Hesychii Alexandrini Lexicon*, ed. by Mauricius Schmidt (Jenae: Sumpibus Hermanni Dufftii, 1867)

Heyns, Peeter (?), *Esbatement moral* (Antwerp, 1578)

Higgins, Iain Macleod, 'Master Henryson and Father Aesop', in *Author, Reader, Book: Medieval Authorship in Theory and Practice*, ed. by Stephen Partridge and Erik Kwakkel (Toronto: University of Toronto Press, 2012), pp. 198–231

Hislop, Alexander, *The Proverbs of Scotland* (Edinburgh: Alexander Hislop and Company, 1868)

Hodapp, William F., 'The Fables of Avianus', in *Medieval Literature for Children*, ed. by Daniel T. Kline (New York: Routledge, 2003), pp. 12–28

Hodnett, Edward, *Aesop in England: The Transmission of Motifs in Seventeenth-Century Illustrations of Aesop's Fables* (Charlottesville: University Press of Virginia, 1979)

―――, *Francis Barlow: First Master of English Book Illustration* (Berkeley: University of California Press, 1978)

―――, *Marcus Gheeraerts the Elder of Bruges, London, and Antwerp* (Utrecht: Haentjens, Dekker & Gumbert, 1971)

Horace, *Satires, Epistles, and Ars Poetica*, trans. by H. Rushton Fairclough (London: William Heinemann, 1932)

Hosington, Brenda M., 'The Role of Translations and Translators in the Production of English Incunabula', in *Renaissance Cultural Crossroads: Translation, Print and Culture in Britain, 1473–1640*, ed. by S. K. Barber and Brenda M. Hosington (Leiden: Brill, 2013), pp. 3–20

Juvenal, *Satires*, in *Juvenal and Persius*, trans. by G. G. Ramsay (New York: G.P. Putnam's Sons, 1928), pp. 1–307

Khinoy, Stephan, 'Tale-Moral Relationships in Henryson's *Moral Fables*', *Studies in Scottish Literature* 17 (1982), 99–115

Kishlansky, Mark, 'Turning frogs into princes: Aesop's Fables and the political culture of early modern England', in *Political Culture and Cultural Politics in Early Modern England: Essays Presented to David Underdown*, ed. by Susan D. Amussen and Mark A. Kishlansky (Manchester: Manchester University Press, 1995), pp. 338–60

Lainé, Pierre, *The princely way to the French tongue as it was first compiled for the use of Her Highness, the Lady Mary, and since taught her royal sister, the Lady Anne: to which is added a chronological abridgment of the Sacred Scripture by way of dialogue: together with a larger explication of the French grammar, choice fables of Aesop in burlesque French, and lastly some models of letters French and English. By P. D. L., Tutor for the French to both Their Highnesses* (London, 1677)

Lerer, Seth, 'Aesop, Authorship, and the Aesthetic Imagination', *Journal of Medieval and Early Modern Studies* 37.3 (2007), 580–94

―――, *Children's Literature: A Reader's History from Aesop to Harry Potter* (Chicago: University of Chicago Press, 2008)

L'Estrange, Roger, *Fables of Aesop and other Eminent Mythologists: with Morals and Reflections* (London, 1692)

Lewis, Jayne Elizabeth, *The English Fable: Aesop and Literary Culture, 1651–1740* (Cambridge: Cambridge University Press, 1996)

Livy, *Livy, in Thirteen Volumes*, vol. 4, trans. by B. O. Foster (London: William Heinemann, 1926)

Loveridge, Mark, *A History of Augustan Fable* (Cambridge: Cambridge University Press, 1998)

Lucian, *Lucian, in Seven Volumes*, vol. 2, trans. by A. M. Harmon (London: William Heinemann, 1915)

Lucretius, *De Rerum Natura*, trans. by W. H. D. Rouse (London: William Heinemann, 1924)

Lyall, R. J., 'Henryson's *Morall Fabillis* and the Steinhöwel Tradition', *Modern Language Studies* 38 (2002), 362–81

Macho, Julien, *Esope. Eingeleitet und herausgegeben nach der Edition von 1486 von Beate Hecker* (Hamburg: Romanisches Seminar der Universitat Hamburg, 1982)

Macrobius, *Commentary on the Dream of Scipio*, trans. by William Harris Stahl (New York: Columbia University Press, 1952)

Mann, Jill, *From Aesop to Reynard: Beast Literature in Medieval Britain* (Oxford: Oxford University Press, 2009)

Melnikoff, Kirk, *Elizabethan Publishing and the Makings of Literary Culture* (Toronto: University of Toronto Press, forthcoming 2017)

Miner, Earl, 'Introduction', in John Ogilby, *The Fables of Aesop Paraphras'd in Verse* (London: Thomas Roycroft for the author, 1668; repr. Los Angeles: William Andrews Clark Memorial Library, 1965), pp. i–xiv

More, Sir Thomas, *The historie of the pitifull life, and unfortunate death of Edward the Fifth, and the then Duke of Yorke, his brother with the troublesome and tyrannical government of usurping Richard the Third, and his miserable end* (London, 1641)

The National Archives of the UK, 'Arthur Golding to Myldemay', 1585, SP 46/33, f. 349, in *State Papers Online, 1509–1714* (Gale, Cengage Learning, 2016) <http://gale.cengage.co.uk/state-papers-online-15091714/part-i.aspx>

The National Archives of the UK, 'Memorandum of money received by Arthur Goldyng for the use of the Earl of Oxford', May 22, 1563,

BIBLIOGRAPHY

SP 12/28, f. 176, in *State Papers Online, 1509–1714* (Gale, Cengage Learning, 2016) <http://gale.cengage.co.uk/state-papers-online-15091714/part-i.aspx>

The National Archives of the UK, 'Petition of Arthur Golding', June 28, 1563, SP 12/29, f. 11, in *State Papers Online, 1509–1714* (Gale, Cengage Learning, 2016) <http://gale.cengage.co.uk/state-papers-online-15091714/part-i.aspx>

The National Archives of the UK, 'Receipt by Arthur Goldyng', May 22, 1563, SP 12/28, f. 175, in *State Papers Online, 1509–1714* (Gale, Cengage Learning, 2016) <http://gale.cengage.co.uk/state-papers-online-15091714/part-i.aspx>

The National Archives of the UK, 'Receipt by Arthur Goldyng', May 26, 1563, SP 12/28, f. 184, in *State Papers Online, 1509–1714* (Gale, Cengage Learning, 2016) <http://gale.cengage.co.uk/state-papers-online-15091714/part-i.aspx>

Nelson, William, 'A Morall Fabletalke', *Columbia Library Columns* 9.1 (1959), 26–32

The New Oxford Annotated Bible: New Revised Standard Version with the Apocrypha, ed. by Michael D. Coogan et al. (Oxford: Oxford University Press, 2010)

Oakley-Brown, Elizabeth, 'Arthur Golding', in *The Encyclopedia of English Renaissance Literature*, vol. 2, ed. by Garrett A. Sullivan, Jr. and Alan Stewart (Chichester: Wiley-Blackwell, 2012), pp. 386–88

Ogilby, John, *Aesopic's: or a second collection of fables, paraphras'd in verse: adorn'd with sculpture, and illustrated with annotations. By John Ogilby, Esq; Master of His Majesties Revells in the Kingdom of Ireland* (London: Thomas Roycroft for the author, 1668)

——, *Aesopicks: or, a second collection of fables, paraphras'd in verse, adorn'd with sculpture, and illustrated with annotations. By John Ogilby Esq; His Majesty's Cosmographer, Geographick Printer, and Master of the Revels in the Kingdom of Ireland. The Second Edition* (London: John Ogilby, 1673)

——, *The Fables of Aesop Paraphras'd in Verse* (London: Thomas Roycroft for the author, 1668; repr. Los Angeles: William Andrews Clark Memorial Library, 1965)

——, *The Fables of Aesop paraphrased in Verse, and adorn'd with sculpture* (London: Thomas Warren for Andrew Cook, 1651)

——, *The Fables of Aesop paraphras'd in verse: adorn'd with sculpture, and illustrated with annotations. The second edition. By John Ogilby, Esq; Master of His Majesties Revells in the Kingdom of Ireland* (London: Thomas Roycroft for the author, 1665)

——, *The Fables of Aesop paraphras'd in verse: adorn'd with sculpture, and illustrated with annotations. The second edition. By John Ogilby, Esq; Master of His Majesties Revells in the Kingdom of Ireland* (London: Thomas Roycroft for the author, 1668)

——, *The Fables of Aesop. Volume 1. Paraphras'd in verse, adorn'd with sculpture, and illustrated with annotations. By John Ogilby Esq; His Majesty's Cosmographer, Geographick Printer, and Master of the Revels in the Kingdom of Ireland. The Third Edition* (London: John Ogilby, 1673)

Ovid, *The Art of Love, and Other Poems*, trans. by J. H. Mozley (Cambridge, MA: Harvard University Press, 1962)

——, *Ovid's Metamorphoses: The Arthur Golding Translation of 1567*, ed. by John Frederick Nims (Philadelphia: Paul Dry Books, 2000)

——, *Tristia*, trans. by Arthur Leslie Wheeler, rev. by G. P. Goold (Cambridge, MA: Harvard University Press, 1988)

Patterson, Annabel, *Fables of Power: Aesopian Writing and Political History* (Durham, NC: Duke University Press, 1991)

Pearcy, Lee T., *The Mediated Muse: English Translations of Ovid 1560–1700* (Hamden, CT: Archon Books, 1984)

Pennington, Richard, *A Descriptive Catalogue of the Etched Work of Wenceslaus Hollar, 1607–1677* (Cambridge: Cambridge University Press, 2002)

Perry, Ben Edwin, *Aesopica: A Series of Texts Relating to Aesop or Ascribed to Him* (Urbana: University of Illinois Press, 1952)

——, 'Fable', *Studium generale* 12 (1959), 17–37

——, 'Introduction', in *Babrius and Phaedrus*, trans. by Ben Edwin Perry (Cambridge, MA: Harvard University Press, 1964), pp. xi–cii

——, *Studies in the Text History of the Life and Fables of Aesop* (Haverford: The American Philological Association, 1936)

Phaedrus, *The Aesopic Fables of Phaedrus the Freedman of Augustus*, in *Babrius and Phaedrus*, trans. by Ben Edwin Perry (Cambridge, MA: Harvard University Press, 1965), pp. 189–369

Physiologus: A Medieval Book of Nature Lore, trans. by Michael J. Curley (Chicago: University of Chicago Press, 1979)

Plato, *Plato: Euthyphro, Apology, Crito, Phaedo, Phaedrus*, vol. 1, trans. by Harold North Fowler (London: William Heinemann, 1926)

——, *The Republic*, vol. 1, trans. by Paul Shorey (London: William Heinemann, 1930)

Plessow, Max, *Geschichte der Fabeldichtung in England bis zu John Gay (1726)* (Berlin: Mayer & Müller, 1906)

Pliny, *Natural History*, vol. 3, trans. by H. Rackham (Cambridge, MA: Harvard University Press, 1940)

——, *Natural History*, vol. 4, trans. by H. Rackham (Cambridge, MA: Harvard University Press, 1945)

——, *Natural History*, vol. 5, trans. by H. Rackham (Cambridge, MA: Harvard University Press, 1950)

——, *Natural History*, vol. 6, trans. by W. H. S. Jones (Cambridge, MA: Harvard University Press, 1961)

——, *Natural History*, vol. 10, trans. by D. E. Eichholz (Cambridge, MA: Harvard University Press, 1967)

Plutarch, *Plutarch's Essays and Miscellanies, in Five Volumes*, vol. 5, ed. by A. H. Clough and William W. Goodwin (New York: The Colonial Company, Ltd., 1905)

——, *Plutarch's Lives*, trans. by Bernadotte Perrin (Cambridge, MA: Harvard University Press, 1954)

Pope, Robert, 'A sly toad, physiognomy, and the problem of deceit: Henryson's *The Paddock and the Mouse*', *Neophililogus* 63 (1979), 461–68

Powell, Marianne, *Fabula docet: Studies in the Background and Interpretation of Henryson's Morall Fabillis*, Odense University Studies in English 6 (Odense: Odense University Press, 1983)

Proverbs, Sentences, and Proverbial Phrases from English Writings Mainly before 1500, ed. by Bartlett Jere Whiting and Helen Wescott Whiting (Cambridge, MA: Harvard University Press, 1968)

Pynson, Richard, *In tyme whenne beestes coude speke the wolues made warre againest the sheepe* […] (London: Richard Pynson, 1500)

Quintilian, *Institutio Oratoria*, vol. 1, trans. by H. E. Butler (London: William Heinemann, 1921)

Romulus: Die paraphrasen des Phaedrus und die Aesopische fabel im mittelalter, ed. by Hermann Oesterley (Berlin: Weidmannsche Buchhandlung, 1870)

Sabino, Georgio, *Fabularum Ovidii interpretatio* (Witeberge, 1572)

Salmon, Vivian, 'John Brinsley: 17th-Century Pioneer in Applied Linguistics', *Historiographia Linguistica* 2.2 (1975), 175–89

——, *The Study of Language in 17th-Century England* (Amsterdam: John Benjamins, 1988)

Seneca, Lucius Annaeus, *Epistles 1–65*, trans. by Richard M. Gummere (Cambridge, MA: Harvard University Press, 1917)

——, *Seneca's Tragedies*, vol. 2, trans. by Frank Justus Miller (London: William Heinemann, 1929)

Sententiae pueriles, translated grammatically leading the learner, as by the hand, to construe right, parse, and make the same Latine; also to get both matter and phrase, most speedily and surely, without inconuenience, trans. by John Brinsley (London, 1612)

Shakespeare, William, *The Norton Shakespeare*, ed. by Stephen Greenblatt et al. (New York: W. W. Norton and Co., 2016)

Sidney, Philip, *The Defense of Poesy*, in *Sir Philip Sidney: Selected Writings*, ed. by Richard Dutton (New York: Routledge, 2002), pp. 102–48

Silcox, Mary V., 'The Emblem in the United Kingdom and America', in *Companion to Emblem Studies*, ed. by Peter Daly (New York: AMS Press, 2008), pp. 369–91

Smith, Paul J., 'Arnold Freitag's *Mythologia ethica* (1579) and the Tradition of the Emblematic Fable', in *Mundus Emblematicus:*

Studies in Neo-Latin Emblem Books, ed. by Karl A. E. Enenkel and Arnoud S. Q. Visser (Turnhout: Brepols, 2003), pp. 173–200

——, '*Dispositio* in the Emblematic Fable Books of the Gheeraerts Filiation (1567–1617)', in *Emblems of the Low Countries: A Book Historical Perspective*, ed. by Alison Adams and Marleen van der Weij (Glasgow: Glasgow Emblem Studies, 2003), pp. 149–70

——, *Dispositio: Problematic Ordering in French Renaissance Literature* (Leiden: Brill, 2007)

Sprat, Thomas, *History of the Royal Society*, ed. by Jackson I. Cope and Harold Whitmore Jones (Saint Louis: Washington University Studies, 1958)

Sturtevant, Simon, *The Etymologist of Aesop's Fables, containing the construing of his Latine fables into English: also the etymologist of Phaedrus fables, containing the construing of Phaedrus (a new found yet aunceint author) into English, verbatim* (London, 1602)

Terence, *Phormio. The Mother-In-Law. The Brothers*, trans. by John Barsby (Cambridge, MA: Harvard University Press, 2001)

Thoen, Paul, 'Aesopus Dorpii. Essai sur l'Esope latin des temps modernes', *Humanistica Lovaniensia* 19 (1970), 241–89

Tiemann, Barbara, *Fable und Emblem: Gilles Corrozet und die französische Renaissance-Fabel* (Munich: Fink, 1974)

Topsell, Edward, *The Historie of Serpents* (London, 1608)

Tung, Mason, 'A Serial list of Aesopic Fables in Alciati's *Emblemata*, Whitney's *A Choice of Emblemes* and Peacham's *Minerva Britanna*', *Emblematica* 4.2 (1989), 315–29

Van Eerde, Katherine S., *John Ogilby and the Taste of his Times* (Swindon: Dawson, 1976)

Virgil, *The Works of Publius Virgilius Maro*, trans. by John Ogilby (London, 1649)

——, *Eclogues. Georgics. Aeneid: Books 1–6*, trans. by H. Rushton Fairclough, rev. by G. P. Goold (Cambridge, MA: Harvard University Press, 1916)

Watson, Henry, *The hystory of the two valyaunte brethren Valentyne and Orson, sonnes vnto the Emperour of Grece* (London, c. 1555)

Wheatley, Edward, *Mastering Aesop: Medieval Education, Chaucer, and His Followers* (Gainesville: University Press of Florida, 2000)

Whitney, Geffrey, *A choice of emblemes, and other deuises, for the moste parte gathered out of sundrie writers, Englished and moralized. And diuers newly deuised, by Geffrey Whitney. A worke adorned with varietie of matter, both pleasant and profitable: wherein those that please, maye finde to fit their fancies: bicause herein, by the office of the eie, and the eare, the minde maye reape dooble delighte throughe holsome preceptes, shadowed with pleasant deuises: both fit for the vertuous, to their incoraging: and for the wicked, for their admonishing and amendment* (Leyden, 1586)

Wilson, Robert H., 'The Poggiana in Caxton's *Esope*', *The Philological Quarterly* 30 (1951), 348–52

Withers, Charles W. J., 'Ogilby, John (1600–1676)', in *Oxford Dictionary of National Biography* (Oxford: Oxford University Press, 2007) <http://dx.doi.org/10.1093/litthe/frm008>

Wortham, James, 'Arthur Golding and the Translation of Prose', *HLQ* 12 (1949), 339–67

INDEX

Absolon, 384
Abstemius, Laurentius, 12
Academics, 422
Acheson, Katherine O., 48
adder, see snake
Aelian
   Historical Miscellany, 431
   Of the Characteristics of
      Animals, 146, 438, 439
Aesop, 1, 2, 4, 6, 7, 8, 9, 10–11,
      12, 13, 18, 19, 21, 22,
      23–24, 26, 27, 31, 39,
      313, 349, 351, 352,
      357, 359, 360, 390,
      397, 411, 413, 414,
      416, 417, 428
   and the Aesopian corpus, 10–12,
      45
   as character, 354–56, 366–68,
      498–99
   as ghost, 23–25, 27, 417, 418,
      498–99
   as storyteller, 315, 316, 317,
      318, 320, 321, 322, 323,
      325, 376, 381, 382
Ajax, 431
Alciatus, Andraeas
   Emblemata, 31–33
Alcides, see Hercules
Alector, 421
Alexander the Great, 465
Alfonso, 11
Alphonsus, Petrus, fabulist, 338,
      340, 343
Altman, Joel B., 9
ant
   and fly, 202–03
   and grasshopper, 88–89
Antony, Marc, 403
ape
   and cat, 188–89
   and fox, 252–53, 410, 447
   and imps (children), 74–75
   and man and monkey, 272–73
   see also monkey

Apuleius
   Golden Ass, 466
Apollo, 76, 337, 355, 356, 365
   see also Phoebus
Apollodorus
   Biblioteke, 110
Apollonius
   Argonautica, 296
Ariadne, 61
Aristophanes
   Avibus (*The Birds*), 421
Aristotle, 5
Ascham, Roger
   Scholemaster, 18, 27
Asclepius, 76
ash
   and reed, 92–93
   see also tree
ass
   and boar, 164–65
   and cock, 68
   and dog, 122–23
   and horse, 130–31, 190–91,
      292–93, 294–95, 407–08
   and lion, 68–69
   and lion and fox, 240–41
   and masters, 268–69
   and ox, mule, and camel,
      270–71
   loaden with provision, 304–05
Athenians, 320
Atalanta, 464
Atropos, 325
Ausonius
   'A Riddle of Number Three',
      421
avaricious man
   and Phoebus and envious man,
      337
Avianus, fabulist, 11, 14, 22, 181,
      337
Aylesbury, Vale of, 389

Babel, 454
Babrius, fabulist, 11, 14, 31

Bacon, Francis, 30
  New Organon, 7–8
  Wisdome of the Ancients, 5
Barlandus, Hadrianus, 11
Barlow, Francis, 15, 26
Barnes, Richard G., 15, 37, 38, 49, 92, 93, 110, 112, 116, 132, 136, 174, 192, 276
bat
  and battle of birds and beasts, 166–67
Batrachomyomachia, see Homer
bawd
  and wife and cat, 340–42
bear
  and bees, 29, 206–07, 449–50
  and forester and skinner, 29, 469–71
  and friends, 120–21
  and lion, 146–47
beasts
  and birds, 166–67
beaver, 31
bee
  and bear, 206–07, 449–50
  and Jupiter, 288–89
  and fox, 116–17
Belin, 488
  see also ram
Bell-Wether, 487
  see also sheep
belly
  and limbs, 35, 327–28, 409, 453–57
Benzi, Ugo, see Hugh of Sienna
Berecynthia, see Cybele
Biblical references (by book)
  Acts, 109, 123
  Apocalypse, 291
    see also Book of Revelation
  Book of Revelation, 291
    see also Apocalypse
  Chronicles, 265
  Colossians, 119
  Corinthians, 87, 113, 147, 177, 253, 269, 301
  Daniel, 117, 125
    see also Susanna
  Ecclesiastes, 71, 99, 129, 155, 173, 225, 311
  Ecclesiasticus, 69, 71, 75, 77, 83, 85, 121, 127, 145, 161, 175, 181, 201, 207, 215, 223, 231, 233, 241, 257, 259, 271, 277, 279, 287, 305
  Ephesians, 73, 309
  Exodus, 63, 115, 171
  Galatians, 131
  Genesis, 285, 454
  Hebrews, 81
  Isaiah, 139, 141, 199, 221
  James, 73, 227
  Jeremiah, 139, 219, 273
  Job, 169, 388, 245
  John, 101, 167, 171, 384
  Jude, 189
  Judges, 168, 329
  Kings, 251
    see also Samuel
  Leviticus, 183, 297
  Luke, 93, 135, 239, 289, 295
  Mark, 353
  Matthew, 103, 167, 185, 211, 220, 235
  Numbers, 229
  Peter, 191, 213, 243
  Proverbs, 65, 67, 75, 76, 77, 79, 89, 95, 97, 131, 133, 137, 145, 149, 151, 157, 159, 163, 187, 201, 203, 209, 217, 237, 247, 249, 261, 263, 267, 275, 281, 283, 293, 303, 307
  Psalms, 137, 143, 153, 179, 197, 205, 274, 299, 310
  Romans, 111, 197
  Samuel, 251, 427
    see also Kings
  Sapience, 91
    see also Wisdom
  Sirach, see Ecclesiasticus
  Susanna, 117
    see also Daniel
  Thessalonians, 193
  Timothy, 105

INDEX

Tobit, 107
Wisdom, 165, 195, 255
   see also Sapience
birds
  and beasts, 166–67
  see also bittern
  see also chicks
  see also cock
  see also cockatrice
  see also crane
  see also crow
  see also cuckoo
  see also dove
  see also dunghillcock
  see also eagle
  see also falcon
  see also goshawk
  see also hawk
  see also hen
  see also kite
  see also milan
  see also nightingale
  see also partridge
  see also peacock
  see also phoenix
  see also puttock
  see also raven
  see also ruddock
  see also sparhawk
  see also stork
  see also swallow
  see also swan
  see also turkeycock
  see also turtledove
  see also vulture
bittern
  and crow, 158–59
blind man, see man
boar
  and ass, 164–65
  and lion and vulture, 244–45
body, see belly and limbs
Boreas, 86
Bracciolini, Poggio, 11, 14, 345
  Facetiae, 345
Brinsley, John, 1, 18–21, 52
  'Epistle Dedicatory', 396

'Epistle to the Reader', 42–43, 394
Fables of Aesop, 29–30, 33, 42–43
Grammar School, 393, 394, 396
Ludus Literarius, 18, 391, 393
translator, *Cato translated grammatically*, 396
  see also Cato
translator, *Corderius dialogues translated*, 396
  see also Corderius
translator, *First Book of Tullies Offices*, 396
  see also Cicero
translator, *Sententiae pueriles*, 396
Bruin, 361, 449, 469, 470
  see also bear
bull
  and mouse, 250–51
  and ram, 218–19
Bullokar, William
  Aesops fabl'z, 21
butcher
  and sheep, 487–89
  see also man

calf
  and ox, 156–57
  with two heads, 345
Calvin, John, 18
  Sermons on Deuteronomy, 82
  Psalmes of Dauid, 274
camel
  and ox, ass, and mule, 270–71
Cancer, 427
Carmelites, 379
Carminum proverbialium, 384
Carnes, Pack, 14
carrier
  and horse, 62–63
  see also man
Carter, Harry, 24
cat
  and ape, 188–89
  and bawd and wife, 340–42

563

and cock, 260–61, 479–80
and fox and dogs, 106–07
and man, 35, 473–76
and mice, 262–63, 483–85
with two heads, 345
Cato, 19, 21
  Distichs, 110
  Cato translated grammatically, 396
    see also Brinsley, John, translator
Caxton, William, 1, 11, 13–14, 50
  Subtle Histories and Fables of Aesop, 22, 25, 29–30, 33, 35, 39–40
Cedars of Libanus, 153
Cerberus, 443, 445
Chaeremon the Stoic, 421
chameleon, 32, 216–18
Chanticleer, 361, 421
  see also cock
Chapman, George
  translator, *Batrachomyomachia*, 26
    see also Homer, possible author
  Widow's Tears, 325
Charles I, see King Charles I
Chaucer, Geoffrey, 13
  Canterbury Tales
    Merchant's Tale, 343
    Miller's Tale, 384
    Nun's Priest's Tale, 361
    Wife of Bath's Prologue, 35, 329
  Troilus and Criseyde, 351
chicks
  and hen, 220–21
child, monstrous, 347
Chrysermus, 431
Cicero
  De Senectute, 70, 196
  Epistles, 437–38
  First Book of Tullies Offices, 396
    see also Brinsley, John, translator
  Sentences, 19

Cilax, 473
Cineas, 437
Cinque Ports, 455
Citherea, see Venus
city mouse
  and country mouse, 402–03
Clark, George, 51
Clyen, Franz, 26
clown
  and satyr, 226–27
  see also man
cock
  and cat, 260–61, 479–80
  and lion and ass, 68
  and partridge, 280–81
  and stone, 35, 162–63, 316, 361–64, 393, 397–98, 421–24
  see also dunghillcock
  see also turkeycock
cockatrice
  and weasel, 72–73
cockerel, see cock
Codrus, 104
Coelum, 429
Coldiron, A. E. B., 13–14, 50
colombe, see dove
Conti, Natale
  Mythologiae, 4, 5, 9, 11
Corderius
  Corderius dialogues translated, 19, 396
    see also Brinsley, John, translator
Corriente, F., 422–23
Corrozet, Gilles, 15
Cotgrave, Randle, 192
Cottegnies, Line, 48
country mouse
  and city mouse, 402–03
countryman
  and snake, 236–37
  and wood, 408
  see also man
cow
  and ox, 156–57
  that gave birth to a serpent, 345–46

INDEX

crane
    and fox, 78–79
    and wolf, 90–91
crow
    and bittern, 158–59
cuckoo
    and kite, 232–33
Cupid, 473
cur, see dog
Cybele, 464, 465
Cyclopes, 429, 434
Cynic, 443

Daedalus, 454
Daly, Peter M., 30–31
Dame Sirith, 340
Danaë, 495
daughter
    and lion and forester, 463–67
    see also woman
Davenant, William, 415, 417
de Dene, Eduard, 15
death
    and man, 70–71
Dick, Hugh G., 36, 37, 116
Diehl, Huston, 31
disciple
    and king, fabulator, and sheep, 338–39
dog
    and ass, 122–23
    and fox and cat, 106–07
    and husbandman, 266–67
    and master, 264–65
    and ox, 128–29, 336
    and reflection, 31–32, 172–73, 394, 401–02
    and sheep and wolves, 82–83
    and smith, 192–93
    and thief, 30, 126–27, 323, 405, 443–45
dormouse, see mouse
doublets, 14, 315, 322
dove
    and kite and sparhawk, 322
    and goshawk, 140–41
    see also turtledove

dragon
    and elephant, 204–05
Du Mornay, Philippe
    Trewnesse of Christian Religion, 116
DuBruck, Edelgard, 48
dunghillcock
    and turkeycock, 296–97
    see also cock

eagle
    and fox, 118–19
    and raven, 160–61
    and snail, 230–31
Eames, Marian, 52
editorial policies, 36–47
educational practices, 8, 9–10, 18–22
Egypt, 141, 297, 416, 453, 454, 455
elephant
    and dragon, 204–05
    and mouse, 438–39
Elizabeth, see Queen Elizabeth
elm
    and oak, 66–67
    see also tree
Elyot, Sir Thomas
    Dictionary of Syr Thomas Eliot, 250
emblems, 15, 30–33, 39
emmet, see ant
Emperor Justinian, see Justinian
English Civil War, 10, 26, 327, 417, 427, 453
Enterline, Lynn, 52
envious man
    and Phoebus and avaricious man, 337
envoi, 351
Epictetus
    Encheiridion, 160
Epicureans, 422
Erasmus, Desiderius, 11
    Adages, 76, 104, 110, 240, 250, 270, 274
Ethiop, 273

Etna, 433, 434
Euphorbus, 433
Euripides
 Hercules Furens, 428
Eutrapelus, 403
exemplarity, 29–30, 33–35

fable
 and education, see educational practices
 and emblems, 30–33
 and fiction or literature more broadly, 5–7, 9, 413
 and falsehoods or deceit, 7, 8
 and the rise of science, 5, 7–8, 30
 formal definition vs historical definition, 2
 reading practices, 10, 28–35, 36
 translations, 13–28
 word, 4, 7, 8
 see also *fabula*
fabula, 1, 2–10, 28
fabulator
 and king, disciple, and sheep, 338–39
Faithorne, William, 26
falcon
 and other birds, 196
Falconer, William Armistead, 196
feet, see limbs
Ferrara, 346–47
Field, Nora Rooche, 37, 49, 92, 110, 116, 132, 136, 154, 162, 180, 192, 216, 220, 251
fieldmouse
 and housemouse, 148–49
 see also mouse
Finch, Chauncey, E., 48
Finch, Heneage, 413
fly
 and ant, 202–03
forester
 and lion, 29, 459–60
 and lion and daughter, 29, 463–67
 and skinner and bear, 29, 469–71
 see also man
Fortune, 160, 166, 198, 222, 232, 292, 375, 388, 408, 454, 471, 487
fowler
 and partridge, 277–78
 and ruddock, 224–25
 and turtledove, 150–51
 see also man
fox
 and ape, 252–53, 410, 447
 and bees, 116–17
 and cat and dogs, 106–07
 and crane, 79–79
 and eagle, 118–19
 and goat, 144–45
 and grapes, 186–87
 and hare and hound, 248–49
 and lion, 64–65, 242–43
 and lion and ass, 240–41
 and raven, 132–33
 and wolf, 246–47, 491–93, 494–96, 497–99
 that lost his tail, 194–95
Fox, Denton, 24, 51
Freitag, Arnold, 16
 Mythologia Ethica, 3, 4, 14, 15, 16, 30, 33, 36–37, 38, 39, 69, 78, 92, 104, 110, 111, 112, 119, 120, 123, 133, 134, 136, 153, 154, 157, 161, 166, 172, 180, 188, 189, 192, 195, 197, 198, 199, 201, 207, 215, 216, 220, 222, 224, 226, 228, 230, 251, 256, 260, 265, 274, 276, 284, 294, 296
friends
 and bear, 120–21
 see also man
frog
 and hares, 184–85
 and Jupiter, wood, and heron, 321
 and mouse and kite, 26, 28, 35, 134–35, 317, 382–89, 394, 400–01, 427–35

INDEX

and ox, 136–37, 168–69
asking for a king, 320, 321
Fudge, Erica, 48
Furthman, Jules, 36

Galbraith, Steven K., 24
Galen, 495, 498
Gaywood, Richard, 26
Geirnaert, Dirk, 15
Gheeraerts, Marcus, the Elder, 15–16, 32–33, 37, 38
goat
  and fox, 144–45
  and lamb and wolf, 200–01
  and wolf, 170–71
  see also shegoat
Golding, Arthur, 4, 14–18, 36–37, 82, 49
  A Moral Fabletalk, 1, 2–3, 30, 31, 32–33, 35, 36–39
Golding, Louis Thorn, 49
Goliath, 427
González González, Enrique, 12
goshawk
  and doves, 140–41
Goudanus, Guilielmus, 11, 19, 42
grapes
  and fox, 186–87
grasshopper
  and ant, 88–89
Gray, Douglas, 51
Green, Ian, 52
Grimalkin, 473
  see also cat

Hale, David G., 37, 48, 50
handicraftsman, see man
hands, see limbs
Hannibal, 460
hare
  and fox and hound, 248–49
  and frogs, 184–85
  and snail, 112–13
harlot, see bawd
Harper, Sir John, 393
hart
  and horse, 142–43
  and reflection, 138–39

hawk, see sparhawk
head, carved
  and man, 254–55
Heal, Felicity, 352
Hector, 431, 494
hedgehog
  and snake, 214–15
  and wolf, 212–13
Helicon, 355
Hellespont, 450
hen
  and her chicks, 220–21
  and woman, 98–99
Henderson, Arnold Clayton, 51
Heninger, S. K., 6
Henryson, Robert, 1, 24, 25, 51, 349, 357, 362, 363, 364, 366, 372, 384, 387
  Morall Fabillis, 22–23, 28–30, 41, 352, 354, 358
Hercules, 403, 428
Hermanus, Guilielmus, 11
Herodotus
  Histories, 450
heron
  and frog, Jupiter, and wood, 321
Hesychius
  Hesychii Alexandrini Lexicon, 421
Heyns, Peeter
  Esbatement moral des animaux, 16–17
Higgins, Iain Macleod, 51
Hippomenes, 464
Hislop, Alexander, 381
Hodapp, William F., 11, 22, 48
Hodnett, Edward, 15, 26, 32, 48, 50, 52
Hogs Norton, 491
Hollar, Wenceslaus, 15, 26
Homer, 432
  Iliad, 431, 494
  possible author,
    Batrachomyomachia, 26, 134, 432
  see also Chapman, George, translator

Horace, 9
  Ars Poetica, 8
  Epistles, 216, 403
  Odes, 134
  Sermones, 162
horse
  and ass, 130–31, 190–91,
    292–93, 294–95, 407–08
  and carrier, 62–63
  and hart, 142–43
  and lion, 76–77, 324
  and sow, 290–91
Hosington, Brenda M., 51
hound
  and fox and hare, 248–49
housemouse
  and fieldmouse, 148–49
  see also mouse
Hugh of Sienna, 345
husbandman, see man
Hymen, 475

Icarus, 454
illustrations, 15–16
Inns of Chancery, 354
Inns of Court, 354
Isgrim, 491–93, 494–96, 497–99
  see also wolf

Jacobs, Joseph, 39, 50
jasp, see stone
jay
  and peacocks, 176–177
Jew's mite, 353
Jove, 168, 240, 268, 437, 439, 454,
    455, 495
  and watersnake, 286–87
  see also Jupiter
Judge Minos, see Minos
Juno, 428, 431, 433
Jupiter, 168, 268, 320, 337, 385,
    429
  and bee, 288–89
  and blind man, wife, and pear
    tree, 343–44
  and frogs, wood, and heron, 321
  and watersnake, 286–87

and wolf which made a fart,
    333–34
  see also Jove
Justinian, 140
Juvenal
  Satires, 104

Khinoy, Stephan, 51
Kindrick, Robert L., 41, 51, 360,
    384
king
  and disciple, fabulator, and
    sheep, 338–39
  requested by frogs, 321
King Charles I, 453
King Midas, see Midas
King Oberon, see Oberon
Kishlansky, Mark, 52
kite
  and cuckoo, 232–33
  and doves, goshawk, and
    puttocks, 140–41
  and doves and sparhawk, 322
  and mouse and frog, 26, 28, 35,
    134–35, 317, 382–89, 394,
    400–01, 427–35
  sick, 31, 298–99
knight
  and widow, 325

Lainé Pierre
  *Princely Way to the French
    Tongue*, 21
lamb
  and goat and wolf, 200–01
  and wolf, 124–25, 393, 398–99
  see also sheep
lar, 444
Laurence, 377
  see also fox
Lely, Peter, 26
Lenaghan, R. T., 11, 39, 50, 315
Lent, 443, 456, 483, 491
Lerer, Seth, 11, 13, 48–49
Lernaean Hydra, 310
L'Estrange, Roger
  Fables of Aesop, 5, 8, 12
Levellers, 453

INDEX

Lewis, Jane Elizabeth, 10, 49, 52
limbs
  and belly, 35, 327–28, 409, 453–57
lion
  and ass, 68–69
  and bear, 146–47
  and boar and vulture, 244–45
  and forester, 29, 459–60
  and forester and daughter, 29, 463–67
  and fox, 64–65, 242–43
  and fox and ass, 240–41
  and horse, 76–77, 324
  and man, 35, 238–39, 329
  and mouse, 35, 84–85, 318–19, 365–75, 404–05, 437–440
  dividing prey, 180–81
  spent with age, 198–99
Livy
  Ab Urbe Condita Libri, 422
Loveridge, Mark, 10, 49, 53, 427
Lucian
  'The Dream, or the Cock', 421
Lucifer, 336
Lucretius
  De Rerum Natura, 250, 421–22
Lyall, R. J., 23, 51
Lynceus, 110

Mab, see Queen Mab
Mabbe, James
  La Celestina, the Spanish Bawd, 340
Macedonian, the
  see Alexander the Great
Macho, Julien, 14, 39, 342
Macrobius, 27, 413
  Saturnalia, 413
man
  and ape and monkey, 272–73
  and cat, 35, 473–76
  and death, 70–71
  and dog, 264–65, 266–67
  and lion, 35, 238–39, 329
  and stork, 282–83
  and sun and northwind, 86–87
  and swallow, 274–75
  and wolf which made a fart, 333–34
  blind, and wife and pear tree, 343–44
  drunken, 276–77
  monstrous, 346–47
  see also avaricious man
  see also butcher
  see also carrier
  see also clown
  see also countryman
  see also disciple
  see also envious man
  see also fabulator
  see also forester
  see also fowler
  see also friends
  see also king
  see also knight
  see also master
  see also neatheard
  see also ploughman
  see also skinner
  see also smith
  see also thief
  see also woodward
Mann, Jill, 22, 49, 51
mare
  and wolf which made a fart, 331
marine monster, see man, monstrous
Marlowe, Christopher
  Tamburlaine the Great, Part 2, 429
Mars, 292, 400, 421, 434
master
  and ass, 268–69
  and dog, 264–65
Mausolus, 453, 460
Meander, 428
Melnikoff, Kirk, 23, 52
Menelaus, 433
Midas, 356
milan, see kite
Miner, Earl, 44–45, 53
Minerva, 355
Minos, 445, 454
Minotaur, 61

Momus, 351
monkey
  and man and ape, 272–73
  see also ape
monsters, 35, 345–47
moral, see narrative and relationship to moral
More, Sir Thomas
  Historie [...] of Edward the Fifth, 375
Morton, William, 427
Mount Etna, see Etna
Mount Helicon, see Helicon
mountain, 152–53
mouse
  and bull, 250–51
  and cat, 262–63, 483–85
  and elephant, 438–39
  and frog and kite, 26, 28, 35, 134–35, 317, 382–89, 394, 400–01, 427–35
  and lion, 35, 84–85, 318–19, 365–75, 404–05, 437–440
  and mountain, 152–53
  and oyster, 228–29
  and ploughman, 222–23
  see also city mouse
  see also country mouse
  see also fieldmouse
  see also housemouse
mule, 100–01
  and ox, ass, and camel, 270–71
Muses, 355, 360, 417, 418
myth, 4, 6
  and mythography, 4–5
  and mythology, 4, 5, 8
  and *mythos*, 4
  see also *fabula, mythologia*
mythologia, 3, 4
Mythologia Ethica, see Freitag, Arnold

narrative
  and emblems, 31–33
  and relationship to moral, 2, 28, 29–30, 33–35
  across fables, 28–29

Nature (character), 68, 70, 80, 81, 110, 113, 136, 164, 220, 234, 262, 270, 273, 300, 385, 427, 443
neatherd
  and idol, 104–106
  see also man
Neckham, Alexander
  Novus Aesopus, 22
  Novus Avianus, 22
Nelson, William, 50
nightingale
  and ostrich, 300–01
  and peacock, 80–81
  and puttock, 234–35
northwind, see wind

oak
  and elm, 66–67
  see also tree
Oakley-Brown, Elizabeth, 18
Oberon, 429, 432
Obsequens, Julius
  Liber de Prodigiis, 433
Ogilby, John, 1, 4, 7, 8, 10, 26–27, 52, 53
  Androcleus, 44, 464
  Ephesian Matron, 44, 325
  Fables of Aesop and *Aesopics*, 28–30, 33, 35, 44–47
  'To the Right Honourable Heneage Finch', 26
  translator, *Works of Publius Virgilius Maro*, 413
  see also Virgil
Orpheus, 355, 357
Orson, 466
ostrich
  and nightingale, 300–01
Ovid, 19
  Art of Love, 162, 180
  Metamorphoses, 1, 4, 12, 18, 166, 308, 432–33, 464, 474
  Tristia, 222
ox
  and ass, mule, and camel, 270–71

INDEX

and calf, 156–57
and dog, 128–29, 336
and frog, 136–37
and stag, 178–79
oyster
and mouse, 228–29

Pan, 355
Panthous, 433
Paphus, 474
Parkinson, David J., 24, 41, 51
partridge
and fowler, 278–79
and cock, 280–81
Patterson, Annabel, 10, 49, 53
Paul's Churchyard, 23, 354, 355
peacock
and jay, 176–77
and nightingale, 80–81
and other birds, 154–55
pear tree
and blind man and wife, 343–44
Pearcy, Lee T., 5
penate, 444
Pennington, Richard, 53
Perry, Ben Edwin, 2, 49, 273, 423
Persian bird, 421
see also cock
Persian water, 353
Petronius
Satyricon, 325
Phaedrus, fabulist, 11, 423
Pharaoh, 63, 141
Phoebus, 365
and avaricious man and envious man, 337
see also Apollo
phoenix, 31, 308–09
Phrygian poet, see Aesop
Physiologus, 32
pig, see sow
pismire, see ant
Plantin, Christopher, 32
Plato, 5
Phaedo, 6, 414
Republic, 7, 9
Timaeus, 196

Plautus
Aulularia (*The Pot of Gold*), 444
Plessow, Max, 44
Pliny, 32
Natural History, 68, 74, 110, 216, 286, 302, 308, 422, 423, 439, 455
ploughman
and mouse, 222–23
see also man
Plutarch
Plutarch's Lives, 353
Poggio, see Bracciolini, Poggio
Pontus, 296
Poge, see Bracciolini, Poggio
Pope of Rome, 347
Pope, Robert, 384
Porphyrius, 421
Powell, Marianne, 52
precious stone, see stone
print technology, 14, 19–21, 24
Proclus, 421
Propetides, 473
Punic Wars, 460
Purple Isle, 453
see also body
puttock
and doves, goshawk, and kites, 140–41
and nightingale, 234–35
Pygmalion, 4, 35, 473–74
Pynson, Richard, 39, 40, 341–42
Pyracmon, 429
Pyrrhus, King of Epirus, 437–38
Pythagoras, 432–33
Pythagoreans, 421, 422, 432

Queen Elizabeth, 352
Queen Mab, 428, 434
Quintilian
Institutio Oratoria, 22

ram, 488
and bull, 218–19
and wolf which made a fart, 331–32

Rastell, John
    Calisto and Melebea, 340
rat, see mouse
raven
    and eagle, 160–61
    and fox, 132–33
    and scorpion, 208–09
    and sheep, 114–15
reed
    and ash, 92–93
Restoration, 453
Reynard the Fox, 491–93, 494–96,
        497–99
    medieval character, 14, 22, 430,
        488
    see also fox
Rimicius, 12
Rojas, Fernando de
    La Celestina, 340
Romulus, fabulist, 2, 11, 14, 22,
        315, 359
rooster, see cock
ruddock
    and fowler, 224–25

Sabinus, Georg
    Fabularum Ovidii interpretatio,
        4, 5–6
Salmon, Vivian, 52
Sampson, 329
Sannio, 402
satyr
    and clown, 226–27
scorpion
    and raven, 208–09
Scorpio, 427
Scotland, 23, 352, 356, 358, 368,
        517
Scots, 1, 24, 41, 358, 359, 362,
        364, 365, 368, 371, 375,
        379–80, 383, 386, 388, 519
seacrabs, 110–11
Seneca
    Epistles, 280
    Hercules Oetaeus, 454
serpent, see snake
servant, see man
Seymour, Henry, 413

shadow, see reflection
Shakespeare, William
    Coriolanus, 35, 327, 453
    Romeo and Juliet, 428
sheep
    and butcher, 487–89
    and king, disciple, and fabulator,
        338–39
    and raven, 114–15
    and stag, 256–57
    and wolf, 182–83, 284–85
    and wolf which made a fart, 333
    and wolves and dogs, 82–83
shegoat
    and wolf whelp, 258–59
    see also goat
shepherd
    and wolf, 94–95
Shirley, James, 418
    'To my Worthy Friend', 4, 27
Sidney, Philip, 10
    Defense of Poesy, 6, 9
Silenus, 431
Silcox, Mary V., 31
skinner
    and forester and bear, 29, 469–71
    see also man
smith
    and dog, 192–93
    see also man
Smith, Paul J., 15, 16, 50
Smith, Richard, 1, 23–26, 27, 51
    'Argument between Aesop and
        the Translator', 23–26
    *Fabulous Tales of Aesop the
        Phrygian*, 28, 29, 33, 41–42
snail
    and hare, 112–13
    and eagle, 230–31
snake
    and countryman, 236–37
    and fowler and turtledove, 150–
        51
    and hedgehog, 214–15
    and stith, 108–09
    monstrous, born from cow,
        345–46
    see also watersnake

INDEX

Socrates, 6–7, 27, 413, 414
sow
  and horse of war, 290–91
  and wolf, 96–97, 406
  and wolf which made a fart, 332–33
spaniel, see dog
sparhawk
  and doves and kite, 322
Sprat, Thomas
  History of the Royal Society, 5, 8
St Paul's Churchyard, see Paul's Churchyard
stag
  and sheep, 256–57
  and oxen, 178–79
Steinhöwel, Heinrich, 11, 14, 22, 39
stith
  and snake, 108–09
stone
  and cock, 35, 162–63, 316, 361–64, 393, 397–98, 421–24
Stonley, Richard, 23, 352
Stoop, Dirck, 26
stork, 302–03, 310–11
  and man, 282–83
  and swan, 306–7
Sturtevant, Simon
  Etymologist of Aesop's Fables, 21, 403
Styx, River, 432, 464
sun
  and northwind and wayfarer, 86–87
swallow
  and man, 274–75
swan
  and stork, 306–07
swine, see sow

Tamburlaine, 429
Tellus, 429
Terence
  Adelphi (*The Brothers*), 402
  Eunuchus, 152, 294

theatricality, 16–17
Theseus, 61
thief
  and dog, 30, 126–27, 323, 405, 443–45
Thoen, Paul, 12
Thraso, 152, 294
Tiberius, 315
Tiemann, Barbara, 15
Tityrus, 250
Topsell, Edward
  Historie of Serpents, 228
Tower of London, 417
translation, 13–28
  and ghosts, 23–25, 27
  and literary production, 22
  and modesty topos, 23
  and pedagogy, 18–22
  and politics, 10, 26–27
  and typography, 24
  cultures of, 1
  double translation, 18
tree
  see also ash
  see also elm
  see also oak
  see also pear tree
  see also wood
Trojan War, 242, 432, 433
Tully, see Cicero
Tung, Mason, 31, 49
turkeycock
  and dunghillcock, 296–97
  see also cock
turtledove
  and fowler, 150–51
Tybert, 361, 430, 473, 483
  see also cat
typography, early, 24, 39, 41, 46, 354, 424, 501

unthrift, see man
urchin, see hedgehog

Vale of Aylesbury, see Aylesbury, Vale of
Vallensis, Laurentius, 12
Van Eerde, Katherine S., 45, 53

Vega, Lope de
  El perro del hortelano (*The Dog in the Manger*), 336
Venus, 344, 421, 473–76
Virgil, 19, 27, 413, 418
  Eclogues, 250
  Aeneid, 429, 443, 464
  Works of Publius Virgilius Maro, 413
    see also Ogilby, John, translator
vulture
  and lion and boar, 244–45

Walter the Englishman, fabulist, 11, 359
watersnake
  and Jupiter or Jove, 286–87
Watson, Henry
  Hystory of the two valyaunte brethren, 466
wayfarer
  and northwind and sun, 86–87
  see also man
weasel
  and cockatrice, 72–73
wether
  and wolf, 102–03, 376–81
Wheatley, Edward, 2, 5–6, 11, 22, 49, 52, 359
White Friars, see Carmelites
Whiting, Bartlett Jere and Helen Wescott, 439
Whitney, Geffrey
  Choice of Emblems, 31–32
widow
  and knight, 325–26
Widow of Ephesus, 325
wife
  and bawd and cat, 340–42
  and blind man and pear tree, 343–44
Wilson, Robert H., 51
wind
  and sun and wayfarer, 86–87
Withers, Charles W. J., 27
wolf
  and crane, 90–91
  and fox, 246–47, 491–93, 494–96, 497–99
  and goat, 170–71
  and goat and lamb, 200–01
  and head, carved, 254–55
  and hedgehog, 212–13
  and lamb, 124–25, 393, 398–99
  and sheep, 182–83, 284–85
  and sheep and dogs, 82–83
  and shepherd, 94–95
  and sow, 96–97, 406
  and wether, 102–03, 376–81
  in sheep's skin, 210–11
  whelp and shegoat, 258–59
  which made a fart, 35, 330–35
woman
  and hen, 98–99
  see also daughter
  see also wife
wood
  and countryman, 408
  and frog, Jupiter, and heron, 321
  and woodward, 174–75
  see also tree
woodward
  and wood, 174–75
  see also man
Wortham, James, 50

Xerxes, King, 450

young man, see man

www.ingramcontent.com/pod-product-compliance
Lightning Source LLC
Chambersburg PA
CBHW071430300426
44114CB00013B/1376